Small Busine[ss]
Networking For D[ummies]

MW00597905

15 Steps to Small Business Networking

1. Identify business goals for your network in the primary categories of cost reduction and revenue enhancement.

2. Name a key employee to act as part-time network administrator.

3. Create a preliminary network budget, including hardware, software, setup, training, and maintenance. Explore financing options.

4. Identify and interview companies that can help you design, roll out, and support your network.

5. Create a schedule, including the tasks of design, rollout, configuration, and management.

6. Weigh the pros and cons of peer-to-peer versus client/server networking and choose a style that fits your company.

7. Choose your networking software from among popular alternatives. If you go with a client/server networking style, you need to choose a Network Operating System for the server, as well as an operating system for your workstations.

8. Choose the language your network will use to communicate between computers. Most companies select either IPX, NetBEUI, or TCP/IP.

9. Choose the plumbing your network will use, including the access method (such as Ethernet) and cabling (such as twisted pair).

10. Install and test the hardware, including cabling, server, workstations, and printer.

11. Install networking software and set it up for file and printer sharing.

12. Set up your network to communicate outside the office, in both the inbound and outbound directions.

13. Apply an appropriate level of security to your network to protect against accidental and intentional damage.

14. Tune your network for the maximum possible speed.

15. Set up a routine for administering and maintaining your network to ensure that it continues to serve your company well for years to come.

12 Keys to a Happy Network

- Stick with industry standards, and add your own company standards. The more standardized your network computers are, the easier they are to manage.

- Build a support system for yourself, including printed and electronic references, vendor support sites on the Internet, and local consultants with relevant experience.

- Take a good class on the kind of network operating system you use.

- Buy workstations and servers with as much stuff preinstalled as possible (Network Interface Cards, disk drives, networking software, and so on).

- Make a map of your network and write down all the settings you made when you installed it.

- Don't skimp on the cabling. Have high quality wire installed by an experienced network cabling contractor and make sure the cable is tested before you use it.

- Spend a day thinking about the worst things that could happen to your network and how you would respond to them. Repeat the exercise annually; serve pizza and beer promptly afterwards.

- Teach your network users how to use the network properly and how to report problems when they occur.

- Perform *full server backups* weekly and *differential server backups* daily. Use the best, fastest, highest-capacity tape drive you can afford, and keep a recent backup set at a safe, off-site location.

- Perform *full workstation backups* monthly and *differential workstation backups* at least weekly.

- Use antivirus software on both servers and workstations, and update it every month.

- Keep tabs on network resource usage so that you can add capacity before it becomes critical.

Small Business Networking For Dummies®

Cheat Sheet

A Network Administrator's Tool Cabinet

- ✔ A set of computer screwdrivers (non-magnetic) including slot, Phillips-head, and *Torx* (the star-shaped variety)
- ✔ A pair of needle-nose pliers and a pair of tweezers, for fishing screws out of tight places (do not use a magnetic grabber for lost screws)
- ✔ An electrical outlet tester to indicate AC wiring faults (you can get one at Radio Shack)
- ✔ A cable tester to check out network wiring, if you don't have a contractor run your cable
- ✔ At least one spare patch cable, Network Interface Card, keyboard, mouse, workstation disk drive, and server disk drive
- ✔ An extra laser printer toner cartridge
- ✔ A baggie with jumper blocks for setting options on Network Interface Cards and disk drives
- ✔ Another baggie with a few extra computer screws for mounting disk drives and securing computer covers
- ✔ Rescue diskettes for starting servers and workstations if a primary hard drive fails — you create these diskettes through your workstation operating system and Network Operating Systems
- ✔ A few "T" connectors and terminating resistors for coaxial cable, if you use it
- ✔ A pocket protector

6 Troubleshooting Questions to Ask

- ✔ Did the task you're trying to perform ever work in the past?
- ✔ What's changed since the task last worked?
- ✔ Is the problem repeatable? If so, what are the steps to recreating it?
- ✔ Does the problem affect every workstation on the network?
- ✔ Does the problem affect every application program, or just one?
- ✔ Do you get an error message? If so, what is it, *exactly?*

11 Troubleshooting Steps to Try

- ✔ Test all cables for good connections with no stress on the connectors.
- ✔ Swap out the patch cable that connects the workstation to the wall plate.
- ✔ Check for plenty of free disk space on both the workstation and the server.
- ✔ Run a computer diagnostics program on the affected machine or machines.
- ✔ Run the Network Interface Card's diagnostics program.
- ✔ Check the network hub lights for indication of failure.
- ✔ Check the status lights on the Network Interface Card for indication of failure.
- ✔ Swap ports at the hub.
- ✔ Check the server's error log or event viewer.
- ✔ Print a test page to the printer.
- ✔ Perform a BIOS upgrade to the workstation computer.

...For Dummies®: Bestselling Book Series for Beginners

™

BESTSELLING BOOK SERIES

References for the Rest of Us!®

Are you intimidated and confused by computers? Do you find that traditional manuals are overloaded with technical details you'll never use? Do your friends and family always call you to fix simple problems on their PCs? Then the *...For Dummies*® computer book series from IDG Books Worldwide is for you.

...For Dummies books are written for those frustrated computer users who know they aren't really dumb but find that PC hardware, software, and indeed the unique vocabulary of computing make them feel helpless. *...For Dummies* books use a lighthearted approach, a down-to-earth style, and even cartoons and humorous icons to dispel computer novices' fears and build their confidence. Lighthearted but not lightweight, these books are a perfect survival guide for anyone forced to use a computer.

> *"I like my copy so much I told friends; now they bought copies."*
>
> — Irene C., Orwell, Ohio

> *"Quick, concise, nontechnical, and humorous."*
>
> — Jay A., Elburn, Illinois

> *"Thanks, I needed this book. Now I can sleep at night."*
>
> — Robin F., British Columbia, Canada

Already, millions of satisfied readers agree. They have made *...For Dummies* books the #1 introductory level computer book series and have written asking for more. So, if you're looking for the most fun and easy way to learn about computers, look to *...For Dummies* books to give you a helping hand.

IDG BOOKS WORLDWIDE ®

SMALL BUSINESS NETWORKING FOR DUMMIES®

by Glenn E. Weadock

Illustrated by
Emily Sherrill Weadock

Foreword by Eric Schmidt,
Chairman and CEO of Novell, Inc.

IDG BOOKS WORLDWIDE

IDG Books Worldwide, Inc.
An International Data Group Company

Foster City, CA ♦ Chicago, IL ♦ Indianapolis, IN ♦ New York, NY

Small Business Networking For Dummies®

Published by
IDG Books Worldwide, Inc.
An International Data Group Company
919 E. Hillsdale Blvd.
Suite 400
Foster City, CA 94404
www.idgbooks.com (IDG Books Worldwide Web site)
www.dummies.com (Dummies Press Web site)

Library of Congress Catalog Card No.: 97-81223

ISBN: 0-7645-0289-1

Printed in the United States of America

10 9 8 7 6 5 4 3 2

1B/RR/QT/ZZ/IN

Distributed in the United States by IDG Books Worldwide, Inc.

Distributed by CDG Books Canada Inc. for Canada; by Transworld Publishers Limited in the United Kingdom; by IDG Norge Books for Norway; by IDG Sweden Books for Sweden; by Woodslane Pty. Ltd. for Australia; by Woodslane (NZ) Ltd. for New Zealand; by TransQuest Publishers Pte Ltd. for Singapore, Malaysia, Thailand, Indonesia, and Hong Kong; by ICG Muse, Inc. for Japan; by Norma Comunicaciones S.A. for Colombia; by Intersoft for South Africa; by Le Monde en Tique for France; by International Thomson Publishing for Germany, Austria and Switzerland; by Distribuidora Cuspide for Argentina; by Livraria Cultura for Brazil; by Ediciones ZETA S.C.R. Ltda. for Peru; by WS Computer Publishing Corporation, Inc., for the Philippines; by Contemporanea de Ediciones for Venezuela; by Express Computer Distributors for the Caribbean and West Indies; by Micronesia Media Distributor, Inc. for Micronesia; by Grupo Editorial Norma S.A. for Guatemala; by Chips Computadoras S.A. de C.V. for Mexico; by Editorial Norma de Panama S.A. for Panama; by American Bookshops for Finland. Authorized Sales Agent: Anthony Rudkin Associates for the Middle East and North Africa.

For general information on IDG Books Worldwide's books in the U.S., please call our Consumer Customer Service department at 800-762-2974. For reseller information, including discounts and premium sales, please call our Reseller Customer Service department at 800-434-3422.

For information on where to purchase IDG Books Worldwide's books outside the U.S., please contact our International Sales department at 317-596-5530 or fax 317-596-5692.

For consumer information on foreign language translations, please contact our Customer Service department at 1-800-434-3422, fax 317-596-5692, or e-mail rights@idgbooks.com.

For information on licensing foreign or domestic rights, please phone +1-650-655-3109.

For sales inquiries and special prices for bulk quantities, please contact our Sales department at 650-655-3200 or write to the address above.

For information on using IDG Books Worldwide's books in the classroom or for ordering examination copies, please contact our Educational Sales department at 800-434-2086 or fax 317-596-5499.

For press review copies, author interviews, or other publicity information, please contact our Public Relations department at 650-655-3000 or fax 650-655-3299.

For authorization to photocopy items for corporate, personal, or educational use, please contact Copyright Clearance Center, 222 Rosewood Drive, Danvers, MA 01923, or fax 978-750-4470.

is a registered trademark or trademark under exclusive license to IDG Books Worldwide, Inc. from International Data Group, Inc. in the United States and/or other countries.

About the Author

Glenn E. Weadock is president of Independent Software, Inc., a Colorado-based consulting firm he founded in 1982 after graduating from Stanford University's engineering school. One of the country's most popular technical trainers, Glenn has taught networking topics to thousands of students in the United States, United Kingdom, and Canada in more than 170 seminars since 1988. He has written six intensive two-day seminars for Data-Tech Institute, including *Windows on NetWare* and *Supporting and Troubleshooting Windows 95,* and has written and presented four Data-Tech computer videos.

Glenn is the author of *Intranet Publishing For Dummies* and co-author of *Creating Cool PowerPoint 97 Presentations,* both from IDG Books Worldwide, Inc. He has also written *Bulletproofing NetWare, Bulletproofing Windows 95* (a *Byte* magazine computer book of the month), *Bulletproofing Client/Server Systems,* and *Bulletproof Your PC Network* for McGraw-Hill. His first book, *Exploding the Computer Myth,* deals with computers and business productivity and is used as a textbook at Rutgers University. Glenn is a Microsoft Certified Professional and member of the Association for Computing Machinery, Independent Computer Consultants Association, and American Society for Training and Development.

About the Illustrator

Emily Sherrill Weadock is the Director of Independent Software's Digital Art Studio. An award-winning computer artist whose work has been featured in international magazines, Emily's talent ranges from technical illustration to broadcast-quality 3-D animation and multimedia development. She has illustrated eight books to date, including *Intranet Publishing For Dummies,* and is the co-author of *Creating Cool PowerPoint 97 Presentations,* both for IDG Books Worldwide, Inc. Before trading brushes for mice, Emily enjoyed success as a mixed-media construction artist, and studied art at SMU and Baylor University.

ABOUT IDG BOOKS WORLDWIDE

Welcome to the world of IDG Books Worldwide.

IDG Books Worldwide, Inc., is a subsidiary of International Data Group, the world's largest publisher of computer-related information and the leading global provider of information services on information technology. IDG was founded more than 30 years ago by Patrick J. McGovern and now employs more than 9,000 people worldwide. IDG publishes more than 290 computer publications in over 75 countries. More than 90 million people read one or more IDG publications each month.

Launched in 1990, IDG Books Worldwide is today the #1 publisher of best-selling computer books in the United States. We are proud to have received eight awards from the Computer Press Association in recognition of editorial excellence and three from Computer Currents' First Annual Readers' Choice Awards. Our best-selling ...For Dummies® series has more than 50 million copies in print with translations in 31 languages. IDG Books Worldwide, through a joint venture with IDG's Hi-Tech Beijing, became the first U.S. publisher to publish a computer book in the People's Republic of China. In record time, IDG Books Worldwide has become the first choice for millions of readers around the world who want to learn how to better manage their businesses.

Our mission is simple: Every one of our books is designed to bring extra value and skill-building instructions to the reader. Our books are written by experts who understand and care about our readers. The knowledge base of our editorial staff comes from years of experience in publishing, education, and journalism — experience we use to produce books to carry us into the new millennium. In short, we care about books, so we attract the best people. We devote special attention to details such as audience, interior design, use of icons, and illustrations. And because we use an efficient process of authoring, editing, and desktop publishing our books electronically, we can spend more time ensuring superior content and less time on the technicalities of making books.

You can count on our commitment to deliver high-quality books at competitive prices on topics you want to read about. At IDG Books Worldwide, we continue in the IDG tradition of delivering quality for more than 30 years. You'll find no better book on a subject than one from IDG Books Worldwide.

John Kilcullen
Chairman and CEO
IDG Books Worldwide, Inc.

Steven Berkowitz
President and Publisher
IDG Books Worldwide, Inc.

Eighth Annual
Computer Press
Awards ≥1992

Ninth Annual
Computer Press
Awards ≥1993

Tenth Annual
Computer Press
Awards ≥1994

Eleventh Annual
Computer Press
Awards ≥1995

IDG is the world's leading IT media, research and exposition company. Founded in 1964, IDG had 1997 revenues of $2.05 billion and has more than 9,000 employees worldwide. IDG offers the widest range of media options that reach IT buyers in 75 countries representing 95% of worldwide IT spending. IDG's diverse product and services portfolio spans six key areas including print publishing, online publishing, expositions and conferences, market research, education and training, and global marketing services. More than 90 million people read one or more of IDG's 290 magazines and newspapers, including IDG's leading global brands — Computerworld, PC World, Network World, Macworld and the Channel World family of publications. IDG Books Worldwide is one of the fastest-growing computer book publishers in the world, with more than 700 titles in 36 languages. The "...For Dummies®" series alone has more than 50 million copies in print. IDG offers online users the largest network of technology-specific Web sites around the world through IDG.net (http://www.idg.net), which comprises more than 225 targeted Web sites in 55 countries worldwide. International Data Corporation (IDC) is the world's largest provider of information technology data, analysis and consulting, with research centers in over 41 countries and more than 400 research analysts worldwide. IDG World Expo is a leading producer of more than 168 globally branded conferences and expositions in 35 countries including E3 (Electronic Entertainment Expo), Macworld Expo, ComNet, Windows World Expo, ICE (Internet Commerce Expo), Agenda, DEMO, and Spotlight. IDG's training subsidiary, ExecuTrain, is the world's largest computer training company, with more than 230 locations worldwide and 785 training courses. IDG Marketing Services helps industry-leading IT companies build international brand recognition by developing global integrated marketing programs via IDG's print, online and exposition products worldwide. Further information about the company can be found at www.idg.com.   1/24/99

Dedication

To Mike Snell, a dedication for dedication.

Author's Acknowledgments

My thanks go to many people at IDG Books Worldwide, including (in alphabetical order) Andrea Boucher, Mary Bednarek, Heather Dismore, Gareth Hancock, Angie Hunckler, Joyce Pepple, Clark Scheffy (editor par excellence), and Joell Smith, as well as to the other IDG employees whom I don't know but who helped with the project. Special thanks go to Gerry Routledge for the technical review and Eric Schmidt for the Foreword. To the software and hardware vendors who helped me learn more about their latest products, my thanks (again alphabetically) to Heather Branan of Exabyte, Tiffany Brown of Network Associates, Diane Carlini of Symantec, Melissa Covelli of Waggener-Edstrom, Pam Crane of Seagate Software, Austin Edgington of Novell, Steve Elston of 3Com, Kristin Gabriel of Symantec, Sophia Gianvecchio of Hewlett-Packard, Marci Pedrazzi Gottlieb of Adaptec, Jim Greene of Novell, Jan Jahosky of Seagate Software, Ken Kark of Artisoft, Patrick Karle of Computer Associates, Jennifer Kissell of The Weber Group, Paulette Passanisi of Castelle, Ned Shipp of Artisoft, and Steve Sturgeon of Seagate Technology. Finally, I thank my wife Emily, whom I'd feel fortunate to have as an illustrator even if she didn't sleep with me.

Publisher's Acknowledgments

We're proud of this book; please register your comments through our IDG Books Worldwide Online Registration Form located at http://my2cents.dummies.com.

Some of the people who helped bring this book to market include the following:

Acquisitions, Development, and Editorial

Project Editor: Clark Scheffy

Acquisitions Editors: Gareth Hancock, Jill Pisoni

Media Development Manager: Joyce Pepple

Permissions Editor: Heather H. Dismore

Copy Editor: Andrea Boucher

Technical Editor: Gerald Routledge

Editorial Managers: Mary C. Corder, Colleen Rainsberger

Editorial Assistant: Darren Meiss

Production

Project Coordinator: Regina Snyder

Layout and Graphics: Lou Boudreau, Angela F. Hunckler, Jane E. Martin, Drew R. Moore, Brent Savage, Janet Seib, Michael A. Sullivan

Proofreaders: Christine Berman, Melissa D. Buddendeck, Nancy Price

Indexer: C² Editorial Services

Special Help

Joell Smith, Media Development Assistant, Ken Ball, Special Sales Manager

General and Administrative

IDG Books Worldwide, Inc.: John Kilcullen, CEO; Steven Berkowitz, President and Publisher

IDG Books Technology Publishing: Brenda McLaughlin, Senior Vice President and Group Publisher

Dummies Technology Press and Dummies Editorial: Diane Graves Steele, Vice President and Associate Publisher; Mary Bednarek, Director of Acquisitions and Product Development; Kristin A. Cocks, Editorial Director

Dummies Trade Press: Kathleen A. Welton, Vice President and Publisher; Kevin Thornton, Acquisitions Manager

IDG Books Production for Dummies Press: Michael R. Britton, Vice President of Production and Creative Services; Cindy L. Phipps, Manager of Project Coordination, Production Proof-reading, and Indexing; Kathie S. Schutte, Supervisor of Page Layout; Shelley Lea, Supervisor of Graphics and Design; Debbie J. Gates, Production Systems Specialist; Robert Springer, Supervisor of Proofreading; Debbie Stailey, Special Projects Coordinator; Tony Augsburger, Supervisor of Reprints and Bluelines

Dummies Packaging and Book Design: Patty Page, Manager, Promotions Marketing

◆

The publisher would like to give special thanks to Patrick J. McGovern, without whom this book would not have been possible.

◆

Contents at a Glance

Cartoons at a Glance

By Rich Tennant

page 279

page 221

page 83

page 169

page 327

page 19

Fax: 978-546-7747 • E-mail: the5wave@tiac.net

Table of Contents

Foreword

· ·

Evolution to Revolution: Small Business in a Networked Age

The computer industry has been marked by tectonic shifts: from the ancient mainframe to the personal computer, and from the personal computer to today's network. This latest shift, more *revolution* than *evolution,* is creating tremors felt by businesses of every kind and size. Whether you have five employees or 5,000, the greatest return on your computer technology investment is in the network. Within the walls of a business, a network allows people to access and share information resources, to communicate and collaborate, and to manage your technology investment. And now, with the rapid growth of the Internet, a network can connect even the smallest business in the next town over from the middle of nowhere to the global economy.

Small businesses, with the help of networks, become big businesses. After you have the right network in place, adding new software applications, computers, and printers becomes relatively easy and cost-effective — a matter of plug and play, not *rip and replace.* A computer network, if sufficiently flexible and *scalable* (able to grow), provides the technology backbone for the future expansion and enhancement of the benefits that a network provides. All you need is the right solution and the right information and support. With the help of this excellent book by Glenn Weadock, you can preserve the value of your technology investments and keep the total cost of owning and running a network to a minimum. As Glenn Weadock explains, the current technology and the abundance of support services make small-business networks affordable, easy to manage, and easy to use.

As you will discover in *Small Business Networking For Dummies,* the revolution starts at the local level, where networks can dramatically increase productivity and improve customer service, making your small business more agile and better able to respond to changing needs. The next level of small business networking is *remote access,* which lets you securely open your network to mobile users over conventional or dedicated phone lines, people working at home, and online services such as information databases, credit verification bureaus, and insurance clearinghouses. And, finally, through the Internet, small businesses can directly connect and interact with customers, partners, and suppliers — anytime, anyplace — without expensive leased phone lines. These techniques can all be applied to better serve customers and keep your business running leaner and smarter.

As networking goes global, the growth opportunities for small businesses are no longer constrained by time or geography. Among our customers at Novell, I constantly become aware of small businesses taking advantage of both internal networks and the Internet to create new categories of applications and new kinds of activities. A parts supplier, for example, has linked itself directly to a major automobile manufacturer and can now quickly and electronically dispatch new orders. A professional hockey team in Florida creates a new profit center by selling T-shirts and other souvenirs over the Internet, with orders coming in from as far away as Japan. A pizza restaurant has fax and phone orders for takeout food go directly into its e-mail system, and then appear on a computer monitor in the kitchen for fast preparation and delivery. *Small Business Networking for Dummies* can help you realize your own vision of competing and winning in a networked world. And please, no anchovies.

As exciting as networking is today, one major use for networks is just starting to gather force. I'm referring to *electronic commerce,* which is computer industry buzz talk for conducting business over the Internet. Electronic commerce is coming fast, and it's a wave that is likely to change the competitive landscape in many different parts of the economy. Increasingly, consumers and business purchasing agents will be drawn to the convenience and speed of the Internet. They will use the technology to comparison shop and customize their orders, make credit card payments and transfer funds. No doubt business still has some way to go before customers feel secure about buying and selling this way, but the good news for small businesses is that they can begin putting the network infrastructure in place today so that they're ready to catch the electronic commerce wave tomorrow.

Some of these technological developments may seem remote from the everyday tasks of running a small business, but they will soon be changing and shaping the world in which we all live and work. One of the chief messages of this excellent book is that the network you install today is your launch pad to the future. Using this book, you can build your small business network into a vital asset, and take control of tomorrow.

Eric Schmidt
Chairman of the Board
Chief Executive Officer
Novell, Inc.

Introduction

● ●

*I*f you want a quick, no-nonsense guide to building a computer network for your small business, you've picked up the right book! In this introductory section, I go over the book's purpose, who I think you are as a reader, and how the book is put together, along with a description of the icons I use to guide you through the material. If you're new to computers and networks, the last part of this introduction explains the basics.

About This Book

The definition of *small business* has changed over the last decade. The term no longer necessarily signifies just a family operation or a company with a dozen or fewer employees — *small business* now generally means under 100 employees. (The U.S. government defines a small business as anything under 500 employees!)

Many people are aware that small businesses account for nearly all the new jobs created in the U.S. during the '90s, and that the number of small business creations is growing faster than business failures. Less well known is the fact that most companies with fewer than 100 employees don't have a computer network.

The reasons for this lack of a computer network among small businesses are many — cost, technophobia, resistance to change, or maybe the company is just too busy — but the stage is set for growing businesses to automate their operations (see Figure I-1). Small business computing is becoming more and more feasible as the cost of personal computer hardware and software decreases and computer literacy among managers and employees (many of whom have home computers) increases. And the fact that the technology gets ever more reliable — reducing the need for dedicated staffs to coddle hardware and tweak software — doesn't hurt either. Finally, small businesses are beginning to compete in global markets, and they need the edge against the established megagiant corporations that technology can provide.

Computer industry marketing gurus are reacting to these changes in the business world and the needs of small businesses for reliable, expandable computer networks. For example, Novell, Microsoft, Apple, and Hewlett-Packard have all recently announced products with "Small Business" in their titles, reflecting the efforts these vendors have made to make products that

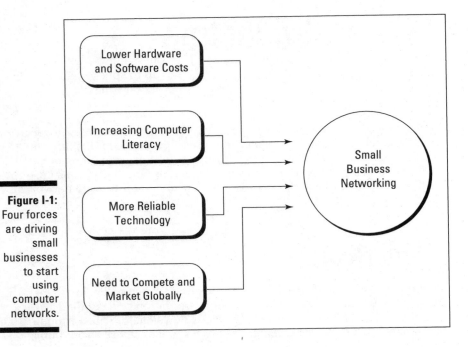

are easier to set up and manage. And as the computer industry targets the small business market more energetically, the variety and quality of computer products for growing enterprises will increase even further.

The main challenge that growing companies must overcome before they begin reaping the rewards of modern computer technology is that most small business managers and employees don't have much (or any) computer networking expertise. If you hail from a large organization, you may have relied on the in-house Information Services department to handle most networking issues. Even businesspeople who have some experience with small computers (for example, with a home PC or notebook machine) find that the technical issues involved in creating a network can be trickier than those involved in setting up a single, isolated PC and cruising the Web.

Depending on your company's size and budget, hiring someone to build and manage a network full time may not be an option. (Network managers with strong experience and training generally command high salaries.) So, the responsibility for managing the network may fall to an office manager or to whoever in the office seems to know the most about computers: "Jane, you know what a modem is? You do? Great, you're our new network manager." (If you substitute "Glenn" for "Jane" in the previous sentence, you know exactly how I got my first network management assignment in my previous life as a solar energy design engineer.)

Fortunately, *Small Business Networking For Dummies* is here to help.

What this book is

In this book, I present the essentials of small business networking concisely, conversationally, and clearly. I quickly bring you up to speed on the key success factors of building and managing a network on which you can rely as a *profitable partner* rather than as a bottomless time and money sinkhole. I cover product-independent concepts that anyone building or managing a small business network must know. What I don't do, however, is tell you all about the rarefied air, computer science Ph.D. networking theory — I only tell you what you need to know in order to make informed purchasing and design decisions.

Small Business Networking For Dummies may be the only book you need to read on the subject if you just need an overview to help you understand the key issues involved, or participate in meetings about the company network. In addition, if you haven't yet decided what network products you want or need, this book is a great place to start, because I don't assume that you have any particular type of network in place. I do, however, discuss some of the popular options for network software and hardware. Finally, I give you many down-and-dirty details for installing everything from cable to computers; configuring servers and workstations for the network; and protecting your network from viruses and failures. Where the material gets too technical to cover in a single book, I point you to other sources for additional help, and suggest whether a consultant, product manual, or commercial book can give you the details you need.

What this book isn't

In some ways, the most important part of any prescription drug label is the part that warns you how *not* to use the product (as in "Do not wash this medication down with vodka"). Well, here's the warning label for this book.

This is not a product-specific book (although I do discuss several hardware and software network products), nor is it a rehash of any computer product manual. This book's content is relevant whether you ultimately install Novell IntranetWare, Microsoft Windows NT Server, Artisoft LANtastic, or some other product. The editors and I are guessing that this book is more useful to you if it doesn't focus exclusively on one networking technology. Instead, I present an overview of what's available, give you a framework for evaluating and deciding what products best fit your needs, and provide tips and techniques that apply to just about any small business network.

So don't try to use this book as a replacement for a particular vendor's network software or hardware documentation. Instead, read this book first, so you better understand the vendor's manuals and have the know-how to make the choices they offer you.

In this book, I don't tell you how to build a large network with a thousand users, either, although much of the stuff I discuss applies equally well to large networks as to small ones. I do discuss some of the network hardware you may need as your network grows, and help you put the types of procedures and technology into place that can expand as your business expands.

Finally, though I mention several specific hardware and software products in this book, please realize that in doing so, I'm not endorsing these products or suggesting that you use them. Ultimately, you have to decide what hardware and software work best for your situation. My job is to prepare you to make such decisions intelligently, either on your own or with the help of a consultant who knows your business.

Who you are

I wrote this book mainly for owners, managers, or soon-to-be part-time or full-time network administrators within a growing business, regardless of job title. You may also get something out of this book if you're a consultant of one stripe or another who doesn't have a computer background and needs to get up to speed with small business networking.

I don't make a lot of assumptions in these pages about you or your business. You can find useful information in this book no matter what sort of business or industry you're in. In fact, for the most part, the country you're in doesn't matter, either. You may already have some so-called _standalone_ computers that don't connect to a network, or you may be embarking on your first computer project altogether. You may have multiple offices, or just one. You may or may not have a full-time network manager on the payroll.

The few assumptions I do make about you are:

- You work in a company with somewhere between 5 and 500 employees.

- You haven't yet set up a computer network, or if you have, the experience was mysterious enough in some way that you now want to know more.

- You may not have any prior experience with computers (if you do, that's fine and it'll help, but experience isn't a prerequisite for understanding this book).

- You're concerned about costs, and would like to spend a minimal amount building a computer network that does what you want it to do.

- You're concerned about your network becoming obsolete, and you want to build a computer network that you don't have to throw away next summer.

- You want your network to be able to grow with your business as painlessly as possible.

> ✔ You don't necessarily want to become a computer expert, and you don't want to spend any more time fiddling with your computer network than is necessary to ensure a successful operation.
>
> ✔ You want to build a network that's as automatic and self-running as possible.
>
> ✔ You're not really a "dummy," you just need the basics on the subject in a hurry.

If this sounds like you, read on!

Who I am

The value of any book depends on the experience of the author, so you're justified in asking who the heck is writing this book — especially because you're about to make some big decisions based in part on my words.

I've run a small computer consulting business since 1982, and I've been a seminar developer and instructor for Data-Tech Institute since 1988. I'm not an electronics genius by any stretch, and I couldn't even tell you how a transistor works anymore (I used to know, but those brain cells are long since defunct). However, I've worked with enough different networks to understand their advantages and pitfalls pretty well, and I've built several dozen networks myself from the ground up. My seminar students have helped me learn a lot over the years about which network technologies and techniques work in the real world, and which don't. I've also had the privilege to work with some of the top experts in computer networking while developing my seminars, videotapes, and commercial books. (Four out of my seven previous books deal with computer networking.)

Although some of my consulting clients are big companies, I've also worked with about 30 different small businesses in the course of my consulting career. These clients include a local wine shop, two real estate developers, a cheese company, a regional lumber distributor, a few law firms, a bail-bonds company, a magazine publisher, a nonprofit senior citizens center, a medical clinic, an engineering firm, an architectural firm, and a credit collection agency. I run a small business of my own, too, which means I've written business plans, wooed bankers, learned about profit-and-loss statements and balance sheets, cursed government paperwork, paid absurd prices for insurance, spent a lot of my life in the car, and eaten way too many fast food meals at my desk while trying to meet one deadline or another. And like most readers of this book, I wouldn't have it any other way!

I've tried to make this the book about the network that I'd want if my small company were just getting into the technology. I hope you'll tell me how you like this book, and how I can make it better for the next edition. You can reach me through my company's Web site, which is at http://www.i-sw.com.

How This Book Is Organized

As with most ...*For Dummies* books, you can dip in and out of specific chapters according to where you are in your project, what your responsibilities and interests are, and what level of knowledge you already have about particular subjects. You can certainly read this book cover to cover, and I do my best to keep it interesting if you do, but each chapter is designed to give you all the information you need on a specific topic and not leave you hanging if you haven't read the entire book up to that point.

The overall book organization follows a logical order: initial planning, key technology decisions, network implementation, and management.

Part I: Assessing the Benefits and Costs

In Part I, I explain how computer networking can help your business cut costs, enhance revenue, and improve communications. If you don't already know what you need a network for, the first chapter in Part I is a great thought-provoker. Even if you do have a specific application in mind, Chapter 1 may suggest some worthwhile additional possibilities. Chapters 2 and 3 present some frameworks for developing cost and time estimates, so you can get an idea of what you need to build and manage your network.

Part II: Four Steps to Planning Your Technology Strategy

Part II identifies and discusses four critical technology decision areas to address before you spend a dime on networking products. First, you pick a networking style — the two primary styles are *client/server* and *peer-to-peer,* and the choice you make has a far-reaching effect on the cost, manageability, and growth potential of your network. Second, you choose the basic system software for your network, based on an overview of today's popular market options. Third, you decide on a network language, another decision to make after careful thought because it has an effect on how easily you can expand and manage your network. And fourth, you make a variety of choices about the nuts and bolts (hardware) for your new network.

Part III: Do It! Setting Up Your Network

In Part III, I walk you through the basic steps of setting up a new network. Chapter 8 goes through the typical hardware installation steps; Chapter 9 covers software installation and configuration, such as creating users and groups, organizing files on the server, and setting up shared print support.

Chapter 10 covers communications: remote access to your network, and how you can use your network to connect to the outside world and the Internet.

Part IV: Running the System — Networking versus Not Working

Part IV shows you how to keep your network up and running securely, quickly, and reliably over the long haul. Small business networking success depends on following through and *managing* the project after you roll it out to users. The chapters in this part deal with setting up a level of network security appropriate for your business, tuning your new network for peak performance, and managing and maintaining your network without the benefit of the full-time network administrative staff that large companies have.

Part V: The Part of Tens

The Part of Tens is a standard feature of ...*For Dummies* books, and this one is no different. The first chapter in this part summarizes ten methods for keeping costs down when rolling out a small business network. Another chapter covers ten useful network troubleshooting steps. Chapter 16 presents ten reasons to build a special type of network called an *intranet,* which is currently the hottest trend in network computing. Finally, Chapter 17 lists ten ways you can use your small business network to connect to the public Internet and develop new markets for your products and services.

Appendixes

This book has three appendixes:

- ✔ Appendix A is a glossary with concise definitions of terms used in the book.

- ✔ Appendix B is a references and resources section that provides details on companies and products mentioned in the book, as well as a list of books and magazines that can help you get more information and stay up to date on networking trends and technology.

- ✔ Appendix C is a description of the software goodies on the enclosed CD-ROM.

Icons Used in This Book

In the spirit of making this book easily accessible, I use several graphical icons to highlight certain kinds of material:

Use this icon to avoid a *gotcha* — a common trap or pitfall. Most of my cautions come from my own experience building and working with small business networks.

The ...*For Dummies* series includes several other excellent books that you may want to consult as you build your network. This icon points you to them.

This icon guides you to other sections of the book where you can find more information relative to the topic at hand.

You get a blockbuster CD-ROM with this book and this icon alerts you that the accompanying text refers to software on that disc.

When you see this icon, you know I've succumbed to the temptation to editorialize a little bit. These rants and exhortations are opinionated and other knowledgeable people may disagree with them, but they *are* based on experience.

This icon points out a bit of knowledge or comment that's worth committing to your long-term memory.

Here's some material you can skip if you don't care about the nitty-gritty details, but may want to read if you like to know a bit more about what goes on inside those off-white computer cases.

Short suggestions, hints, and bits of useful information appear next to this icon. My tips are usually based on actual experience working with small companies.

What Is a Computer Network, Anyway? (The Basics)

This section is for readers who are new to it all — computer networks, computers, and books about computers. If you already know what terms like *LAN, CPU,* and *Ethernet* mean, please feel free to skip this section and proceed directly to Chapter 1 (or whatever chapter you need). Otherwise, read this section to get the scoop on computers and networks so that the rest of this book makes sense.

Networks are collections of computers, software, and hardware that are all connected to help their users work together. However, before I explain what a computer network really is, I need to spend a little bit of time explaining the bare-bones basics of computer categories, software and hardware.

Computer categories

Lots of different types of computers exist — you've probably heard terms like *supercomputer, mainframe,* and *minicomputer.* Supercomputers and mainframes aren't generally used by small businesses; they're used for applications like predicting the weather and handling airline reservations. However, minicomputers may enter the picture for some small businesses.

A *minicomputer* is a machine for multiple users (generally 2 to 200), each of whom typically uses a *dumb terminal* to send information back and forth to the central machine. (A dumb terminal simply means that the keyboard-and-screen workstation that connects to the minicomputer doesn't have any computing power itself — it just displays the computing results of the minicomputer to the user, and acts as a window into the central machine which does all the work.) Minicomputers can also connect to other kinds of computers (other minicomputers, PCs, and so on). Minicomputers typically have high levels of security, lots of computing power, and excellent reliability (usually better than PC networks). Today, most minicomputers cost anywhere from $10,000 to $200,000. These machines have been around for years and a very wide variety of programs run on them. If you need stringent security and very low downtime, minicomputers remain a viable choice, but they generally cost more and require more technical support than PC networks.

Digital Equipment Corporation single-handedly created the minicomputer, but its famous VAX machines are no longer as popular as they were 10 or 20 years ago. IBM makes a popular minicomputer called the AS/400. Today's larger minicomputers aren't really "mini" in any real sense — they're very powerful computers capable of running medium and large businesses. Some people call minicomputers *midrange* systems, which is a better term.

Sorry about names like AS/400 and VAX, but one thing about the computer industry is that it calls products by techie-sounding names. Personally, I wish that every computer had a nonnumeric name, like *Sirius* or *Lisa* or even *Datamaster* — those were all real computers, by the way — but the fact is that most of the computer industry uses boring, hard-to-remember numbers and letters instead of names.

Most likely, your computer network will use *microcomputers* rather than minicomputers. Microcomputers, also known as *personal computers,* are small, individual-sized computers for one user at a time — and the micro-computers have a full allotment of processing hardware and software (the opposite of a *dumb terminal*). Microcomputers are less expensive than minicomputers (although not necessarily on a per-user basis), generally costing between $1,000 and $10,000. Examples of microcomputers are IBM-compatible PCs, Apple Macintoshes and their clones, and Unix *workstations.* (A *workstation* is typically a microcomputer on the high end of the power scale, fast enough to do demanding work such as product design and high-speed graphics.)

Microcomputers trace their popularity to the debut of the Apple II in 1977 and to the entry of IBM PCs into the market in 1981. Since 1981, these small computers have doubled in speed seven times, meaning that today's micro-computers are about 100 times faster than the original IBM PC.

More types of computers exist, including *minisupercomputers* and *superminicomputers* (I am not making these up), but minicomputers and microcomputers are the ones you really need to understand for most small business network setups. Chances are good that if your company has fewer than 50 employees, you'll stick with microcomputers for your computer network.

In the case of microcomputers and minicomputers used for small business applications, the computer's capability to compute is no longer its strongest or most interesting capability. Although we're stuck with the term *computer,* think of the device as a *data tool* that can do more than just crunch num-bers. Computers accept, store, move, and produce just about any kind of data — and then modify or manipulate that data in just about any kind of way.

Hardware

Now that you've got a handle on the main computer categories, it's time to discuss a few basic terms about *hardware* — the parts of a computer you can touch, see, and break. (Just kidding — computer hardware nowadays is actually pretty difficult to damage.)

The central part of a computer — the box containing the core components of the machine — is called the *system unit*. The system unit is the enclosure that has to be opened up if you ever need to add memory or disk storage to the computer. The system unit connects to the screen, printer, keyboard, mouse, and other devices by means of a variety of cables. Because these cabled devices exist along the outside (periphery) of the system unit, they go by the name *peripherals* (see Figure I-2).

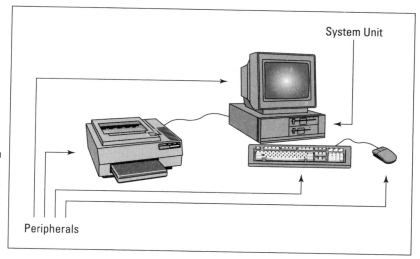

Figure I-2:
A computer
system unit
and
peripherals.

If you remove the system unit's cover, you see one or more thin, flat, plastic boards, called *circuit boards,* that plug into a larger circuit board called the *system board* or *motherboard*. The motherboard usually contains one or more slots called *expansion slots* into which you can plug additional circuit boards in order to add new features to the computer. For example, in the case of a computer network, you have to add a special circuit board called a *Network Interface Card* (NIC — say "nick") that allows the computer to connect to your new network — more on that in Chapter 7.

On the motherboard is a large black plastic chip, an inch or so square — it may lie hidden underneath a knobby metallic plate, or *heat sink,* which acts like a radiator to cool the chip (sometimes you see a little cooling fan instead of a metal plate). This chip is called a *microprocessor* — it contains millions of tiny on-off switches (transistors) etched into the silicon wafers contained inside the chip's black case. More specifically, it's the Big Kahuna of microprocessors known as the *CPU* (Central Processing Unit), which directs most of the data traffic throughout the computer. (Incidentally, many people use the term *CPU* incorrectly to refer to a computer's *system unit.*) A number of the other circuit boards also have microprocessors that perform specialized tasks to help out the CPU.

Also inside the system unit is a sealed metal box containing several disk-shaped platters stacked one above the other on a common spindle that's connected to a motor. The metal box also contains a movable arm assembly that can move in toward the center of the disks, or out toward their edge. This box is the *hard drive* (see Figure I-3), and the platters are magnetized so that they can store information even when no power is flowing to the device. The computer can change the magnetic fields (and the data they contain) at any time by magnetizing the *read/write head* on the tip of the movable arm, and directing that arm across the specific areas on the disk that the computer needs to change. The process is basically the same one that audio cassettes use to store music, only on a much finer scale, and on a disk instead of a tape. You can use the hard drive to store information you want to keep, and you can reuse the hard drive's platters to store different information over time. (Of course, you don't have to manually etch magnetic data to the disk — you just click the Save command in your programs, and the CPU takes care of the work.)

Figure I-3:
A hard drive cutaway, showing disk platters and read/ write head.

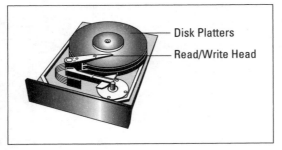

Disk Platters

Read/Write Head

Even a really fast hard drive isn't fast enough to do the computer's daily work, however. The computer's motherboard contains several rows of identical *chips* (little computing circuits), smaller and much simpler than the CPU, called *memory chips* (or *RAM* chips, which is short for Random Access Memory). These devices provide high-speed data storage, typically about 20 times faster than a typical hard drive — this is where most of the computer's work takes place.

RAM chips can't account for all the storage in a computer for two reasons: First, they're much more expensive than the magnetic hard drive, so a typical computer only contains as much RAM as is necessary to store the information that a user is working on at any given moment. Second, without power, the contents of RAM disappear — when a user enters or changes information using RAM (for instance, while writing a memo in a word-processing program), the user must copy that information to the hard drive (that is, *save* the memo) so that it is available later.

Think of the hard disk as your filing cabinet; RAM is like your desktop where you work. Remember to save your work in the filing cabinet, because when you turn off the machine at night, it's like having the cleaners come through and wipe everything off your desk.

Software

Software is a set of instructions that tells a computer to do something. Think of hardware as the brains and body, and software as the intelligence and instinct of the computer system.

All software comes on diskettes, CD-ROMs, or magnetic tape. Software becomes active when the computer reads (or loads) the information from the magnetic or optical medium into the computer's main memory (RAM). Think of the process of loading software as the computer's waking into consciousness. Computers forget everything they know the moment you turn them off, so every time a computer is turned on, it needs to load a complete set of software instructions all over again.

This book spends a lot of time talking about two main categories of software: *system software* and *application software.* Let me briefly explain what these terms mean, and then I can move on to a definition of a computer network (which I get to eventually, I *swear*).

System software

The basic software that allows the computer to move information from point A to point B and communicate with devices like the keyboard, screen, disks, and printers is called the *operating system.* Operating systems store information and programs on disks in organized data structures called *files.* Most operating systems use a *branched file structure* that allows data and program files to be grouped into *directories* — directories organize disks pretty much the same way manila folders organize file drawers. In fact, depending on the kind of computer you use, directories may even be called *folders.*

You can have directories within other directories — this manila folder within the file drawer is called a *subdirectory.* For example, on the computer I used to write this book, I have a directory called "Books" (the file drawer) and, underneath it, subdirectories for each particular book project (the manila folders). Each subdirectory, in turn, contains the chapter and illustration files (see Figure I-4).

Operating systems do more than just organize files and move data around inside the computer; they provide a standard way for other programs to do the same things. For example, if you're using a word-processing program to write a letter and you tell the program to print the letter, the program issues commands to the operating system to handle the printing. If the computer were an office building, then the operating system would be the superintendent,

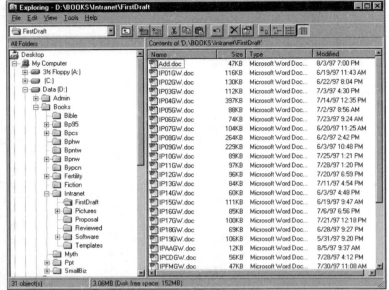

Figure I-4:
Operating
system
software
enables you
to organize
files into
directories,
or folders.

doorman, and delivery boy all rolled into one; he's at the beck and call of all the tenant programs and when they need something delivered to the hard disk or printer, he's the one who does the work.

All computers have an operating system, and some computers can run multiple operating systems, but only one at any given time. IBM-compatible PCs, for example, can run Windows 95, PC DOS, and Unix.

You may need more than a single operating system if you want to connect computers together. You may, for example, need another layer of software called a *Network Operating System* (NOS — pronounced "noss"). A Network Operating System (such as Windows NT Server) may run on a special computer called a *server,* which "serves up" shared files, programs, and printers, while a workstation operating system (such as Windows 95) may run on the computers at employee desks.

You also need housekeeping software, called *utility software,* to handle daily chores and help the operator or administrator manage the computer's resources. Utility software includes programs for monitoring and trouble-shooting computers; making backup copies of the data they store in case of hardware failure; and protecting computers against software viruses that can damage data.

The sum total of the workstation operating system, Network Operating System (on the server), and utility software makes up the so-called *system software* (see Figure I-5). Users may not interact directly with system software, and may not even know that it's there. However, like the foundation that supports a building, you have to have it before you can build much of anything else.

Application software

Programs that enable users to do useful and specific jobs with the computer, such as word processing, financial management, and simulated golf, make up *application* software — so called because they permit a human being to *apply* the computer to a useful task. Application software "talks" to system software to get things done, things like saving a user's work or printing a document. Users don't necessarily see the separation between the application and the operating system, and there's really no reason they should.

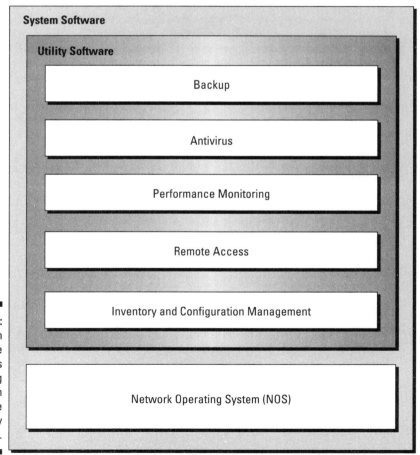

Figure I-5:
System software includes operating system software and utility software.

Computer designers have worked hard in the last several years to make things simpler and hide as much of the system software as possible from the average computer user.

However, to build and manage a computer network, you have to know a fair amount about the system software as well as the application software that you use. In fact, understanding system software is the biggest difference between being a computer *user,* and being a computer *administrator.*

Application software starts the same way system software starts: The computer loads it from a disk or other storage device into the computer's RAM, a procedure called *running* or *executing* the program. But, a computer has to load its system software first, before it can run application programs. (Remember, the application software uses the system software to get things done.)

Application software breaks down into two main categories: *horizontal* (or *horizontal market*) applications, which apply to a wide variety of industries and businesses, and *vertical* (or *vertical market*) applications, which address a particular business type. For example, a spreadsheet program is a horizontal application; a videotape rental-tracking program is a vertical application. Some examples of horizontal applications include

- ✔ Bookkeeping and Accounting
- ✔ Inventory
- ✔ Word Processing
- ✔ Desktop Publishing
- ✔ Spreadsheet
- ✔ Communications and E-Mail
- ✔ Groupware (Scheduling, Collaboration, and so on)
- ✔ Database
- ✔ Computer-Aided Design (CAD)
- ✔ Project Management
- ✔ Graphics Design

Vertical applications often combine elements of horizontal market software with special features for a particular industry's needs. For example, a real estate property management program that tracks tenants, leases, and payments is a specialized version of a horizontal application called a *database.*

Networks and information systems

Designers originally built microcomputers to allow one person to do one job at a time on one machine. Today, microcomputers that connect to networks form a strong alternative to the minicomputer or mainframe.

A network connects computers by means of cabling systems, specialized software, and devices that manage data traffic. A network enables users to share files and expensive resources, such as high-quality printers, as well as send messages electronically (*e-mail*) to each other. I mention in the "System software" section that any computer that offers resources for use by other networked computers is called a *server;* on the flip side of the coin, any computer that uses a shared network resource is called a *client.* Sometimes, computers can act as a server and a client at the same time.

Networks have both hardware pieces (Network Interface Cards, cables, cable connection boxes, and so on) and software components (the Network Operating System, and network management utilities like performance monitoring software and antivirus software). Microcomputers, midrange systems, and mainframes *can* all participate on the same network, although achieving this level of integration isn't necessarily a cakewalk.

In a network involving microcomputers, the intelligence or processing power of the system is divided out among the various computers on the network. (However, remember that processing power is concentrated in a single, centralized, high-speed computer with a network based on a minicomputer or mainframe computer.) Because microcomputers have become much more powerful over the last few years, such a *distributed processing environment,* as it's called, now brings a great deal of computer horsepower to bear on solving business problems and streamlining operations.

Computer networks fall into two main types: *client/server* networks and *peer-to-peer* networks. Chapter 4 discusses these in greater detail, but for now, just know that a client/server network uses one or more dedicated machines (the servers) to share files, printers, and applications. A peer-to-peer network allows any user to share his or her files with any other user, and doesn't require a central, dedicated server.

Most of the discussion in this book has to do with *Local Area Networks,* or *LANs* for short. A LAN connects computers within a single geographical location, such as one office building or office suite. By contrast, *Wide Area Networks* (WANs) span different cities or even countries, using phone lines or satellite links. You may hear other acronyms, such as *Metropolitan Area Network* (MAN) or *Campus Area Network* (CAN), but this book doesn't spend much time on those multiple-site network types because I assume you're setting up a network in a single location. Besides, I think the industry is getting a little carried away with all these acronyms. Before long we'll be discussing BLANs (Big Local Area Networks) and GLANs (Giant Local Area Networks).

Networks are often categorized in other ways, too. You can refer to a network by what sort of circuit boards the computers use to link to each other — *Ethernet* and *Token-Ring* are the most popular choices. You can also refer to a network by how it packages data for transmission across the cable, with terms such as *TCP/IP* (Transmission Control Protocol/Internet Protocol) and *IPX/SPX* (Internet Packet eXchange/Sequenced Packet eXchange). Don't worry if these terms are new to you — I explain them all in Chapters 5 through 7.

Finally, I should mention that the term *network* usually refers to the techno-logical components (hardware and software) and excludes the human components (*wetware,* so called because the human brain is bathed in blood — apologies to squeamish readers). An *information system,* on the other hand, is a computer or computer network coupled with its human user(s). A successful network information system, in my opinion anyway, is one that does at least three of the following:

- ✓ **Reduces costs:** A network enables sharing of expensive computer equipment.

- ✓ **Helps you make better decisions:** Gets accurate operating information more quickly.

- ✓ **Opens new revenue opportunities:** Links your company with global markets.

- ✓ **Frees you and your colleagues from tasks with low added value:** No more hunting for information on paper documents in file cabinets or in the trash can.

- ✓ **Improves internal communications:** Employees relate better with each other (though not necessarily with their inner children).

- ✓ **Improves external communications:** Suppliers, contractors, and customers can now depend on a reliable system.

This book is dedicated to helping you achieve six out of six!

Part I

Assessing the Benefits and Costs

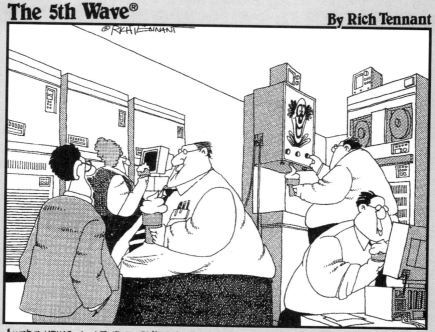

The 5th Wave® By Rich Tennant

"WE'RE USING A 4-TIERED SYSTEM - PC, TO MINI, TO MR. SMOOTHY, TO MAINFRAME."

In this part . . .

*B*usiness investments are all about benefits and costs, and that's where this book starts. How can a computer network help your David company compete with the Goliaths out there? In Chapter 1, I explain the three main ways — cutting costs, enhancing revenues, and improving communications — and offer some examples. In Chapter 2, I go out on a limb and try to give you an idea of what computer network technology actually costs, both up front and over the long haul.

When you launch a new project, you budget time as well as money, and Chapter 3 helps you plan your schedule. The *who* of a schedule is as important as the *when*. Most small companies don't have full-time computer gurus on staff, and therefore don't want to (or can't) do all the technical grunt work in-house (although with this book you can do much more than you think). So, in Chapter 3, I also offer some insider's tips on how best to use consultants in order to speed up the rollout schedule and help you make key technology decisions.

Chapter 1

I Just Sell Widgets. Why Do I Need a Network?

● ●

In This Chapter

▶ Competing on a global scale (why your small business may have to)

▶ Using computer networking to reduce operating costs

▶ Opening markets and generating new revenue with your network

● ●

*"M*odern computers can do everything from ruining your credit rating forever to landing a nuclear warhead on your porch." (Dave Barry, *Bad Habits*, Henry Holt)

A TV commercial that ran a few years ago featured several business executives in somber poses, contemplating their obviously dire business problems, until one executive looked at another executive across a conference room table and said, with a deep and very serious voice, "What we need . . . is a network." Sort of the same way James Earl Jones says, "This . . . is CNN."

I do think that a well-designed computer network can significantly help most businesses today. However, I would never suggest that any company take that on faith, or that a computer network is a cure-all for company problems. A small company with intelligent and responsive management, motivated employees, and a product or service that meets customer needs can benefit from a *Local Area Network* (LAN), but a company without these essentials shouldn't expect a computer network to vault it to success. (Incidentally, a LAN is a network in a single location — the kind this book discusses.)

In this chapter, I present a few reasons why you may need a LAN, along with several ways a network can help you reduce costs and enhance revenues. Even if you've already made the mental commitment to build a computer network (or your boss has made that commitment and strongly encouraged you to share it), this chapter may be helpful in suggesting how you can use the network once you get it in place. This chapter is not exhaustive, because the number of possible business applications for a computer network is huge, but it does get you thinking along some profitable lines.

Check out *Small Business Web Strategies For Dummies* by Janine Warner and *Small Business Internet For Dummies* by Greg Holden (both from IDG Books Worldwide, Inc.) for more on this topic.

You're Not in Kansas Anymore (If You Ever Were)

The days of innocence when a small business could operate successfully in a geographically limited market, grow at its own pace, and not worry much about competition or technology are probably gone forever. Your business may never have known that sort of world — but if it did, bid it a fond farewell. You're not in Kansas anymore, Dorothy.

The globalization of small businesses, the increased intensity of competition in almost every industry, and the tighter operating parameters of small business versus big business all challenge you to do more productive work in less time than you ever have before. A computer network is no guarantee of greater competitiveness, but it's fast becoming a requirement for staying in the race. (As an old math teacher of mine would have put it, computer networks are becoming *necessary* if not *sufficient*.)

Your business is global (whether you realize it yet or not!)

The last time I went skiing at a Colorado resort, I wore a jacket made in Brazil, a sweater made in Mexico, ski pants made in Germany, and thermal underwear made in Austria. The Japanese-owned resort imported the chairlift from Switzerland. About the only thing completely American made in the whole experience was the snow, and you could argue that it was imported to some extent, too.

The small, neighborhood business is finding itself competing against the giant corporate entities that seem to be infiltrating every vacant commercial lot. If you're a retailer, you may have to compete against the Wal-Marts and the Home Depots. If you're a restaurateur, you may have to compete against the McDonald's and Domino's chains.

Today's small business doesn't merely compete with large domestic-based companies, either. Some of your competitors are companies based outside your own country. If you're a winemaker, for example, you have to compete with products from Chile and Australia and Spain, as well as those from your neighbor down the valley.

Another factor leading to the globalization of markets is the ready availability of fast shipment via air express. Almost every product you can imagine is now available for next-day delivery through one of the thousands of mail-order catalogs that keep postal services across the globe operating in the black. If your business markets a product that's physically smaller than a jet engine, you probably have mail-order competition. The computer industry itself is a good example: One of the top three microcomputer manufacturers is a mail-order company.

The disintegration of the Iron Curtain has accelerated international trade. The former Soviet Union, eastern Europe, and China are now participating in international business to a much greater degree than they did ten years ago. The move toward a European economic union promises to streamline business in what has traditionally been a more or less fragmented collection of individual markets.

The bottom line is that small business is up against big, international business at every turn — but being up against the big guys doesn't mean that you can't profit by marketing the craftsmanship, personal service, quick market response, and innovative design that small businesses often bring to the market. What it does mean, however, is that you now have competition from every corner of the globe, and your products and services have to deliver more value than those offered by international companies with much greater resources. (Globes don't really *have* corners, but you get my drift.)

The globalization of business holds great opportunities, too. Your company may have a potentially much larger market than you ever thought you had — if you can somehow get the word out to that market.

You need every edge you can get

If the globalization of business means more competition on the one hand, and exciting new market opportunities on the other, you need every edge you can get. A lean-and-mean computer network can help provide that edge.

Having said that, please understand that even with the best advice and guidance, and even with today's more user-friendly networking products, building a reliable, cost-effective, easy-to-use computer network takes a certain amount of time and effort. Creating a network *increases* your workload in the short term for long term benefits, as shown in Figure 1-1.

You have to put time in at the outset to learn the computer networking technologies and products available so that you can make smart purchasing decisions. Someone in your organization (and that person's backup) has to learn the networking products well enough to install them properly and

Figure 1-1:
Creating a
productive
computer
network
involves an
up-front
investment
of time,
effort, and
dollars
before you
see any
rewards.

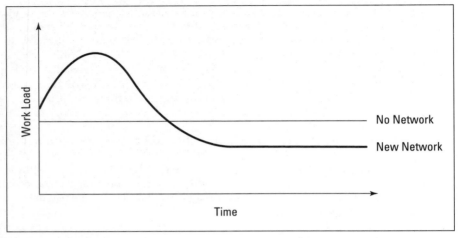

manage them over time. Employees have to devote some time to learning how to use the software applications you place onto the network. If you understand that computer networking isn't something that you can (or even should) build overnight, you're well on your way to building a system that can boost your business.

You can't afford big-business inefficiencies

You've probably heard some variation of the old cliché that goes like this: When a big business makes a mistake it stubs its toe, but when a small business makes a mistake, it stubs its head. (You *can* stub your head, I looked it up.) The adage contains much truth — big businesses have resources that allow them to survive inefficiencies and mistakes, at least up to a point. IBM didn't go out of business when its ill-conceived PCjr home computer flopped (typing on the tiny "Chiclet" keys was next to impossible). Such a complete product failure would wipe out most small businesses — if you're going to be small, you have to be better.

Anyone who's ever worked for a large company has seen firsthand the enormous inefficiencies a big bureaucracy can impose. Many small business managers and employees are working in a smaller company now because they grew frustrated with those inefficiencies. Three examples of common big-company ills are *left-hand-right-hand syndrome, redundant information,* and *incompatible computer systems.*

The left-hand-right-hand syndrome is where one employee does something unproductive or counterproductive because he or she didn't know what others in the organization were already doing.

> A computer network can help you avoid left-hand-right-hand syndrome by enhancing internal communications, for example, with e-mail.

Another big-business inefficiency is creating and maintaining redundant information. In any large corporation, the same information often exists in many different places, even if it's in computerized form. For example, the marketing department may maintain a list of customers, and the finance department may maintain precisely the same list. This means twice as much work goes into keeping the customer lists current.

> A computer network can help you avoid redundant information by providing a central storehouse for key operating information.

Large companies often merge with or acquire other companies that use different computer systems. So, a third big-business inefficiency is coordinating, reconciling, and combining information from information systems that don't talk to each other.

> You can reduce your chances of running into the compatibility problems of multiple computer systems by designing a network that adheres to industry standards and uses popular hardware and software.

No doubt you can think of other ways big companies operate inefficiently, but the point here is that *you* can't afford to operate that way. Your computer network must help you reduce redundant and unnecessary effort so that you can get the most from your employees — and level the playing field with the big, lumbering companies. A fast, efficient, well-designed network can be one of the stones you use to knock out Goliath — or at least distract him for a time, while you make enough money to build yourself a bigger slingshot.

Cutting Costs

Most small businesses are acutely aware of how important cash flow is to their continued existence. If the incoming cash flow isn't enough to cover operating expenses, loan repayments, coffee machine rentals, and other financial obligations, companies can fail even as they sell product and gain market share. Unlike large companies, small businesses can't necessarily rely on cash from other fat-profit-producing divisions in order to stay afloat. I've seen small companies close their doors due to cash flow concerns even in the midst of a sales upswing, and the irony can be truly tragic.

You've probably heard about some of the amazing things that businesses have done in order to cover cash shortfalls. Fred Smith, the president of Federal Express, once went to a casino in order to win enough to make payroll (he did). Most small business managers prefer not to have to resort to such measures to keep the cash flow positive, especially if you have trouble even *pronouncing* "baccarat."

A big part of keeping the cash flowing is keeping operating costs low. Carefully designed and well-managed computer networks can help you do that in several ways, especially when compared to running your business on a few *standalone* (unnetworked) computers that don't connect to each other.

Sharing expensive resources

If your small business already has some computers, linking them together can reduce costs by allowing you to share resources such as printers, tape drives, phone lines, and even software. If you don't have any computers but are thinking about buying some, you can probably spend less on hardware and software by building a network. The more users your network has, the more your cost savings increase from networked resource sharing.

Printers

Laser printers certainly cost less now than they did a decade ago, but you can still find yourself spending a few thousand dollars on one, especially if you need highly detailed graphics, large paper sizes, or color capability. And even if you don't need a fancy model, why spend $1,800 on three printers when one $600 printer will do?

The dollar savings from printer sharing may grow even more if you use other kinds of printers for special purposes. You may use a dot-matrix printer for multiple-part forms, or a color inkjet printer for low-cost color prints. You can hang these kinds of printers off your network just as easily as laser printers.

Portable computer users can share networked printers, too, by plugging into the network. Unless your users have to be able to print while they're on the road, they can connect their *notebooks* (small portable computers) to a network cable in the main office and print whatever they need. If most of the notebook computers your users have (or will have) are the same kind, you can even set up a *docking station* on your network. A notebook user can connect his or her computer by just sliding it into the docking station, and instantly have access to all shared network resources. The docking station is always connected to the network, but only becomes active when it has a notebook computer connected to it.

Modems, faxes, and phone lines

Computer networks allow sharing of other resources, too. For example, your employees may need access to electronic information services such as America Online, CompuServe, the Internet, or other remote computer systems belonging to customers or suppliers. Rather than buy a modem for each employee, and run a separate phone line to each computer, you can set up one or more shared modems on the network. Network users can then connect to a shared modem over the network cable.

You can also set up your network to share fax capabilities. You may already do this if you have a single fax machine in the office that everyone uses, but if you have enough employees to warrant more than one fax machine, having a computer network can save you some money. A network fax server can also save time by allowing users to fax documents directly from their computers without having to print the document on a laser printer and then feed it into a fax machine for scanning and transmission.

Finally, having a network makes remote access easier on the inbound direction, too. A remote user can call your network from a customer location, or from home, without your having to dedicate a computer in the office to handle the connection and act as a "slave" machine. The remote user can simply dial into a shared network modem and enjoy full access to your network. (For more on dial-up communications, see Chapter 10.)

Storage devices (and computers with no storage devices at all)

Most microcomputers today come with pretty large hard drives for storing programs and data files. Your employees are unlikely to ever need an extra hard drive. However, you may want to consider buying a new kind of micro-computer (called a *network PC* or *netPC*) that doesn't have a hard drive at all. In doing so, your network allows you to share a central set of hard drives with all the users on the network, saving in the range of $100 to $200 per user computer.

Network PCs have some drawbacks that you need to consider, as I discuss in detail in Chapter 4.

Computers that do have their own hard drives need some way of storing the information they contain on a removable medium, such as tape, magnetic cartridge, or optical disk, just in case the disk drive inside the computer decides to burn out a bearing and self-destruct. (Copying computer data to a removable medium is called making a *backup*.) With a network, you can buy a single tape drive or cartridge device that all the network users can share, instead of installing one at each computer.

More and more useful business databases are coming out on CD-ROM (Compact Disc Read-Only Memory) discs, which are similar in construction to the music CDs you buy for your home or car stereo. The difference between the two is that the CD-ROM stores computer data rather than music. You may find that setting up a shared CD-ROM drive (or two, or three) on a network server is less expensive than buying microcomputers that each sport their own CD-ROM drive.

Software

As far as software goes, *network licenses* or *site licenses* often save you money when compared to buying a separate copy of each program for each computer in your office. For example, with a network license, the vendor can sell you one set of disks and manuals, along with a license that permits a certain maximum number of users to run the software over the network. The vendor's costs are lower, and the vendor usually passes some of the savings along to you.

You can also save because network licenses usually specify a maximum number of *concurrent* users rather than total *possible* users. That is, even though ten employees may use program X, you can buy a license that lets five employees use it at the same time (concurrently) and probably meet everyone's needs without spending as much money as if you had bought ten separate single-user copies.

Now, I wasn't born yesterday, as the gray around my temples bears annoying witness, and I know that some readers are probably now saying to themselves, "Heck, we only buy one copy anyway and just install it on each machine." Some others are saying, "Buy software? Who *buys* software? I have a buddy at SuperCorp who lets me have copies of what I need." I understand the temptation, but I've also seen companies get slapped with fines of $10,000 *per copyright violation* for using illegally copied software. (Incidentally, it's usually the company who pays, not the employee.) I believe most managers prefer to do the right thing and pay for the software they use — network licenses make it more affordable to do just that.

If you decide to keep your application software (user programs) on a network server, you may also save time and money over the long run. If your software resides on the network server, you can update it once on the server, and everyone enjoys the benefit of the new software. If a separate copy of the software resides on each individual user's computer, you have to go around and update everyone's copy individually.

Other stuff

The previous list of shared resources isn't comprehensive. Depending on what your business does, you may also be able to share specialized computer hardware, such as document *scanners* (which read paper documents and convert them to computer-storable documents).

Improving internal communications

I'm often amazed at how miscommunications can occur even in an office of just a few people, especially if those people are extremely busy and don't spend much time in the break room swilling java and chatting with their coworkers. When employees work in separate locations, spend significant time traveling, or when their number is in the dozens or hundreds, miscommunications and missed communications tend to become more frequent.

I'll go out on a limb here and say that improving internal communications is the greatest single potential benefit of having a computer network.

Communicating with e-mail

The telephone has evolved into a sophisticated set of cutting-edge technologies that is unparalleled in its ability to confuse mere humans. Okay, that's an exaggeration, but how many of you reading this book *really* know all the commands your phone system offers? Even your *cellular* phone? I'd be surprised if I knew half the commands for either.

Despite the fact that I now have more and fancier telephones than ever, I still have a hard time actually reaching a person when I dial. Telephone tag may be the biggest time-waster in business today. (The second biggest is *voice mail,* in which you hear a recorded message that you've heard 200 times before, that drones on forever, and that eventually asks you to leave a message, and in the middle of doing so, you are disconnec)

E-mail to the rescue

Fortunately, your small business network can provide an alternative channel of communication: LAN-based electronic mail, or *e-mail,* as shown in Figure 1-2.

E-mail systems let you create an electronic *post office* that stores messages and also forwards them to the account (or *mailbox*) of each network user. E-mail differs from voice mail in several ways:

- ✔ **You can leave as long a message as you want.** Some voice mail systems offer this too, but who wants to sit and listen to ten minutes of rambling babble?

- ✔ **You can attach any sort of computer file to an e-mail message,** including word processing documents, graphic images, and even programs.

- ✔ **Sending a message to multiple recipients at once is easy** (perhaps too easy).

- ✔ **You can write an e-mail message today, and tell the computer to send it later.**

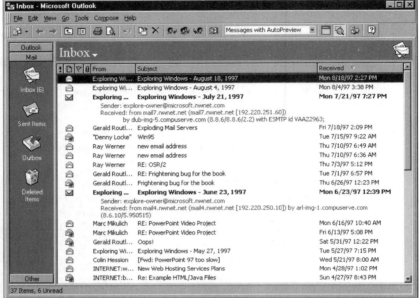

Figure 1-2:
Microsoft
Outlook 97
is an update
of the
Exchange
e-mail
client
program
and works
with
Windows 95
and
Windows
NT.

✓ **E-mail messages are easy to forward to other parties.** If you need to "bring someone into the loop" on an e-mail conversation, you simply send the message their way.

✓ **E-mail is great for global communication.** If your e-mail system communicates with the outside world (that is, over the Internet or some other online service), sending an e-mail to a customer, contractor, or supplier can be cheaper than a phone call, fax, or letter.

✓ **You can indicate the priority of your message as a sender, and sort messages by priority as a recipient.**

✓ **You can also sort messages by sender, by date, and various other ways.**

✓ **You can request an electronic "return receipt" to make sure that the recipient got your message.**

✓ **You can create a short subject description to help the recipient know at a glance what your message is about.**

✓ **E-mail messages are easy to keep for later reference.** You can store and organize your messages in different electronic "file cabinets" for more convenient retrieval.

✓ **You can set up an e-mail system to keep a copy of every message for a company communication archive.**

E-mail guidelines

E-mail can be great, but it works even better when you lay down some guidelines for its use. For example, although e-mail can be used to reduce their frequency somewhat, it probably shouldn't be used to completely replace face-to-face meetings, and you may want to address this in your e-mail usage guidelines. If e-mail replaces face-to-face meetings too often, employees may use e-mail to work out all but the thorniest day-to-day business issues, and then before long, every face-to-face meeting becomes difficult and potentially confrontational.

Another problem you may want to address through usage guidelines is that e-mail can become even more of a time drain than voice mail if employees overuse it. A relevant policy here, for example, may be "no sending e-mail to everybody on the network unless absolutely necessary." Another helpful policy is to urge e-mail senders to help recipients save time by including brief subject matter descriptions (some e-mail users routinely delete messages with no subject stated, assuming they're junk e-mail) and by designating message priority. Most e-mail systems offer the capability to do both.

Many e-mail systems allow you to block messages from specific individuals. Consider banning the use of this feature, which destroys one of e-mail's biggest advantages — increasing the flow of communications. Instead, state as policy that if someone is bothering someone else over the network cables, the two parties should sit down face to face and resolve the matter.

Urge your e-mail users to be honest online. Specifically, if someone receives a message sent with the cyberspace equivalent of a "return receipt requested" card, the recipient shouldn't electronically acknowledge the message without actually reading it first. Also, when a manager writes a reminder e-mail message with a delayed posting of weeks or months later, the message should reflect the date the manager actually created the message.

Finally, educate your LAN users about e-mail etiquette. It can be tempting to fire off an e-mail in anger or frustration, but for some reason, the written word has more of an ability to incite nastiness than the spoken word. Few LAN activities are more counterproductive than a heated exchange of antagonistic e-mails, that is, a *flame war*. A good guideline for everyone is to stop sending e-mails and meet face to face the moment an e-mail exchange begins to get testy.

Some e-mail systems

Some popular e-mail systems include the following (see Appendix B for contact information):

- ✔ Lotus cc:Mail
- ✔ Microsoft Exchange, Outlook 97

   ✔ Novell GroupWise

   ✔ Qualcomm Eudora Pro

Collaborating with groupware

E-mail is mainly for person-to-person communications. When you want to give your e-mail system the capability to allow multiple users to share the same messages and add comments to them, you want a class of software called *groupware*. Imagine a shared corkboard where employees can tack up memos, and then other employees can add sticky notes to the memos over a period of time, and you begin to get the idea.

The groupware term also encompasses *group scheduling software,* which allows multiple users to check each other's electronic calendars, and *task management software,* which is, essentially, shared to-do lists. Group scheduling is especially handy, because you can punch in the names of individuals you want to include in a meeting, and the software hunts for blocks of time during which each of those people is available. (Of course, this only works if everybody keeps their personal electronic calendars up to date — and that can be a big "if.")

Scheduling groupware has become fairly sophisticated. You can designate assistants to log on to the network and make appointments for you. You can control what other users on the network see — appointment details, for example, or just whether or not you're busy at a given time. If you don't want certain people to see your schedule at all, you can make it totally private, although that sort of defeats the purpose of network calendars.

The line between e-mail and groupware is really more of a blur than a line. For example, some e-mail systems, such as Microsoft Exchange, provide a mechanism for "public" discussions as well as group scheduling — these are traditionally groupware features that Microsoft has added to its e-mail system.

The semantics of *groupware* versus *e-mail* are ultimately less important than what the software does for you. I tend to favor groupware products that integrate well with (or come bundled with) e-mail systems, because they usually involve less work to set up and manage.

Some popular groupware systems include the following (see Appendix B for contact information):

   ✔ Lotus Notes

   ✔ Microsoft Exchange

   ✔ Netscape Collabra Server and Calendar Server (part of the SuiteSpot bundle)

   ✔ Novell GroupWise

Reducing paperwork

Every piece of paper your business must create, duplicate, distribute, file, or mail costs you money — not just for the raw material itself, but also for the time and special equipment involved. Copy machines, fax machines, postage meters, and binding machines all cost money, both to purchase and to keep fed. Every minute your coworkers spend in front of (or, during repairs, underneath or inside) these devices is a minute they could be spending in more productive pursuits.

You can certainly say the same thing about the time employees spend in front of their desktop computers, but electronic documents are generally less expensive than paper documents over the long run, in terms of both time and materials. For example, a letter that you send by the regular postal service costs about $2 when you figure in paper, postage, and handling time; the same document sent by e-mail costs about one-fourth as much, not counting the amortization of network hardware and software. (This cost discrepancy is one reason the U.S. Postal Service gives when raising rates: E-mail is taking a big bite out of their business — and this situation soon becomes a self-fulfilling prophecy, because higher postal rates just increase the cost advantage that e-mail already enjoys.)

The *paperless office* remains an elusive goal except in the most tightly managed offices. Whether a computer network reduces paperwork or adds to it depends greatly on the network's design, how much you and your colleagues trust its ability to stay running and not trash vital information, and whether you can adjust work habits to spend more time with electronic information and less time with paper.

How close you get to a paperless office relates strongly to the size and quality of the monitors you buy for network users. People are more likely to read documents online if they don't get eyestrain when doing so.

Even if your computer network does reduce paper flow, whether that reduction translates into time and cost savings depends largely on how adept your employees become with the automated systems, and how well they can avoid the temptation to fritter away lots of time perfecting documents (such as e-mail messages) that don't have to be perfect. E-mail systems with built-in spell checking can reduce the fritter factor, but they don't eliminate it.

Word processing

Word processing is the horizontal software application most small businesses know best. Its popularity is partly due to the fact that word processing is an evolutionary step up from the typewriter (remember typewriters? I still have one, for those tax forms that say "This Report Must Be Typed, Even If You Have Really Good Handwriting"). Word processing is also popular partly because every business creates documents, for everything from business plans to correspondence.

Network-based word processing can reduce paperwork. For example, revising a document can occur online instead of on paper — you don't need to print out a draft for a colleague to revise; you can simply post it in a public area on the network server, or send it as an e-mail attachment. Once your coworker has commented on your document, or actually made some revisions to it, he or she can transmit it back to you via the network. You can then choose to accept the revisions, change the document based on the comments, or even send the document to someone else for additional reaction. The beauty of it is, you don't have to actually print the thing until it's finished (see Figure 1-3).

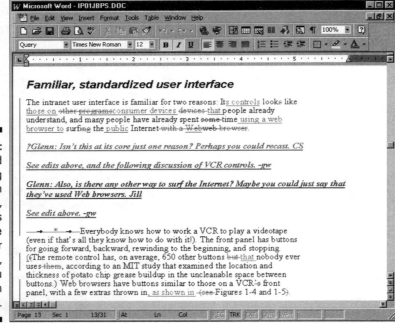

Figure 1-3:
With a word processing program on a network, colleagues can make revisions or comments, which you can then review.

The word processing software tracks who made each comment and revision, which is handy when multiple people have worked on your document. Technically, you can edit documents collaboratively with standalone microcomputers by shuttling files back and forth on diskette, but people tend not to bother with such "sneakernet" data exchange. The network makes document collaboration easy, saving time, paper, and money.

Managing money

Every small business has to manage its accounts, whether you work out of a corporate checkbook or use a more sophisticated double-entry bookkeeping system. Many growing companies get their first taste of computing when they buy a system to handle the general ledger, accounts payable, accounts receivable, order entry, and so on. Often, a small business buys a standalone computer to perform these money-management chores.

However, when you put your automated financial systems on a network, you enjoy several benefits over the standalone single-computer configuration. For one, you can now have several bookkeepers keying data into the system simultaneously. The software manages this simultaneous access and also prevents two people from updating the same information at the exact same time through techniques called *file locking* and *record locking*.

Another benefit, and one that saves paper, is that anyone in the company who has the appropriate network security clearance can look up operating financial data at any time. You no longer have to distribute giant sheaves of green-bar paper to everyone in your organization who needs access to financial data. Whether you're an account manager, chief financial officer, credit manager, or bookkeeper, with a computer network you can create whatever report you need on the fly. You also benefit by getting more timely information than you can from a paper printout because the information on the network is the most up to date available.

You don't even have to print checks anymore, at least not for payroll. You can set up your network to make electronic payments directly into employee checking accounts. This is a boon for employees who are tired of the lame smart-aleck remarks their bosses make when handing out paychecks ("Don't spend it all in one place" and so on).

Publishing documents online

Another excellent way to reduce paperwork is to post commonly requested information on the network. For example, you can use your e-mail system to place documents in a *public folder* that you make available to everyone. A few candidates for document publishing are

- **Employee directory,** including phone numbers, addresses, e-mail addresses, and so on

- **Benefits information,** including insurance, profit-sharing, employee stock purchase, retirement plans, what new cool pens are available from the office supply cabinet, and so on

- **Product information,** such as specifications, photographs, and price lists

> ✔ **Standard proposals and contracts** (the so-called *boilerplate*)
>
> ✔ **Company newsletter** (generally useful for companies having over 50 or so employees)
>
> ✔ **Technical support information** (how to use programs on the network, frequently asked questions, and so on)

A kind of computer network that's especially effective at reducing paperwork is called an *intranet,* which is a private network based on the same technology used on the public Internet. You may want to set up an intranet server computer that shares documents users can view using the same software they use to browse the World Wide Web (for example, Microsoft Internet Explorer or Netscape Navigator).

Setting up an intranet server on your network is fairly easy if you choose *TCP/IP* (Transmission Control Protocol/Internet Protocol) as your networking language. Much of the software for setting up such a server comes free with both Microsoft Windows NT Server and Novell IntranetWare, two popular Network Operating Systems.

Chapter 16 looks at intranets in greater detail, and Chapter 6 explains TCP/IP.

Telecommuting

Telecommuting is the practice of employees working from their homes while linked electronically to the main office. Some employees work from home only a few days a month; others do it almost full time, coming to the office only for important meetings. A small business computer network can allow telecommuters to tap into your network from home and exchange documents or pick up and send e-mail just as if they were physically in the office.

One branch of American Express Travel Related Services was able to reduce its office rent by one-third by equipping agents with the necessary home computer equipment and letting them work from home part of the time. Most of the agents were happy with the arrangement because they didn't have to waste as much time in their cars and on trains — which is becoming a bigger deal to many employees because you just can't find a good radio station anymore. The state of California even gives tax breaks to companies whose employees work from home (it keeps the smog down and reduces the number of bullets flying around the expressways).

Depending on the office and home environments, some workers may be more productive at home because fewer distractions exist (office politics, endless and unnecessary meetings, phone calls, and so on). You may even find that you are able to keep certain talented employees on the payroll whom you couldn't keep otherwise. Examples include employees who want to live in an area that's prohibitively far from the office, those whose mobility is restricted for medical reasons, or those who have small children at home and want to stay close to them. Reducing employee turnover by keeping valued workers is a major way to reduce costs and keep productivity high.

Extending this thought a bit further, you can hire contractors or consultants in other cities and then communicate with them through the network. When I moved from Dallas to the Denver area six years ago, I was able to continue providing computer consulting services to several clients because I could easily link in to their networks. Having a network in place means that you can work with contractors outside your local area, who, when compared to local resources, may be less expensive, better qualified, or both.

On a related point: In addition to facilitating telecommuting, a small business network can also make it less necessary for employees to come to the workplace after hours. If an emergency situation arises, employees may be able to handle the problem by dialing up the office network from home.

Chapter 10 discusses the different ways remote users can connect to your network, and the software and hardware you need to make telecommuting practical.

Enhancing Revenue

Many businesspeople think of computer networks mainly as a way to reduce operational costs, as I explore in the previous section. Small business networking can often reduce those costs enough to justify the required investment in time and money. However, in addition to cutting costs, small businesses can use computer networks to enhance revenue as well, by shortening payback time and increasing return on investment. Maybe the most important realization to which businesses have come in the last decade is that computer applications, and especially networks, aren't just for the "back office" anymore — they can make every aspect of daily work more efficient.

Speeding up business processes

Small businesses enjoy a tremendous speed advantage over large businesses. Without the overhead of bureaucratic layers, the lengthy decision-making process and stifling turf battles, small companies can be fleet of foot while their elephantine competitors are slogging along in slow motion. An efficient computer network can help you fully realize this advantage.

Designing your products

If your small business creates a physical product of some sort, you can use a computer network to help design the product. The speed advantages of designing products on a computer system include the following:

- ✔ **Collaboration.** Multiple people in different locations can contribute to the design process by sharing documents like product technical drawings and specifications. Concurrent engineering can be much faster than older, sequential models of product design, because it involves employees in engineering, manufacturing, marketing, and finance from the early design stages.

- ✔ **Testing.** Some engineering design software allows you to perform limited product testing on the computer, instead of in a laboratory or physical test bench setup. And with a network, you can share test results with design and manufacturing engineers immediately.

- ✔ **Streamlined drawing changes.** You can use the computer to generate drawings and specifications for new models rapidly, for example, by making small changes, or by scaling a drawing up or down by a uniform percentage.

- ✔ **Integration between design and manufacturing.** You can use the computer design files to "feed" automated manufacturing equipment, such as a sheet metal press, across the network — saving a step in manually programming the equipment.

"What if...?" (Evaluating alternatives)

Decision support is an entire class of software that tries to help you run your business more effectively by presenting information in useful, action-oriented ways. Many specialized decision support programs exist, but I want to take a look at a common and generic one: the *spreadsheet* program.

Most businesspeople are familiar by now with computer spreadsheets — tools that enable you to create tables of information arranged in a row and column format, and to set up numerical relationships between spreadsheet *cells* (a cell being the contents of a particular row and column location). In fact, the first microcomputer spreadsheet program, VisiCalc, made the Apple II a viable business computer in addition to a fine platform for playing games like Pong and Beer Hunter. VisiCalc's successor, Lotus 1-2-3, more or less single-handedly spurred the popularity of the IBM PC in the business world. Today, the most popular microcomputer spreadsheet is Microsoft Excel, although Lotus 1-2-3 retains a place in the market along with Corel Quattro Pro.

You may already be using spreadsheet software for a variety of purposes: budgeting, forecasting, even creating small lists or databases. I have a small enough business that I did my profit-and-loss statements and balance sheets on a spreadsheet program for years. As an author, I also use a spreadsheet to analyze the contract terms publishers offer for the books I propose to them, terms that can get pretty complicated if you're trying to figure them out in your head. Spreadsheets are great for playing these "what if?" games, because you can vary the assumptions and let the spreadsheet program calculate the results based on those changed assumptions.

The benefit you realize when you install a computer network is that you can easily share your spreadsheet models with others in your company, soliciting comments and refining the model more rapidly than you could do otherwise. Today's spreadsheet applications provide the ability for multiple people to comment on your assumptions and formulas, and even attach comments to specific cells in your model ("Gina, you assume here that 100 percent of our customers will pay their bills within 30 days. Is that realistic? — Jane.") as shown in Figure 1-4.

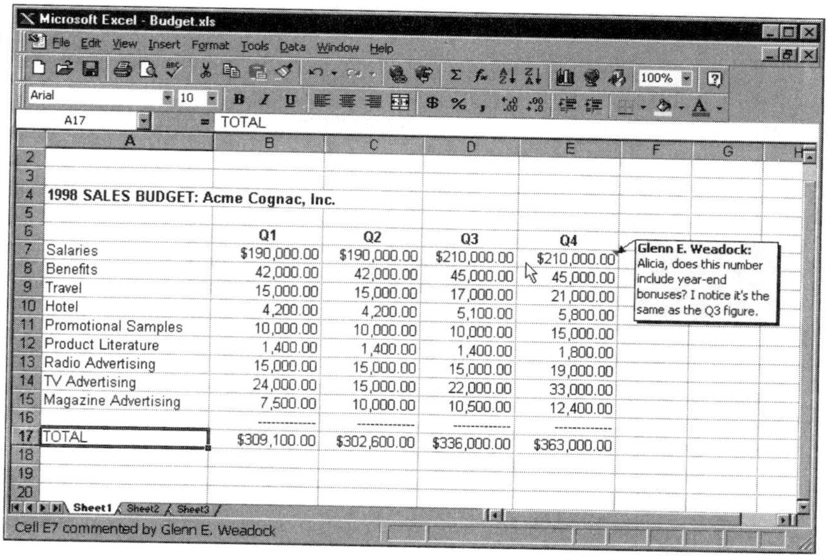

Figure 1-4: Spreadsheet users on a network can make comments that pertain to specific cells. You view the comments by passing the cursor (pointer) over the cell.

One reason that using the network to share spreadsheet models is more effective than poring over printouts is that in their electronic form, spreadsheets show the spreadsheet formulas and numerical relationships. A printout, on the other hand, does not easily show this information. (You *can* print the formulas, but you may not be able to see both the formulas and the numbers at the same time.)

Another advantage to networking is that you can link the contents of one spreadsheet to another. For example, you can create a spreadsheet model on your workstation, for your own use. That model can be set to reference sales data stored in a spreadsheet on a shared server machine. You can set up your private spreadsheet to link to specific rows and columns on the shared spreadsheet so that you don't have to re-enter that information by hand. To make things even easier, your spreadsheet is also automatically updated when the sales data on the shared machine changes.

Enabling growth

Many small businesses reach a point at which they must grow internally in order to achieve greater financial success. That growth may take the form of hiring more employees for the main office, establishing branch offices in different areas, or partnering or merging with other companies. In any case, a well-designed computer network can ease the growing pains in the following ways:

- New employees can get up to speed with the business by studying shared documents such as business plans, budgets, financial projections, contracts, and so on.

- A computer network can help train new employees in how to use your company's software, and potentially in other areas as well.

- A network-based employee database can provide an efficient structure for managing tax-related information, insurance data, and benefits, so that as the payroll grows, the effort in administering such data does not grow proportionally.

- Network communications (e-mail, groupware, and so on) make doing business with remote offices easier.

- A properly designed network makes administrator tasks such as adding new user accounts and assigning appropriate security privileges easy.

- Most networks allow you to easily accommodate staff growth by letting you add shared devices such as modems and printers.

- Managing software on a network can be simpler than managing a growing number of individual standalone computers, because much of the software remains in one place.

Connecting with customers

Your network can be a useful way to build closer relationships with customers and markets, in addition to streamlining internal communications and reducing operating costs. Tracking customer information, providing better service, marketing your products and services, and analyzing market trends are four ways your network can enhance your company's ability to generate revenue.

Tracking and sharing customer data

By maintaining a shared database of customer data on your network, you help everyone in your company get the latest information on customer contacts, orders, projects, quotations, and so on. Shared customer data helps avoid left-hand-right-hand syndrome, such as one employee calling a customer to pitch a new product that the customer's already ordered.

Keeping customer data on a network is also a good way to let your customers know that they matter to you. If a customer who hasn't done business with you for months or even years puts in a call to your office, the person who takes the call can consult the network. He or she can bring the customer's order history up on the screen and ask questions like, "How did those curtain rods you ordered back in 1994 work out for you, Mr. Dunbar?" and "Are you still at 1414 Interior Designer Way?" The customer not only feels important, but he or she also gets the impression that you're on top of things (which, with a computer network, you definitely are).

The software you use for applications like this shared customer database is called *database* software (surprise!). With database software, you create structured *records* containing information about customers, products — almost any information you want. For example, a simple customer database can include company names, addresses, and phone numbers. Using the database program, you add a record for each customer using on-screen *forms*. You can later search, retrieve, and view those records, and print reports based on them, sorted any way you like.

You can buy *horizontal* database software, which you must tailor to your own needs, or *vertical* database software that a vendor has customized for your particular industry. You can also choose to use a small *desktop database,* which is generally suitable for under a dozen simultaneous users, or a larger, more expensive *server database* that requires its own computer, but can handle many more users.

Some popular network desktop database products include the following (see Appendix B for more information):

- Claris FileMaker Pro
- Corel Paradox
- Lotus Approach 97
- Microsoft Access 97

- ✔ Microsoft Visual FoxPro
- ✔ Oracle Corp. Personal Oracle Lite
- ✔ Sybase SQL Anywhere

Popular server database products include

- ✔ Informix OnLine Dynamic Server
- ✔ Microsoft SQL Server
- ✔ Oracle Corp. Oracle 7 Server
- ✔ Sybase SQL Server System 11

Offering cyberservice

You can also improve customer service by being able to deliver information to customers as soon as they ask for it, instead of saying, "I'll have to get back to you on that." If your business involves calling on customers at their locations, small business networking can help you provide more information to those customers. When your employees are out in the field, they can tap into the central network and consult product specifications, inventory, pricing, shipping schedules, and customer credit status.

You can also make your network directly available to customers for online product ordering and for checking order status, something that is difficult to achieve with standalone microcomputers. A *fax-back* information delivery system is another possibility (take a look at Chapter 10 for details).

Sometimes speed is a critical part of delivering a service. Say, for example, that you run a medical clinic. When a patient calls with a question about a drug interaction or a poison, your network can enable the employee to provide the information quickly (for example, from a shared network CD-ROM drive containing discs with drug and poison databases) without having to run around asking everyone if they have the CD-ROM.

To take a less dramatic example, say you work in an auto parts store, and you spend a great deal of time each day flipping through those giant product books to answer customer questions over the phone ("Have you got a window switch for a 1992 Ford Explorer?"). You can buy CD-ROM catalogs that require much less searching time, in turn freeing up your business to devote more employee time to the people actually in the store with wallets at the ready (and sick vehicles in the parking lot).

Yet another benefit and service you can offer to customers is tracking after-sale complaints or support calls using your small business network. Besides the direct benefit of ensuring that you track and follow up on customer requests by using a formal network-based documentation tool, you can realize some surprising side benefits. For example, if several customers report the same problem with a new product, you may have a design or manufacturing defect on your hands. The computer database can alert you to this sort of problem by generating periodic reports summarizing customer calls. Individual employees may not notice the problem, for example, if four different people take four different complaint calls.

Marketing with your network

Small business computer networks aren't just for internal consumption. You can use them, with appropriate security measures, to broadcast information about your company's products and services to the entire world, via the Internet. The Internet is a public, global network of millions of computers — while it was originally used for academic and military purposes, it is now okay to use it for shamelessly commercial purposes (see Figure 1-5).

The *World Wide Web* is the Internet service that most businesses use — it allows you to post pages of information about your products and services, using text, graphics, and even sound and animation. The nice thing about the Web from your standpoint is that just about any computer, anywhere in the world, can connect to it.

Most small businesses don't set up their own so-called web servers in-house. (A *web server* is a computer on the public Internet that makes your promotional pages available to the general public.) You normally contract

Figure 1-5: My own small business site on the World Wide Web allows potential customers worldwide to learn about my books and seminars.

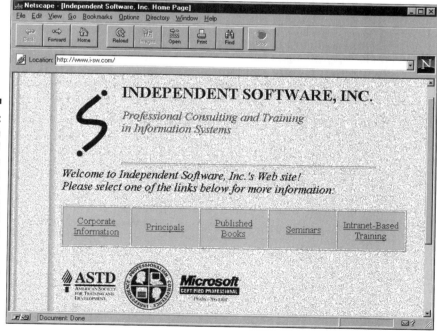

with a third party, called an *Internet Service Provider* or ISP, to host your Web site (a site being a collection of Web pages). Web hosting services don't have to be expensive — the site shown in Figure 1-5 costs my company $50 a month and generates roughly ten times that in additional revenue.

The benefit you realize from having your own computer network is that you can put several employees to work designing, refining, and updating your Web pages, and then sending those new pages to the ISP via a dial-up modem connection.

If you need a reference that covers the ways in which computers can help your small business before you investigate how a small business network fits in, take a look at *Small Business Computing For Dummies* by Brian Underdahl. *Small Business MS Office 97 For Dummies* by Todd Stauffer and Dave Johnson covers the Microsoft business applications like Word and Excel and can be another handy book to have around as you put together your small business network. Both books are from IDG Books Worldwide, Inc.

Although the Internet can be a great and relatively inexpensive way to market your business internationally (see Chapter 17 for more on using the Internet), you don't have to establish an Internet presence in order to use your network for marketing purposes. For example, you can also use a computer database to manage mailing lists that you either build or buy. By having your mailing lists on a multiuser network, any employee can update information at any time, from his or her own desktop.

By tracking customer orders on the network, you can easily generate custom mailing lists, and then use the lists for things like sending a promotional flyer to customers you haven't done business with in a certain number of months. Or, you could send a discount coupon to customers who have placed recent orders, as a way of saying thanks and building customer loyalty.

Responding to market changes more quickly

If you know what the market is doing, you can respond to it more rapidly. A computer network can give you market information from your own operating data as well as from outside sources.

Your internal operating data can tell you a great deal about what your customers are buying, and what they're buying more of this year when compared to last year. The longer you use your computer network to manage daily operations, the larger a history you build and the more useful the network becomes in identifying trends, growth patterns, and potential new opportunities.

If you use your small business network to provide employees with Internet access, or access to other online information services like CompuServe, your employees can conduct their own market research. Demographic information, market reports, and even detailed information on your publicly traded competitors are all available in cyberspace.

Chapter 2
Networking on a Budget

● ●

In This Chapter

▶ Taking advantage of lower computer hardware and software costs

▶ Exposing those hidden life-cycle costs

▶ Figuring out how you're going to pay for a network

▶ Keeping your network in fine form (and not spending a fortune)

● ●

"*W*hen I was young I used to think that money was the most important thing in life; now that I am old, I know it is." (Oscar Wilde, Irish playwright)

Every now and then, I hear an industry guru comment that you don't really need to cost-justify a computer network anymore, because everyone knows it's a requirement for doing business, just like a telephone or an office or stationery. This statement contains a grain of truth, as long as you take it with ten grains of salt. The small business managers I know scrutinize expenses on telephones, offices, and stationery pretty darned closely — I know I do. The scrutiny of network expenses doesn't have to be a detailed, formal cost-benefit analysis, but you do need to take a careful look at the costs in light of the expected benefits.

If you made it to this chapter, and you aren't sure what benefits a network can bring to your company, check out Chapter 1.

The position that you should simply regard the cost of a computer network as the cost of doing business in today's world, *regardless of the amount,* is most definitely *not* true. You may need a computer network to help you compete, and I make a case for that position in Chapter 1. However, you may be able to do just fine with a $15,000 network as opposed to a $150,000 network.

Most books about computer networking barely mention costs, and for a good reason: Costs change rapidly in this business, even in a relatively mature field such as small office networking. No author wants to have a reader pick up a book a few years down the road and read something like, "You can now buy a good laser printer for only $30,000."

My guess is that you're sophisticated enough to know that anything anybody says about costs in a computer book is likely to change almost as soon as the book hits the streets. So I try to give you some idea of what networking is going to cost you, on the understanding that the numbers are likely to change over time. Ultimately, you must do your own shopping to get a really solid cost estimate at any particular point in time.

The Good News: Networks Are Cheaper than Ever

Setting up a computer network has never been less expensive than it is today. As if that isn't good news enough, the hardware and much (if not all) of the software is faster, easier to set up, and more reliable than ever before.

You've probably read statements in business magazines saying that you can now fit a computer in your briefcase that has the same processing power as a 1960 computer that would have occupied a building the size of Bermuda, contained 90 million vacuum tubes, required its own hydroelectric generating station, and cost so much that Oprah Winfrey could not have afforded it, even if she went in on it with Steve Forbes.

You have to watch out for this sort of comparison because it is a little misleading. First of all, Bermuda is not all that large. Furthermore, today's software is much less efficient than software written in 1960 — as hardware becomes more powerful, software companies have less incentive to write really fast and efficient programs. This said, today's run-of-the-mill computers really can do just about anything a typical business needs them to do, taking up amazingly little space and for amazingly little money.

Hopping off the fence

Businesspeople new to the computer industry sometimes worry that as soon as they buy hardware or software, it will become obsolete. My response to this concern has five parts:

✔ **You're right.** Heck, sometimes computer products are obsolete *before* you buy them. (A strong sign is when a computer retailer promotes a big sale with heavy discounts. The vendor is probably poised to replace those products with newer models in a matter of days or weeks, and the retailer won't be able to sell the older models as easily once the newer ones hit the streets.)

✔ **So what?** Obsolescence is a fact of life in the computer industry and is not likely to change anytime soon. The pace of technological development hasn't slowed in the last 15 years — if anything, it's accelerated.

✔ **Take the road *most* traveled.** You can protect yourself to some degree against obsolescence by purchasing in the mainstream, paying attention to industry standards, and buying expandable hardware.

✔ **Wallflowers miss out on the party.** The time you spend waiting for the optimum moment to buy, in order to ensure the longest possible technological life for your computers, is time that you could have been enjoying the productivity benefits of a network — benefits that are probably much more valuable than the cost of product obsolescence.

✔ **Obsolete is a state of mind.** If you buy something today that works well for you, it will probably still be working well for you a year or two later, even if it's outmoded in some technical respect. Obsolete doesn't usually mean useless. If last year's car model still gets you to market, its "obsolescence" is moot.

I used to advise companies to buy hardware right after a new processor came out on the market, because you could get a good deal on the slightly older processor models but still not lag too far behind the technology curve. Nowadays, with new processors coming out on the market every couple of months, that advice holds less water.

Bottom line: Hop off the fence, buy what you need, and cheerfully accept obsolescence as a fact of life, like death and taxes. (Well, maybe more cheerfully than *that*.) Just make sure that you're buying products that adhere to industry standards and that you can upgrade later as new technology becomes available. I cover the industry standards you need to know about, as well as upgradability issues as they pop up, in Chapters 5, 6, and 7.

Computers as status symbols

While some businesses require persuading to invest in a computer network, other companies go overboard and buy more computer horsepower than they need out of a desire to feel technologically current and impress customers and colleagues. I still hear this attitude crop up at conferences and seminars. One consultant says, "Yeah, after you use a 300-megahertz workstation, everything else just seems stuck in the mud." Another replies, "I know, I felt that way as soon as I got my 350-megahertz system. How do you put up with that older bucket of bolts?" At that point, I like to jump in and say, "I use a 166-megahertz system" (piteous looks) "and with the money I saved, I bought a hot tub" (confused looks as they try to calculate whether they could have done the same thing).

Many people are easily swayed by technolust. Computer magazines tend to extol the virtues of the latest technology while deriding the limitations of last month's obsolete clunkers. New hardware can be intriguing and showy. And hey, if your competitors have it, you'd better have it too, right?

Not necessarily: Buying today's hot technology can be more of an expression of management's *desire* to progress than of a well-thought-out *plan* to progress. Having the latest stuff can even backfire with both hardware and software (see the "Release zero syndrome" sidebar).

I'm not saying that you should never buy the latest and greatest technology. Just make sure that if you do, you buy it for the right reasons. Technological one-upmanship can be needlessly expensive, and it may also drive you to spend your company's money where it doesn't necessarily do you the most good — that is, on hardware instead of software. I get more into the hardware-versus-software issue later in this chapter.

The Bad News: Price Isn't the Whole Story

So, the good news is that computer hardware and software are cheaper and more powerful than ever, you can still reap great productivity benefits even though the technology is advancing rapidly, and you don't have to buy the latest, greatest stuff to build a great network. The bad news is that what you pay up front for these products is a small fraction of what your computer network is going to cost you over the long haul.

Many computer market research companies, including the Gartner Group, Nolan, Norton and Company, Datapro, and others, have done studies on the total cost of computer systems over their useful business life. Depending on which study you read, the up-front purchase price is somewhere between 10 and 20 percent of the total life-cycle cost. So, if your hardware and software budget comes to, say, $15,000, you can plan to spend anywhere from $60,000 to $135,000 more on your system over the next five to ten years — that is, if you're a typical business.

The best advice here, then, is this: Don't be a typical business! By knowing and understanding the hidden life-cycle costs and by planning to minimize them, you can cut these numbers in half or even less. For example, you may be able to spend a little bit more up front for better network wiring, and save a lot more over the next decade on troubleshooting cable-related problems. (In the worst case, you need to replace your network cabling entirely, for example, in order to move to a higher network speed.)

The hidden life-cycle costs of a computer network include

- Network manager training
- Network user training
- Hardware maintenance

Release zero syndrome

Software companies assign version numbers to their products, in the optimistic view that customers will buy enough of them to justify an improved version down the road. Although the specific notation varies from one vendor to the next, most use the *X-point-zero* notation to denote a major upgrade instead of a minor bug-fix release. That is, NetWare 4.0 is a major upgrade, and NetWare 4.01 is a minor upgrade.

I almost always advise computer customers to avoid *release zero* of anything. New major upgrades are likely to be buggy because the vendor changes so much of the program. Don't software vendors test their products? Sure, but today's software is so complex that no vendor can take the time to do really complete testing and still keep the new products flowing fast enough to compete with other vendors. Also, no vendor can test their software in combination with all the other software customers use, and many release zero bugs are really problems that stem from interactions with other software.

Any company that absolutely must have the latest, greatest software must put up with more defects and incompatibilities than a company that waits until version X.01 or X.1 or X.0a (I call this latter strategy *release point one*). Buying a *release zero* version may be a good tradeoff if your company is technology driven, but you should at least be aware that early software adopters pay for their head start advantage with greater troubleshooting and support expenses, as the *leading edge* becomes the *bleeding edge*.

Release zero syndrome can affect hardware as well as software. One example from the PC world is the *VESA* (Video Electronics Standards Association) *local bus,* or *VL bus,* which was a new kind of slot for high-speed circuit boards. Companies that rushed out and bought computers with VL bus technology have since watched that technology all but vanish, meaning that they can't use their VL bus network cards with today's computers (which use a similar but incompatible technology called *PCI,* or *Peripheral Component Interconnect*). Generally, in the hardware world, customers must wait at least a year after a new technology debuts before they can be reasonably sure it won't quickly become orphaned. Unfortunately, hardware doesn't come with version numbers to help you with the hardware variety of release zero syndrome!

✔ Hardware upgrades

✔ Software tech support

✔ Software upgrades, both direct cost and time to install and configure

✔ Configuration and setup for user accounts, security, backups, and so on

✔ Troubleshooting time and services

✔ Insurance for both hardware and data

✔ System documentation

✔ Subscriptions to electronic information services or Internet access services

✔ Extra phone lines for inbound and outbound communications

This chapter covers some of these less obvious costs. My point here is that you need to consider the hidden costs along with the purchase price of hardware and software if you want to create a realistic budget and ensure fewer surprises down the road. A one-year network budget isn't nearly as helpful as a three- or five-year budget that covers your total system costs.

So What Do Networks Cost?

This section presents some ballpark figures so you can begin to prepare a network budget. But before I get into the numbers, I need to speak a bit about the options that you have in paying for your network.

Financing your network

Buying network hardware and software outright makes sense in several ways: You don't have to spend time negotiating and qualifying for leases or loans, you don't add financial obligations to your balance sheet, and you can buy exactly what you want.

Many small companies can *expense,* or write off, some or all of a computer investment the same year that they make the investment, using the tax code's Section 179 exemption. Expensing a computer network purchase has tax advantages over *capitalizing* the investment and depreciating it over several years. Your accountant can advise you about these matters in greater detail.

If you can think of better uses for the cash, or if the cash isn't readily available, you may not have to come out of pocket for many of your small business network costs. For example, leasing companies can help you spread the costs out over several years, and that can be a real boon for a small business that has good growth prospects but not much cash on hand. Here are a couple of tips if you decide to go the leasing route:

- ✔ **Figure out what's included.** Many leasing companies cover hardware, but not software. However, if you buy systems that *bundle* (that is, come with) much of the software you need, you may be able to apply the lease to the entire system cost, simply because the leasing company doesn't know how to break out the software costs separately.

- ✔ **Look down the road.** The option to purchase network hardware at the end of a lease term may not be all that important, because after five years, you may want to replace most of your network hardware anyway. Unlike a lease on a Mercedes, your computer hardware probably won't be worth much on the resale market after five years. The option to purchase may affect how you can treat lease payments on your company tax return, too; you may have to depreciate the payments if you ultimately buy the goods, while you may be able to expense the payments if you don't.

You may be able to obtain bank financing, also, although the help of a bank can be harder to come by than a lease arrangement. Small business failure rates being what they are, many banks don't want to suddenly become the proud owners of old equipment with little market value. Here again, banks don't typically lend money for software, but you can do the bundle thing and possibly work around this problem, to some extent. Your bank may offer a collateral loan, in which you put up your network equipment as collateral, but due to the quick depreciation of computer hardware, such loans rarely extend past two or three years.

Leasing companies and banks may both apply some restrictions to the hardware you purchase. For example, they may not work with you if you want to buy from *second-* or *third-tier manufacturers*. (Generally, second-tier computer manufacturers have recognizable brand names but they aren't among the top vendors in sales, while third-tier manufacturers are those that make so-called *no-name clones*.)

Software

Almost invariably, company managers have a harder time convincing themselves to pay more for high-quality software than they do to pay for high-quality hardware — probably because to most people, hardware is tangible and software is abstract. Even those of us who've worked in the business for a long time may subconsciously feel a little let down when we pay $1,000 for a program and all we get is a tiny manual and a CD-ROM. Pay $1,000 for a laser printer, on the other hand, and we get a big, solid-looking piece of equipment that we can barely even lift.

Fight this natural tendency to undervalue software! Software is by far the most important part of your computer network: Software determines what you can and cannot do with your system, and accounts for most of the long-term costs, in terms of configuration, maintenance, technical support, and training. In fact, software is so important that you don't even want to think about hardware until you've chosen the software that you need.

REMEMBER

Rule #1 of small business network design: Always select your network software first, based on the business processes you want to automate, and then build your hardware around it. Think of hiring an employee: You look for the skill set and personality first — not physical appearance.

You may see guidelines in the trade press or in business publications that say things like, "Spend 75 percent on hardware and 25 percent on software." If you ever do read an article or a book that includes advice like this, put it in a plain brown envelope and mail it to a competitor whose operation you would like to undermine, because it's complete drivel. I've seen (and built) successful networks where the software costs exceeded the hardware costs. The appropriate ratio of software cost to hardware cost depends completely on what you want to do with your network, and it should not be a primary concern for you as you create your LAN (Local Area Network) budget.

System software and licensing

Network Operating System software (sometimes called *NOS* for short — say "noss") is generally sold with per-user licensing options. The more users you want put on the network at one time, the more expensive the license. Table 2-1 presents ballpark U.S. prices for four popular small business NOSs.

Table 2-1	Approximate U.S. Network Operating System (NOS) Costs			
Maximum Number of Users	**Novell Intranet-Ware for Small Business**	**Novell IntranetWare 4.1.1**	**Microsoft Windows NT Server 4.0**	**Artisoft LANtastic 7.0**
5	$600	$650	$730	$350
10	$800	$1,300	$1,000	$350
25	$1,400	$2,300	$1,500	$600 (unlimited)
100	N/A	$4,400	$3,700	$600 (unlimited)

If you decide to use Novell NetWare as your Network Operating System, you have a choice between the full version (IntranetWare) or the small-business version (IntranetWare for Small Business). At the time I write this, the costs aren't greatly different for a very small 5-user network, but they diverge as you add users, and you must upgrade to the full version once you get past the Small Business product's 25-user limit.

One of the nice aspects of IntranetWare for Small Business is that you can add one-user licenses ($50), whereas with the larger product you can only purchase licenses in discrete jumps. You can also add one-user licenses with Microsoft Windows NT Server ($35 for each user over ten) and Artisoft LANtastic ($70 for each additional user).

I don't list the Windows 95, Windows NT Workstation, or Macintosh operating systems in Table 2-1 because these products include built-in networking capability. Incidentally, these built-in capabilities are for peer-to-peer networking, in which each computer can both share files (be a server) and use other computers' files (be a client). See Chapter 4 for more on network types.

The NOS is only one piece of the entire system software puzzle, although it's usually the biggest piece. You may need separate software packages for virus protection, data backup, network management, and web server software (if you want to create an intranet — see Chapter 16). The following list gives some ballpark prices for these system software components, based on name-brand software and support for ten network users:

- ✔ **Antivirus software:** $400 to $500. This purchase is absolutely necessary to keep your network safe and reliable.

- ✔ **Data backup software:** $250 to $400. Another must-have piece of software.

- ✔ **Network management (troubleshooting, inventory, and software installation utilities):** $700 to $900. Troubleshooting software can save you a lot of time down the road.

- ✔ **Web server:** Free to $300. A web server is crucial if you plan to create an intranet, or create a presence for your company on the Internet.

You need system software for your individual user workstations, too, but you generally don't pay separately for it when you buy new computers — they usually come bundled with the necessary software such as Windows 95, Windows NT Workstation, MacOS, and so on.

Application software

Without knowing the details of a specific business and how it plans to use its network, making an accurate estimate of software costs is almost impossible. However, estimating the costs for common *horizontal applications* (applications that apply to a wide variety of industries and businesses) such as word processing, spreadsheet, and database access is fairly easy.

Although the prices I discuss here apply to new purchases, the software industry aggressively discounts its products when customers make a so-called *competitive upgrade* — that is, if you switch from one brand of word processor to another, you may be able to get savings of more than 50 percent (if you qualify). Usually, when you install the new software, it looks around on the hard disk for competitor files. (No files, no install.)

The least expensive way to buy workstation-based software is to buy a suite of products bundled together in one package. Table 2-2 presents per-user prices for some popular office automation suites. Typically if you need more than ten user licenses, you qualify for quantity discounts. If you don't need most of the bundled applications, the suite is not so suite, and you can buy the individual programs separately for around $100 each.

Table 2-2   Approximate U.S. Workstation Software Costs

Suite Name and Components	Cost Per User
Microsoft Office 97, Small Business Edition (includes Word, Excel, Outlook, Publisher, and Financial Manager)	$410
Microsoft Office 97, Standard Edition (includes Word, Excel, PowerPoint, and Outlook)	$450
Microsoft Office 97, Professional Edition (includes Word, Excel, PowerPoint, Outlook, Access, and Bookshelf Basics)	$540
Corel WordPerfect Suite 8 (includes WordPerfect, Quattro Pro, Presentations, CorelCentral, Photo House 2, Envoy Viewer, QuickView Plus)	$300
Lotus SmartSuite 97 (includes 1-2-3, Freelance, Word Pro, Organizer, Approach, and ScreenCam)	$410

Your business can probably benefit from *vertical market applications,* that is, software written specifically for your industry. Unfortunately, vertical market applications vary greatly in price. Your best bet is to survey the marketplace (any good computer consultant can help you here) and look at the specific applications available for your kind of business.

Give greater weight to commercially available software than to custom software. Unless your company is so highly specialized that no decent commercial software exists, or you're willing to spend a premium (both now and down the road) in order to gain a significant competitive edge, commercial software is the way to go. Good custom software is expensive, both to maintain and to have designed, and makes your company vulnerable to a variety of risks, including the following:

- **Programmers can be fickle.** Your programmers take more attractive jobs elsewhere, after the project is finished, in which case you may never be able to modify it, or before, in which case you've made progress payments with no benefit.

- **Programmers are . . . accident prone?** Your programmers get hit by a beer truck crossing the street on their way to the local Internet café and must spend two years in traction.

- **Programmers are *programmers*.** Your programmers don't create proper documentation, either because they didn't want to or you didn't want to pay them to. When they move or get hit by a beer truck, you're stuck with a useless system.

✔ **The future is obsolete.** Your custom software, which worked fine on Windows 95, doesn't work properly on Windows 2001, and you have to pay big bucks to update it because the programmers can't spread the cost among multiple customers.

✔ **Programmers can be money-grubbers.** Your programmers get cocky and triple their prices overnight, after you're already heavily committed to the project. (Happens rarely, but does happen.)

I'm not suggesting that custom software is always a bad idea for a small company. Heck, I used to write custom programs for clients from time to time, especially back when good commercial microcomputer software was scarce. However, good commercial microcomputer software isn't scarce anymore. If you go the custom route, make sure you hire a firm with several programmers on staff, so you are at least somewhat protected from personnel changes. Also, insist on thorough documentation, even if it's expensive. Good documentation (design notes and program source code) is your best assurance that you are able to switch programming firms in the future if you need to, without having to throw away everything done up to that point.

Hardware

The primary hardware costs for your network are the servers, the users' computers (workstations), the cabling and hubs that connect the server to the workstations, and the peripherals.

You can save anywhere from 30 to 50 percent of the cost of new equipment by buying used or reconditioned hardware. The savings sound tempting, and some of my consulting clients have gone this route in the past, but it's not as attractive as it used to be. Used hardware can cost much more money than it saves. You don't usually get warranty coverage and you usually end up with a hodgepodge of systems that is more expensive to install, configure, support, and troubleshoot. Generally, I suggest that you don't buy used microcomputers for your business unless

✔ You can buy as many of the same make and model as you need (25 identical machines are cheaper to maintain than 25 random purchases).

✔ You can have someone knowledgeable run extensive tests on them.

✔ You can get at least a 30-day return guarantee.

✔ You can verify that the units are no more than a year old.

✔ You can get a service contract that doesn't wipe out the cost savings.

Even with these suggestions in mind, get some outside expert advice before you commit. I've always bought new computers for my own company, and I sincerely believe that I've saved money in the long run by doing so.

Servers

Not all small business networks have dedicated, single-purpose *server* computers that act as a central location for the computer network structure. Some networks, called *peer-to-peer* networks, allow every user's computer to share files and printers. However, if you do decide to go the route of the server computers and devote one or more computers completely to the task of sharing files and printers and so on, read on.

I discuss peer-to-peer networks in depth in Chapter 4.

For most businesses, the server computer should be the most powerful on the network, because everyone else on the network shares its power. You used to be able to actually use a less expensive machine for a server than you used for user workstations. Today, however, networks tend to place more and more responsibilities on the server, responsibilities beyond mere file and print sharing. For example, many small business network servers do double duty as a database engine to keep track of financial information, customer information, and so on.

You don't necessarily have to buy one large, powerful server — two smaller servers that divide the labor between them may cost a little more, but provide some useful redundancy you don't have with a single machine (that is, if one server crashes, you can limp happily along with the other instead of being completely shut down).

If your network may grow rapidly, definitely buy a server that can support more than one CPU (Central Processing Unit), even if you don't actually buy a second CPU until later. Most servers (and even some high-powered user workstations) can use multiple CPUs on the same motherboard.

The following list gives some ballpark U.S. costs for low-end, midrange, and high-end small business servers. Remember that these are examples, not recommendations. The type of server your business requires depends on the actual software you want to run.

- ✔ **A low-end server** that may be suitable for a network of 25 or so users has 32MB of memory (of course, more is always better), a couple of reasonably large hard drives (1GB at least), and one CPU running at a speed of at least 166MHz. You can expect to pay $2,000 to $3,000 for a computer like this, excluding the monitor.

- ✔ **A midrange server** that may be suitable for a network of 50 or so users has 64MB of memory, four fast SCSI (Small Computer Systems Interface) hard drives, and two CPUs running at 200MHz or faster. Such a machine costs around $3,000 to $4,000 (also without monitor).

- ✔ **A high-end server** that may be suitable for a 100-user network has 128MB of memory, eight fast SCSI hard drives, and four CPUs. Now you're getting into the $8,000 to $10,000 territory (without monitor).

The keyboard and mouse that come with the server should be fine. You may need to buy a monitor, but most businesses don't spend very much for a server monitor because there really isn't much to see — you're not going to use the server to cruise the Web for the latest 3-D video games. A relatively inexpensive 15-inch monitor for $300 to $400 should do just fine.

I often suggest an *external disk drive enclosure* (a separate box with bays for anywhere from 2 to 16 hard drives) for network servers, so that you can quickly move disk drives from your primary server to a backup server if the primary server fails. Figure on anywhere from $500 to $1,000 for a unit with dual power supplies and space for eight disk drives. If you do purchase a backup server for emergencies, and you use an external disk enclosure, you don't have to buy any disk drives for the backup server — and that can save some substantial bucks.

You also need a *battery power backup* unit for your servers, so they can keep running through brief power cuts. Figure on about a $400 unit for a low-end server and $800 or so for a high-end server, using the examples in the bulleted list earlier in this section.

Your users' computers

Today's microcomputer *workstations* (the individual computers you connect to a network) are truly amazing bargains. Not all that long ago, I bought my company's first microcomputer, which had under a megabyte of memory, a 20MB hard drive, a barely-color monitor, and a 6MHz CPU — and it cost me $7,000 (which, at the time, corresponded to about a year's salary).

Today, you can expect to buy a name-brand desktop computer with 16 to 32MB of memory, a single fast (but not state-of-the-art) Pentium-class CPU, 1 to 2GB of hard drive storage, a CD-ROM drive, network card, and reasonably fast color video circuitry for $1,200 to $1,500, plus the cost of a monitor.

The keyboards that come with nearly all desktop microcomputers are the straight rectangular variety, which are fine for occasional use. However, you may want to consider buying ergonomic keyboards for users who spend a great deal of time typing at the computer; these units typically cost from $100 to $150. Sometimes you can upgrade the keyboard at the time of purchase, and save some money.

The mouse, or pointing device, generally comes with a new computer and is of adequate, if not inspirational, quality.

The monitor is a key technology choice and often doesn't come bundled with a new computer. A poor monitor leads to user discomfort, so much so that some users may try to avoid using the computer network rather than deal with eyestrain and headaches. An excessively small monitor may not allow users to work effectively with the technology. For example, a windowing computer operating system (such as Windows 95 or Macintosh OS) is less useful when the monitor only permits the user to use one window at a time. A good 15-inch monitor for general business use costs from U.S. $300 to $400. A good 17-inch monitor costs from $600 to $800. Larger monitors become cost prohibitive for most businesses, although if your company employs a design engineer or in-house advertising designer, you may want to look at a 21-inch monitor, which typically costs at least twice as much as a 17-inch unit.

Portable computers cost 50 to 100 percent more than desktops on an apples-to-apples basis, because everything has to be smaller and more rugged. I usually recommend overbuying on notebook computer disk drives and memory, because after-sale upgrades tend to be fairly expensive.

Cabling and hubs

You have to connect those servers and user computers (workstations) together, and so you can plan on needing some cabling and hubs.

You may be fortunate and have network-grade cabling already available in your central office, but if not, you're looking at materials and labor costs to run the cable, install wallplates, and so on. Plan on around $350 to $450 per thousand feet of *Category 5 twisted-pair* cable (the most common kind for small networks) that's fire-rated for running through walls and over drop-ceilings. You can spend less than half that for nonfire-rated cable, but it's not nearly as safe, and the local fire marshal may shut down your business if you run the cheaper cable where local fire code prohibits it.

The cable installation generally costs five to ten times the cost of the actual wire, depending on the layout of your particular office. You can save here, too, by hiring a phone cable installer instead of someone with computer network cabling experience, but this may be penny-wise and pound-foolish. Something like 10 percent of all small network problems end up being cable related, so you're much better off having a network cable expert run the wires for you. This person needs to have specialized test equipment to verify the integrity of your cable runs before you even connect the first two computers together. Ask the installer whether he or she has such equipment *before* you authorize the job.

Because the labor is such a large part of network cabling costs, many companies go ahead and wire up every room in the office, including conference rooms, offices that are now vacant but may be occupied later, and so on. You've got the installer on-site, and the incremental cost of wiring up a few extra wallplates isn't usually large compared to the cost of getting the installer back out to the office a few months later. Pull somewhat longer lengths of cable than you need, too, as long as you don't exceed the maximum specifications (such as 100 meters for twisted pair) — that way you can adjust for a bad connection at the wallplate or other mishap because you have a bit of cable to spare.

Network *hubs,* the boxes that actually link up the computers in your network, vary widely in cost depending on their speed, sophistication, and expandability. *Switching hubs,* or *switches,* are fancier than regular hubs because they juggle your network connections on the fly for faster data transmission. *Fast Ethernet* hubs run up to ten times faster than regular Ethernet hubs. Table 2-3 provides some cost ranges for these different types of small network hubs. The wide cost range within each category reflects the dramatic difference between *managed* and *unmanaged* hubs. Managed hubs include remote control and remote diagnostics capabilities that you probably don't need in a small network, but may want in a larger network.

In Chapter 7, I discuss cabling, hubs, and switches in more detail.

Table 2-3	Approximate U.S. Network Hub Costs
Hub Type	*Cost*
Ethernet hub, 8 ports	$100-$500
Fast Ethernet hub, 8 ports (10x faster than Ethernet)	$300-$500
Ethernet hub, 16 ports	$220-$700
Fast Ethernet hub, 16 ports	$700-$1,800
Ethernet switch, 8 ports	$850-$1,700

Peripherals

Peripherals are all the devices on a network that aren't computers or hubs. Laser printers are usually the most expensive peripheral in a small business network. So-called *network* laser printers are rated for high *duty cycles* (a large number of pages per month — say 50,000 to 100,000). However, you may find that a so-called *desktop* laser printer can handle the workload that your office generates. For example, the $1,300 desktop laser printer I use at work has a 35,000 pages-per-month duty cycle, more than enough for most small businesses. If you need large paper formats (bigger than legal size), or really fast graphics printing, you're probably looking at $2,500 to $4,500, depending on the speed.

I don't usually recommend *personal* laser printers for network use. They're inexpensive (as low as $400) but they're pretty slow, have smaller paper trays, and are not as sturdy as desktop or network printers.

Color printers range all over the price map. Color laser printers, which produce medium quality output that's fine for most business applications, run from $3,000 up. You can easily spend twice that on a photographic-quality dye sublimation printer, and you may want to if you're in a business such as advertising and you rely heavily on visuals. A nice quality color inkjet printer runs about $300 to $500; inkjets produce the least impressive results but are unbeatable in terms of "wow" per dollar.

Watch the cost of printer consumables: toner, ink cartridges, and special paper (if required). Laser toner cartridges are rated for anywhere between 5,000 to 20,000 pages. The longer-lasting units cost about the same on a per-page basis, and take less of your time fiddling around with the printer.

The following list gives some ballpark figures for other shared network peripherals you may need. These devices are designed specifically to "hang off" the network directly and run at full network speed, rather than link to the network through a connected computer. Please note that in a small network, you can save money by buying a workstation (personal) version of some of these peripherals and sharing it across your network:

- ✔ **Network modem:** $1,500 to $2,500 for a four-port unit

- ✔ **Network CD-ROM drive:** $400 to $800 for a four-disc unit

- ✔ **Network tape backup:** $1,000 to $3,000, depending on capacity, speed, and autochanger options with multiple tape cartridge handling

Setup

Installing your network can be a big job, even after the cable has been run and the machines are plugged in. I take you through the major installation steps in Chapters 8 through 11, but you may still elect to hire out the work. In any case, you can benefit by reading these chapters so that you have a good idea of what you're buying. If so, plan on spending roughly 10 percent of the total hardware and software cost on network setup and configuration.

Training

Most growing companies have two sets of computer training requirements: one for the person or persons who build and manage the network, and another for the users. The cost of training varies depending on the delivery method, but technical education for the network manager is almost always much more expensive than for network users.

In Chapter 13, I discuss network management and end-user education in more detail.

For network managers

Public, independent seminars put on by professional training companies for network managers can cost as little as $200 for a light, one-day class. An intensive two-day class with hands-on demonstrations may cost as much as $1,000. Highly product-specific seminars designed to prepare network managers for formal certification exams can run a week long and cost $2,000 to $4,000. These courses may be overkill for the typical small company, but hiring a less-experienced person and running that person through such a course may be less expensive than hiring someone who already has the certification. (Of course, once your network manager completes the course and becomes certified, don't be surprised if he or she asks for a raise, or at least a corner cubicle.)

Vendor-provided classes generally cost about the same as public, independent seminars. The advantage is that the network manager can learn a lot of specifics about the particular network he or she is administering; the disadvantage is that the course may not cover as much (or any) third-party software.

Consultants can provide one-on-one education for your network manager. Figure in the ballpark of $600 to $800 per day for a good consultant, although the going rate varies by geographical region and consultant experience. You may be able to bring in colleagues you know from other companies who can freelance for you on a weekend or in the evening for much less money because they already have a salaried "day job." Beer and pizza (or wine and cheese) can lower the hourly rate further.

Videos, CD-ROMs, and books all cost much less than personal instruction. Some vendors package all three media together in one bundle. Technical videos can range from $100 to $400 apiece, and running times vary widely. A good instructional CD-ROM falls in the same price ballpark. Books are good options at $20 to $50 each, especially if you buy them at a discount through mail order or Internet-based services. Note, however, that these self-study techniques require a lot more discipline than formal training sessions.

For network users

User education is a lot less expensive, fortunately. Public seminars on popular horizontal software applications (word processing, spreadsheet, and light database) are available for $50 to $100 a day. Many community colleges offer evening and weekend classes for $50 to $100 a *course,* which includes several sessions. Most user-oriented videos on typical software applications run $30 to $75 per application, and CD-ROM instructional titles run in about the same price range. (Let me also not forget to mention the bargain pricing of the fine *...For Dummies* series of computer books!)

Maintenance, troubleshooting, and upgrades

Keeping a network running, fixing problems, and improving hardware and software over time can be more expensive than your initial network setup. However, these ongoing costs are not entirely beyond your control.

The more *consistency* you can build into your network, the less expensive hardware and software maintenance becomes. Any big-company Help Desk analyst can tell you that troubleshooting a network with microcomputers from three different manufacturers is nearly three times as time-consuming as troubleshooting a network where all workstations are the same make. Also, for hardware maintenance, keeping spare parts (circuit boards, power supplies, and so on) for one brand is much cheaper than keeping spare parts for a bunch of different makes and models of computer.

You can reduce the time, effort, and dollars required to maintain both servers and workstations by obtaining Internet access. Many vendors, including Novell, Microsoft, and Sun, offer a variety of technical support services on their public World Wide Web sites — including downloadable software updates that you may otherwise have to pay for.

I explain network maintenance and management in depth in Chapter 13.

Hardware

Hardware maintenance costs are low during the warranty period, which ranges from one year to three years depending on the manufacturer and the particular product. However, most small computer warranties only cover carry-in (also called *depot*) service. If you want on-site service, you may have to pay extra. Some manufacturers provide on-site service during the first year, but then you have to pay extra for it in subsequent years. As a general guideline, plan on spending from 5 to 10 percent of the hardware's purchase price per year for a hardware maintenance contract after the warranty expires.

On-site service rarely lives up to customer expectations — it only means that a technician shows up within X hours of your service call. The time to *response* (X) isn't the same as the time to *repair!* The technician may show up, tell you that you need a spare part that's out of stock and has been on back-order for two months, and still meet the service contract's obligations even though you're stuck with a dead box for eight weeks or more. (Imagine that a fire engine responds to your emergency call within a quick five minutes, only to have the chief advise you, while you watch your office building turn to carbon, that the fire hose is on order from Omaha.) The moral is that if you rely heavily on your network, consider stocking some spare parts yourself, especially if you don't have a backup server or spare workstation.

Some small businesses do without a maintenance contract and just buy an extra workstation for every 10 or 15 employee computers. You spend the same or even less, and if something breaks, you have a machine you can "cannibalize."

Some companies buy a *cable tester* to troubleshoot network cable problems. A good cable tester is pretty expensive, though (in the hundreds of dollars), and it may be cheaper to just have whoever installs your cable in the first place come out to test it if you suspect a problem. If you use an installer who has networking experience, that person probably already has a high-quality cable tester (and knows how to use it).

As far as hardware upgrades go, if you purchase machines that don't have much performance headroom to begin with, you may need to make some enhancements later — such as adding a CPU to a server, for example. You may also need to add server disk capacity: A fast SCSI 2GB hard drive costs in the $500 to $600 range at the time I write this. Whoever adds such bits and pieces to a computer needs to be familiar with the necessary safeguards — reading Chapter 8 is a good start.

Software

You may not think that you have to have maintenance contracts for software, but they can be a good idea. Troubleshooting software problems can be a very complex and time-consuming undertaking. Unfortunately, software maintenance and support contracts have become very expensive. Some vendors charge $100 per incident after the free support period expires — and that free-support period is generally only 30 to 90 days. Unlike hardware maintenance contracts, software support contracts can easily cost more than the software's purchase price for a mere year of technical support and free upgrades, although 15 to 25 percent is more typical.

If the free support period clock starts ticking the day you buy the product, test the bejeepers out of the software immediately after you buy it, so that you can work with the vendor on any major problems during the initial free support period. If you have X days of free support, counting from the first time you call the vendor, but with no limit on how many questions you can ask, save up your questions for awhile. By doing so, you can delay that first phone call or e-mail and wring the most value out of the free period.

You can often get quick answers to technical questions from a software vendor's Internet site, particularly if the vendor sponsors a *newsgroup* (electronic discussion forum) where customers can share questions and problems with each other. Often, these newsgroups are fairly well organized and you may even be able to search them for particular difficulties. Check out the vendor's Internet support resources before deciding on a software support contract. CompuServe offers newsgroup-like forums that may be even better than Internet newsgroups because CompuServe has traditionally targeted the computer professionals market.

You can update your software at no cost when a vendor releases bug-fix *maintenance releases*. These software *patches* or *service packs* (as they are also sometimes called) usually ship upon request for free or for a small shipping fee, and you can also generally download them from the Internet. You have to stay in touch with the vendor, though, because you won't receive a postcard in the mail alerting you to such maintenance releases if you haven't been in contact with the vendor.

So-called *major upgrades* are another story. The software industry updates its products frequently, so you are best off budgeting for new and improved versions of both Network Operating System software and application software. You can generally plan on upgrading everything every two to three years, for an estimated cost of 30 to 50 percent of the original purchase price. (Upgrades used to be a smaller percentage of the original price, but the software industry has saturated many markets and is now looking to the upgrade market to boost profits. Also, original purchase prices have dropped a great deal over the years.)

Chapter 3

Networking on a Schedule

. . . .

In This Chapter

▶ Designing and building your network

▶ Planning your network design time schedule

▶ Administering a network

▶ Choosing and using consultants to help you build your system fast and right

. . . .

"*T*ime is money," so they say — but this statement cuts two ways when it comes to computer networking. You sure don't want to spend more time than you need to build your network, but if you don't spend enough, you'll pay for it later — in both time *and* money.

"More software projects have gone awry for lack of calendar time than for all other causes combined."
(Fred Brooks, *The Mythical Man-Month,* Addison-Wesley)

Replace the word "software" with the word "network" in this quotation, and you've got an equally true statement. Almost every computer network project comes in late — even the small ones. Why?

The main reason is that small businesses always (and I mean *always*) underestimate how long it takes to build a computer network. The computer industry is partly to blame here: It's famous for promising easy, quick installation. However, your actual "out-of-box experience" always entails more time and effort than advertised (plus a few phone calls to technical support hotlines, which are never all that hot).

Rule #1 of network planning: Don't take the computer industry hype without a railcar full of salt. If you think of a small business network as more like a model train set than a toaster oven, you're on the right track. (Readers sensitive to my daft humor may groan now.)

Another reason computer network projects run over schedule is that some small businesses want to do everything in-house. For a small network, that's fine — computer hardware and software has become easier to set up in recent years, and with this book you can reasonably go the DIY (Do It

Yourself) route. But if your network is moderately complex or bigger than a dozen users, doing everything yourself takes more time (and may cause you a lot more headaches) than if you get a little expert help. Tasks that sound simple ("Install the Network Operating System") can be complex in real life if you've never done them before.

How can you keep your network on schedule? Here are five tips:

- ✔ **You're off to a great start by reading this book.** Many of the suggestions sprinkled throughout these pages can help you save time and avoid mistakes you have to correct later.

- ✔ **Set a realistic schedule at the outset.** This chapter helps you identify the tasks in rolling out a new network, and estimate how much time they should take.

- ✔ **Take the Alfred Hitchcock approach.** Hitchcock would envision an entire movie in his mind before filming the first scene. Reading most of this book before you start buying products is a great idea. (Your network administrator should read it twice.)

- ✔ **Shortcuts aren't.** Whenever you feel the temptation to take a shortcut ("Do I really need to have the installer test this cable? It sure looks good to me"), lie down somewhere quiet until the feeling goes away. Doing things right is always faster in the long run.

- ✔ **Ask for help.** Don't be shy about getting some technical help for your network project. I give you a lot of advice in this chapter about your help options, and they don't have to be expensive.

Scheduling Your Project

A small business network isn't a nuclear reactor, and you probably don't need a formal schedule if all you're doing is setting up a super-simple *Local Area Network* (LAN) for four users. However, all networks go through roughly the same steps in terms of design, rollout, and management — steps that this section details in the following paragraphs.

If you're setting up a network with more than a dozen or so users, I recommend that you use a computer program to help you set the schedule, delegate the tasks, and monitor your progress. If you have at least one PC in your office already, snag a copy of Microsoft Project (shown in Figure 3-1) or Primavera Project Planner (Appendix B provides vendor details). These tools let you set up key tasks, assign people to them, and identify which tasks depend on others (so-called *critical path* items). Both of these programs are easy to use, and may come in handy for many of your other business-related projects.

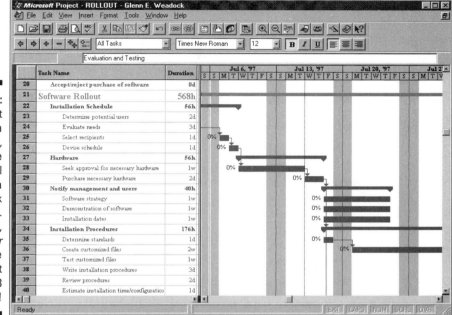

Figure 3-1:
Microsoft
Project is a
good,
inexpensive
planning tool
for a
network
project.
Don't worry,
your
software
rollout won't
take 568
hours!

Designing your network

Spend a little time on design, even for a four-computer network, and I
unconditionally guarantee you'll be glad you did (there — you even have it
in writing). Start by reading the chapters in Parts II, III, and IV of this book.
Then, plan on the design phase to take anywhere from one to three working
days, depending on how much help you have and how big your network is.
Here are the key tasks:

✔ Settle on a peer-to-peer network or a client/server network (Chapter 4)

✔ Pick your network system software (Chapter 5)

✔ Pick a network language (Chapter 6)

✔ Figure out what hardware you need (Chapter 7)

✔ Decide what degree of information security you need (Chapter 11)

✔ Choose software and hardware solutions to handle day-to-day management chores (Chapter 13)

Rolling out your network

Rolling out your network requires the following steps, covered in detail in Chapters 8 and 10:

1. **Run and test network cable.**

2. **Install the server or servers if you're setting up a client/server network. (If you are setting up a peer-to-peer network, you typically don't have to worry about any dedicated servers.)**

3. **Set up the workstation hardware.**

4. **Plug in and cable the *Network Interface Cards* (NICs — these connect the computers to the LAN).**

5. **Install the hub or hubs (if you're using twisted-pair cable).**

6. **Install printers.**

7. **Load up the server software (the NOS, or *Network Operating System*) if your network is a client/server type.**

8. **Install the workstation software.**

9. **Install modem hardware for remote dial-up (if you want your users to be able to dial into your network).**

10. **Install the programs you want to run (application software).**

How long does all of this take? The time you need to run the cable is hard to estimate because offices vary so widely in their physical layout, but one to two hours per computer is a good guideline. Getting a computer up and running (hardware only!) takes about one to two hours per machine (most of which you spend ripping into the plastic bags that computer makers feel strangely compelled to wrap around every single little component). Ditto for printers and hubs.

Installing server system software, that is, the Network Operating System (NOS), can take anywhere from no time (if it comes preinstalled) to an afternoon (if it doesn't).

The user workstation operating system (such as Windows 95) usually comes preinstalled. However, if it doesn't, expect to spend about an hour per machine installing it.

Allow 30 to 45 minutes to install each Network Interface Card (NIC), unless your workstations are "network ready" and come with a NIC preinstalled. In either case, the NIC usually requires some configuration time.

Putting a modem on the network takes from one to two hours, not counting the time necessary for the phone company to run a line where you want it. You may want to schedule an appointment with the phone company early, in case they are running a long backlog.

The time required to load up your application software is almost impossible to estimate, because it depends on where you're installing the software (on the server or on the workstations) as well as on the individual product. Find someone who has some experience installing the programs that you want to run, ask that person for a time estimate, *and then double it.*

Configuring your network

What the heck is *network configuration?* The term technically means all the stuff you have to do to customize the network for your own use. The typical steps, all covered in Chapter 9, include

- ✔ Creating network accounts for your users (names, passwords, groups)
- ✔ Creating areas on shared disk drives for users to share data files
- ✔ Creating areas on shared disk drives for users to share programs (unless everyone runs programs from their own computer)
- ✔ Setting up print queues (the software that lets users share networked printers)
- ✔ Installing network support on user workstations, so they can "talk" to your network
- ✔ Installing screen saver software that displays inspirational messages such as "Teamwork is the patty in the hamburger of success"

Plan on anywhere from one to three days for the first four items. Installing the network software on user computers shouldn't take more than about a half hour per computer.

Managing your network

Setting up your LAN for convenient ongoing management is a step many small companies skip in order to save time. Don't fall into that trap. The work you do right after your LAN is up and running and configured can save you huge amounts of time in the coming months. Building a good network management setup includes the following tasks:

✔ Mapping your network for easier management and troubleshooting (Chapter 9)

✔ Setting up appropriate security measures to protect against accidental and intentional harm (Chapter 11)

✔ Tuning up your LAN so that you get the best possible speed from it (Chapter 12)

✔ Creating company standards for adding hardware and software, so you don't have nagging compatibility problems later (Chapter 13)

✔ Putting backup systems in place so that you have copies of data and programs if your hardware fails (Chapter 13)

✔ Installing some monitoring and diagnostic software so that you can check on your network's health and get an early warning of impending problems (Chapter 13)

✔ Figuring out how you plan to handle troubleshooting — educating your LAN administrator, setting up a support contract with a software vendor, and so on (Chapter 13)

Plan on about a week's worth of work to put a solid network management structure into place, but future time savings pay off many times that amount.

Who Does the Work?

Many of the steps involved in designing and building a small business network can happen at the same time, and that's a great way to shorten the time frame between the time you bought this book and the time you can start to use your network. An important part of scheduling your network project, then, is determining who does what, and how much (if any) of the work you need to assign to outside contractors in order to get connected as quickly as practical.

Outsourcing, partnering, or insourcing?

Most small companies find that doing all the work of designing and building a computer network in-house saves money, but may take too much time. Hiring everything out to a consulting firm can save time, but may cost too much money. Partnering — that is, hiring a professional company to do some of the hard work in cooperation with your employees, and adding some of your own "sweat equity" — is a middle-of-the-road option that works well for many small businesses (see Figure 3-2).

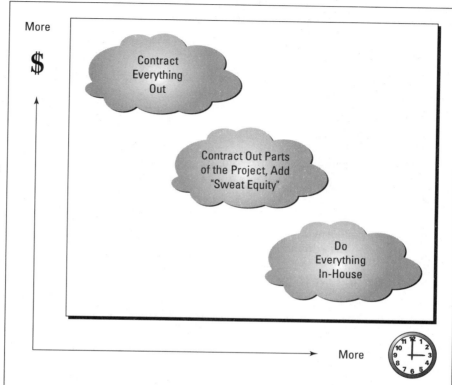

Figure 3-2:
Outsourcing,
partnering,
and
insourcing
are all valid
approaches,
depending
on whether
you have
more
money than
time or
verce visa.

Outsourcing

Outsourcing just means contracting with other companies for a service. You may want to outsource some or all of your networking project. If you need your network yesterday, and you don't have any computer-savvy employees on the payroll, outsourcing may be your best bet. Consultants have the advantage of working with multiple companies and applications, so they bring a valuable perspective to your project. They're also less tied to your own internal company politics. Finally, when you outsource, you don't add to your company payroll, and so you save the fringe benefit costs that salaried employment may impose.

When considering the outsourcing option, ask yourself these questions:

- How soon does this network have to be ready?

- How complicated is the network I have in mind — how many users, how many printers, is it client/server or peer-to-peer, does it require dial-up remote access, and so on?

- ✔ What skills does it require that my company doesn't have in-house? ("All" is an okay answer.)

- ✔ How long would it take to acquire those skills, either through hiring or training interested employees?

- ✔ Can we conveniently outsource part of the project, such as the hardware installation, rather than the whole ball of wax? (Note that partial outsourcing isn't quite the same as partnering. With partial outsourcing, your company does task *A* and the contractor does task *B*, whereas with partnering, you both do *A* and *B* together.)

The biggest drawback of outsourcing everything, aside from the cost, is that you miss out on an opportunity to gain experience by doing. Your part-time or full-time network administrator won't understand your network as thoroughly as would be the case if he or she was involved in building it. A secondary drawback is that outsourced personnel may not have as solid an understanding of some of your company's inner workings (politics, information flows, and so on).

Partnering

Partnering differs a bit from outsourcing, and has the following characteristics:

- ✔ The outside company shares work with your in-house network administrator, and works at your location most of the time.

- ✔ The hired partner educates your employees as the project goes along, meaning that the transition to running your network in-house can be much smoother.

- ✔ The process usually takes somewhat longer than straight outsourcing because of the training time.

- ✔ The end result is not only a completed project, but also the expertise your organization gains.

Partnering may be either more or less expensive than outsourcing, depending on how quickly your in-house staff picks up concepts and can start doing productive work on the project. You may find partnering to be a good middle-of-the-road option if you want to learn about and get trained in computer networking, but need to get a specific project off the ground faster than would be possible by relying on in-house expertise and personnel alone. Partnering is a little bit like building a house with a general contractor, but jumping in to hang drywall, nail up some of the framing, lay tile, clean up after the general contractor, and so on.

Insourcing

Insourcing means you do everything yourself. If you read this book fairly carefully, you can build a small network (under a dozen users, say) yourself. If you have one or more computer-savvy people in your organization, you may be able to build a bigger network on your own.

Just because this book lays out the main steps in building a small business network, I don't want to imply that you don't need to consider outside help for part of the project. Think of a manual for building a redwood deck onto your home. Reading such a manual can help you get your money's worth from a contractor, if you decide that a contractor can do the work faster and less expensively than you could. Or, the manual can help you build your deck yourself if you feel you have the time, general construction skills, and inclination. You can use the book you're reading now either way, too — it's up to you.

You can get helpful advice from consultants on a less formal basis than outsourcing or partnering. For example, you can hire a firm to take a gander at the network you've built, and make some suggestions for performance, reliability, or security improvements. Sometimes, consultants are also useful for pointing out new technology that you may not know about. Finally, they can get your boss to pay attention to what you've been saying for weeks. (I've done a few jobs like that, where my final report to my client basically says, "Your network administrator is right! Do what she says!")

You can (and should) listen to technical advice from other sources, too — Chamber of Commerce meetings, community business assistance programs, friends in the computer industry. Just remember that the pros have experience that may give you an edge over the company getting its advice from the owner's nephew, who is taking a college computer course to meet the science requirement for his degree in Postmodern Tibetan Ritual Dance.

Designating a key employee

Whether you outsource, partner, or insource your network project, you need to assign one key employee to track and stay on top of the project. Ideally, this employee is the same person who manages the LAN after it's up and running — your future *network administrator.*

Your network administrator will probably have other job responsibilities in a company with fewer than 40 or 50 employees, and will probably manage your network full time in a company with more employees than that. In either case, the network administrator does the following:

- ✔ Manages the network project's budget and schedule
- ✔ Acts as your company's primary contact with any outside contractors, hardware vendors, and software vendors
- ✔ Helps to train employees in the use of the network
- ✔ Takes care of day-to-day network management and troubleshooting chores (Help Desk-type support)
- ✔ Coordinates network expansion to handle new employees and new programs (adding user accounts, installing software)
- ✔ Manages network security (monitoring network log files, staying up to date with software security concerns and the latest security technology)
- ✔ Calls in help when necessary

Chapter 13 provides more details on network management.

Choosing and Using Consultants

The second half of this chapter presents guidelines to help you choose and use consultants who'll help you meet your project schedule. Most growing companies get at least some degree of outside help when building a network, but precious few networking books offer tips on how to do so, so the subject seems worth a few pages.

Good network consultants usually cost money, but rarely more than a good plumber or electrician. You wouldn't trust your water pipes or electrical wiring to a shoddy contractor because you know you end up paying more later to get the work done properly. Approach networking consultants with the same attitude. Plan on the neighborhood of $50 an hour — if you pay much less than that, you may not be getting someone with good training and experience; if you pay much more, you may be buying more consulting horsepower than a small business network requires.

To save money, you can go with an individual consultant, even someone working out of his or her home. Thousands of excellent consultants work independently, and enjoy keeping their overhead low. However, you do get some advantages in exchange for the higher cost of a consulting firm with more than one employee. Such a firm can put more people on the job to get your project finished sooner, and you have more than one person to call if something goes wrong. And, statistically speaking, the company's a little more likely to be around next year. Whether those advantages are worth the extra cost, which may be $10 to $20 more per hour, is something only you can decide. If you expect to build a long-term relationship with a company that can continue taking care of your network as your business grows, you may lean toward the company with multiple employees.

Choosing professional professionals

How do you qualify a computer consulting firm? With so many companies hanging out computer consulting shingles these days, you need some guidelines for selecting a company that has the expertise and experience to do a proper job and not waste a lot of time correcting its own mistakes. The network experts at "Bill and Ted's Excellent Computer Consulting Firm" may seem smart, but you need more than just smart. You need smart, experienced, fast, and professional. Look for certification, professional affiliations, referrals, and interview performance.

Bona fide and certified

Unlike civil engineers, dentists, lawyers, and (I'm guessing) beekeepers, computer consultants don't have an industry board that confers an industrywide certification. Some argue that in a field with so much specialization, a certification test similar to the test engineers take to achieve Professional Engineer, or P.E., status would be impractical, and the resulting credential would be so broad as to be meaningless. Others make the point that the "state of the art" changes so rapidly in the computer field that a computer consultant certification would have to be renewed every year in order to retain any value.

These arguments contain some truth, but the problem for business customers is that you have no single, convenient guarantee of a minimal level of competence when hiring a computer consultant or consulting firm. However, the fact that no *single* certification test exists doesn't mean that no certification tests at all exist. *Au contraire.*

Microsoft certification

Microsoft, for example, has assembled a comprehensive set of certification exams for consultants working with its products. Different levels of certification exist in the Microsoft curriculum, all conferring the status of Microsoft Certified Professional (MCP):

- ✔ A *Microsoft Certified Product Specialist (MCPS)* must pass at least one core exam covering a Microsoft operating system, such as Windows 95 or Windows NT. This credential assures you that the consultant has a fairly good knowledge of a product that you intend to use on your network.

- ✔ A *Microsoft Certified Systems Engineer (MCSE)* must pass six exams. This credential lets you know that the consultant has a wide enough range of expertise to help manage an entire networking project.

- ✔ A *Microsoft Certified Solution Developer (MCSD)* must pass four exams with an emphasis on programming. This certification is useful when you're looking for someone to design a custom information system for you, such as a database program.

✔ A *Microsoft Certified Trainer (MCT)* is someone who wants to teach official Microsoft courses, and must pass the relevant exam plus demonstrate training skills. You'd give this credential weight if you were hiring someone to train an in-house network administrator.

How tough is it to attain Microsoft certification? A consultant doesn't have to be a superexpert to pass any given test, but does have to know the product reasonably well; even superexperts have a hard time scoring 100 percent. Also, the tests are monitored, closed-book, and the questions vary from test to test, so cheating is difficult (although if you write really small on your forearm and wear a jacket to the test — but I digress).

If a consultant proudly states that he or she has Microsoft certification for the Windows for Workgroups product, throw that consultant out of your office and don't validate. Windows for Workgroups is old and tired and you don't want it. If you have it, you need to run, not walk, to the computer store and upgrade to Windows 95 or Windows NT *before* you set up your network.

If you have access to the Internet, you can get more information on current Microsoft certification tests and requirements at `http://www.microsoft.com/train_cert`.

Novell certification

Novell also has set up a highly organized and popular certification structure for everyone from salespeople to installers and instructors. The Novell certifications divide out as follows:

✔ A *Certified Novell Salesperson (CNS)* has passed one test covering Novell products and how to position them. Frankly, this certification doesn't mean a great deal to a consulting customer.

✔ A *Certified Novell Administrator (CNA)* must pass one technical test on NetWare or GroupWise. This credential indicates a good enough understanding of the specific product to install and manage it.

✔ A *Certified Novell Engineer (CNE)* must pass seven technical tests. CNE certification is more rigorous than CNA certification and indicates a very thorough understanding of the product. The CNE program has been very popular, with some 100,000 individuals certified.

✔ A *Master Certified Novell Engineer (MCNE)* must pass at least 15 (!) difficult and specific technical tests. MCNE certification means that your consultant is likely to know everything backward, forward, and sideways (and charge accordingly, so watch out).

✔ A *Certified Novell Instructor (CNI)* must have teaching experience, pass two to three technical tests, and pass an instructor performance evaluation. You'd give this credential weight if you were hiring someone to train an in-house network administrator.

> ✔ A ***Certified Internet Professional (CIP)*** must pass tests from one of five tracks covering the Internet and intranets. Note the lack of the word "Novell" here: This curriculum is a joint venture of Novell and Netscape, and is both less product specific and less technical than other Novell certifications. CIP certification may matter to you if you want to put your business on the Internet (see Chapter 17).

How well do the Novell tests indicate technical competence? Very well. Like the Microsoft tests, the pass/fail Novell tests are closed-book and monitored, so fudging is just about impossible. The CNA certification parallels the MCPS Microsoft certification: Neither is very hard to achieve, but both guarantee a minimal level of competence. The CNE certification is analogous to the MCSE "degree" — you're looking at a consultant who really knows the material.

If you have Internet access, you can find out more on Novell certification at http://education.novell.com.

If your business is in a small town, the nearest testing facility may be some distance away, so local consultants may know their stuff but don't want to drive 200 miles to take a certification exam. They may also be too doggoned busy installing networks to go through the formal certification process, which in the case of MCSE and CNE certifications, requires a major time commitment (and a few grand, too). For these reasons, don't absolutely rule out a consulting firm because of a lack of industry certification. Past experience and references from happy customers count as much, if not more, than any certification.

Other network software vendors have their own certification programs, too. Space prohibits discussing them all here, but if you're looking at a network from someone other than Microsoft or Novell, check out the available certification programs and find out what the different levels are. This way, you can evaluate consultant credentials intelligently.

Well connected

Consulting firms that are active in the industry are more likely to be up to date on current technology trends. Of course, any consulting firm with a few hundred bucks can join just about any industry association. However, professional associations sponsor newsletters, meetings, and conferences that can help consulting firms stay on top of the industry. Some also have codes of conduct that members must agree to uphold. So, as with professional certifications, membership in industry groups is a plus even if it's not a deciding factor.

Some of the industry groups that computer consulting firms can join include

- The Association for Computing Machinery (ACM)
- The American Society for Training and Development (ASTD — for consulting firms that also do training)
- The Independent Computer Consultants Association (ICCA)
- The Institute of Electrical and Electronic Engineers (IEEE)

Well regarded

Referrals outweigh certifications and trade group memberships when you're selecting a consulting firm. The candid comments of other customers are very helpful in determining how a consulting firm performs in real life — not just how well its members take tests and pay membership dues.

Getting candid comments is a little easier with contractor references than it is for employee references. Some companies adopt a policy of not commenting about former employees beyond confirming dates of employment, so the companies can protect themselves against pesky lawsuits ("You ruined my career by telling my interviewer about that office fire I started when you laid me off!" and so on). However, most companies are more forthcoming when it comes to commenting about contractor performance.

Some questions you may want to ask former customers of the consulting firms you're considering include:

- Did the consultants listen carefully to your descriptions of your operations and business needs?
- Did they help draft a detailed contract?
- Did they meet their obligations on time?
- Did they stick to the budget, allowing for change orders?
- Did they provide detailed invoices, so you knew what you were paying for?
- Did they steal sandwiches from the mini-frig in the break room?
- Did they follow up regularly after the project was complete to see how the network was doing?
- Were they responsive to your questions and problems during rollout and afterward?

Your gut feel

Interview a potential network contractor as thoroughly as you would any new employee candidate. Ideally, you want to build a relationship that can benefit your business over a period of years, not just weeks. Spend at least an hour with each prospective contractor. If you deal with a company with multiple employees, make sure that you speak with the person who'll do the actual work, not just a company salesperson.

During the interview, take a few minutes to explain your business and what you expect your new network to accomplish for you. Talk about your budget, too. Then let the contractor tell you about past experience, work habits, time and cost estimates, and so on. Ask if the contractor resells hardware and software, or makes a living solely on consulting (the answer could affect the contractor's inclination to recommend certain products over others). Don't expect a lot of free advice — advice is what these companies sell for a living — but do get an idea as to how the contractor would approach your project. Your "gut feel" is just as important as strong references when deciding on a network contractor.

Pros and contracts

You may feel that a contract isn't necessary for a small business network consulting deal. I don't care how small your network outsourcing project is or whether your consultant is a lifelong buddy who's moonlighting for you as a favor — write up a contract! A good contract spells out everyone's responsibilities, sets a timetable, specifies costs, lets your contractor know you're serious about the project, and protects both parties against unpleasant surprises. Your contract doesn't have to be long and involved; a one- or two-page letter agreement may be all you need. Ninety-nine times out of a hundred, the planning required to put the job description down on paper is more valuable than the resulting document.

I've seen several networking projects that suffered from the lack of a contract, but none that suffered because of one. Further, I have yet to see any computer professional refuse a job — even to build a TAN (Tiny Area Network — yes, some books use this term!) — solely because the customer wanted to put it in writing.

Don't make the mistake of handing a contract over to a consulting firm and then not speaking to your consultant until project review time (see Figure 3-3). Even in a small project, plan to touch base at the design review, hardware test, and software test/demo stages (see Figure 3-4). You don't want the project to get too far under way before you realize it's not going the direction you anticipated.

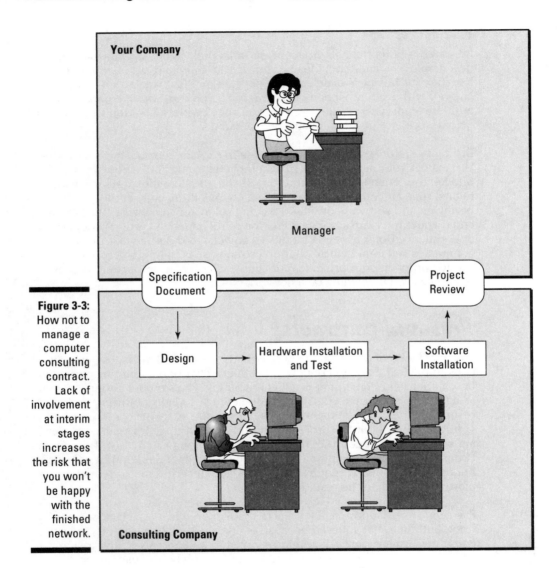

Figure 3-3: How not to manage a computer consulting contract. Lack of involvement at interim stages increases the risk that you won't be happy with the finished network.

Project scope

This paragraph of the contract lays out what the contractor agrees to do for you. Make the project scope as specific as possible: Is the contractor responsible for installing hardware, or just software? Network software, or applications, too? If applications, which ones?

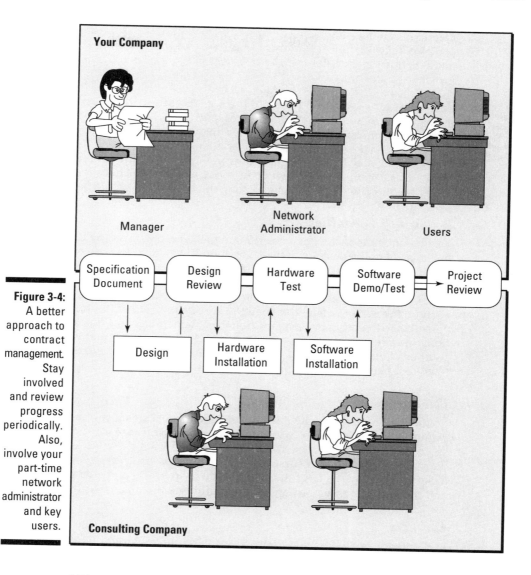

Figure 3-4: A better approach to contract management. Stay involved and review progress periodically. Also, involve your part-time network administrator and key users.

Milestones and deliverables

You may think that I'm silly to talk about *milestones* (also called *checkpoints* or *target dates*) for a one- or two-week project, but those consulting hours and dollars can rack up quickly and you want to make sure that they're being put to good use. I usually recommend setting very specific milestones for the following deliverables: detailed network design, hardware installation and test, network system software installation and test, and application software installation and test. Questions that arise during these checkpoint meetings can not only raise concerns about your network's limitations, but can also suggest opportunities for improvement that may be easier to implement sooner rather than later. Milestones are also convenient dates for progress payments.

Your contract should entitle you to the contractor's work notes, project management schedules, internal memos, and so on. You can learn something from these materials, but most outsourcing arrangements don't include them in the package. Make sure that system documentation is part of the arrangement, too. If you ever take over your network and run it entirely in-house, this documentation (which includes a map of the network and a list of key technology decisions made along the way) can be a big help.

Bonuses and penalties

You can include penalty clauses for late delivery, to reflect the cost to your business of not getting its network built on time, if you feel the need. Two cautions, though: If the penalties are too strict, the consulting firm you choose may reject the job, especially if the firm's been working long enough to know that many project delays are caused by customer change orders. Second, the carrot is mightier than the stick, so offset late-performance penalties with early-performance bonuses. Remember how quickly construction crews rebuilt the highways after the 1994 Northridge earthquake in southern California? A big part of the reason was that the contractors stood to collect performance bonuses if they finished the job ahead of schedule.

Contingencies

Computer projects usually change after the parties sign a contract. You may want to add computers to your network, change software, or run more cable as you get into a network installation. You don't want the contract to limit your ability to make midcourse corrections. So your contract needs to provide a clause allowing the consulting firm to do more work, and change the cost and time estimates accordingly, if you authorize the change order in writing.

Conflicts

In the list of small business distractions, lawsuits rank right up there with office romances and IRS audits. As a consultant, I've often worked with an arbitration clause to help reduce the chance of getting tied up in court if a contract goes utterly sour. Different opinions exist about independent arbitration, but it's at least an option to consider if you have better things to do than spend time and money on court cases and lawyers.

Preempt common conflicts by including both a conflict-of-interest clause and a paragraph on nondisclosure. Your consultants get to see some sensitive material, and you want them to treat it professionally.

Part II

Four Steps to Planning Your Technology Strategy

"THE TROUBLE-SHOOTERS FROM THE VENDOR AND THE PHONE COMPANY ARE HERE."

In this part . . .

Most small business managers I know are high-energy, action-oriented people. When such people decide to build a computer network, their impulse is to run down to the computer store, buy several thousand dollars' worth of equipment, and say, "Let's install it this evening! Tomorrow, we'll be in the Information Age, using words like *surf* and *boot!*" (This impulse is why so many networks are such a mess.)

It takes some restraint, but before you buy anything, you need to lay out a technology strategy so that you get the most bang for your networking buck. The strategy has four key parts, each corresponding to a chapter in Part II. First, choose a networking style: *client/server* or *peer-to-peer*. Second, choose the Network Operating System software. Deciding which network language to use comes next. And finally, you need to make several choices about the nuts and bolts (hardware) for your new network. Put all of these decisions together, and you are on your way!

Chapter 4

Networking Styles and Business Personalities

*E*very computer network has a certain style, and that style needs to reflect the personality of the company that uses it. In this chapter, I discuss the two primary network styles and their pros and cons.

Say what? Business personalities? Isn't this supposed to be a book about small business networking? Yes, it is — and personality is a big part of your network. You need a computer network that fits your company's style. Pick a network that goes against your company's grain, and you may find yourself struggling to work for your network instead of having your network work for you.

When you buy clothes, whether you're male or female, you make decisions like the following:

✔ High-priced and durable versus low-priced and replaceable

✔ Suits versus separates

✔ Snug-fitting for now versus loose-fitting for a few years from now

✔ Follow fashion trends or go your own way

✔ Fancy stores with personal service versus no-frills stores with no service

If you already know your preferences about these matters, shopping becomes a lot easier because you can greatly narrow your list of choices. Similarly, if you know your preferences about business computing (which actually involves the same basic questions), shopping for network products becomes a lot easier, too. To recast the previous list of issues in a business light:

- ✔ Is your company more inclined to spend less money now and possibly replace pieces of your network in a couple of years, or lay out more cash up front for a system that will run for a longer period?

- ✔ Are you more comfortable getting products that you know work well together because they're from the same vendor? Or would you prefer to invest more time, save some money, and mix and match network components?

- ✔ Is your company growing, and if so, do you want a network that can expand along with it? Or would you rather have a network that's easier to set up, but that may not let you easily expand in the future?

- ✔ Do you want to stick with established standards and industry trends, or do you want to set up a network that may flout those trends but that works more the way you want it to — at the risk of finding yourself with products that are out of the mainstream?

- ✔ Do you want to get the best deal on hardware and software even if it means you have to figure out how to put everything together yourself and rely on your own resources for troubleshooting and support?

I address all of these points throughout the book, and at each point you can easily see how the style issues crop up. For now, the biggest style decision you need to resolve is whether to go with a *peer-to-peer* network or a *client/ server* network.

This decision not only involves most of the style issues in the preceding list, but it also involves your company's management style: wide open versus security-conscious, free-wheeling versus structured, multiple teams versus one coordinated group, ad-hoc versus planned.

You can have both peer-to-peer and client/server components in a single network (called a *hybrid* network), but doing this in a small company is a bit unusual. Chances are that you're best off going one route or the other, and worrying about a hybrid network if and when you grow beyond a few dozen employees. In the rest of this chapter, I describe peer-to-peer and client/ server networking styles, along with a few words about hybrid networks, to help you get the best "fit" for your company.

Peer-to-Peer Networks: Digital Democracy

"As I would not be a slave, so I would not be a master." (Abraham Lincoln, in *The Collected Works of Abraham Lincoln,* edited by Roy Basler)

Lincoln believed in a peer-to-peer society, in which slaves and masters do not exist and no one governs another without that person's consent. In a peer-to-peer network, similarly, no one computer has priority over any other, and no user can take control over someone else's work without that person's consent. In this networking setup, any user can be both a client and a server — a true digital democracy, as shown in Figure 4-1.

To quickly recap the terms *client* and *server:*

- ✔ A network *client* is a user workstation (computer) that connects to a shared resource on a server.

- ✔ A network *server* is a computer that makes a resource (such as a program, a data file, a printer, and so on) available for sharing by clients.

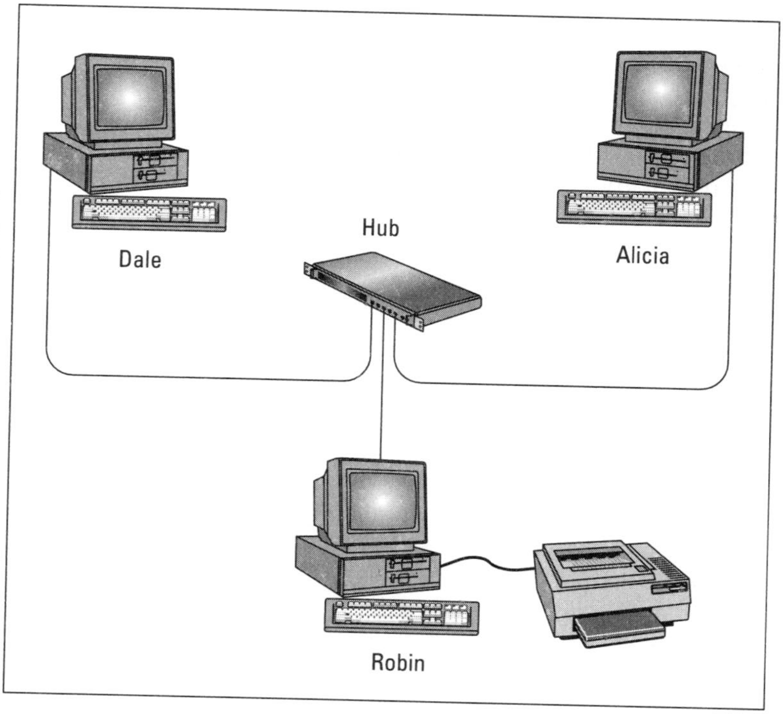

Figure 4-1:
Any computer can share resources and connect to shared resources (including the printer) in this peer-to-peer Local Area Network (LAN).

Dale

Hub

Alicia

Robin

Remember Windows for Workgroups?

If you remember the Microsoft product *Windows for Workgroups,* and assume from the name that it was designed for peer-to-peer networking, you're absolutely right. The fact that the original Windows for Workgroups (version 3.10) was a flop in the marketplace reflects the concern many big corporate network managers had about the security of peer-to-peer networks in general ("Mi hard disk es su hard disk"), something I cover in the "Security concerns" section later in this chapter. Windows for Workgroups 3.11 was very popular, not because of its built-in network, but because it ran hard drives faster.

 If you already know something about network software, don't concern yourself too much with the specific products at this point — such concern can be a bit misleading. You can often use so-called client/server networks (such as Novell NetWare) in a peer-to-peer fashion, and you can also often use so-called peer-to-peer products (such as Artisoft LANtastic) in a client/ server fashion. Chapter 5 deals with today's popular network products, but for now I keep the discussion product independent.

Direct sharing

Peer-to-peer networking may be a closer fit to the way people actually share information in your organization than other networking methods. Your company may have two or more reasonably independent teams working on different projects or different aspects of the business — for example, a small group may work on the design of a new product while another group concentrates on marketing and promotion, and so on. Such teams often go by the name *workgroup.*

In a company with multiple teams or workgroups, team members may not need to share information with everybody on the network; rather, they may need to share information only with the other members of their team. With most peer-to-peer networks, setting up different workgroups is as easy as typing in a workgroup name at each computer; the connected computers then automatically look around the LAN for other PCs in the same workgroup.

Looking back at Figure 4-1, suppose Robin has a spreadsheet that she'd like to share with Dale. In a peer-to-peer setup, all Robin has to do is perform two or three steps:

1. **Mark the directory in which the spreadsheet is stored as *sharable* (for example, in Windows 95, right-click the directory in Windows Explorer, choose S̲haring, and then click S̲hared As).**

2. **Give the directory a *share name,* which can be (but doesn't have to be) the same as the directory name.**

   The share name is how the directory appears to Dale and other workgroup users.

3. **Specify a password, if desired.**

   With Windows 95, Robin can specify a *full access* password or a *read-only* password, depending on whether she wants other users to be able to change the files in the directory, or just be able to view them. She can even specify two separate passwords, one for read-only access and one for full access.

Members of other workgroups don't see the spreadsheet directory when they browse their own workgroup resources, which is fine, because they have their own jobs to worry about and don't *want* to see Robin's spreadsheet.

Robin can make life easier for herself by setting up a particular directory on her hard drive for all her shared files. This way, if she wants to share any file, she can simply move it into the shared directory, where it automatically becomes available to other network users.

In this example, notice that Robin doesn't have to move or copy her spreadsheet to a different computer. She doesn't have to worry about where on a server the spreadsheet should go in order for Dale to be able to see it. And she doesn't have to copy the spreadsheet to another computer every time she changes it, either. Sharing a file on a peer-to-peer network is equivalent to putting a paper document in a desk drawer and telling somebody else where it is. The only difference is that with a network, Dale doesn't have to hike over to Robin's office (and Robin doesn't have to see Dale's ugly mug) every time he wants to look at the document.

Seems like a natural way to share information, right? And it is. Direct sharing on a peer-to-peer *Local Area Network* (LAN) doesn't involve a lot of steps — it's intuitive and easy, and it may be the most important single advantage of peer-to-peer networking.

Peer-to-peer network users can share entire disks, printers, CD-ROMs, and even modems in the same basic way. In Figure 4-2, for example, Windows 95 indicates that Robin has shared her entire CD-ROM drive (shown by the little hand underneath the CD-ROM drive icon). If Robin's computer has a slick laser printer connected to it, and Dale doesn't have a printer at all, Robin can share her printer with Dale, or even with everybody in the workgroup. (The printer sharing setup may not be quite as convenient as sharing the directory containing the spreadsheet document, though, because Robin is interrupted every time somebody needs to go to her office and collect a printout.)

Figure 4-2:
Robin has
shared her
entire
CD-ROM
drive. The
hand is like
a waiter or
waitress
"serving
up" the
drive.

Smooth setup

One key advantage of a peer-to-peer network is that it's easy to set up. Installing the hardware and software for a *dedicated server* in a client/server network, on the other hand, can be fairly complex. (*Dedicated,* by the way, means that a computer does just one thing. A computer set up as a *dedicated server* can't chew gum and walk at the same time — that is, it can't function as a user workstation because it's acting just as a server.)

There are some gray areas here. For example, you can use a Windows NT Server machine as a workstation at the same time (although it's very slow if you do so) even though Windows NT Server is usually considered a *dedicated* server. A Novell server (another dedicated type) can't run as a workstation, period (how's that for dedication?).

With the simplest sort of peer-to-peer network, you just use the built-in networking that comes with your operating system (Windows 95, MacOS, and so on) and you have very little software to set up — even less if you buy computers that have the operating system preinstalled, as most computers do these days.

You need to skip over to Chapters 7 and 8 if you don't yet have your network hardware (cabling, wallplates, and so on) installed.

The first thing you need to do is activate the necessary network software pieces. For Windows 95, the basic steps to setting up a peer-to-peer network are as follows:

1. **Sketch out your workgroup map.**

   You can make your network setup procedure a lot easier if you have an idea of where everyone in your workgroup sits. In Steps 3-10 in this list, you have to go to each computer on your workgroup map and tell it that it is now a part of the new workgroup that you've sketched out. You may want to put a check mark next to each computer on your map as you complete the next steps for each workstation.

2. **Figure out a naming convention (set of rules for naming individual computers).**

   Often, the easiest way to set this up is with the employee's first initial and last name. For example, I would set my computer to GWeadock, and my editor's computer to CScheffy, and so on.

3. **Go to the first computer on your network and click Start⇨ Settings⇨Control Panel.**

   The Control Panel pops up.

4. **Double-click the Network icon to display the Network dialog box.**

5. **Click the Configuration tab (if it isn't already in the foreground).**

6. **Click the File and Print Sharing button.**

   The File and Print Sharing dialog box appears with a checkbox option for sharing files and another for sharing printers.

7. **Click both checkboxes so that they appear checked, and then click OK.**

   The computer is now set up to share its files and printer(s) with other users.

8. **Click the Identification tab.**

   The window in Figure 4-3 pops up.

9. **Make the computer a member of the workgroup by typing the workgroup name in the** Workgroup: **text box.**

   The workgroup name needs to be *exactly* the same for each computer in the workgroup you're setting up so that they all know to share files and printers with each other.

10. **Give the computer a unique name in the** Computer name: **text box.**

    Use the naming system you decided on in Step 2.

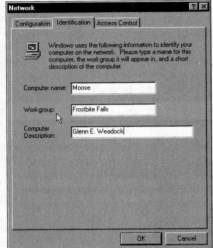

Figure 4-3:
Assign
each
computer
in a
Windows 95
network a
workgroup
name and a
computer
name in the
Network
control
panel. You
can go up
to 15
characters.

11. **Repeat Steps 3–10 for each workstation in your new workgroup.**

12. **Teach all the network users how to share files, directories, and printers, as I explain in the "Direct sharing" section in this chapter.**

You may also want to let everyone know when to use passwords, how to choose them, and what *read-only* means as opposed to *full access*.

And that's about it!

Low cost

Another key advantage of peer-to-peer networking is that you don't have to buy a computer that nobody can use as a client workstation (something that client/server networking requires), as Figures 4-1 and 4-4 illustrate. The cost of a dedicated server in a client/server network isn't as big of a deal as it used to be, but server computers are still more expensive than your average user workstation because of the extra horsepower they deliver, so the savings can amount to two or three thousand smackers (or even more).

Peer-to-peer networking offers other cost advantages, too:

- ✔ **The software is usually free.** It either comes bundled with the workstation operating system, such as Windows 95 or the Macintosh operating system, or is an inexpensive addition (such as LANtastic).

- ✔ **The software is simple.** You don't have to spend the money and time required to train someone to learn a complex, full-featured Network Operating System like Microsoft Windows NT Server or Novell IntranetWare.

- ✔ **Administration is easy.** Each user is a small-scale network administrator, responsible for whatever that user's computer shares on the network. As a result, your part-time or full-time network administrator can spend less time managing the LAN and more time doing other things for your company, possibly saving you from spending bucks on one extra employee.

With all these advantages, why would anybody build any other kind of small business network? Well, peer-to-peer networking has its limitations too, as the following section discusses.

Users = administrators?

The moment Robin shares a file or other computer resource with her workgroup members, she becomes a *network administrator,* if only on a small scale. This may not be a job Robin really wants.

For example, assume Robin and Dale are on flex time, and Robin works from 7:00 a.m. to 3:00 p.m. while Dale works from 10:00 a.m. to 6:00 p.m. If Robin turns her computer off when she leaves the office, Dale can't get to the spreadsheet anymore. Also, Dale and whoever else normally has access to Robin's printer can't print anymore, either. All of a sudden, Robin's personal computer isn't quite so *personal,* and she must consider the fact that other team members depend on her keeping that thing turned on and running.

Another example has to do with making *backup copies* of important computer files. Robin's hard drive is a mechanical device, and as a fact of computer life, one of these days that drive is going to self-destruct, probably taking all the data it contains with it. Robin can and needs to keep important files on her computer, but she also needs to remember to regularly make backups of those files (for example, to a diskette drive, or — better and faster — to someone else's computer on the network) just in case her hard drive decides to commit silicon suicide. (See Chapter 13 for more on backups.)

Finally, if Robin chooses to set up shared directories so she doesn't have to share each file explicitly and individually, she has to keep track of those directories and make sure that the files she wants to share are stored in the proper directories. Conversely, if Robin has some files that she doesn't want other employees to see, such as her personal calendar ("Did you hear? Robin's dating Antonio in Accounting!"), she has to make sure that she doesn't store those files in the shared directories. In short, Robin has to be a little more careful about file and directory management on her computer — something many computer users would prefer not to worry about.

Incidentally, Artisoft LANtastic permits individual file sharing, but Microsoft Windows 95 by itself only allows directory sharing. You can still move specific files to a shared directory, so the distinction isn't a big one.

Security concerns

The main reason that many larger companies don't use peer-to-peer networks extensively is that the security isn't exactly ironclad. (You could call it chiffonclad.)

Unless the network offers provisions to the contrary (such as the *system policies* in Windows 95, as I discuss in Chapter 11), any user on the network has the authority to share any file on his or her computer with anyone else on the network. If every single user isn't sensitive to security concerns, someone may share files that others shouldn't see — especially because sharing an entire directory or hard drive is a lot easier than sharing individual files. Whether sharing certain information is a problem for your company depends on your management style: Does your business operate on a need-to-know basis, or a need-to-withhold basis? (Those small business style issues crop up again.)

Another security issue has to do with the number of passwords involved. A well-known fact of computer security is that once you reach a certain number of passwords that users must know to do their work, the users start writing those passwords down — often on stick-on notes that they affix to their monitors. At this point, your security model becomes practically useless. Because peer-to-peer networks assign passwords to each shared resource, rather than to individuals, the number of passwords is sure to be higher than in a client/server network, where the user only has to remember one password in order to have access to everything on the network.

Chapter 11 discusses computer network security in more depth.

Growing pains

The larger a peer-to-peer network becomes, the more of a chore it can be to keep it running well for everyone. The number of shared resources and passwords can quickly get out of hand. Resources that were shared a year ago never get "unshared." Naming shared resources so that they don't conflict with other names becomes more of an issue. And changing the passwords for protected shares becomes more involved, because the users sharing those resources have to notify more people.

Security hassles

Consider what you have to do when someone quits to go to work for a competitor (an event that happens six times every minute in Silicon Valley). Everyone who has shared a file, directory, or even an entire hard drive that the departed employee used should really change the passwords for those resources — and that can be a fair number of resources and passwords.

You can manage this situation in a small network where employee turnover is a rare event, but as your company grows, keeping a peer-to-peer network secure can become a headache. When you consider that you also need to change passwords anytime one person in a workgroup gets reassigned to a different project, that headache becomes a *migraine*.

Speed bumps

As a peer-to-peer network grows, performance (speed) can become an issue as well. If Robin shares a printer or a directory that more and more people want to use, her computer has to give more of its attention to servicing those network requests. The result may be a noticeable slowdown in the performance of the programs she uses. (Few things are more disconcerting than to be typing along when the computer suddenly stops showing letters on the screen for few seconds, and then catchesupallofasudden.)

An iffy solution

Earlier in this chapter, I comment that you can set up a computer to act as a dedicated server in a peer-to-peer network, and creating such a dedicated computer is one way to deal with the performance problem. Employees *could* use such a machine for client activities — you just get everyone to agree not to, and put up a sign on the screen saying "DO NOT USE — DEDI-CATED SERVER ONLY" (or, better, unplug the screen). However, this solution has its problems.

For one thing, you give up one of the cost advantages of peer-to-peer networking (see the "Low cost" section in this chapter), because you're dedicating a computer to sharing services. For another, operating systems (like Windows 95 or Macintosh OS) that support peer-to-peer networking are not optimized for sharing resources exclusively (that is, being a dedicated server — see the "Smooth setup" section in this chapter). The result is that a peer-to-peer networked computer that you designate as a dedicated server can't give all of its attention to resource sharing, even if no one runs any client programs on it or so much as glances in its direction. Think of using a four-seater sedan as a two-seater sports car: Even if you never use the back seat, it's still there, taking up weight and space and making your sports car a little less sporty.

Some industry gurus argue that peer-to-peer networks have no place in computing anymore because of the drawbacks I list in this section. I understand their position, but I don't agree that *no* small business should ever consider peer-to-peer networking. As long as you have a network of a dozen or so users or less, security isn't a big concern, your users' workstations are zippy enough to handle the occasional performance drag, and your users are quick to cotton on to the administrative chores they must undertake to manage a peer-to-peer network properly, this sort of network is a good, cost-effective way to go.

Client/Server Networks: Silicon Socialism

"There are just two rules of governance in a free society: Mind your own business. Keep your hands to yourself." (P. J. O'Rourke, in *Age and Guile Beat Youth, Innocence, and a Bad Haircut,* Atlantic Monthly Press)

Client/server networks help network users mind their own business and not have to be network administrators on top of their regular jobs. This type of network also helps users (especially unauthorized ones) keep their hands to themselves. Client/server networks are the most popular kind of network for companies with more than a dozen or so users. They take the approach that a little government can be a good thing, much like a social democracy. I'm not much of a liberal, personally, but whatever your politics, a little social democracy makes a lot of sense for computer networking.

Resource sharing

The client/server network model for resource sharing falls somewhere between a peer-to-peer network, where everyone has a personal computer that can act as client and server at the same time, and a minicomputer/dumb terminal network, where all the computing work takes place on a central machine. In client/server networks, users have powerful workstations, just like in a peer-to-peer network, but much of the heavy lifting takes place on the central server, just like in a minicomputer/dumb terminal network.

In a client/server network, you have a computer dedicated to being a server, as illustrated in Figure 4-4. Sharing resources is all that the server computer has to do — nobody uses it for word processing or reading e-mail.

In the client/server network model, resource sharing isn't quite as straight-forward as it is in the peer-to-peer model. For example, if Robin wants to share her spreadsheet with Dale, she has two choices: She either has to copy it from her own hard drive to a hard drive on the server, where Dale can get at it (and remember to copy it again every time she changes it), or, because this method of resource sharing is rather awkward, she can store the main copy of the spreadsheet on the server, where she and Dale can both work on it — just not at the same exact time. The second approach is usually what people do in a client/server network. Most "network-aware" programs won't let two users try to work on the same file simultaneously, so Robin doesn't have to call Dale on the phone to ask, "Are you using the spreadsheet?"

What if Robin doesn't want Dale to be able to modify the spreadsheet, but rather, just be able to look at it? To achieve this goal, the network needs to "know" that Robin has more network *privileges* with that particular file than Dale does.

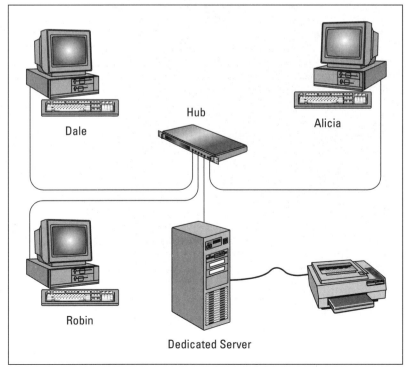

Figure 4-4:
Client/
server
networking
brings
specialization
to the
network. A
computer
becomes a
dedicated
server
and is
unavailable
for use as a
client.

Hub

Dale

Alicia

Robin

Dedicated Server

In most networks, the author of a document can set privileges for the document, specifying who can and cannot make changes to it. Client/server networks typically ask employees to identify themselves before gaining access to the network by logging in with their own unique user names and passwords (a process called *authentication*). The server maintains a database of users and the resources they are allowed to use. The network administrator can control the security database, setting privileges user by user, or even for groups of users with similar access needs.

Finally, sharing application programs over a peer-to-peer network is usually difficult, if you can do it at all. However, you can share programs fairly easily over a client/server network. In fact, many companies use dedicated servers as a way of easing the ongoing burden of keeping applications up to date. If everybody shares a server-side copy of a word processing program, when it comes time to update that program, the network administrator has to update just one computer instead of several (or several dozen).

Cost and complexity

A client/server network is likely to cost more than a typical peer-to-peer network because you have to devote an entire computer (and maybe more than one, depending on the size of your network) to hosting shared resources. That extra computer is also extra expensive, because it needs to hold everyone's files. You also need a *Network Operating System* (NOS) that runs on the server — an additional software cost. Finally, a client/server network requires more network knowledge and experience to set up than typical peer-to-peer networks, and you may want to throw in a class or two for your part-time network administrator.

Centralized administration

Compared to a peer-to-peer network, a client/server network is easier to administer, especially when you have a large or growing network because all of the shared resources are in one place. All network traffic flows through the server, and shared programs and data files reside on the server as well. On a client/server network, procedures like adding or removing users, upgrading shared applications, and backing up company data can all be done from one computer. On a peer-to peer network, on the other hand, these procedures need to be repeated on every user's machine.

When your network grows to the point that you have to add a second server, many client/server Network Operating Systems let you hide that fact from users so that they still only see "the network." Ideally, you don't want users to have to know if the stuff they need is on server X or server Y. This is a big advantage over peer networks ("Where the heck is that spreadsheet — on Robin's computer or Dale's?").

The less users have to remember, the more successful your network.

Better security

Peer-to-peer LANs are notorious for being difficult to secure because any file on any computer can be shared, and each user must monitor passwords and privileges for files on her workstation. In the client/server model, users can only share files residing on the server — a setup that offers several pluses:

- **Centralized network privileges.** The network administrator can assign privileges to a particular set of files and know, for example, that no one is allowed to modify those files, or that only a particular group may modify them. Achieving the same level of confidence in a peer-to-peer network is more difficult.

- **Centralized network passwords.** The convenience of having only one password to remember — one password that unlocks all of the resources on the network (except the ones for which the user does not have access privileges) — is not only great for users, but it reduces the likelihood that users will write down their passwords on pieces of paper in their top desk drawers.

- **Easy physical security.** When you consider physical security, a client/server setup is safer than peer-to-peer, as well. You can put a dedicated server in a locked room, but putting every user workstation in a locked room isn't all that practical!

Comprehensive reporting

How's your network performing? This question is much easier to answer for a client/server network than a peer-to-peer network. You can look at one machine and get most of the information you need: how busy the server CPU is, which data files get the most use, which users are the busiest, who logs on when, what network errors are occurring, and so on.

When one machine controls access to all shared resources, you can use network management utility software to track server activity and provide comprehensive reports. Such software may come with the NOS, or you may have to buy it separately, but you probably can't get convenient network-wide statistics on a peer-to-peer network at any price.

Better overall speed

Client/server networks generally run faster than peer-to-peer networks for three reasons:

✔ **Sharing is caring.** Server software designers optimize client/server NOSs for sharing resources as opposed to serving double duty as both a server and a client.

   Note: Windows NT Server does have client capabilities, but the Microsoft programmers made client services far subordinate to the main goal of sharing resources. If you don't believe me, try running some application software on an NT Server that's busy sharing files with other users — it's like watching corn grow.

✔ **Fewer growing pains.** You can throw all sorts of high-performance hardware into a dedicated server, such as really fast hard drives, lots of RAM, and high-speed CPUs, and everyone on the network reaps the benefit.

✔ **Workstations get to be selfish.** User workstations can run faster if they don't have to worry about sharing stuff in the background.

Types of client/server networks

Client/server networking is a broad term, and several different types of client/server networks exist: traditional *file and print servers, application servers, intranets,* and *thin-client networks.*

File and print servers

Early client/server NOSs concentrated on providing file and print sharing, and these are still the most important functions for most small business networks. Put a data file on the server's hard drive, and other users on the network can use it. Hook a printer up to a server machine, and others can use it, too.

Client/server networks can get pretty sophisticated about these two activities. You can set up different areas on the server hard drive for different groups or users to store their data files, and you can easily secure one area from another. You can separate data areas from program areas for ease of performing backups (you need to back up data more often than programs). You can hide some areas from users' view — for example, you may want to hide an area of the hard drive that contains files and programs that only a network administrator needs.

On the printing side, you can create print *queues* that allow everybody to print whenever they want to, even if you only have one network printer. The queue is an area on disk where print jobs wait until the printer's available. Nobody gets a "busy signal" — if the printer's tied up, the server processes your print job in a first-come, first-served manner. You can even assign two printers to the same queue, so that if one printer's busy, the server automatically routes an incoming print job to the other printer.

Application servers

As networks evolved, computer professionals realized that merely putting programs and data files on a file server where everyone can use them isn't necessarily the most efficient way of doing things. For one thing, especially with database work, all the traffic between server and workstation can bog down a network's speed. Enter the *application server*.

An application server is a special-purpose server that supports users of a specific application program, most often a database. As with all servers, an application server receives a request from a client computer, processes the request, and sends back a response. However, requests sent to application servers are generally more complex than those sent to file servers. The bottom line is that application servers don't just share resources as file servers do, they do some of the computing as well. Explaining this in words is a little like trying to describe a spiral staircase without using your hands, so Figure 4-5 illustrates the situation.

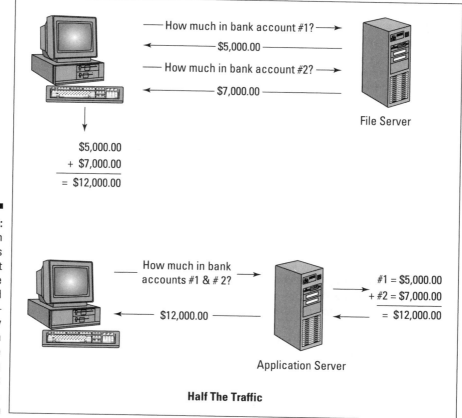

Figure 4-5:
Application servers don't just share data and programs— they perform some of the computing chores as well.

In Figure 4-5, a user needs to know how much cash is on hand in the company's two bank accounts. If the account data is on a regular file server, the user computer does all the processing: It has to read the amount in account #1 from the file server, read the amount in account #2 from the file server, and then add the two.

However, if the account data is on an application server, such as a database server, the user computer asks the server for the sum of the balances in both accounts — a request that a simple file server doesn't know how to handle. The database server does the lookups *and* the math, and then returns the sum to the user. In this simple example, the application server puts half as much traffic on the network as the regular file server does.

Application servers can (and usually do) coexist with more traditional file servers. You may not need an application server for a small network of one or two dozen users, but for a larger network, or if your small network grows, an application server or two may be the best way to beef up your LAN.

Database servers aren't the only kind of application server. You can have specialized servers to handle e-mail, remote access, and even an internal "companywide web," or *intranet,* as the following section discusses.

The company intranet: New kid on the block

An *intranet* is really a special form of client/server network that uses the technology and *TCP/IP* network protocols of the Internet. (TCP/IP is just a networking language computers use to communicate; I explain it in detail in Chapter 6.) The client in an intranet is usually a workstation running a web browser program such as Microsoft Internet Explorer or Netscape Navigator — the same program you use to surf the World Wide Web. The web browser communicates with a web server to request information. The web server spits out the requested information, and then the browser displays it. Sometimes the workstation runs programs *inside* the web browser, too, and the web server may hand over certain programming chores to another server on the same network.

Thanks to the Internet frenzy, one can now literally buy a web server in a box — web server software also comes bundled with all major Network Operating Systems. Since *Business Week* ran a cover story on intranets in February 1996, nearly every Fortune 500 company has rolled out at least one — some have dozens — and the trend is gaining momentum.

To set up an intranet, you don't have to expose your networks to the dark alleyways of the public Internet, and you don't have to rely on the Internet to move data and programs around. An intranet can leverage all the cool technology developed for the Internet without incurring the security risks and traffic problems that beset the information superhighway.

Intranets are typically built on top of an existing peer-to-peer or client/server network. Any benefits or drawbacks that you get from running an intranet are in *addition* to the features of your existing LAN setup, and only apply to the intranet component of your LAN. For example, though I mention in the following bullet list that print support for intranet documents is fairly poor, you still get all the great print support features of your regular Network Operating System and other application software.

What's different about an intranet compared to a traditional client/server network, like Novell NetWare or Microsoft Windows NT Server? Here are some key distinctions:

- **Open architecture:** Intranets, for the most part, use *open* (public, not controlled by a single company) standards for their operation. Traditional networks often use proprietary (private, controlled entirely or primarily by one vendor) standards, such as the Novell *IPX* (Internet Packet eXchange) network communication language. Open standards mean your intranet is not tied to any one vendor, and you have more products from which to choose.

- **Web publishing:** Until recently, traditional NOSs haven't offered an integrated web server with which you can publish documents for users to view with their browsers. However, Novell, for example, recently added a web server in its IntranetWare for Small Business product.

- **Platform independence:** Intranets generally work with any computing platform that works with the Internet. Intranet web servers, for example, can automatically support PC, Macintosh, and Unix workstations. Traditional networks are more limited and typically do not support a wide variety of workstations "out of the box," and when they do, administrators often have to contend with compatibility problems. Being able to move information between platforms can help businesses approach the goal of the paperless office, which previous computer revolutions have mostly hindered rather than advanced (the PC and LAN revolutions were the two biggest windfalls for the paper industry since movable type).

- **Poorer print support:** Internet/intranet technologies were designed for on-screen use and have never been too concerned with printing. On the other hand, traditional networking technology arose largely so that users could share expensive printers (laser printers used to cost $100,000!). The bottom line is that you don't get precise document formatting and quality print output from intranet documents.

- **Weaker security:** The Internet, where intranet networking technology developed, is a public place for information sharing. Traditional NOSs, such as Novell NetWare and Microsoft Windows NT Server, are built for companies that need to protect their data from within and without, and have extensive security systems in place to restrict what data users can access and what they can do with that data.

Although intranets are in many ways better than traditional client/server LAN setups — for example, because of their use of open versus proprietary standards — what makes sense for Fortune 500 companies doesn't necessarily make sense for all small businesses. Growing companies can (and sometimes should) use intranets, but this type of network is best suited for companies with more than a couple dozen employees, companies where the employees are geographically scattered, or companies where different employees need to use different computing platforms.

Chapter 16 takes a closer look at intranets, if you're *intrasted.*

Skin-and-bones clients

In the lingo of client/server networking, a *thin-client* setup puts only the *user interface* component on the *client,* keeping all the process logic (that is, number crunching, database work, and so on) and data storage on the *server.* This is the principle behind the application server, as I mention in the "Application servers" section (duh) in this chapter.

If you take the thin-client concept a step further, you arrive at the so-called *network computer,* or (as I call it) a *skin-and-bones* client. IBM, Microsoft, Netscape, Oracle, Sun, and many other vendors are hyping the network computer concept feverishly. In a nutshell, the network computer is just a workstation with no disk storage. Anything the computer needs, from programs to data files, it gets from the network (see Figure 4-6).

Variations on the theme exist. Sun, for example, is building the *JavaStation,* a microcomputer that runs the Java programming language from an internal chip.

Why strip out the disk drives, especially these days, when their cost is so low? The big reason is *maintenance.* Consider these advantages:

- ✔ **Network computers are easier to update with the latest software.** When user workstations run programs from their own disk drives, updating those programs is a Class A migraine, even with today's clever network management utilities.

- ✔ **Keeping network computers in sync is easier.** When users store data files on local disk drives, those data files can get out of sync with copies other users are working on. If everyone works on the same data file, presuming the supporting network software only lets one user change the data at a time, the latest version is always available.

- ✔ **Network computers are less prone to user error.** When users add their own programs, or modify configuration information on their own computers, they can make mistakes that hurt the computers' ability to run reliably (if at all). They also create a computing environment with very little consistency, which makes the job of troubleshooting and support much more difficult.

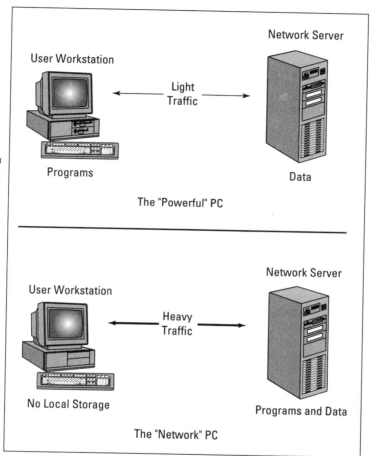

Figure 4-6:
The Network PC has no hard drive or CD-ROM drive, and must retrieve programs and data from a network server, in contrast to the more typical "powerful PC."

Organizations are struggling to balance the power of full-fledged user workstation computers against the cost of maintaining and managing those distributed systems. Democracy is great, but it's expensive (check your latest tax return). Moving to a benevolent dictatorship where users have powerful workstations, but must run *approved* programs and get *approved* data from a central source, has great appeal. However, the scheme has a few catches:

✔ **The increased traffic on the network is a major drawback.** Today's programs are huge — the industry term is *fatware* — because their creators assume that workstations have plenty of local disk space to hold them.

> ✔ **Users may resist losing control, choice, and flexibility over what programs they run.** They may perceive the network computer as a thinly veiled return to the dictatorial mainframe/dumb terminal dark ages.
>
> ✔ **Users are helpless during system crises.** Overall, system fault tolerance can suffer: A network computer can't do a darned thing if a needed server is down.

For a small network, administration isn't as much of a hassle as it is for a network of a few hundred (or few thousand) workstations. My suggestion is to wait on the network computer concept, and go ahead and buy workstations with their own hard drives. You may, however, want to consider removing the diskette (floppy) drives, for security reasons, as I discuss in Chapter 11.

Hybrid Networks: Social Democracy

"Democracy is the wholesome and pure air without which a socialist public organization cannot live a full-blooded life." (Mikhail Gorbachev, in a 1986 speech)

I hinted in the introduction to this chapter that you can actually combine elements of a client/server network with elements of a peer-to-peer network. I have a hard time imagining why you'd want to do this in a network with only a dozen or two users, but if your small business network will have more than that, you may want to know about the *hybrid network* — an attempt to combine the virtues of silicon socialism and digital democracy into a sort of European social democracy.

Figure 4-7 illustrates a hybrid network. Alicia, Robin, and Dale all belong to a peer workgroup. These three can share each other's files and devices just as in a straight peer-to-peer network. Glenn and Emily aren't part of the workgroup, but they can use resources on the server just as they would in a straight client/server network. To top it off, Alicia, Robin, and Dale can all use server resources too.

Why would you want to set things up this way? A couple of reasons: If the workgroup members are sharing directories among themselves, but Glenn and Emily don't need to see those directories, the workgroup network keeps the directories off the server, lightening the server's workload. (Companies sometimes use workgroups in order to keep an overworked server from becoming hopelessly slow until the company can afford a new or extra server.) You can put onto the server only those files and programs that every employee needs, or that require tight security, and let the workgroup manage its own project files. Or, you may be moving from a peer-to-peer network to a client/server network, and want to use the hybrid structure as a stepping-stone — putting more and more services on the server network until everybody gradually gets used to it.

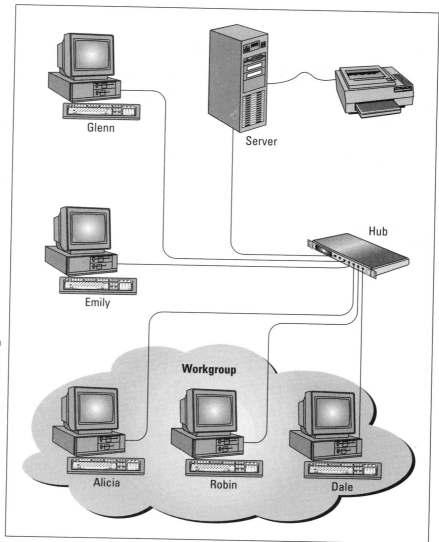

Figure 4-7:
A hybrid network combines aspects of a peer-to-peer network and a client/server network.

One cool capability you may have for your hybrid network, depending on the specific software you choose, is leveraging the server's user-level security to make administering the peer-to-peer workgroup easier. For example, in the pure peer-to-peer example shown back in Figure 4-1, if Robin wants to share the directory containing her now-famous spreadsheet file to Dale, but not to Alicia, then Robin needs to specify the password and privileges for that directory, and then privately (and in hushed tones) give Dale the password and make sure she keeps it secret from Alicia.

In the hybrid network shown in Figure 4-7, Robin can specify exactly who has rights to see that spreadsheet by specifying a name from the server's user list (clicking Dale's name, but not Alicia's), instead of having to engage in playground games with passwords for every shared folder. Finally, if for some reason Robin wants Emily to be able to use the spreadsheet, she can specify Emily as a bona fide user of the file, too, even though Emily isn't technically part of the workgroup.

Got all that? (I don't hold it against you if you have to read the previous couple of paragraphs twice. I had to rewrite them about three times.)

To accomplish the preceding bit of wizardry in a network with Windows 95 workstations and a Novell NetWare server, Robin has to install *File and Printer Sharing for NetWare Networks* on her computer — easily done through the Network control panel. She also has to be using the Microsoft client software for NetWare, rather than the Novell Client32 program (which doesn't support this sort of peer resource sharing). I talk more about network client software in Chapters 5 and 9.

What's the drawback to a hybrid network? You've probably guessed it already: Keeping track of what's going on can become pretty complicated, and the workgroup part of things has most of the same performance, security, and administration limitations of a straight peer-to-peer LAN. However, you may come across occasions when you want such a setup, and I thought I should at least give you an understanding of the basics of how a hybrid network can work. If, instead, I've just given you a mild headache, kindly forget everything in this section and don't read it again until you need it — which may be never.

Chapter 5

Operating System Software:
Choose It Like a Business Partner

- -

In This Chapter

▶ Making sense of the Microsoft Windows product family

▶ Discovering Antisoft LANtastic, a peer-to-peer network with security features

▶ Finding out about Novell IntranetWare and IntranetWare for Small Business

▶ Understanding Unix

▶ Getting the scoop on the Apple Macintosh

- -

"First off, you need an *operating system,* which is the 'Godfather' program that operates behind the scenes, telling all the other programs what to do, making sure they cooperate, and if necessary leaving the heads of virtual horses in their beds." (Dave Barry, *Dave Barry in Cyberspace,* Crown)

As a group, the software that runs your network is called *system software,* and the most important piece of system software is the *operating system*. An operating system is really a collection of programs that runs the basic housekeeping functions in a computer: moving files around, communicating with the keyboard, display, and mouse, loading and running application programs (such as spreadsheets and word-processing programs) and so on.

In addition to the operating system, system software also includes programs such as antivirus and backup utilities (see Figure I-5 in the Introduction), but I cover those programs in other chapters (11 and 13, respectively).

The operating system or systems that you choose go a long way toward defining how your network looks, feels, and acts. In part, the operating system defines which application programs you can use, as well as what they can do. Your choice of operating systems has a great impact on the reliability, security, and speed of both your workstations and your network as a whole; it also affects how easily you can set up your computers and manage and expand your network over time. Select operating system software as carefully as you'd select a business partner, because that's really what it is.

In a *peer-to-peer network,* you can simply choose an operating system for your workstations (for example, Windows 95 if you use PCs, or MacOS if you use Mactintosh) and you're done. The operating system in a peer-to-peer network takes care of the workstation functions (keyboard and mouse controllers, and so on), as well as the network functions (file serving, file sharing, and so on).

However, in a *client/server network,* you have two decisions to make: server operating system (that is, the *Network Operating System,* or NOS — say "noss"), and workstation operating system (sometimes just called the OS — say "oh-ess"). Choosing a NOS may be the single most important decision you make when designing a new network.

If you haven't read Chapter 4 yet, you may want to do so before diving in to this chapter. Chapter 4 outlines the differences between peer-to-peer networking and client/server networking. You may also want to take a gander at Chapter 6, which covers networking languages, and Chapter 11, which covers security in detail (including file-level security, share-level security, server security, and so on). These chapters address and explain a lot of the alphabet soup that I throw around here.

By necessity, this chapter is a little bit of a laundry list of features, so the narrative flow isn't exactly as gripping as a Patricia Cornwell novel. I didn't even have room for many bad jokes. The way to use this chapter is to skim it lightly, and then read carefully the sections about the products you think may work for your network. Table 5-1 summarizes the key features of the operating systems I discuss in this chapter.

MS-DOS

Forget it! (I've waited ten years to be able to write that!) MS-DOS (PC-DOS to you IBM users, or just DOS for short) is *history* as a workstation operating system, and it was never a viable server operating system. (DOS used to stand for *Disk Operating System* but now I think it stands for *Defunct Operating System.*) DOS served long and reasonably well, but it's an anachronism in today's world of cheap memory, big programs, and *graphical user interfaces* (that is, the *windows* of Windows). If you ever have to run a DOS program, you can run it from Windows 95/98, but every program you could conceivably *want* to run on an IBM-compatible PC runs under Windows 95/98.

Windows

Nobody would have believed it based on the near-total market rejection of Microsoft Windows 1.04 — a product that accomplished so close to nothing that most industry watchers just assumed Microsoft would drop it in utter embarrassment — but Windows has taken over the desktop and is making loud noises in the server market, too. Before long, we'll all probably be running some version of Windows on our wristwatches and VCRs and toaster ovens. In the meantime, however, the key versions of Windows you need to know about are 3.*x*, 95, 98, NT Workstation, and NT Server. (And thankfully, my watch still just tells the time.)

Windows 3.x

I thought about not even writing a section on Windows 3.*x* for this book. But then I thought that if I didn't, some up-and-coming business may not know about the problems associated with it, base its network around it, sink all sorts of time and money into making it work, neglect the core business, go bankrupt, and deprive the world of some valuable product that I could really use, such as heated ski goggles.

Windows 3.*x* (Windows 3.1 and its quicker sibling, Windows for Workgroups 3.11) enjoyed very strong market acceptance as workstation operating systems, selling dozens of millions of copies. Windows 3.*x* popularized the graphical user interface (GUI), provided a way for programs to use more memory than they could before, allowed users to switch rapidly between tasks, relieved the need to set up a printer from within every single application program, and provided a way to cut and paste data between different programs. Windows for Workgroups added built-in peer-to-peer networking capability on top of Windows 3.1. All these features are good and useful things.

Table 5-1	Operating Systems				
	Windows 95/98	**Windows NT Workstation 4.0**	**Windows NT Server 4.0**	**LANtastic 7.0**	**IntranetWare for Small Business**
Type of Operating System	Workstation, peer-to-peer network (dedicated or non-dedicated server)	Workstation, peer-to-peer network (dedicated or non-dedicated server)	Client/server NOS (dedicated or non-dedicated server)	Peer-to-peer network (dedicated or non-dedicated server)	Client/server NOS (dedicated server only)
Compatible CPUs	Intel & compatible only. 80386 and higher; Pentium or Pentium II preferred	Intel, DEC Alpha, MIPS (Microsoft no longer supports MIPS)	Intel, DEC Alpha, MIPS (Microsoft no longer supports MIPS)	Intel & compatible only	Intel & compatible only
Can the OS Handle Multiple CPUs?	No	Yes (2)	Yes (4)	No	Yes (32)
Minimum Practical RAM Required	16MB	24MB	32MB	16MB	20MB
Typical RAM for Small Business Use	32MB	32MB	64MB	16MB	64MB
Maximum RAM	4GB	4GB	4GB	4GB	4GB
Which Network Protocols Are Supported?	TCP/IP, NetBEUI, IPX/SPX	TCP/IP, NetBEUI, IPX/SPX	TCP/IP, NetBEUI, IPX/SPX	NetBIOS	TCP/IP, IPX/SPX
Maximum Disk Storage	137GB per drive	408TB (1TB = 1024GB)	408TB	137GB per drive	32TB
Maximum Size of a Single File	2GB (95), 2TB (95b/98)	408TB	408TB	2GB	4GB
Maximum Open Files Per Server	Unlimited	Unlimited	Unlimited	Unlimited	100,000
Security System	Minimal share-level security	Excellent	Excellent	Good share-level and some user-level security	Excellent

	Windows 95/98	Windows NT Workstation 4.0	Windows NT Server 4.0	LANtastic 7.0	IntranetWare for Small Business
Clients Supported	Windows NT, Windows 95, Windows 3.x, DOS	Windows NT, Windows 95, Windows 3.x, DOS, Macintosh, OS/2	Windows NT, Windows 95, Windows 3.x, DOS, Macintosh, OS/2	Windows 95, Windows 3.x, DOS	Windows NT, Windows 95, Windows 3.x, DOS, Macintosh, OS/2
Modem Sharing?	No	Yes	Yes	Yes	Yes (via NetWare Connect)
Fax Sharing?	Yes	Yes	Yes	Yes	Yes (via NetWare Connect)
Internet/Intranet Server Software?	Yes, limited (Personal Web Server)	Yes, powerful (Internet Information Server, 10-user license)	Yes, powerful (Internet Information Server, keyed to NT Server license)	No	Yes, powerful (Novell Web Server) but no FTP service
Internet Link Sharing?	No	Yes	Yes	Yes	Yes (via NetWare Connect) but no IP-IPX gateway
PC Card Support?	Excellent	Limited	Limited	Yes, via Windows 95	Limited
General Peripheral Device Support	Excellent	Limited to the Microsoft Hardware Compatibility list	Limited to the Microsoft Hardware Compatibility List	Excellent, via Windows 95	Very Good
Plug-and-Play Support?	Yes	Poor	Poor	Yes, via Windows 95	No, but good auto-detection of common hardware

That said, the time for Windows 3.x has passed. The "new" Windows 3.x, Windows for Workgroups, debuted in 1992 (the computer industry's Cretaceous Period). Compared to Windows 95 or Windows NT Workstation, Windows 3.x in a network setting is slow, prone to crashing, slow, difficult to set up properly, and slow. You have to add a fair amount of third-party software to a Windows 3.x computer for it to become even moderately reliable, functional, and secure. Besides, it doesn't run any of the new and better programs you want for your business, and nobody is writing new software for Windows 3.x anymore. I don't care if 100 million copies *are* still in use. You don't want it.

Unlike companies that continue running Windows 3.x in the face of much better alternatives, you're in a small business that probably hasn't sunk tens of thousands of dollars into outfitting a big staff with this software. If you already have Windows 3.x running on your PCs, close this book right now and upgrade to Windows 95, preferably with the help of someone who's done it a few times before. Let the big companies continue to fret and fiddle with Windows 3.x while you get up to date and kick their butts.

Windows 95/98

You'll almost certainly run Windows 95 on your workstations if you're setting up a new PC network. Windows 95 is an excellent network client, nearly twice as fast in that role as the older Windows 3.x. Windows 95 works well as a peer-to-peer server also, without requiring any additional software. It doesn't live up to the ridiculously inflated expectations created by Microsoft's 1995 marketing blitz — Microsoft even reportedly took some industry reporters in France out to sea in a submarine to illustrate what life would be like without "windows" — but then again, nothing could.

Here are some facts about Windows 95, in no particular order:

- **Widely compatible.** Windows 95 works with just about every hardware device available, and its software compatibility with older Windows 3.x and MS-DOS programs is good, too.

- **Easily networkable on a client/server network.** As a network client, Windows 95 can connect to just about any kind of server: another Windows 95 machine, Windows NT (Workstation or Server), Novell IntranetWare, LAN Manager, Banyan VINES, Pathworks, you name it.

- **Easily networkable on a peer-to-peer network.** The built-in peer-to-peer networking in Windows 95 is easy to set up and manage using *share-level security* (see Chapter 11). It's also mature and reliable, having evolved from Windows for Workgroups.

✔ **Easy to troubleshoot.** You can perform remote troubleshooting and management of Windows 95 PCs — from across the network or even over a dial-up connection — with Windows utilities such as the Remote Registry Editor and System Monitor, as long as you use Windows 95 in a client/server network. (You can't run the Remote Registry Editor in a pure peer-to-peer LAN.)

✔ **Easy to link with a modem.** The *Dial-Up Networking* (DUN) feature of Windows 95 lets you connect to most network servers over a modem link, and works well. You can set up a Windows 95 machine as a host for incoming connections, allowing employees to dial in to your network from the road or a home office. To do so, however, you need the Plus! add-on product, which is often included with new PCs.

✔ **Easy to install new hardware.** Windows 95 makes installing hardware easier with Plug-and-Play, a technology that enables you to set up new devices with less fuss and muss than with Windows 3.*x*.

✔ **Easy to install.** Installing Windows 95 is accomplished with a *wizard*, a program that asks you a few easy questions and then configures the system based on your answers. Also, Windows 95 automatically detects about 2,000 different devices during setup, so just about any piece of hardware you have connected when you start installing Windows 95 will be recognized and ready to roll when you're done.

✔ **Windows 95 doesn't really have its own security system.** Although you can restrict what users can do on their own workstations with a utility called System Policy Editor, Windows 95 leverages the security database of another network server (IntranetWare or NT Server) for access control in its user-level security mode.

If you choose Windows 95, make sure you're running at least the "a" release, which appears in the System control panel as 4.00.950a (click Start➪ Settings➪Control Panel, and then double-click the System icon to check). If you have the original release (called 4.00.950), download the free Service Pack 1 from http://www.microsoft.com and run it — it fixes a number of annoying bugs.

Windows NT Workstation

More and more often, companies are considering Windows NT Workstation (NTW) in place of Windows 95/98 for desktop use. NTW makes a fine client operating system and can function in a peer-to-peer network just like Windows 95/98 (actually, probably a little better, because it's closer to being crashproof). NTW uses the same graphical user interface that Windows 95 does, so it's comfortable for those familiar with Windows 95.

What about Windows 98?

Windows 98 is very similar to Windows 95 under the hood, and you can run a peer-to-peer network with Windows 98 in much the same way as with Windows 95. Windows 98 provides the option, available now separately for Windows 95 as the *Active Desktop,* to use the Internet Explorer 4.0 user interface in place of the regular Windows 95 interface, so users who are comfortable surfing the Web should feel right at home. It can access your hard drives faster than the original Windows 95 does, although probably not faster than the "b" release of Windows 95 that started shipping on new computers in early 1997. It also introduces the ability (with extra hardware) to run TV shows in a window right alongside your general ledger program, a feature that seems likely to undermine whatever productivity gains you hoped to glean from a computer network in the first place.

Windows 98 is evolutionary rather than revolutionary. You don't want to start using it until it's been out in the commercial marketplace for several months, so that the technical types have some time to figure out what can go wrong and publish articles and books to help you work around its problems. If Windows 98 is not yet available when you read this, my advice is not to wait for it if you're thinking about installing a Windows 95 network today. You'll be able to upgrade later if you want to, and Windows 95 should still be able to run nearly all programs written for Windows 98.

Why does Microsoft sell two workstation products? In a nutshell, the Windows 95/98 products are for general business use and work with just about every conceivable peripheral device, while NTW is for users who require very high reliability, security, and data processing power, and don't mind more limited hardware choices (and a somewhat higher price tag). These two product lines are becoming more like each other with every new release, and Microsoft has pledged that they will merge into a single product by the year 2000.

Because so much confusion exists about these two product lines, here's a list outlining how NTW differs from Windows 95/98 beyond the information in Table 5-1:

- ✔ **More stable (good).** NTW crashes far less often than Windows 95/98.

- ✔ **More secure (good).** NTW offers its own reasonably airtight security system, while Windows 95/98 depends on network servers to impose workstation security.

- ✔ **Offers more limited choice of peripherals (not so good).** Windows 95/98 works with a much wider variety of hardware, and with Plug-and-Play, can usually figure out how to install and support new hardware automatically. Try installing hardware that isn't on the Microsoft Hardware Compatibility List for NTW, and you'll be lucky if the computer even boots. In addition, NTW supports Plug-and-Play only in a very limited way, although NTW 5.0 (not yet released as I write this) provides much better support.

✔ **More difficult to install.** Windows NTW is a bit more difficult to install than Windows 95/98 for nontechnical users.

Windows NT Server

Although it has a separate name, package, and price, Windows NT Server (NTS) isn't all that different under the covers from its workstation twin. Frankly, the main difference is in how Microsoft licenses the product and what extra software goodies Microsoft throws in. In addition, the NTS version supports four CPUs rather than the two allowed with NTW, and it offers *domain services* to enable you to divide up your network (NTW doesn't let you set up domain services, although it can certainly use them if an NT Server is running on the same network).

Although NTS is a relatively young product as Network Operating Systems go, Microsoft has devoted a great deal of time, energy, and talent toward enhancing it since its undistinguished debut with versions 3.1 and 3.50. (Microsoft never released an NT version 1 or 2. Yes, Microsoft cheated, but you can do that if you're the software industry's 800-pound gorilla.) NTS 4.0 is the current version as I write this, and although many consultants feel that it still isn't quite ready for prime time as a general-purpose server for very large networks, it's a strong choice for a small business.

Here are some of the most interesting features of Windows NT Server, over and above the features I mention in the previous section on NT Workstation:

✔ **Capable of running a couple of different file systems.** NTS can run the FAT (File Allocation Table) file system (a method of organizing disk space), which DOS, Windows 3.x, and Windows 95 use (except for the "b" release of Windows 95, which may come with a different file system called FAT32). However, NTS comes with its own preferred file system, NTFS (NT File System), which offers the advantages of file-level security and disaster recovery.

✔ **Solid security.** NTS offers solid security and is certified by the U.S. Department of Defense. You can set up users, groups, workgroups, and domains, and you can set up directory and file-level security. (For more on security, take a look at Chapter 11.) NTS comes with the C2 Manager to implement its security model.

✔ **Easy to integrate with Novell stuff.** NTS integrates very well with existing Novell IntranetWare servers, allowing NT clients to see IntranetWare resources and allowing IntranetWare clients to see NT resources. (This is a bigger deal with larger companies having a variety of servers; I don't recommend that small companies mix and match server types without a compelling reason.)

✔ **Helps manage IP addresses.** NTS comes with most of the utilities you need to handle IP (Internet Protocol) addressing issues. (For more on this, cruise over to Chapter 6.)

✔ **Supports remote access for your employees on the road or at home.** The NTS *Remote Access Service* (RAS) is a mature and competent communications tool for outbound or inbound access.

✔ **Lots of compatible, useful software.** Microsoft makes a number of companion products available for NTS in the BackOffice product family, including a database (SQL Server), e-mail server (Exchange), and management software for larger networks (Systems Management Server).

Microsoft is devoting a lot of resources to enhancing NTS, and it's a safe bet for a small business client/server network. Most growing companies should put NTS on their short list, along with Novell IntranetWare (see the "NetWare" section later in this chapter).

LANtastic

Until Windows 95 came along, LANtastic from Artisoft was a very popular choice for a peer-to-peer small business network, and it's still quite popular. The built-in networking capabilities in Windows 95 make LANtastic a less compelling choice than it used to be, and the company has undergone some painful downsizing as a result. The product includes some nifty features that Windows 95 doesn't, although in some respects (such as e-mail), it's still tied to outdated DOS/Windows 3.*x* technology.

LANtastic software (in version 7.0 at this writing) offers the following capabilities, in addition to those listed in Table 5-1:

✔ **Convenient installation.** You can conveniently install LANtastic on workstation computers using a single diskette that you create on the first workstation you set up.

✔ **E-mail software included.** You get an e-mail package, too, although it requires at least one computer on the network to run Windows 3.*x* or DOS — a requirement that leads me to recommend against LANtastic mail.

✔ **That's not all!** You also get . . . an Internet gateway, based on the separately available i.Share product. You set up one computer, running Windows 95 and TCP/IP with an Internet link, and all the other workstations can connect to the Internet through that gateway computer.

✔ **Remote management.** LANtastic includes a DOS-based utility for remote management (so that you can administer the network from a dial-up connection), but only of DOS, Windows 3.*x*, or dedicated LANtastic servers.

✔ **Good security.** LANtastic offers much more in the way of security than the Windows 95 peer-to-peer network. You can set up logon security with password and time-of-day restrictions, network accounts at one of four management security levels, and file and directory security that overrides account security — much like you can do on client/server networks like Windows NT Server or IntranetWare.

If you read Chapter 4 and you think that peer-to-peer networking is the way to go, put LANtastic on your short list along with Windows 95. And even if you don't see that LANtastic offers enough benefits over Windows 95 to warrant the extra dollars, take a look at the separate products ModemShare and i.Share, anyway — these two products provide modem and Internet connection sharing for Windows 95 networks. (I discuss these products in more detail in Chapter 10.)

NetWare

The Novell NetWare product family has been synonymous with small business networking for many years, and the biggest slice of the Network Operating System pie still belongs to "Big Red." NetWare is no longer the "no-brainer" decision it once was, though, and Novell has lost some market share in recent years to Windows NT Server. While Novell was making some widely publicized management missteps in the mid-90s that distracted it from its core networking business, Microsoft was doggedly advancing on the learning curve that began with the unsuccessful MS-Net and LAN Manager products.

Today, Novell has written off its dalliances with WordPerfect and UnixWare, and is more focused on what it does well. Novell still has a strong asset in the form of its NetWare Directory Services (NDS), and the IntranetWare for Small Business (ISB) bundle is very competitive with Windows NT Server in terms of capabilities and price. Novell has also taken some strong steps to make the ISB product easier to install, an area that was never NetWare's strong suit in the past (one of the reasons Windows NT Server made inroads in the market, in fact). Novell is making IntranetWare more Internet-friendly, and less closely tied to the IPX/SPX network language that it developed to run with NetWare. Finally, there are still many more NetWare experts out there than Windows NT Server experts, so the pool of consulting and support resources is bigger.

Considering these factors, the small business Network Operating System market is more competitive now than it has been for a long time, and that's good news for consumers. Regardless of what the long-term future holds for the NOS wars, certainly some flavor of NetWare should be on your short list if you plan to create a client/server network today. ISB is probably the logical choice for most readers of this book, but I tell you about versions 3.12 and 4.11 also so you can make up your own mind.

All current versions of NetWare share one key advantage over most other Network Operating Systems: They're specialists. IntranetWare doesn't run as a workstation operating system, and it doesn't run "on top" of other operating systems (as, for example, LAN Manager does on Unix or OS/2). Novell designed IntranetWare to do one thing, and do it well.

IntranetWare 4.11

IntranetWare 4.11 (which I'll shorten to IW 4.11 from now on) is a full-featured, industrial-strength, mature, and highly scaleable NOS. Like all versions of NetWare, IW 4.11 runs on Intel and Intel-compatible processors only. The networking nuts and bolts are basically the same as those in what Novell used to call NetWare 4.1, but Novell has added software for Internet and intranet features and given the product a new name in the process.

With capability comes complexity, and IW 4.11 is not the sort of software you pull out of the box and install in one afternoon. Novell designed this product to be able to support hundreds of users per server and several servers per network. IW 4.11 is arguably the best NOS around for such a large Local Area Network (LAN), and its NetWare Directory Services (NDS) method of organizing LAN resources handles big networks better than the Windows NT Server domain model. NDS is a single database containing information about every user, group, and printer on the network, along with all access permission information (see Figure 5-1). However, as a small business, you don't have a large LAN, and IW 4.11 is probably overkill.

Here are some of the salient features of IW 4.11:

- **Users conveniently log on to the entire network using a single account name and password.**

- **Easy application distribution.** An administrator can distribute new application software to IW 4.11 users relatively easily with the NetWare Application Launcher (NAL).

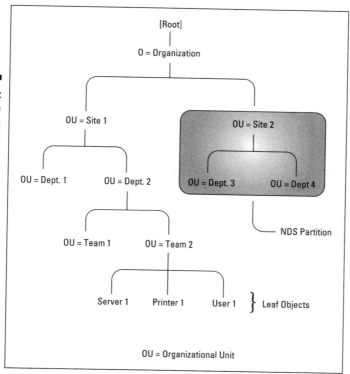

✔ **Many printer connection options.** You can set up network printers that connect to an IW 4.11 server, to the network itself via a *Network Interface Card* (NIC), to the network via a parallel-to-network conversion device (such as the Castelle print server that's part of the 3Com OfficeConnect product line), or to a workstation.

✔ **Easy Internet connection for workstations.** IW 4.11 includes an IPX-to-IP gateway that lets you run your LAN on the IPX network language and connect to the Internet, which uses the IP network language, without having to install IP software on each workstation.

✔ **File compression.** The IW 4.11 automatic file compression options enable efficient use of disk space, and are more sophisticated than those of Windows NT Server.

✔ **High reliability features.** The network comes with features to ensure reliability, such as automatic recovery from disk defects, *disk mirroring,* and *disk duplexing* (I discuss these features in Chapter 8). At extra cost, you can even create mirrored servers for very high reliability.

✔ **Tweak while hot.** In contrast to Windows NT Server, you can make a lot of changes to an IW 4.11 server while leaving it up and running.

IntranetWare for Small Business

IntranetWare for Small Business (ISB) is basically IntranetWare 4.11 with the following changes:

✔ **It's got NEAT (which is neat).** In addition to the NWADMIN management tool, ISB includes a simplified version, the *Novell Easy Administration Tool* (NEAT), which (if I may editorialize) lives up to its acronym: NEAT it is. You also get a little program called QuickStart, which steps you through the process of setting up network users and groups. You use QuickStart to set things up at first, and NEAT to make changes later on. For more on NWADMIN and NEAT, see Chapter 13.

✔ **Includes remote connection software.** ISB throws in an 8-port version of NetWare Connect, which is software for inbound and outbound communications. NetWare Connect (which does not come with IntranetWare 4.11) makes it easy for your NOS reseller to log on and perform maintenance functions remotely, and many Novell VARs (Value Added Resellers) provide such services. Read Chapter 11 on security before you set this up, however.

✔ **Does not include Internet gateway.** ISB doesn't include the IPX-to-IP gateway that regular IntranetWare includes, nor does it include the MultiProtocol Router. However, if you want to link to the Internet, you can get IPX-to-IP gateways from other companies. Some companies, such as 3Com, throw in such a gateway with their ISDN-capable hubs for one-stop Internet connectivity. See Chapter 17 for more info.

✔ **Less complex than its big brother.** Novell deactivated some of the more complex features of NetWare Directory Services (NDS) in order to make the NDS network tree easier to understand and navigate in a single-server setup. If you move to a multiserver network later and upgrade to IntranetWare 4.11, you can turn these features back on.

✔ **Different licensing than its big brother.** The licensing and pricing arrangements are different; in particular, you can buy one-at-a-time licenses for ISB, which you can't do for IntranetWare 4.11, and ISB has an upper limit of 25 concurrent users. If you grow beyond that size, Novell lets you upgrade to the "big" version of IntranetWare.

As with IntranetWare 4.11, ISB works well with Windows 95, but you have a choice between using Microsoft software or Novell software in order to add the necessary network software to your workstations. If you stick with the Microsoft client, you need to add NDS support in the form of two files — MSNDS.EXE and SHELUP.EXE — that you can download from the Microsoft Web site (`http://www.microsoft.com`). These programs come with their own help files, and while not difficult to install, you may find the Novell client (the so-called Client32) easier to set up. Client32 comes with the ISB CD-ROM, along with client software for DOS (yecch), OS/2, and Macintosh.

If you're thinking about a small client/server network, ISB is very competitive with Windows NT Server. I'd lean a bit toward ISB if you mainly want file and print services, and a bit toward NT if you want to run database software on your server. In the end, you really can't go wrong with either one.

NetWare 3.12

You can still buy NetWare 3.12 in some places, and up until the release of IntranetWare for Small Business, it had a certain appeal. NW 3.12 is easier to set up for a single-server LAN than IntranetWare 4.11, and a ton of software is available for it from third-party vendors as well as Novell. Further, even now there are probably more consultants who know NW 3.12 like the back of their hands than IntranetWare 4.11.

NW 3.12 doesn't use the vaunted Novell NetWare Directory Services (NDS) structure for organizing the network's database of users, groups, and printers. Rather, it uses a server-centric database (called the *bindery*) that works fine for one server, but becomes a bit of a pain to manage for multiple servers. You have to set up accounts in each server's bindery if you want users to have full access to those servers.

IntranetWare for Small Business (ISB) is easier to set up than NW 3.12, and includes many goodies to make your shared disks run more efficiently. Therefore, I don't recommend that a small business install NW 3.12 today. If you already have a NW 3.12 network, I recommend upgrading to ISB.

Personal NetWare

Personal NetWare was a little peer-to-peer operating system that fixed some of the problems with its predecessor, NetWare Lite. If you want peer-to-peer, though, I suggest you go with Windows 95, Windows NT Workstation, or LANtastic. Personal NetWare never really caught on, and Novell is busy working on other things these days.

OS/2

OS/2 comes in two flavors: OS/2 Warp, and OS/2 Warp Server. Originally, IBM and Microsoft worked together on OS/2, and you can see similarities between OS/2 Warp and Windows NT. However, OS/2 Warp never caught on as a workstation operating system, and I don't recommend it for a new small business network. OS/2 Warp Server is a very competent choice for a client/server network, but it doesn't bring any killer advantage that would set it apart from more popular choices like Windows NT Server or IntranetWare for Small Business. OS/2 runs on the NetBIOS and TCP/IP network languages, but not IPX/SPX. OS/2 Warp Server supports a variety of clients, including DOS, Windows 3.*x*, Windows 95, Windows NT Workstation, and Macintosh. If you're a big IBM fan, take a look at OS/2 Warp Server, but make sure you have local consulting support for it — by no means a given.

LAN Manager

LAN Manager was Microsoft's training ground for Windows NT Server. Microsoft licensed the product heavily during LAN Manager's heyday, and much of its code appears in variants like DEC Pathworks and IBM LAN Server. Unlike IntranetWare, LAN Manager runs on top of a general-purpose operating system — usually OS/2, Unix, or Windows NT. LAN Manager crops up in many forms and from many different vendors, including (in addition to DEC and IBM) Hewlett-Packard, NCR, and Santa Cruz Operation (SCO). Today, organizations wanting a Microsoft network generally choose Windows NT Server, but LAN Manager is far from dead in the Unix world (see the following section on Unix).

Unix

Unix grew from its roots at AT&T Bell Labs to become the most popular software around for running scientific and engineering workstations, such as those made by Sun Microsystems and IBM, and for running servers on the public Internet. The Unix networking system, NFS (Network File System), can function as a client/server or peer-to-peer network. Unix offers the useful ability of running the user interface on one computer while running an underlying application program on another computer, making it a good operating system for remote computing.

Unix is common in large organizations that need to manage big databases or perform real-time transaction processing. However, you don't see Unix too much in small business networks outside the computer industry. Unix requires more computer knowledge to set up and manage than Windows NT Server or IntranetWare for Small Business. Rampant version-itis has also hurt the Unix cause, with dozens of more-or-less incompatible variants vying for attention in the marketplace. The Unix world doesn't offer nearly the variety of business application software that the Windows world does, and although you can run Windows software on some Unix machines, doing so is slow and limited.

Having said that, the popularity of the Internet has led to a resurgence in the Unix market. TCP/IP, the network language (protocol) of the Internet, has its roots in Unix, and more World Wide Web servers run Unix than any other operating system. Unix servers, therefore, make a good choice for companies setting up *intranets* (see Chapter 16 for more on these "company-wide webs").

So, if your business is heavily involved with the Internet, if you plan to set up an intranet, or if your company employs a gaggle of design engineers and scientists, take a close look at Unix. Just make sure you have someone on the payroll who has some familiarity with it. Unix isn't for beginners.

HP-UX

The Hewlett-Packard version of Unix is called *HP-UX:* It takes second place in popularity to Sun Solaris, and runs on HP and Motorola processors. HP-UX supports NFS and also offers a Unix version of Novell NetWare for file and print services; using the latter setup, NetWare users can also run server-based Unix programs. HP also offers LAN Manager for Unix, a Microsoft-style network.

IBM AIX

The IBM Unix flavor goes by the name *AIX* and runs on PowerPC and Intel CPUs. It lags behind Sun Solaris, HP-UX, and SCO in sales, but not by much. AIX has a number of appealing features, one being that you can make a variety of changes to an AIX setup without bringing down the network. LAN Server for AIX provides network file and print services, and it supports DOS, OS/2, Windows 3.*x,* Windows 95, Windows NT, and Macintosh clients. LAN Server for AIX can run on the TCP/IP and NetBEUI network languages.

Sun Solaris

Sun Microsystems dominates the Unix workstation operating system market, offering powerful server and workstation software under the name *Solaris*. Sun Unix servers support a variety of client workstations, including DOS, Windows 3.*x*, Windows 95, and Windows NT. Solaris runs on Intel CPUs, and more commonly, on the SPARC CPUs found in Sun SPARCstation computers. Solaris can link to NetWare and LAN Manager networks, and has a strong Internet server.

SCO Unix

SCO (Santa Cruz Operation) Unix is the most popular version of Unix for Intel-compatible computers, though it ranks third overall on all hardware platforms, behind Solaris and HP-UX. SCO Unix runs on the TCP/IP, IPX/SPX, and NFS network languages. With the appropriate client software installed, users running SCO Unix can access NetWare and Windows NT Server resources, and a wide variety of Internet and intranet software is available.

Linux

Linux is a freeware version of Unix, begun by a Finnish student in 1991 and since enhanced and improved by dozens of programmers worldwide. Linux has gained popularity not only because it's free, but also because it runs on a wide variety of hardware, including PCs and Macintoshes. It is available commercially on CD-ROM, and comes with extra utility software. Linux isn't easy to install, and you should have someone in your company who is at least moderately familiar with Unix systems if you choose Linux. Check out the Linux information page at `http://www.linux.org`.

Macintosh

Dismissing Apple and the Macintosh as dead ducks is a popular thing to do these days. I don't go that far, but Apple is certainly far less competitive than it used to be for general small business networking, and it's a shame. The Macintosh network has so much going for it that Apple's continued decline in the microcomputer marketplace is all the more distressing.

Even with the well-publicized cash infusion from Microsoft in late 1997, most industry watchers agree that Apple has become a niche player for the graphics and design professional market, and the Macintosh product line holds little hope of regaining the broad viability it once enjoyed versus

Windows/Intel ("Wintel") computers. Some even suggest that Microsoft's investment in Apple is more a way to ward off antitrust investigations than a vote of confidence in Apple's objective viability. Although I would hesitate a long time before recommending that a company build its network around Macintoshes, I have to say that the Apple networking model is just about the simplest and easiest around, and the Mac excels in graphics and design work for less moola than Unix workstations.

Advantages to networking with a Macintosh network include the following:

- ✔ **Every Macintosh has built-in networking capability, from the operating system to the hardware, and can function as both client and server.**

- ✔ **Macintoshes support TCP/IP as well as the AppleTalk networking language.**

- ✔ **Yes, they do support Ethernet.** You don't have to use the slooooow LocalTalk hardware (or the third-party PhoneNet hardware) that leads many people to wrongly dismiss Mac networking. Mac networks support Ethernet (which Apple calls EtherTalk).

- ✔ **Macintosh invented Plug-and-Play.** Adding new hardware to a Mac network is generally a piece o' cake. Mac had Plug-and-Play long before Windows 95 brought it to PCs.

- ✔ **Mac networks support dividing the LAN into workgroups (Apple calls them *zones*) for easier administration.**

- ✔ **Easy to use.** Many experts still give the Macintosh highest marks for ease of use among all small computers.

The main disadvantages to building a Macintosh network are as follows:

- ✔ **Software updates.** Application software for Macs lags behind application software for PCs by months and sometimes years.

- ✔ **Cost.** Mac hardware always seems to cost more than similar PC hardware.

- ✔ **Company resources.** Apple doesn't have the resources that Microsoft, Novell, and Unix vendors have to invest in advancing its network technology.

If you believe, as I do, that Apple will be around for quite some time (at least in some form), if you don't mind paying somewhat more for your computers and peripherals, and if you can live with the fact that Macs generally don't run the latest and greatest application programs, then take a look at a Macintosh network. You'll spend less time getting it going than you would a Windows NT Server or IntranetWare system, and you'll find that the Macintosh systems offer a certain *je ne sais quoi* that makes them feel just a little more polished and intuitive than their "Wintel" counterparts.

Chapter 6
Picking a Network Language

- -

- -

"**I**f other people are going to talk, conversation bcomes impossible." (James McNeill Whistler, in *The Portable Curmudgeon,* NAL Books)

On a network, other people *are* going to talk, so the network needs some rules to govern the conversation. Most people planning a new network know that they need to choose a NOS, such as Novell IntranetWare (the latest in the Novell NetWare product family) or Microsoft Windows NT Server. They also know that they need to choose a hardware setup, such as Ethernet or Token Ring (see Chapter 7 for details). What they may *not* know is that another technology layer lurks in the middle of the network cake: the language, or *protocol,* that your network speaks. In some ways, choosing a network protocol is just as important as the other two decisions.

Rules of the Road

Opening a file (say, a spreadsheet) that resides on a network server would seem to be a fairly simple operation — and it is, to the user anyway. Under the hood, opening the file involves a complex set of interactions between the spreadsheet program, the networking software (such as Windows or IntranetWare), the network language (protocol), the *Network Interface Card* (NIC), the cable, and many of those same bits and pieces on the server computer. This section describes each set of interactions in complete detail, and defines the 94 different acronyms the computer industry uses to describe them. (Just kidding, of course. What I describe here is the *least* you need to know about network communications.)

OSI versus WINK

One aspect of computer networking you probably already know about is the fact that many different companies make network software. In order for one company's software to work with another's, all the companies have to agree on some rules of the road. The main framework for these rules is a layer-cake model called Open Systems Interconnect (OSI), created by an international standards organization called (get ready!) the *International Standards Organization* (ISO). Most computer network books describe the seven different layers of the OSI model. However, at the risk of upsetting technical purists (none of whom should be reading this book anyway), I'm squashing these seven layers into three big, delicious layers because that's all you need to worry about and it's a whole lot easier to explain.

Figure 6-1 shows the three layers in the *Weadock Integrated Network Knowledge* model (or *WINK* for short, which you can tell is not a "real" computer industry acronym because it's easy to remember).

The network driver

The bottom layer of software, the *network driver,* handles the job of sending and receiving information to and from a particular kind of Network Interface Card, or NIC (say "Nick"), and spewing that information out to the network cable. When you plug a NIC into the inside of a computer, you have to make sure the computer also has the right network driver for that kind of NIC. Most NICs you encounter in a small network use Ethernet or Token Ring, but in special circumstances, you may use *Fiber Distributed Data Interface* or *FDDI* (pronounced "fiddy"). Chapter 7 talks about these kinds of NICs in more detail.

You can think of the network driver layer as the trucks, trains, and planes that move mail through a postal system. This layer mainly concerns itself with the physical movement of information from point A to point B.

The transport protocol

The middle layer of software is the network language (the more formal name is the *transport protocol,* which I sometimes shorten to simply *protocol*). Figure 6-1 shades this layer in gray because it's the layer I talk about in this chapter. You can think of the middle layer as the language (English, French, Bronx) you use to write the letter you're mailing. Just as the sender and receiver of an actual letter have to speak the same language in order to understand each other, so do two communicating computers.

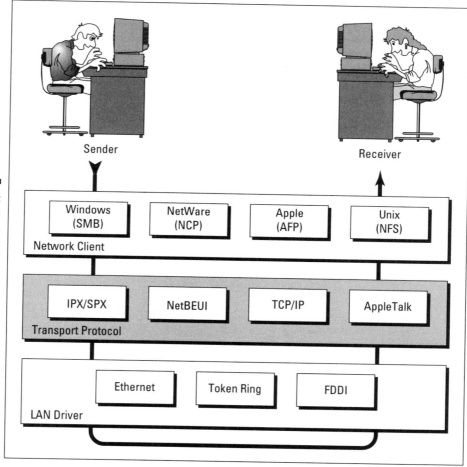

Figure 6-1: WINK: the three layers of network communications you need to understand. A sending computer communicates from the top down, a receiving one from the bottom up.

The transport protocol doesn't really care about the network driver in the bottom layer. You can send a physical letter through the mail, write it in whatever language you like, and the letter doesn't care whether it goes by truck or train or plane. These layers are independent from one another, which is how different companies can write software for different layers and it all still works together (usually, anyway!).

The network client

The top layer of software is called the *network client* on a user workstation, and is the heart of the Network Operating System (NOS) on a server computer (if you use one). The network client is in charge of maintaining a map of the network and making sure information goes to the right place — network disk drives, shared printers, and so on. The network client is a bit like the routing and distribution equipment a postal service uses to make sure your letter goes where it's supposed to go. This layer is the one that knows how to find that spreadsheet file the user is opening, for example. This top layer also handles security issues, such as whether the user has the right to access the spreadsheet file. (The postal service has those X-ray machines for security, too — this analogy is holding up pretty well, huh?)

Chapter 5 covers the network client layer.

The network client and Network Operating System generally don't care about the network language, and the network language doesn't care about the network driver; just as a post office can route your letter to the right place, whether you write the letter in English or Serbo-Croatian.

Mixing and matching

So, now you know the three WINK layers. With a couple of exceptions, which I discuss in a minute, you can mix and match within each layer and still have a functioning network. For example, you can run a Windows NT network (top layer) over the NetBEUI transport protocol (middle layer) and the Ethernet driver (bottom layer), or you can run Windows NT using the TCP/IP transport protocol and the Token Ring driver.

Being able to mix and match is great for customers who want a lot of flexibility, but it means you've got more decisions to make. Chapter 5 covers choosing the software in the top layer. In this chapter, I show you how to select the software for the middle layer — the transport protocol. Choosing the software in the bottom layer depends on the kind of network hardware you decide to set up, as I discuss in Chapter 7.

Does the transport protocol you choose really matter? After all, some introductory networking books don't even discuss the issue. Take it from me — it's a key decision. Transport protocols are not all equal in terms of speed, reliability, industry support, simplicity, and ability to grow with your network.

Following Protocol

A *protocol* is a language computers agree to use in order to communicate. More formally, it's a set of rules, specifications, and standards that controls and manages the creation, maintenance, and termination of data transfer between computers. The options in the middle layer of the WINK model in Figure 6-1 are all protocols.

Slicing and dicing

When you write a letter, you conceive entire thoughts and then chop those thoughts up into individual words for "transmission" via paper. The person who receives your letter then reassembles those words to form the sentences and thoughts you originally conceived. Similarly, network protocols chop up data files into tiny pieces at the sending side, and then painstakingly reconstruct data files at the receiving side, as Figure 6-2 illustrates.

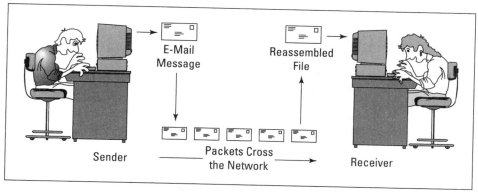

Figure 6-2: A network protocol takes care of cutting up, packaging, sending, and re-assembling your data.

Why perform such seemingly unnecessary surgery, which you would think would slow data transmission to a crawl? Two reasons:

- **First, all sorts of mishaps can befall data zipping across network wires.** If a tiny piece of a computer file doesn't make the journey intact (known as a *transmission error*), the receiving computer can request that the sending computer resend it. Resending just a tiny piece of a file is a whole lot faster than resending the whole darned file.

- **Second, the network is shared among multiple users.** If everybody had to wait around until a large file crossed the network before they could use the wire, their computers would seem to be much slower. With little pieces flying around instead of big ones, each user can send his or her own little pieces of mail intermixed with everybody else's.

So, chopping up data actually makes things work faster rather than slower — one of the little ironies of computer networking. However, chopping up the data into tiny pieces places a special demand on the receiving computer, which has to know which pieces go together, and in what order. How does it do this?

The only way the receiving computer *can* know this is if every piece of information carries with it some instructions for reassembly. You can think of this process as the protocol scribbling these instructions on the back of each tiny envelope that it sends over the wire. Different protocols specify a different set of rules and regulations for how the sending computer specifies the reassembly instructions, and how the receiving computer interprets them.

At this point, I should start using the correct term for the tiny envelopes and their contents: These are network *packets*. A network packet not only contains a piece of the original data file, but also source information (the tiny envelope's return address), destination information (the "send to" address), and reassembly instructions. Figure 6-3 shows a very simple little network packet diagram.

Managing addresses

For these network packets to include source and destination addresses that mean anything, every computer has to have a different address.

Different protocols manage computer addresses differently, as the following sections explain, but the point to make here is that each computer's address must be unique — just as each mailing address must be unique in order for a letter to find its proper destination. You need to know about network addressing, because it has a direct bearing on how easily you can manage your network over time. The "Popular Protocols" section later in this chapter discusses how different protocols deal with addressing.

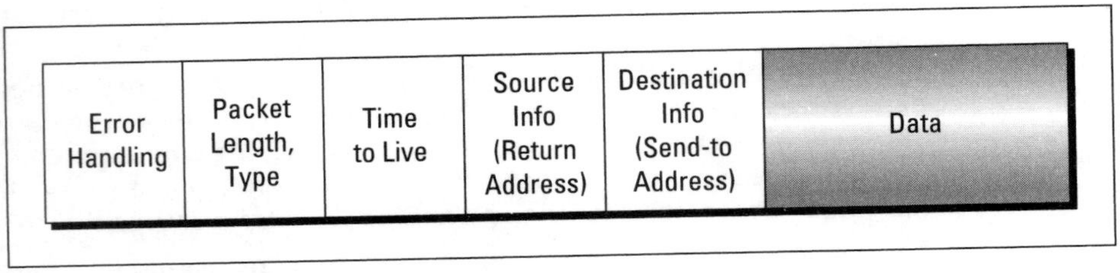

Figure 6-3:
A network packet is a unit of data transfer on a network.

Error Handling	Packet Length, Type	Time to Live	Source Info (Return Address)	Destination Info (Send-to Address)	Data

A time to live . . .

Another issue the transport protocol handles is *timing*. If a packet doesn't reach its destination promptly, the receiving computer asks the sending computer to resend it. Problems arise if the original packet eventually does arrive at the receiving computer after the sending computer has already re-sent it. The receiving computer then gets two identical packets and doesn't know what to do with them. (Computers are a little slow this way; you have to tell them how to handle every little situation.)

The transport protocol handles this timing problem by stamping a "time to live" indicator onto each packet. The receiving computer ignores a packet that arrives after its expiration date, assuming that the sender has already re-sent it. You don't have to worry too much about timing issues in a small network, but I mention it in passing because it helps explain some of the cabling restrictions I bring up in Chapter 7.

Popular Protocols

Now that you have a basic idea about what a transport protocol does, you have to choose one. This section spells out the options, and Table 6-1 summarizes which popular protocols are supported by popular Network Operating Systems.

Table 6-1	Network Operating Systems and Transport Protocol Support			
Transport Protocol	*Novell IntranetWare for Small Business*	*Novell IntranetWare 4.1.1*	*Microsoft Windows NT Server 4.0*	*Microsoft Windows 95*
IPX/SPX	Yes	Yes	Yes	Yes
NetBEUI	No	No	Yes	Yes
TCP/IP	Yes	Yes	Yes	Yes

Transport protocol software is generally included in the price of the operating system. For example, Windows 95 comes with about a dozen different transport protocols right out of the box.

IPX/SPX: Easy and popular

IPX/SPX stands for *Internet Packet eXchange/Sequenced Packet eXchange.* The great popularity of this particular protocol in small networks traces its roots to the great popularity of Novell NetWare, for which Novell designed IPX/SPX. Even though you can run Novell networks with TCP/IP nowadays, IPX/SPX remains an integral part of Novell *Local Area Network* (LAN) software and most Novell networks today run IPX/SPX.

Why the slash in the middle of the name? In brief

✔ **The IPX part may be all you need in a particular network, but it doesn't guarantee packet delivery.** That is, it's up to the application software to detect if a packet is missing. Also, IPX may send packets out of order. Network gurus call IPX a *connectionless* protocol because of the unordered and unguaranteed transmission method.

✔ **The SPX part runs on top of IPX and provides error checking and flow control to make sure that packets reach their intended destination accurately and in the correct order.** Some data backup, diagnostic, and communications applications (such as videoconferencing) require the SPX component. SPX is a *connection-oriented* protocol because it sends packets in sequence (hence the name) and sets up a sort of conversation between the sending and receiving computers.

Fortunately, you don't have to worry about whether your software needs SPX — when you set a computer up to use IPX, the SPX software comes along for the ride, and if a program requires it, it usually uses SPX automatically.

Aside from its convenient integration with NetWare and IntranetWare, my favorite aspect of IPX/SPX is its no muss, no fuss addressing technique. Every Network Interface Card (NIC) comes with a number, sort of like a serial number, called a *MAC address,* burned into a silicon chip on the card. The NIC manufacturers go to great pains to ensure that every single NIC in the world has a unique MAC address. IPX/SPX uses this number as the computer's mailing address — you never have to worry about it.

IPX/SPX is also a *routable* protocol, meaning that it can work in a larger network that uses devices called *routers* to connect smaller networks together. Routers help reduce traffic across the LAN, like a post office sub-sorting station.

Does IPX/SPX have any drawbacks? One is that IPX/SPX isn't the fastest protocol on the block, especially for programs that use the SPX part. However, it is a respectable performer and does fine for a small network. More important, IPX/SPX doesn't do especially well in *Wide Area Networks* (WANs). Novell has made some improvements over the years to address this problem, but if you plan to connect two networks over a long-distance link, IPX/SPX is definitely at a speed disadvantage compared to TCP/IP *(Transmission Control Protocol/Internet Protocol),* as I discuss later in this chapter.

As I write this, Novell is working hard to separate IPX/SPX from the rest of its network software so that shops using Novell networking software can just as easily choose a different transport protocol. Novell says that it plans to continue supporting IPX/SPX for a long time, although personally I doubt the company is devoting major resources to its enhancement. For now, though, IPX/SPX remains a logical choice if you use IntranetWare.

The fact that both Microsoft and Novell support IPX/SPX makes this protocol a safe choice. Incidentally, Microsoft's fully compatible version of IPX/SPX goes by the name *NWLink.*

Your network software may provide all sorts of options for fine-tuning IPX/SPX, but 99 times out of 100, the standard settings are fine.

NetBEUI: Easy and fast

NetBIOS Extended User Interface, or NetBEUI (pronounced "net-BOOie"), has the distinction of being the fastest protocol in the bunch. IBM introduced NetBEUI in 1985, and Microsoft used it as the default (standard) transport protocol for the peer-to-peer network system built into the old Windows for Workgroups product line. Older networks like Microsoft LAN Manager and IBM LAN Server used NetBEUI, too.

Although consultants don't recommend NetBEUI as often as they used to, I still like it for a small, Windows-based network that you're fairly sure will stay small (under a couple dozen users). Windows NT Server runs NetBEUI very quickly.

NetBEUI handles computer addressing simply and easily, though not quite so easily as IPX/SPX. On a NetBEUI network, you have to give each computer a name, called a *NetBIOS name*. (NetBEUI is based on NetBIOS, as I discuss at the end of this chapter.)

NetBIOS really sounds more complicated than it is: Usually, giving a computer a NetBIOS name is a simple matter of running a little control panel program on the computer and typing in the name. You do have to make sure each NetBIOS name on the network is unique; you can't use spaces; and you can't go over 15 characters.

If you go with NetBEUI, figure out a standard way to name the computers in your network. Basing the computer names on employee names is okay if you have low personnel turnover. You may want to start each server name with an "S" and each workstation name with a "W" to make life easier.

NetBEUI has two big drawbacks. First, it isn't a *routable protocol,* meaning that you can't grow your network by adding a *router* to connect multiple subnetworks, or segments. However, NetBEUI can cross *bridges,* another kind of network connection device. The bottom line is this: Once you get more than two or three dozen users on your LAN, you've probably outgrown NetBEUI as your transport protocol and you have to switch to something else. Second, NetBEUI doesn't work with Novell servers, so if you go with Novell IntranetWare, you must use IPX/SPX or TCP/IP.

TCP/IP: For today and tomorrow

IPX/SPX and NetBEUI are fine solutions for small networks that stay within a single location. However, they both have their problems when a Local Area Network grows into a Wide Area Network. Enter TCP/IP (Transmission Control Protocol/Internet Protocol).

Overview

TCP/IP (pronounced "tee-see-pee-eye-pee," not "tick pip") works well on large networks as well as small ones, and on slow remote connections as well as fast local ones. TCP/IP also makes two network jobs much easier: connecting to the Internet, and creating an *intranet* (kind of like a private Internet inside your own company). Of all the network transport protocols, the widest variety of computers support TCP/IP — PCs, Macintoshes, engineering workstations, and so on. If you run a Unix network such as Sun Solaris, TCP/IP is usually the logical protocol to use.

Chapter 16 discusses intranets, and Chapter 17 discusses the Internet.

Most industry analysts agree that the world is moving to TCP/IP. Some go so far as to say that all the other transport protocols are as dead as disco. I would agree if it weren't for two facts: TCP/IP involves a complex method of assigning computer addresses, and its use on Novell servers — while certainly possible — involves significant additional overhead and a speed sacrifice. However, if you want to set up a company *intranet* or build a WAN, TCP/IP is the way to go.

TCP/IP is actually a set of network protocols for file transfer, network management, and messaging. Developed in the early '70s by the Defense Advanced Research Projects, TCP/IP became a formal standard in 1982, and is now used on the public Internet, company intranets, and in many educational, engineering, and governmental areas. One of the big advantages of TCP/IP is that it originated in the public sector, so its specifications are public, and no one vendor controls it — the benefit for you is that many companies create software that uses TCP/IP, giving you more options and keeping the price of software competitive.

As with IPX/SPX, the slash in the name indicates different pieces of software that do different jobs:

- ✔ **TCP** breaks apart and reassembles packets in the correct order, and resends packets if errors occur — a guaranteed-delivery protocol similar to SPX (see the previous section on IPX/SPX).
- ✔ **IP** handles basic addressing, routing, and transmission.

As with IPX/SPX, you typically install the TCP and IP software at the same time.

Addressing

The hassle with TCP/IP is that it manages addressing in a more complex way than either IPX/SPX or NetBEUI does. With TCP/IP, any computer on the network can have one of a variety of *IP addresses,* each of which is a series of four numbers with periods between them, for example `207.68.137.40`. As with other protocols, this address must be unique for each connected computer at any given moment.

If you don't want to know about IP addressing, even a little bit, please skip down to the "Remember" icon at the end of this section.

A few different methods exist for maintaining and managing IP addresses:

✔ **The network administrator can keep track of them, and ensure uniqueness when issuing new addresses.** In this scenario, any new user must request a fixed, or *static,* IP address from the network administrator, who then types that number in the appropriate control panel on the user's workstation. This approach can work well for small shops, but it becomes labor intensive for medium-sized businesses.

✔ ***Bootstrap Protocol,* or *BootP* (pronounced *boot-pee*) comes from the Unix world and allows the system to make on-the-fly IP address assignments from a predefined pool of addresses as users connect to the network.** BootP works a little like a motor pool: You need a jeep, you take a jeep — it doesn't much matter which one you get. This method beats the heck out of trying to manage several dozen addresses manually. Windows 95 workstations, however, don't support BootP.

✔ ***Dynamic Host Configuration Protocol,* or *DHCP,* does pretty much the same thing as BootP but it's a little more automatic (and it does Windows, too).** When a user links to your network, a server running DHCP automatically *leases* the user an IP address for a specified period. When the user is done using the network, that particular IP address becomes available for another user. DHCP makes sure that no two active users have the same IP address. For example, when you dial up an Internet Service Provider, you get a TCP/IP address good for the duration of your call, and when you hang up, someone else can use it.

You can build easier maintenance into your network by using BootP or DHCP on the network. Most Unix networks use BootP; Microsoft and Novell networks use DHCP, as does OS/2 Warp Server.

Besides making sure that users get unique IP addresses, maintaining a TCP/IP network also means making sure that those numeric addresses match up properly with user-friendly *domain names* such as acme.pub.com. (You've used these names on the Internet if you've done any World Wide Web surfing or used e-mail.) Sending mail to Bill@thirdfloor.com is much easier than remembering his IP address of 127.46.112.22, especially if that IP address can change.

A small business can choose to manage its domain name match-ups manually, for example by typing the associations into a special workstation file named HOSTS anytime the associations change. Medium-sized (or just busier) businesses appreciate having the name associations handled more automatically and centrally, with the help of a *Domain Name Server* (often redundantly called a *DNS Server*). A DNS server sits on your network and simply maintains a list of IP addresses and the associated domain names, so that every time a user enters a domain name (again, like acme.pub.com) in an application, your network can find the IP address (like 207.68.137.40).

Finally, on Windows networks, computers find other computers on the network using special names called *NetBIOS* names (see the discussion of NetBIOS in the preceding "NetBEUI: Easy and fast" section). Windows networks use NetBIOS names even if they don't run the NetBEUI protocol, and just like the domain name, NetBIOS names need to match up with IP addresses, too. Just as with domain names, you can manage NetBIOS names manually with workstation text files (called LMHOSTS) or automatically with a specialized server (*Windows Internet Naming Service,* or *WINS,* is the most popular choice for NT Server networks).

You don't have to have separate machines running address-management services like DHCP, DNS, and WINS. For example, on a Windows NT server, you can run all three on the same computer. (I can hear a collective sigh of relief.)

✔ DHCP is only available if you have a server; peer-to-peer LANs can't use it. Also, WINS is only useful if the entire network is Windows-based.

✔ If you use TCP/IP with Novell networking products and Windows 95 workstations, you may need to use the Novell networking client (called *Client32,* free from Novell) on the top layer of the WINK cake, rather than the Microsoft client for NetWare that comes with Windows 95. I've heard more than one LAN administrator report trouble with TCP/IP and the Microsoft client. It's a shame that both Microsoft and Novell offer different client-layer software for Novell networks, but in this business companies don't always work together as we all would like them to.

If all of this sounds fairly complicated, rest assured that it gets even more so in real life! Assuming that you don't want to know all the gory details about IP addressing — that is, that you are *sane* — I suggest you get some help from a consultant in setting up the addressing system for a TCP/IP network. Experienced network consultants do this sort of thing in their sleep, and once the system is in place, you don't have to worry about it — setting up the addressing system is a one-time expense and well worth the day or so of consulting time required. (Chapter 3 covers the details of choosing and using a consultant to meet your needs.)

Summing up

You now have enough information to make an informed decision as to which network transport protocol makes the most sense for your network. To sum up, the generally accepted industry guidelines are as follows:

✔ **If you choose a Novell network for the upper WINK layer,** use IPX/SPX for best performance, and TCP/IP if you want to set up an intranet (Chapter 16). Use IPX/SPX and an IP-to-IPX gateway if you want your users to have Internet (Chapter 17) access, it doesn't have to be super fast, and you don't want to mess with IP addressing.

✔ **If you choose a Windows network for the upper WINK layer,** use IPX/SPX if you also have a Novell server in the mix, or if you don't have any interest in the Internet or intranets but you think your network may grow beyond a couple dozen users. Use NetBEUI for speed if your network is under two dozen users and likely to stay that way. Use TCP/IP if you plan on growth and you may want to set up an intranet (Chapter 16) or connect to the Internet (Chapter 17), now or in the future.

✔ **If you choose a Unix network for the upper WINK layer,** the most likely protocol choice is TCP/IP. Unix can accommodate other protocols if necessary.

✔ **If you choose a peer-to-peer network, such as Windows 95 or Windows NT Workstation,** and you plan for it to stay small (under two dozen users), use NetBEUI. If you think your peer-to-peer network will grow larger, don't use a peer-to-peer network; start with a client/server network such as Novell IntranetWare or Microsoft Windows NT Server.

Changing Protocols

What if your work environment changes over time, and you want to make a network change? For example, what if you choose NetBEUI for a small network because of its fast performance, but your business grows faster than you ever imagined, and you need to switch to IPX/SPX or TCP/IP?

In most cases, you can make a transport protocol change without changing any of your Network Interface Cards (NICs) or *hubs* (the black boxes that manage network traffic). You can switch protocols simply by reconfiguring the software on the individual computers connected to your network. Changing protocols on a network server can be more involved than making the change on user workstations, but again, in most cases you don't have to buy any new hardware. You probably do have to add new software for the server, though.

If you change from either NetBEUI or IPX/SPX to TCP/IP, you have to handle the addressing challenges that come along with TCP/IP (as I cover in the "TCP/IP: For today and tomorrow" section in this chapter), and (probably) install some new software to help automate the address-management chores.

If and when you switch transport protocols, my suggestion is to switch every computer on the network at the same time (say, over a long weekend). While you may be technically able to run multiple protocols on every computer as a way of stretching out the transition, doing so makes support and troubleshooting much more complex, and slows performance. Large companies sometimes have to run multiple protocols because of the mishmash of computers they have, but you are not a large, lumbering company (or you wouldn't be reading this book) — use your small business advantage!

Another option to consider that's not quite as drastic as changing every computer's transport protocol is to install a *gateway,* that is, an interpreter that can translate between protocols in real time (much like those headset-equipped United Nations translators you sometimes see on TV). For example, an IPX-to-IP gateway can allow user workstations running IPX to access the Internet via the gateway, without having TCP/IP installed on the workstations. A gateway can be an extra program running on a network server, or a dedicated computer running gateway software; you'd choose the latter if your existing server is already really busy. Chapter 17 lists some gateway vendors and provides an illustration of how they work.

Other Protocols You May Bump Into

Although IPX/SPX, NetBEUI, and TCP/IP are the protocols that small businesses are most likely to use, various other protocols exist.

AppleTalk

The original Macintosh network protocol, AppleTalk, is very convenient (it comes built in with all Macintoshes) and highly standardized (Apple is the only supplier). Originally, AppleTalk networks ran at a very slow speed (230 Kbps, or about one-fortieth the speed of regular Ethernet) over a hardware layer called *LocalTalk,* causing many to brand AppleTalk as a slow network. However, you can now run the AppleTalk transport protocol on top of Ethernet (Apple calls this *EtherTalk*) or on top of Token Ring (yup, *TokenTalk*) for good Local Area Network (LAN) performance.

Remember the WINK layers! (See Figure 6-1 for a refresher.) A transport protocol can run at different speeds, depending on that bottom layer. . .

Nowadays, Macintosh networking is moving gradually away from AppleTalk as a transport protocol and toward TCP/IP. Macs can also run IPX/SPX to participate in a Novell network. Various Apple managers have confirmed that the company doesn't plan to keep enhancing AppleTalk. However, you may need to use the protocol with older Macintoshes that don't support TCP/IP easily, with Apple printers that require AppleTalk connections, or with a new Macintosh network that you want to keep simple and easy.

Banyan VINES

Banyan VINES is a NOS that has enjoyed popularity in really big networks, but that small businesses very rarely use. VINES has its own protocol.

DEC PathWorks

If you use Digital Equipment Corporation's PathWorks network, for example, because you bought one lock, stock, and barrel in a bankruptcy sale, you should install the PathWorks protocol. Different versions exist for TokenRing and Ethernet networks.

DLC

DLC *(Data Link Control)* is a transport protocol used to communicate with some network-equipped printers and large (minicomputer and mainframe) machines. DLC can run over Token Ring or Ethernet.

If you have a network printer that uses DLC (such as a Hewlett-Packard LaserJet with a JetDirect network card built in), you generally don't have to install DLC on every computer on the network — just the computer that's acting as the *print server* (that is, the one that queues up user print jobs and feeds them to the printer). For more on print queuing, see Chapter 9.

NetBIOS

NetBIOS (short for *Network Basic Input/Output System*) was made popular by IBM and Microsoft, and is required today for certain application programs. Its successor, NetBEUI, is more popular, but some networks still use NetBIOS (Artisoft LANtastic, for example) and some versions of Lotus Notes require it as well. Also, if for some reason you use an older network, like LAN Manager or LAN Server, you may have to add (through the Windows 95 Network control panel) the NetBIOS protocol to user computers.

Because NetBIOS tends to slow performance, don't add it to another protocol, such as IPX/SPX, unless you know you need it.

PC-NFS

If you plan to use PCs with Unix servers that don't run Banyan VINES, you can install the PC-NFS transport protocol (the NFS stands for *Network File System,* the Unix standard for network communications — not "Not For Sale," as you'd see at the antique dealer).

SNA

SNA *(Systems Network Architecture)* includes protocols for IBM and compatible mainframes and midrange computers. Unless you have a mainframe or midrange computer system in your small business, you don't need to worry about SNA.

Chapter 7

Choosing Network Hardware: The Least You Need to Know

. . . .

In This Chapter

▶ Choosing between Ethernet, Fast Ethernet, and Token Ring signaling methods

▶ Selecting a cable type

▶ Specifying server and workstation computers

▶ Buying backup devices, network printers, modems, and CD-ROM drives

. . . .

*A*fter you choose a networking style, network software, and communications language for your company network, you need to make some decisions about the computers, peripherals, and cables (hardware) that make your network a concrete reality.

Hard•ware (härd'wâr') *n.* The parts of a computer network that you can hit with a hammer. (*Weadock's Practical Computer Dictionary,* not yet written)

Good news: Computer hardware is more reliable than ever. Bad news: When the hardware does fail, it tends to fail in a big, inconvenient way. If a computer, cabling system, or hub costs less but fails more frequently than an alternative, or takes longer to get repaired when it does fail, you probably got ripped off. So, when buying hardware, look at the *lifetime* cost, not just the initial cost. A big part of the lifetime cost is the time, effort, and downtime that hardware failure brings. Buy name-brand hardware that's a notch or two below the state of the art (saving big bucks), but that is much more reliable than bargain-basement hardware.

Paying for the very best makes sense with certain things — doctors, smoke alarms, and beer come to mind. Think of the popular Swatch wristwatch — those plastic Swiss watches work very reliably for about five or six years and cost around a hundred bucks. A Swatch costs at least 30 times less than a Rolex, so when a Swatch breaks, you can replace it without taking out a loan or borrowing from your in-laws (always a bad idea).

Similarly, you should expect good computer hardware to serve you very reliably for about five or six years. Technology advances so fast that in five years you may want to replace your computers, anyway. The bottom line: Unless you have very special needs, state-of-the-art computers aren't worth the substantial price premium over merely excellent computers.

Whatever you spend, when network hardware works properly, it becomes invisible. Your goal is to choose hardware that you can take for granted and not even *think* about again for years after you install it. Good hardware hardly ever breaks or gives you problems, and when it does, it's unlikely to trash your data or cripple your entire network — and you can fix or replace the hardware easily and quickly. Good hardware does its job without undue delays, and lets you easily expand it to accommodate network growth. This chapter helps you choose good hardware; Chapter 8 helps you install it.

Network Plumbing

The physical structure of your network occupies the bottom layer in Figure 7-1, the not-yet-famous Weadock Integrated Network Knowledge (WINK) model that I introduce in Chapter 6. You can think of this layer as your network's *plumbing* (in fact, many networking professionals call it just that), moving the sparkling water of data through efficient pipes of cable to reach the gleaming faucets of user workstations, the water towers of network servers, and perhaps even the vast churning storm sewers of the Internet.

This section deals with the plumbing choices you must make before you whip out the company credit card and start laying on the debt burden. The first decision is whether to go with the Ethernet, Fast Ethernet, or Token Ring *signaling method*.

Signaling methods

Your network's *signaling method* (also called the *access method*) specifies how computers gain access to the network cable. The signaling method you choose determines a great deal about how fast your *Local Area Network* (LAN) can run, how much it costs, and how easily it can grow. You can usually choose a signaling method independently of the *Network Operating System* (NOS) software and the network language (or *transport protocol* — see Chapter 6). For example, a LANtastic network doesn't care if you use Ethernet or Token Ring.

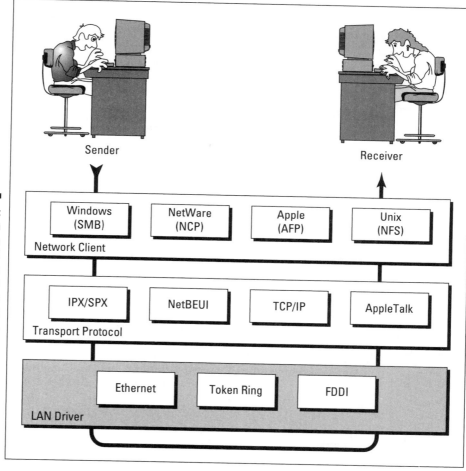

Figure 7-1:
The bottom layer of the WINK model deals with network plumbing design, including signaling schemes, cabling, and Network Interface Cards (NICs).

Ethernet

Ethernet is by far the most popular signaling method for small networks — it provides good performance at low cost, works with just about any cable type, and runs on nearly every kind of computer. Ethernet's standard transmission speed is 10 Mbps (Megabits per second), although in practice, you rarely see more than 7 Mbps.

With the Ethernet access method, anytime a computer wants to send data over the network, it first "listens" to the cable. If no other computer is trying to send anything, then fine: The transmission occurs. If another computer tries to send at that same exact moment, both computers back off for a random period of time and then try again. The idea is that on the next attempt, one of the computers will beat the other to the punch because of the differing delays. The acronym for this scheme is *CSMA/CD,* for *Carrier-Sense Multiple Access/Collision Detection.*

The only big drawback to Ethernet is that once your network reaches a certain size (usually 50 to 75 users), more and more collisions occur, and network performance falls off fairly rapidly unless you start dividing up your LAN with *bridges* and *routers*. Small companies aren't likely to bump into this problem, but if you do (and a good monitoring tool can tell you — see Chapter 12), you may want to consider Fast Ethernet.

Fast Ethernet

3Com, Digital Equipment Corporation, Intel, and Sun (among others) got together and enhanced Ethernet with a new standard called *Fast Ethernet*. Fast Ethernet works pretty much like regular Ethernet: CSMA/CD and all that, as I describe in the previous section. The main difference is that Fast Ethernet is somewhat more particular about the type of cable it runs on, and it goes ten times faster at 100 Mbps (though the practical maximum speed is more like 70 Mbps). You need Fast Ethernet-compatible hubs and *Network Interface Cards* (NICs) to enjoy the greater speed.

Most small companies don't need Fast Ethernet, at least not to every computer. Some hubs (the boxes to which your computers connect) allow you to use Fast Ethernet for a server, and regular garden-variety Ethernet for workstations (see the section "Hubs and switches" later in this chapter), which makes a lot of sense given that your servers are transmitting and receiving information much more frequently than your workstations.

When buying Ethernet NICs for your workstations, price units that can handle Fast Ethernet too. The cost difference may not be large, and combo NICs can run at the faster speed if you decide to get a Fast Ethernet hub.

Fast Ethernet puts more of a strain on your cabling system than regular Ethernet. Be sure to have an experienced contractor check out your cabling and connectors if you go to 100 Mbps. Also, be sure to read the "Cabling options" section later in this chapter for more information.

Token Ring

Token Ring is still in widespread use, but it's a distant second to Ethernet. Most Token Ring networks are in companies that have traditionally bought whatever IBM was selling — IBM developed and promoted Token Ring. Token Ring is common in the financial services industry and in manufacturing environments where company networks are often used to control automated equipment. Token Ring's advantages include predictable response, fault tolerance, and the ability to add computers without decreasing performance as rapidly as with Ethernet.

Here's how Token Ring works: Computers connect to a central *Multistation Access Unit,* or MAU, (rhymes with "cow") and forms the center of a star-shaped wiring layout. However, electronically (inside the MAU), Token Ring isn't a star but rather a ring, in which computers pass *tokens* — electronic data buckets — from one to another in round-robin fashion. When any computer wants to send data to any other computer, it waits until an available token (an empty bucket) makes the rounds, and then send its data. Strict limits on token availability ensure that each computer has a chance to send data within a well-defined timeframe — something not always guaranteed on Ethernet.

Consultants rarely recommend Token Ring for small office applications. The hubs and NICs are too expensive, and you don't have as many products from which to choose as with Ethernet. If you need better speed than Ethernet, Fast Ethernet runs faster than Token Ring for about the same money. However, if you come across a great deal on a Token Ring setup, it's solid technology, and if for some reason you have to hook up with an IBM midrange computer such as an AS/400, Token Ring may be the way to go. Just make sure you get the 16 Mbps flavor rather than the slower, 4 Mbps second version.

Other

Here are five other network signaling methods that you may hear about. Most small companies normally wouldn't use any of these for a Local Area Network, but things can change fast in this business, and your company may have unique needs that one of these methods can meet.

100VG-AnyLAN was developed by Hewlett-Packard and AT&T, and runs at 100 Mbps over all four twisted pairs in Category 3 cable. Fast Ethernet has whupped 100VG-AnyLAN in the marketplace, but apparently nobody's told HP, who continues to promote it.

FDDI (Fiber Distributed Data Interface) connects computers in a dual counter-rotating ring that can survive a complete cable cut. Its access method is similar to Token Ring, and despite the name, you can run FDDI on copper cable. FDDI is fast (100 Mbps), cool, very reliable, immune to electro-magnetic interference and general bad vibes of any kind, expensive, and overkill for 99 percent of small businesses.

Gigabit Ethernet is a developing standard that outpaces even Fast Ethernet. A typical small business network doesn't need the speed; however, you may want to follow this technology if your business does intensive graphics or multimedia work. I predict that by the turn of the century, "gig" will be big.

ATM (Asynchronous Transfer Mode) is another fast signaling method that beats out Fast Ethernet and Token Ring, but costs a lot more and is very rare in small networks. You can run ATM at up to 622 Mbps, although a small network would likely stick to 25 Mbps cards for workstations and 155 Mbps cards for servers. ATM can transmit data, voice, and video simultaneously. Consider ATM only if Fast Ethernet isn't fast enough for you, and then only after consulting with a network expert.

ARCNet (Attached Resource Computer Network) is a 2.5 Mbps network standard that enjoyed a good reputation for reliability and moderate cost. It has fallen out of favor because it's so slow compared to Ethernet and Token Ring. I mention ARCNet only so that you know to avoid it — even if someone offers it to you gratis.

Cabling options

Depending on the signaling method you choose, you may have several options for the cabling and connectors that tie your network together.

Twisted pair

Twisted-pair network cable looks a lot like everyday telephone cable, although it's not exactly the same (see Figure 7-2) — it's thicker and uses the larger RJ-45 connectors instead of the small RJ-11 connectors that phone cable uses. Twisted pair comes in two main flavors. *Unshielded Twisted Pair* (UTP) is by far the more popular type; it consists of pairs of copper wires twisted around each other and covered by plastic insulation. *Shielded Twisted Pair* (STP) adds an encircling metallic jacket around the twisted pairs for better resistance to electromagnetic interference. STP uses different connectors than UTP, is more expensive, and requires careful grounding in order to work properly. (The twists, incidentally, improve the electrical characteristics of the cable.)

Twisted-pair networks use a *star topology,* that is, a wiring layout in which cables radiate from a central *hub* (as opposed to thin coax, which operates without a hub) to each workstation computer (see Figure 7-3). The length of each hub-to-computer cable can't exceed 100 meters. The best feature of twisted pair is that damage to any given cable is likely to affect only a single computer, not the whole network.

Various categories of UTP exist:

- **Category 1** is suitable for voice but not data.
- **Category 2** is suitable for data, but at such slow speeds (4 Mbps) that you don't want it.

- ✔ **Category 3** is suitable for data at up to 10 Mbps; you can use it for Ethernet, but I don't recommend it. You can run Fast Ethernet over Category 3 cable, but you need all four of the provided wire pairs.

- ✔ **Category 4** is better than 3, not as good as 5, and rarely used for new networks. It can move data at up to 20 Mbps and is most often found with Token Ring networks.

- ✔ **Category 5** is your best choice for networking purposes. It costs a little more, but it can support Ethernet with no problem and, as long as the installation is sound, Fast Ethernet, ISDN, and ATM, too. "Cat5" includes four pairs of wires, although Ethernet and Fast Ethernet only use two of the pairs.

Figure 7-2:
Twisted-pair cable with an RJ-45 connector.

Figure 7-3:
A twisted-pair, star topology network layout joins several computers at a central hub.

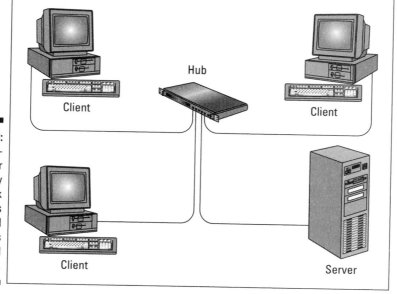

Your landlord may advise you that Category 5 twisted pair is already installed, but the patch panels and connectors may or may not meet Category 5 specifications. Get a network-savvy cable contractor to run tests for you.

When you run regular Ethernet on twisted-pair cable, you're using what the techies call *10Base-T*. Fast Ethernet on Category 3 or 4 twisted pair uses all four wire pairs and goes by the name *100Base-T4*. Fast Ethernet on Cat 5 twisted pair is *100Base-TX*.

Coax

Coaxial network cable (*coax*) comes in two varieties, both using a central insulated copper conducting wire, an encircling jacket shield, and a rubber, plastic, or plastic-and-Teflon outer layer. The older variety, called *ThickNet, Thick Ethernet,* or *10Base-5,* is not something you're likely to use. It's bulky, expensive, hard to install, a pain to tap into, and generally not appropriate for small business networks. ThickNet may be worth considering if you have to have a long cable run (up to 500 meters) in an electrically noisy location, although I prefer fiber optic cable in these situations (see the following section "Fiber"). You may also use ThickNet if you work in a building that already has it installed, for example, between floors. Thin Ethernet (or *ThinNet* or *10Base-2*) coax cable (see Figure 7-4) is superior to Thick Ethernet for small networks because it's thinner, cheaper, easier to install, and comes in prebuilt lengths with connectors already attached. Thin coaxial computer cable looks like TV cable, but it's different. You need RG58A/U type coax for computers.

Figure 7-4:
Coax
cable "T"
connector,
cable with
connector,
and union.

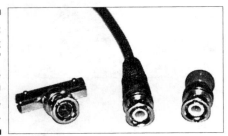

The big advantage of coax over twisted pair is better resistance to electrical and magnetic noise. You can run coax in environments that would bring twisted-pair cable to its little copper knees, which is why you see coax where heavy machinery generates big-time interference, or in research labs where scientific equipment creates a similar, electrically noisy environment.

Thin coax is also a common way of connecting multiple hubs together, so you probably need to know about it for this reason even if you don't plan to use it to connect workstations to your network.

The big problem with a thin coax network is that it isn't what computer designers call *fault tolerant*. Thin coax networks use a so-called *bus topology*, a fancy way of saying that they basically form a straight line (see Figure 7-5). This layout seems smart at first glance, because you don't have to use a hub, and you use less cable than in a star topology (see Figure 7-3). Saving a few hundred bucks is appealing, but it isn't worth it. If the cable has a problem, it affects everybody on that cable run. Cut, bend, or break a coax cable, or even jiggle the connection at the back of the computer, and everybody on that segment loses the network connection.

I rarely recommend coax except for a very simple network of two computers. (After all, if a cable fails in a two-computer network, you're pretty much sunk whether you're using coax or twisted pair.) If you have three or more computers, use twisted pair, and use coax only for hub-to-hub connections. (By the way: Coax *doesn't* support Token Ring.)

As far as the nuts and bolts go, thin coax connects to Network Interface Cards using *BNC* "T" connectors that link with a push and a twist, much like many small bayonet-style automotive light bulbs. You can connect one thin coax cable to another with BNC unions, but the less you do this the better because every connection is a possible trouble spot. Each segment of thin coax cable must have a 50-ohm terminating resistor at each end, can't run over 185 meters total (from resistor to resistor), and can't have over 30 computers on it.

Figure 7-5:
A bus topology network segment joins several computers in a single, linear cable run.

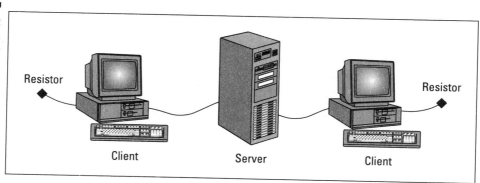

Resistor   Resistor

Client   Server   Client

Wireless networking

The coolest, if not the fastest, network cabling isn't cabling at all, but a wireless link. The two common types are infrared and radio frequency. Both are trés handy for notebook computers that need an occasional connection to the network, because you don't have to fiddle with wires and circuit boards, and because notebook docking stations can be pricey and bulky.

All you do to create an infrared link is plop your infrared-capable notebook a couple of feet in front of a $300 to $400 infrared network station such as Hewlett-Packard's NetBeamIR, which links to your network through a regular twisted-pair connection, and log on! (Getting everything set up and working right may take some doing, though, as infrared networking is still pretty new.) The big problem with infrared has traditionally been pokey performance. However, in 1995, the Infrared Data Association (IrDA) came out with a standard that supports up to 4 Mbps — perfectly acceptable for light, occasional duty. (Some notebooks still only support the older standard of 115 Kpbs, though, so buyer beware.) Microsoft supplies the necessary software for notebook users running Windows 95 to connect to an infrared port. You can use infrared with Ethernet and Token Ring networks.

A radio frequency (RF) link costs more and doesn't run any faster than an infrared link, but RF allows much greater flexibility in locating the notebook — the user doesn't even need to know exactly where the network-side link (called the *access point*) is. The access point costs from $500 to $2,000 depending on the range you need, but even the least expensive device covers a 200-foot radius. Client-side hardware runs about $600 per machine, so RF is an expensive solution compared to infrared. Unlike infrared, multiple RF clients can link to the same access point at once. Proxim is the leading vendor.

Fiber

Fiberoptic cable is unquestionably the best kind if cost is no object. You run zero risk of electromagnetic interference shifting decimal points around in your spreadsheets because you're not moving electricity around, you're moving pulses of light. You can also have very long cable runs of up to 2 kilometers (about 1.25 miles). Fiber is great for running between buildings, not only because of the distance issue but because you don't need to worry about electrical grounding. In addition, eavesdropping on a fiber network is very difficult, so a network running this type of cable is highly secure.

The gotcha isn't so much the cost of the thin glass cable itself; it's the cost of the NICs, hubs, and the technician to connect them. A Fast Ethernet fiberoptic NIC (techie term: *100Base-FX*) runs $100 to $300 more than a twisted-pair Fast Ethernet NIC. Installing fiberoptic NICs requires special skills. Testing fiber requires expensive equipment. You can plan on about $500 per computer as a minimum total cost for fiberoptic connections.

If you know that you're going to be in the same building for awhile (such as, for example, if your company owns it), go ahead and pull fiber at the same time you install twisted-pair cable. Maybe in a few years the cost of fiber-optic NICs will have come down dramatically, and if so, you won't have to incur the labor cost of running new cable.

Lamp cord

You can't really use lamp cord to wire a computer network. I just threw this in to see if you're reading.

Network Interface Cards

The *Network Interface Card,* or *NIC* (pronounced "nick"), is an extremely important little piece of hardware (see Figures 7-6 and 7-7). Every bit (pun intended) of network traffic that a device sends or receives must pass through the device's NIC, which handles the coding and decoding of cable signals. Good NICs make your LAN easier to set up, faster, and more reliable. Bad ones can save $20 to $50 per computer and make your network administrator's life a living heck. (Not as bad as a living hell, but *bad.*)

Any device that wants to communicate on the network has to have a NIC. Servers, workstations, and directly connected modems, printers, and CD-ROM drives all must have a NIC that ties them to a LAN cable. (Any device that has a NIC becomes a so-called network *node.*)

The NIC may come built in to a device, thus reducing your installation time, or you may have to install it yourself. In the latter case, you have to buy a NIC that connects properly to the device (such as a computer) on the one

Figure 7-6:
A typical desktop computer NIC plugs into the computer's main circuit board.

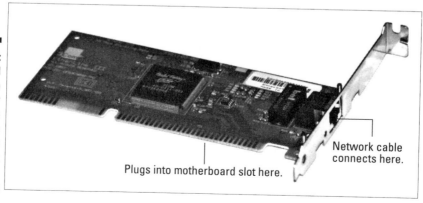

Plugs into motherboard slot here.

Network cable connects here.

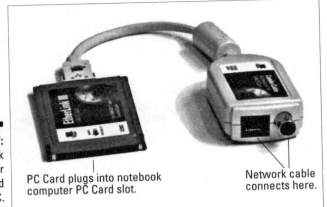

Figure 7-7:
A notebook
computer
PC Card
NIC.

PC Card plugs into notebook
computer PC Card slot.

Network cable
connects here.

hand, and to your network cable (for example, Twisted Pair), on the other hand. The NICs you buy must also work with your chosen network signaling method (Ethernet, Fast Ethernet, or Token Ring).

TIP

You can hedge your bets a little by paying a tad more and getting NICs that support multiple cable types — many support both thin coax and twisted pair. I prefer to get NICs that only work with twisted pair if that's my chosen cable type; it's one less software setting that can go wrong, and you're not likely to change cable types after you wire your whole doggoned office.

As far as the way the NIC fits into your workstations and servers, your choices are *ISA, PCI, EISA, MCA,* and *VLB.* (Sorry for the alphabet soup — see the Glossary for the expanded terms if you must.) These are the different kinds of slots computers offer for NICs to plug into. However, I can simplify things a little here: Today's computers typically use either ISA or PCI. If you're buying new equipment, you can probably forget about EISA, MCA, and VLB.

Many new computers offer both ISA and PCI slots. Which kind of NIC should you buy?

✓ **For servers, always choose PCI.** The server NIC is often a bottleneck, so you want the fastest connection possible: PCI is faster than ISA. If you have an older server, it may use EISA slots and require an EISA-compatible NIC for best results.

✓ **For workstations, you can choose ISA if you use regular Ethernet, but choose PCI if you use Fast Ethernet.** ISA slots don't let you take maximum advantage of Fast Ethernet's speed (the slot is actually slower than the Fast Ethernet network). You can use either ISA or PCI for Token Ring — PCI may provide slightly better speed, but the difference usually isn't dramatic.

Before you buy your NICs, check to see whether a given slot type is physically available on the computer. The computer maker may advertise PCI slots, but they may all be occupied by video and multimedia cards, leaving only ISA slots free for the network card.

Older NICs may require you to flip switches or juggle *jumpers* (little plastic connectors that slide over pins that stick out from the board) to configure the card's options. (I discuss these options, such as the interrupt settings and memory location, in more detail in Chapter 8.) Late-model NICs allow you to configure all the options by running a software program, which is so much easier that I recommend you not even *consider* buying a NIC that still makes you fiddle with switches or jumpers.

Hubs and switches

A *hub* (see Figure 7-8) is a device at a central location to which two or more cables connect in a star configuration. Hubs are usually separate boxes, but they can be circuit boards that plug into a server (you don't want this kind; so-called *internal hubs* require that you bring the server down for at least an hour to replace them, they don't offer the benefit of diagnostic LED lights, and they're less reliable). Hubs may also include network management software (so-called *intelligent* or *managed* hubs) that lets you monitor their status from a remote console. Typically, small businesses with a single location use unmanaged hubs, which are less expensive. If you see the acronym SNMP, you're looking at a managed hub. Some hubs let you buy the management capability separately, so you can get it later if you need it.

In a twisted-pair Ethernet network, the hub basically makes the network look like it's sharing one big cable. The hub receives a message from one computer and then rebroadcasts it to all the other devices connected to the hub, so the message's recipient can pluck it off the wire. This rebroadcasting is why you sometimes see Ethernet hubs referred to as *multiport repeaters*. (Personally, I prefer "hub.")

A *stackable hub* is one that you can easily connect with other hubs, usually with a coaxial cable, to form a *daisy chain* (a string of two or more computer devices connected together in a row) that the network thinks is a single, larger hub. Some stackable hubs can connect with each other using Fast Ethernet for better performance, even if the rest of the network is using regular Ethernet. Hub vendors include 3Com, Bay Networks, Cisco, and Intel, among others.

A *switch* differs from an ordinary hub in that it can chop your network into smaller pieces for better performance when network traffic forms a bottleneck at some point in the system. Switches can perform this segmentation on an as-needed basis, essentially reconfiguring your LAN on the fly to meet current traffic demands. Switches can also link network segments having different speeds (for example, Ethernet to Fast Ethernet).

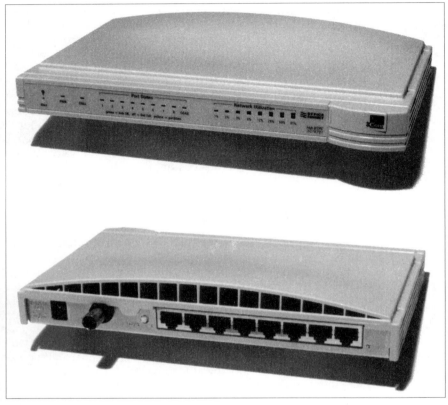

Figure 7-8:
An 8-port
10Base-T
hub in
3Com's
OfficeConnect
product
family.

Your LAN may need a switch if employees need to move large files or multimedia programs on the network. A company doing computer graphic design work, computer-based training development, or digital video work may benefit from the greater data transmission speed a switch can provide.

You can use a switch different ways, depending on your budget. For example, you can put a Fast Ethernet card in a server and link that server to workstations running regular Ethernet via a switch. This setup is an appealing way to improve network performance without incurring the cost of upgrading all the workstations to Fast Ethernet NICs. For an even more demanding situation, just about the fastest (and most expensive) way to plumb a small network is for every computer on the network to use Fast Ethernet *and* connect to a switch. Ethernet switches cost more than Ethernet hubs, but less than Token Ring switches.

Bridges and routers

You probably don't need to know about these devices unless you're a big small business ("huh?") with a few dozen workstations or multiple offices. If you find yourself bumping into cable length limitations or traffic problems, or if for some reason you have to connect multiple types of networks, you may want to consider adding a *bridge* or a *router*. You may also need a router if you hook up to the public Internet. I suggest you look up a good networking consultant if you need to investigate the use of routers and bridges beyond the scope of this book, but here are some concise definitions.

A *bridge* is usually a device that connects two networks of the same type (see Figure 7-9) and can be as simple as a computer with two NICs installed. I say "usually" because so many different kinds of bridges exist that the term has become impossible to define precisely. This much I can say, though: Having a bridge allows you to run more cable and workstations, because it actually creates two physical networks (one on either side of the bridge), each of which has its own maximum distance and workstation limits. A bridge also divides up traffic: It knows whether a packet originating on one side needs to go to the other side and lets it cross, but it doesn't let through packets that are addressed to a computer on the same side of the bridge. However, bridges do let *broadcast* messages (which go to everybody) cross over, so a faulty NIC sending out tons of broadcast messages (called a *packet storm*) can bog down both sides of a bridge.

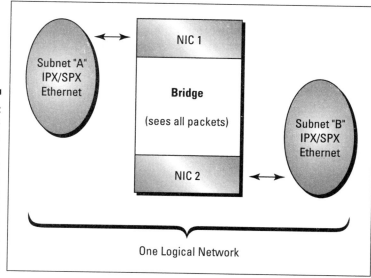

Figure 7-9:
A bridge joins two physical networks so that they appear as one logical network to the network software.

A *router* can connect two networks of different types, for example your LAN and the public Internet, and provides better traffic isolation because it doesn't forward broadcast messages. You can program a router to let only certain kinds of traffic flow across the device, which makes routers useful for security purposes (see Chapter 11). Routers are handy for *Wide Area Networks* (WANs) that connect smaller networks over large distances, and Internet connections. Routers talk to each other over the network, so they learn about your network's connections and can even figure out how to send information along the fastest route (hence the name).

Server Hardware

The information in this section applies to server computers in a client/server network, and to machines acting primarily or solely as servers in a peer-to-peer network.

Server machines

You don't necessarily have to buy computers that say "server" in the model designation or the marketing materials. Many desktop computers work well as a server as long as the specifications are appropriate — I've successfully used so-called "workstation" computers as servers on many occasions. Having said that, models with the server moniker sometimes offer useful advantages, such as preinstalled networking software, sophisticated diagnostic software, and extra bays for adding disk drives.

CPU

Not so long ago, network consultants routinely advised clients that the CPU, or *Central Processing Unit,* inside their server computer didn't make a lot of difference because it was almost never a performance bottleneck. Things change. Modern Network Operating Systems (NOSs) handle many more chores than mere file and print sharing: shared communications, application services (such as database programs), intranet and Internet connectivity, and so on. Also, faster network communications (for example, with Fast Ethernet) mean that servers no longer spend most of their time twiddling their electronic thumbs while waiting for NICs to deliver data.

So, pick up a server computer with a reasonably quick processor (166 MHz is considered rock bottom at this writing) and the option to add at least one extra CPU later on. Here are a few other specific suggestions:

 ✔ **If you go with an Intel CPU, I suggest Pentium Pro or Pentium II processors, which run Windows NT Server noticeably faster than the regular Pentium or Pentium MMX.**

> ✔ **Digital Equipment Corporation (DEC) makes the Alpha line of CPUs —
> they're fast and they run NT Server very well.**
>
> ✔ **If your network is a Unix type, then you have a variety of CPUs from
> which to choose.** Among them are Sun SPARC processors, IBM RS/6000
> chips, and so on. Unix servers tend to ship with CPUs that are plenty
> fast for small business networks.

Memory

Server memory is even more important than the server CPU is. Of the LANs
that I've seen, more run slowly because of too little server RAM than any
other cause. For most networks, 32MB is rock bottom, 64MB is better, and
consider 128MB if you have more than 75 users and only one server. As far
as the different types of memory go, SDRAM is faster than EDO, which is
faster than FPM (the meanings of these abbreviations are absolutely unim-
portant). Go with SDRAM or EDO.

Sophisticated companies like Novell and Microsoft, and sophisticated
network consultants, offer detailed equations you can pore over to determine how much RAM a server should have, depending on how many users
and printers and programs the server must handle. These formulas were
more important when memory cost $1,000 per megabyte, but they still offer
useful guidance if you want to get scientific about things.

Disks

A server machine definitely needs to have a diskette drive (otherwise known
as a floppy drive, although the diskettes don't flop anymore) and a CD-ROM
drive. You usually need a CD-ROM drive to install software onto the server,
and a diskette drive to create emergency startup diskettes to get things back
on track if anything happens to the server hard drive(s).

The hard drives on server machines are vital to your network's success in
three respects: capacity, performance, and reliability. In at least the first two
areas, *SCSI,* (pronounced "scuzzy") disks beat out the major competitor,
EIDE disks, although the gap is narrowing (see the Glossary for expanded
terms). I still recommend SCSI for server hard drives. Two main variations
exist: *Fast SCSI* (a subset of the SCSI-2 specification) is the most popular kind
with a top data transfer rate of 10MB/second, and *Ultra SCSI* (a subset of
SCSI-3) is somewhat more expensive but doubles the maximum transfer rate
to 20MB/second. Both come in so-called *wide* versions that double the non-
wide transfer rates, but require twice as much cabling.

Installing SCSI devices can get a little complicated. Chapter 8 provides some
helpful details.

In terms of disk drive capacity, every network is different; a very small
network (under eight users) may be okay with 2GB, but a 100-user network
may require ten times that amount. Just be sure that you can easily add

hard drives to your server in case you underestimate your capacity requirement up front. After working with your network for a few months, your LAN administrator will acquire a good feel for capacity needs.

SCSI CD-ROM drives tend to be less problematic with Windows NT Server than EIDE CD-ROM drives. If you run Novell software, either SCSI or EIDE CD-ROM drives work fine.

External hard drive enclosures are handy for servers using more than one hard drive. You can replace hard drives much more easily when they break, because you don't have to tear into the server system unit.

NIC

A small network of under 25 users can probably get by with a single *Network Interface Card* (NIC) in the server, but I definitely recommend a NIC that plugs into a PCI slot rather than an ISA slot (see the "Network Interface Cards" section earlier in this chapter for more information). Also, a NIC that offers *bus mastering* will perform better than one that doesn't; bus mastering just means that the NIC can move data around without bothering the server CPU about every little detail. For a heavily used server, you may want to use a switching hub with one Fast Ethernet port, and connect that port to a Fast Ethernet NIC in the server. The other hub ports can then connect to workstations running regular Ethernet NICs. You can also use multiple NICs for larger networks, as Chapter 12 discusses.

Battery backup

Every server should have a battery backup unit to keep the server running in case of a power cut. Chapter 8 discusses how to properly size and connect an *Uninterruptible Power Supply* (UPS). These devices not only provide battery power, they also provide protection against potentially harmful voltage surges and irregularities.

Data backup

Somewhere you need to have hardware that can create copies of the operating data that resides on server hard drives, in case a server drive ever fails. A few years ago, you had one choice: magnetic tape. That's still the best option for most small businesses, but you now have the new choices of removable magnetic disks and writable optical disks (see Figure 7-10).

Figure 7-10:
Tape,
removable
cartridge
disk, and
optical disc
media each
have unique
advantages
and dis-
advantages.

Tape

Magnetic tape technology has evolved to provide high reliability, high
capacity, and the lowest cost per megabyte of any backup device. Today's
small business networks can use a variety of tape technologies for backing
up servers (and even workstations). Here are the main ones:

✔ *Quarter Inch Committee* **(QIC)** is an organization that creates standards for drives using 0.25" wide tape. Defined standards go all the way
   up to 13GB, and many variants exist. The most popular is *Travan,* an
   inexpensive standard using 0.315" tapes (I know, not 0.25", but it's still
   considered QIC) with longer lengths and higher densities than regular
   QIC tapes. Travan capacities range from 800MB to 10GB, competing
   with low-end 4mm drives (see next bullet), and can move data at rates
   from 10MB per minute to 20MB per minute. Most Travan drives don't
   perform *Read-After-Write* (RAW) verification, an important data integrity check, and are slower than 4mm or 8mm tape.

✔ **4mm or** *Digital Audio Tape* **(DAT)** is a popular Sony-licensed technology offering high capacity and good price/performance using small
   cartridges (2.9" x 2.1" x 0.4"). Cartridge capacity ranges from 4GB to
   24GB, and the speed of data transfer goes up to 2.4MB per second.

✔ **8mm** tape drives from Exabyte, Seagate, and Sony offer higher tape
   capacity than 4mm drives on slightly larger cartridges (3.75" x 2.5" x
   0.5"). Cartridge capacity ranges from 7GB to 25GB, and the speed of
   data transfer ranges from 0.5MB per minute to 6MB per minute.

✔ *Digital Linear Tape* **(DLT)** is a half-inch format using cartridges about
   twice the size of 4mm and 8mm tape with supporting capacities from
   10GB to 35GB and transfer rates of 1.25MB per second to 5MB per
   second. DLT is becoming a popular alternative to DAT and 8mm.

Tape drives can mount inside network servers or workstations, they can be self-contained external units that connect to a computer with a cable, or they can connect directly to the network with a standard twisted-pair or coax connection. If your network has just one server, installing an internal tape drive right into the server is simple, convenient, and inexpensive; use a SCSI connection for optimum speed. If you have more than one server, consider a drive that *hangs off* (cool networking slang for *connects directly to*) the network cable.

Despite their popularity, QIC and Travan aren't the best choices for network backups, although these technologies are fine for workstation backups and notebooks. Your network backup device really should have Read-After-Write (RAW) verification built into the hardware so you know without a doubt that your backup tapes are good. Whether you use 4mm, 8mm, or DLT for server backups depends on which you can get the best deal on; all three are excellent for small businesses.

If you're building, or already have a smaller network (total server hard drive capacity of 8GB or less), you're best off getting a tape drive that can back up an entire server (or at least an entire disk) onto a single tape so that you don't have to mess with manual tape swapping or *autoloaders*. Larger servers and networks benefit from autoloader tape drives that can load several tape cartridges without manual intervention, but you pay an extra thousand bucks or more for the convenience, so you may prefer to leave tape rotation up to the network administrator.

Top tape drive vendors include Exabyte, Seagate Technology, Hewlett-Packard, Iomega, and Sony.

Digital Versatile Disc (DVD)

The latest technology in the writable optical disk arena is the *Digital Versatile Disc,* or DVD. Unlike CD-R and CD-RW discs, DVD discs use both sides for recording. They also pack about four times as much information per square inch than CD-R and CD-RW do. The combination results in a capacity of between 5.2GB to 6.0GB for rewritable media. Because DVD discs are more rigid than CD discs, they can spin faster, providing fast data transfer rates.

Two specifications for rewritable DVD are fighting for market acceptance. *DVD-RAM* specifies 2.6GB per side and is supported by Toshiba, Hitachi, and Matsushita. *DVD-RW* specifies 3.0GB per side and is supported by Sony, NEC, Hewlett-Packard, and Philips. Time will tell which standard wins out, so it's early yet to be buying DVD for your network, but the technology is worth watching. DVD drives that adhere to the MultiRead standard will be able to read CD-ROM, CD-R, and CD-RW discs; the DVD-RW standard is more likely to support these earlier optical formats than the DVD-RAM standard.

Removable magnetic disks

Several companies have worked to advance removable magnetic disk technology in recent years. In particular, the Iomega Zip drive has set a new level of price/performance for cartridge disks; 100MB cartridges for Zip drives cost about $15 at the time of this writing, and the drives go for about $150. You can buy higher-capacity removable disks, such as the Iomega Jaz drive (1.0GB) and the Syquest SyJet (1.5GB), at proportionally higher cartridge costs. These devices can connect to a computer's parallel port or to a SCSI card inside the computer.

The cost per megabyte for these devices is much higher than tape, but disk cartridge drives are also much faster than comparably priced tape drives. If archival storage is all you need and you don't expect to do a lot of file recovery, tape or optical disk media is much less expensive over the long run. Tape and optical disk vendors provide better customer support, too. Removable magnetic disks are handy for backing up workstation data files and notebook computers, and they're a good way to mail files too large to fit on a diskette, but the disks are still too expensive to replace tape as your primary network backup technology.

Writable optical disks

Optical disks have several advantages over tape: Magnetic fields don't bother them, restoring files is faster, and the disks last longer (some vendors say 100 years, but no one's really sure). The drive and media cost is still higher than tape on a per-megabyte basis, but not dramatically so, and the media is much less expensive than removable magnetic disks.

Drawbacks? You may have to swap disks to do a full server backup, because these devices top out at about 650MB. The drives are much slower than 4mm and 8mm tape and magnetic cartridge drives. And the hardware doesn't perform automatic Read-After-Write checks, so you have to use backup software that performs a separate verification step, which takes as long as the backup itself, if you want to be sure your files copy accurately.

- ✔ ***Compact Disc-Recordable* (CD-R)** drives create discs that any CD-ROM drive can read, but you can only write data to them once; the discs aren't reusable like tape or magnetic cartridges. CD-R drives are in the $500 range, and the 600MB discs cost between $2 and $5.

- ✔ ***Compact Disc-ReWritable* (CD-RW)** drives are newer than CD-R and permit reuse of the same disc. CD-RW drives can also read regular CD-ROMs and CD-R discs. Regular CD-ROM drives can't read CD-RW discs, though, because CD-RW discs aren't as reflective as CD-ROMs or CD-Rs. Next-generation CD-ROM drives with *MultiRead* technology will be able to read CD-RW media. CD-RW discs cost much more than CD-R discs at $25 and are good for about a thousand reuses.

Vendors of CD-R and CD-RW drives include Hewlett-Packard, Philips, Yamaha, and Smart and Friendly. (Yes, that's actually the company's name.)

Workstation Hardware

The computers you choose to be user workstations can be less powerful in some ways than your server computers, and more powerful in other ways. Here are the ways that workstations typically differ from servers:

- **A lonesome CPU.** Typical business workstations need only a single CPU. In the Intel world, a Pentium works fine with Windows 95, a Pentium with MMX works better for users running multimedia applications, and a Pentium Pro or Pentium II works better with Windows NT Workstation.

- **Less RAM.** You can get by with 16MB of RAM on a workstation, but for the extra hundred bucks or so, 32MB runs noticeably faster. Most users can't tell the difference between 32 and 64, though.

- **Slower hard drive.** EIDE hard drives are fast enough for most workstations; you don't need SCSI in your workstations unless users are doing something unusual. One gigabyte of storage capacity is fine for most users.

- **Slower NIC.** The Network Interface Card can plug into an ISA slot in user workstations. Users who spend a lot of time moving files to and from servers may need a NIC that plugs into a PCI slot and may want Fast Ethernet rather than regular Ethernet. If you use Token Ring, use the 16Mbps variety.

- **No UPS.** User workstations rarely have battery backup units (also called *UPSs,* or *Universal Power Supplies*), but you may want to install them if you have frequent power cuts. You can get a good one for $100 or so.

- **More creature comforts.** Consider an ergonomic (angled) keyboard for your workstations if it's an upgrade option. These are great for users who spend a lot of time typing.

- **Less need for a dedicated backup device.** Workstations don't usually need their own backup device. You can set up your network to perform workstation backups across the wire. However, portable 2 to 3GB QIC Travan tape drives costing only $200 to $250 for the drive and $20 to $30 for tapes may have some appeal, especially for notebooks. These connect to a workstation's parallel port and manage around 10MB per minute. Vendors include Iomega and Seagate.

- **More bleary-eyed scrutiny.** Workstations *do* need good monitors. Today's software benefits from 17" screens, but if you can't afford those, don't go any less than 15".

Printers

Nearly all small companies use a shared laser printer for most of their printing needs, and (as I mention in Chapter 1) sharing such an expensive device is one of the key advantages of a Local Area Network (LAN). You can add a dot-matrix impact printer if you need to print multiple-part forms. If you need color printouts, color inkjet printers provide cost-effective medium-quality output, and more expensive devices (*color laser, thermal wax,* and *dye sublimation* printers) offer more accurate, higher-resolution output that may be useful if your business does art and graphic design.

Laser printers with the "network" designation can handle 50,000 to 100,000 pages per month, which may be overkill for your LAN. A high-end desktop laser printer that handles 20,000 to 40,000 pages per month may do just fine. However, I don't recommend so-called *personal* laser printers for shared network use — they're usually slow, not sturdily built, and have paper trays that are too small for anyone who wants to stay sane.

The laser printer resolution you need depends on whether you print graphics or just text. For text, 300 dots per inch (dpi) looks fine and 600 dpi looks great; for graphics, 1,200 dpi looks noticeably crisper. The higher the resolution, the more memory your printer needs, the more network traffic you have, and the slower the printer spits out pages, so don't use 1,200 dpi unless you need it.

As for speed, most businesses are happy with a rated text speed of 12 pages per minute (ppm) or faster. If you don't do a lot of printing, you can go with a slightly slower printer and save some bucks, but check the page per month rating on any models you consider to make sure it's adequate for you.

Your business will likely depend heavily on your network laser printer. Get a good unit from an experienced vendor such as Lexmark or Hewlett-Packard. You probably don't have to get their fastest or most rugged model, but you'll be glad you went with a reliable brand.

Printers that come with their own Network Interface Card (NIC) built in save you a step during installation, but you can usually get a cheaper NIC through a mail order service if you don't mind installing it yourself. If you buy a printer that doesn't work with a NIC, you can still put it anywhere on the network by buying a printer sharing device (3Com and Hewlett-Packard sell them). Such a device hooks to the network on one end, and to your printer's parallel port on the other.

Modems

You can install a modem in a network server and share it among all network users with the help of software, as I discuss in Chapter 10. You can also connect some modems directly to a network cable; these more expensive devices have the name *network modem* (a prominent vendor is Shiva). If you find that a single shared modem isn't enough, you can set up a shared group of modems, called a *modem pool*. You can buy a modem pool with four to eight modems on a single circuit board that plugs into a computer expansion slot, or you can get a rack-mounted system that lets you add modems as needed to meet demand. A bundled package consisting of a computer, network connection, and modem pool is called a *communications server*.

Whatever route you go, if you use regular dial-up modems, your two-way communications speed is limited to 33.6 kilobits per second (Kbps) at the time of this writing. Newer and not-yet-standardized technology permits 56 Kbps in the receiving direction only.

Modems vary widely in their ability to deal with line noise, so if you want to connect at near the 33.6 Kbps speed, check out recent tests in computer magazines.

If you connect your network to the public Internet, you may want a faster link than a plain dial-up connection. If so, consider an *ISDN (Integrated Services Digital Network)* line, which your local phone company can install — presuming you work in an area where the service is available (most major cities). ISDN connections support speeds of up to 128 Kbps by using digital connections at both ends, and use special hardware at your office called a *terminal adapter*. You pay a monthly fee for the ISDN line, and if you move your office, the line doesn't go with you; you have to run a new one to your new location. (The phone companies are wealthy for a reason.)

CD-ROMs

If you want to share certain CD-ROMs with various network users, you have several options. You can hook several CD-ROM drives to a file server, you can share several workstation CD-ROMs in peer-to-peer fashion, or you can install a network CD-ROM drive sharing unit.

If you don't require instantaneous access, consider a CD-ROM changer, or *jukebox*. Units that hang directly off the network and can handle four disks are available for under $500. Faster systems use multiple single-disk drives stacked in a tower, but they're more expensive. Make sure that whatever you buy comes with software for your Network Operating System.

Follow licensing agreements when sharing CD-ROMs among multiple users. Vendors may sell CD-ROM software with a single-user license or a network license; you want the network license if you plan to share the software on a networked drive. Some single-user license products don't even work if you attempt to run them as shared software.

Part III
Do It! Setting Up Your Network

The 5th Wave®   By Rich Tennant

"I guess you could say this is the hub of our network."

In this part . . .

Installing a computer network involves many steps that you can do yourself, and a few that a little expert help can make much easier. Today's hardware and software vendors are making strides in the ease-of-use department. They're learning that they need to make network setup simpler if they want to attract small businesses, because most of you don't want to hire expensive consultants to do the whole thing for you. By doing what you feel comfortable doing yourself, and getting some assistance with the trickier bits, you can save big bucks and gain a much better understanding of your network in the process.

My goal in this part's three chapters is to lay out the main steps you need to take in order to set up any network, so that when you read the installation instructions for your specific products, you can smile knowingly ("Yeah, I remember Glenn telling me about this") rather than frown in confusion ("What in blazes is a *terminating resistor?*"). First, I go through the basics of installing network hardware, from running cable to plugging in Network Interface Cards. Next, I discuss setting up network software to enable both peer-to-peer and client/server networks to share files and printers. The last chapter in this part helps you link your network to the outside world. Have at it, and have fun!

Chapter 8

Put on Your Jeans and Grab a Screwdriver

. . . .

In This Chapter

▶ Cabling your network

▶ Installing the server and workstation computers

▶ Setting up a shared printer

▶ Testing the hardware installation

. . . .

*W*ith a little planning, a gung-ho attitude, and a couple of colleagues to lend a hand, you can probably install your server and workstation hardware in a day. Read this chapter first, though — maybe read it twice.

> "There is no point in paying other people to screw things up
> when you can easily screw them up yourself for far less money."
> (Dave Barry, *The Taming of the Screw,* Rodale Press)

My father was visiting me one day at the research lab where I used to work as a design engineer. The facility reeked of fresh paint, and he commented that he loved that smell. I didn't understand then, but I do now: Fresh paint smells like progress. I feel a little bit the same way around fresh new computers — all those cardboard boxes, shiny monitors, cables, and metal boxes really *do* mean progress. You're doing something that will help your business communicate, compete, and succeed. It's all kind of exciting (especially if you drop a really expensive component on the floor).

Computer hardware can be a little intimidating, but installing all this stuff really isn't too hard anymore. The instructions now come in bona fide English and not badly translated Taiwanese ("The cable please keyboard into round connection delightfully connect with pushing"). Some computer vendors even give you a big printed cardboard sheet with numbered, illustrated steps, so you may not even need the manual at all. I do recommend at least skimming the manual, though, even if you've done this sort of thing before. Reading the manuals is *de rigeur* if you're doing something fancy like installing your own hard drives.

The key point to remember when installing computer hardware is to give yourself enough time so that you don't have to rush. I like to do this sort of work on a weekend — the phones don't ring and you can focus on the work at hand. You don't have to unseat employees from their workspaces, you can wear cutoffs and a T-shirt, and you can have a drink or two (see chapter title). If something doesn't go right, you can get on the phone Monday and fix it Monday evening.

Buy computers with most of what you need already installed. If you can get your supplier to put in the right amount of memory, disk space, and a *Network Interface Card* (NIC) in each machine, you can skip much of the more technical stuff in this chapter and the installation goes *much* faster.

So now you're ready to get to work. You need a pocketknife and one of those little computer screwdriver kits that you can pick up at most computer superstores or Radio Shack. You may also want to have a flashlight on hand for looking inside the computer when you install the NICs, or for peering across the false ceiling if you run wires up there.

Don't use magnetized screwdrivers! They can damage certain computer parts. You need to get a nonmagentized screwdriver kit that is specifically for use with electronic and computing devices.

Running the Cable

You can run your network cable even before you start buying computers; doing so is wise because by running the cable first, you can test the network connection when you set up the server and workstations. The simple steps are to place the hub, decide if you want permanent or temporary wiring, run the wire, and test it. See Chapter 7 for details on all the hardware — things like *coaxial cable, hubs, twisted-pair cable,* and so on — that I mention in this chapter.

Placing the hub

The *hub,* remember, is the box into which all your computer network cables connect. You need to put it where you can get to it easily for troubleshooting purposes, but preferably not somewhere that sees a lot of foot traffic or indoor office whiffle golf. Most important, place your hub as centrally as possible, because you can't run twisted-pair cable more than 100 meters between hub and workstation. That sounds like a long run, but remember that network cable doesn't generally run as the crow flies: It makes right-angle turns and has to go over ceilings — all of which adds length.

If you need more distance, you can place two hubs in your office and link them with thin coaxial cable, effectively creating a single hub as far as the network software is concerned. Most hubs come with a special connector for this purpose. The coax run can extend to 185 meters, giving you a setup similar to the one shown in Figure 8-1. Many hubs let you *daisy chain* them (that is, connect them in series) with twisted-pair cable, but you can't place them as far apart as you can with thin coax, and you use up two connection ports that you could otherwise use for computers.

Installing permanently, or for the time being

Running cable through the walls makes for a cleaner installation, gets the cabling away from places where people can damage it, and reduces the likelihood of someone breaking his or her neck. However, the decision of whether you go for in-wall cable or a more temporary arrangement depends on how long you think you'll stay in your present location. I usually advise companies to go permanent if they plan to stay put for at least two years.

If your office isn't already wired for networking and you want to run cable through the walls, negotiate the cost with your landlord. Some will split it with you, as it's a permanent improvement that makes the space more attractive to future tenants. If the landlord doesn't go for this, you can at least take the wallplates and patch panel with you when you move out (along with the light bulbs, doorknobs, and that little roller the toilet paper goes on).

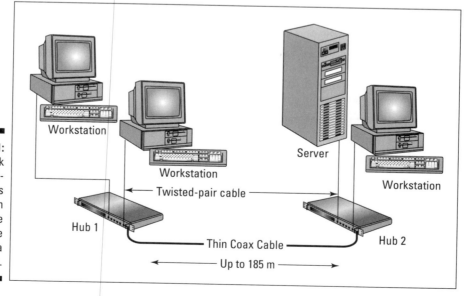

Figure 8-1:
You can link two twisted-pair hubs with thin coax cable if distance is a problem.

Running the wire

If you go for a permanent installation, I suggest contracting it out to an experienced cable installer. Professionals have expensive test equipment that's necessary in order to ensure a solid end-to-end connection that meets industry specs. Testing is especially important when you have wallplates and patch panels in the picture (see the following tip). Installers also have specialized tools for fitting cable wire ends onto *RJ-45 modular plugs* (the kind that look like telephone plugs, only slightly larger).

Tell the installer you want *wallplates* (jacks on the wall, a lot like a telephone jack) at each computer location. Make sure they meet your cable specifications (typically *Category 5* — see Chapter 7). Connect computers to the wallplates using prewired *patch cables,* which are simply short network cables with a plug at both ends — one for the wallplate and one for the NIC in the computer. You can buy them from places like Data Comm Warehouse (http://www.warehouse.com). That way, if the part of the cable between the wall and the computer gets damaged, you don't have to splice cable or run new wire through the walls; you just replace the patch cable.

The multiport wallplate that you want near the hub goes by the name *patch panel.* Some installers may suggest putting in a *punch-down block* as well (a wire connector panel similar to what you'd find in a phone wiring closet), but I've happily wired many networks without one.

The 100-meter distance limitation applies to the total length of cable between the computer and hub, *including* the patch cable.

Here are a few do's and don'ts if you decide to run the wiring yourself:

✔ **Make sure everything you buy, from cable to connectors to wallplates, is Category 5 compliant.** (The cheaper stuff isn't.)

✔ **If you aren't running your cable through walls, get prewired cables of the correct length.** That way, you don't have to bother with putting plugs on the cable. Always get a slightly longer cable than you think you need.

✔ **If you go for temporary cabling, look into that plastic WireMold stuff that you can buy at the home improvement centers.** (WireMold looks like a little speed bump with a groove in the bottom to hide the cabling.) You can cover the cable with the WireMold to protect it and everyone in the office. This method is much better than running cable under carpeting — the carpet tacks can puncture the cable jacket.

✔ **If you *are* running through walls (the wiring, that is), install wallplates and a patch panel, just as a pro would do.** You can use a short-bladed jigsaw to cut through the wallboard, and plastic or metal anchors to seat the mounting screws. Unbent coat hangers are handy for fishing the cable.

- ✔ **Don't run LAN cable near anything electrical or magnetic.** This includes copiers, refrigerators, big coffeemakers, fluorescent lights, and elevator motors. I heard of one do-it-yourselfer who ran LAN cable through the same holes in the concrete roof support beams where the fluorescent lighting power cables ran. Every time anyone turned the lights on or off, the network went down!

- ✔ **If your network is going into a space with heavy manufacturing equipment, consider using *Shielded Twisted Pair* (STP) or thin coaxial cable rather than *Unshielded Twisted Pair* (UTP).** See Chapter 7 for more on these cable types.

- ✔ **Use Teflon-coated, fire-resistant cable if you plan on running the cable through walls or over false ceilings.**

- ✔ **Avoid sharp-angle bends.** Cable turns should have at least a 2-inch radius, and tie down the cable every few yards with plastic *wire ties* or *zip ties* (you can buy them at any hardware store).

- ✔ **Label the cable ends so that you know which one goes where.**

Testing the cable

If your cable runs consist of single prewired lengths of twisted-pair cable that you run along baseboards or over false ceilings, and you've taken care to keep the total runs under 100 meters, you can probably get by without testing. If you run LAN cable through walls and use wallplates, a patch panel, and patch cables, test the cable for compliance with the Category 5 specs — especially if you built the connectors onto the cable yourself. (No offense — I know that I'm a klutz when it comes to wiring connectors.)

Cable testing is best left to experts, but if you want to do your own tests, beg or borrow a good LAN cable tester, such as those made by Fluke or Microtest. These devices measure *resistance* (how much the cable resists the flow of electricity), *attenuation* (loss of signal over time and distance), and *noise* (interference). If the cable tester indicates a problem, fix it now, before you start hooking up computers. You may have a bad connection, an overly long cable, or a cable running too close to other electrical devices.

Don't Let Power Corrupt

Before you actually install the hardware, verify all the outlets in your office for correct wiring. The procedure is super easy. Hop over to Radio Shack or another electronics store and buy an outlet tester (the "electrician's night light") for $10. The tester is a little plastic gizmo that plugs into a wall socket and lights up. The lights tell you if the electrician wired the outlet properly. (If you use extension cords, especially antique ones, you should also use the tester to verify *their* wiring.)

If the lights tell you that one or more outlets has a problem (common in older buildings), or if you can't plug in the tester without sawing off the third prong, do *not* plug in your computers. Go directly to the phone, and have your landlord get a licensed electrician to fix the wiring and/or ground the outlets. Reversed polarity can have three possible results: sporadic communication problems between devices, total destruction of one of the devices, or (if you touch both devices simultaneously) death. Yes, I'm trying to shock you (sorry).

You shouldn't have to pay for fixing bad wiring. Drop the hint that bad wiring is a fire and safety hazard, and the building manager should take care of it pronto — as long as the owner hasn't spent a lot of time at the racetrack recently and taken out a large fire insurance policy (in which case I recommend moving). The last thing you want to have to troubleshoot is electrical power problems or electrocuted employees.

Installing the Server

After the cabling is in and the AC power checks out, you can set up your computers.

This book doesn't cover all the nuances of hardware installation for specific computer types. If you use PCs in your network, check out *Upgrading and Fixing PCs For Dummies* (Andy Rathbone, IDG Books Worldwide, Inc.), which provides more details and diagrams.

Before you start, if you work in a carpeted office, get barefoot and shed your sweater. That way, you get into the bohemian spirit of things, and on a more practical level, you're less likely to fry circuit boards with static electricity. Also, take off any jewelry you're wearing around your neck or wrists or on your hands; it can scratch and sever the electrical traces on Network Interface Cards. In the next section, "Adding disk drives," I include an additional Remember icon that deals with static when you are actually working inside the computer.

Here are the typical steps to install a server machine:

1. **Unbox everything and throw away all those annoying plastic baggies and twistees.**

   Gather the pieces of paper together and read any that scream in large type READ ME RIGHT NOW. Be sure to keep all the paper documentation together and out of harm's way.

2. **Even though you may need to install a Network Interface Card, tape drive, or additional disk drives, test the computer first *as shipped*.**

Place the system unit (the main part of the computer) vertically on the floor if it's a tower, or horizontally on a desktop if it's a desktop — but in any case, place the unit so that you can easily get to the back panel. I usually like to pull a desk away from the wall so I can walk around both sides of the computer for access. And be sure to put the system unit where it doesn't wobble. *Don't plug it in yet. . . .*

3. **Plug the round keyboard cable into the keyboard connector on the back panel. Do the same with the mouse, which usually has a similar round connector.** If the mouse is a serial type, which is less common, it has a "D"-shaped nine-pin connector.

   If these cables aren't color-coded to the sockets on the computer's back panel, study the back panel for little stamped or printed icons that look like a bad artist's rendering of a keyboard and mouse.

4. **Set the server monitor near the computer at roughly eye level and connect it to the computer.**

   The monitor has two cables: one that goes to a connector (usually a "D" type shell connector with screws on the side to hold it in place on the computer, and one for AC power). Connect them in that order, and then turn on the monitor. Let it warm up a minute.

5. **If your server is preconfigured with a Network Interface Card, connect a patch cable between the network connection on the back panel and the wallplate.**

   Make sure the connectors are clean (blow on them to remove any dust) and that you leave plenty of slack in the cable.

6. **Plug in the computer, turn it on, and watch the messages that pop up on the screen.**

   Don't worry if many of them are meaningless to you at this point. If you bought a machine designated as a server, you may see instructions on the screen for setting up your Network Operating System, or the Network Operating System itself may load into memory.

7. **Shut down the server.**

   Always shut down a server with the keyboard first, before you turn off the power switch. Choose an *Exit* or *Quit* command if you see one on the screen. If the Network Operating System itself has started, then the command to shut down the server depends on the network: Type **down** to shut down a Novell server, or click Start➪Shut Down for a Windows NT server. When all is quiet, kill the power.

If your server is preconfigured with adequate disks, a Network Interface Card, and tape drive, then skip to the "Power backup connection" section later in this chapter. If you have to add equipment to your server, read on.

Adding disk drives

If you buy a server that doesn't have as much disk capacity as you need, you have to add a disk drive or two to the machine. The server should already have the appropriate circuitry installed (a *SCSI,* or *Small Computer Systems Interface,* circuit board). If not, you need to install one. Adaptec is the market leader, and its SCSI controllers come with an excellent configuration program called EZ-SCSI that makes the job of adding new drives and other SCSI equipment a cinch.

I suggest using an external disk enclosure for your hard drives. Even in a small network, keeping your hard drives in a separate box makes replacing them much easier when they fail, because you don't have to rip into your server machine. The basic steps are as follows:

1. **Install the SCSI controller in the server.**

2. **Install the drives into the external enclosure.**

3. **Connect the drives to each other in a *daisy chain* (in series, with the first drive in the series connected to the disk drive controller, the second drive connected to the first, and so on) with the supplied flat ribbon cables.**

4. **Connect the disk enclosure to the SCSI controller using the thick and ungainly SCSI cable you can buy from the enclosure vendor.**

   Use the shortest external SCSI cable you can in order to minimize problems; the SCSI-2 specification puts the maximum combined length of all cables in the chain at 6 meters (about 18 feet) but I prefer to keep the total run to 12 feet or less.

Your controller user's manual and hard drive installation instructions should cover all the details of installation that are specific to your particular device. If your hard drive doesn't come with printed installation instructions, you can usually find them on the manufacturer's Web site.

Whenever you do anything inside a computer's system unit, take precautions against static electricity. Do the work at one sitting, and frequently touch the computer's metal frame to ground yourself. The pros use an *antistatic wrist strap* that clips to the computer frame, which is an even better idea if you can find a computer store that sells one. Sometimes you get a disposable wrist strap with a new hard drive.

To install a new drive, you typically remove a plastic front cover, slide the drive into an available bay (either in the server, or in an external enclosure as I recommend), and secure it with two to four mounting screws — then again, every drive can be a bit different. For example, you may also need to ground the device with a separate wire if the computer has plastic mounting rails instead of metal ones. In any case, here are the key points unique to SCSI drives:

✔ **If your computer contains both PCI and ISA slots for adding new circuit boards, buy a SCSI controller that works with PCI and install it into a PCI slot.** Simply remove the plastic or metal slot cover at the slot's back edge (save the screw!), place the board's connector into the slot, and push down while gently alternating pressure from the board's top left edge to its top right edge until it snaps into place (you can usually hear or feel it *kerchunk* into place when the board is properly seated in the slot). Secure the board with the screw.

✔ **If you're using PC hardware, assign the SCSI controller its own unique *interrupt number* when you run its configuration program.** The interrupt number (also called the *IRQ*) ranges from 0 to 15, and specifies a particular wire the controller uses to communicate with the computer's CPU *(Central Processing Unit)*. Your computer manual should tell you which interrupts are available; 10 and 11 usually are. If the manual doesn't say, the diagnostics diskette that comes with most computers should be able to tell you. If the SCSI controller is compatible with the Plug-and-Play standard, be glad, because Windows 95 selects an appropriate IRQ number automatically.

✔ **If you're using PC hardware, assign the SCSI controller its own unique *upper memory address* when you run its configuration program.** The upper memory address is a specific location in the PC's memory space that the SCSI controller uses for managing read and write activity. No two devices in a PC are allowed to use the same upper memory address. Again, if the SCSI controller is compatible with Plug-and-Play, Windows 95 handles this assignment for you. Otherwise, the controller setup program lets you try different addresses until you find one that doesn't prompt an error message. The controller manual should offer a variety of specific addresses you can try.

✔ **If you're using Mac hardware, you already have a SCSI connector on the back of the computer, as well as one inside.** You don't have to worry about the interrupt number, but you do have to pay attention to the following two bullets.

✔ **A SCSI device chain must have electrical termination at both ends, but not in between.** First, make sure that the controller is terminated (most are — the manual should say). Then, install a *terminating resistor* on the last disk in the chain, and remove the resistor from any disks in the middle of the chain. The resistor is usually a tiny electrical component with a single row of little pins that plug into a socket on the disk drive; sometimes it's enclosed in a plastic plug-in module. You usually get a terminating resistor in the box with your SCSI hard drive.

✔ **Make sure each device has a unique *SCSI address* ID, a number from 0 to 7.** Usually, the SCSI controller (also called the *host adapter*) uses 7, the first disk in the chain starts at 0, and additional disks go up from 0 in sequence. You set the ID using little plastic jumper blocks that slide over protruding pins on the disk drives; refer to the drive documentation for the details.

Figure 8-2 shows a sample SCSI disk setup with three hard drives. I don't show it in the figure, but you also need to connect power cables to the disk drives so that they get electricity to drive the motors. The power cord connectors usually have a white plastic shield with two beveled corners; most computers have two or three unused ones flopping around inside the system unit.

If all this seems way too complicated, get some expert help. But if you tackle the job yourself, don't worry; most of the cables only connect one way, and it's hard to damage a SCSI device merely by connecting it improperly.

Disk striping

Disk *striping* (not *stripping*) allows you to set up your server so that it treats multiple hard drives as a single, large hard drive, which some network administrators prefer in order to simplify the server file system organization. Striping involves writing data across two or more disks, but it isn't the same as *mirroring* or *duplexing* (see the next two sections), and it doesn't provide *fault tolerance* (the ability to operate without interruption during a software or hardware component failure). A group of striped drives that

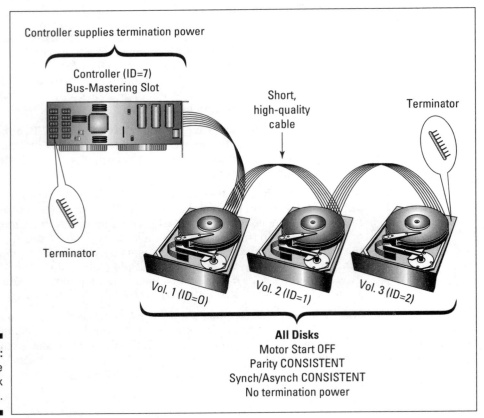

Controller supplies termination power

Controller (ID=7) Bus-Mastering Slot

Short, high-quality cable

Terminator

Terminator

Vol. 1 (ID=0)   Vol. 2 (ID=1)   Vol. 3 (ID=2)

All Disks
Motor Start OFF
Parity CONSISTENT
Synch/Asynch CONSISTENT
No termination power

Figure 8-2:
An example SCSI disk chain.

appear to the server as a single drive is called a *stripe set*. Windows NT Server supports disk striping, and you can specify that you want it when installing the Network Operating System.

Disk mirroring

In a simple server disk setup, you're living life dangerously. If one drive or controller fails, the server doesn't work, and you have to fix or replace the device while the server is down. Such a failure can be inconvenient, because everyone on the LAN uses the server. Fortunately, you have several options, including disk mirroring (see next paragraph), for making your server more *fault tolerant,* as the technicians say. These options all involve having more than one hard drive in the server, and fall under the generic acronym *RAID,* which stands for *Redundant Array of Inexpensive Disks.* (The opposite of RAID is *SLED,* which stands for *Single Large Expensive Disk.* A *Beat-up Old Broken Single Large Expensive Disk* is a . . . never mind.)

RAID Level 0 is disk striping (see previous section). *RAID Level 1* is disk *mirroring,* in which you install a twin for each hard drive in the server. The disk controller, usually a *SCSI host adapter* (see the "Adding disk drives" section) writes data to each drive in the mirrored pair more or less simultaneously, so that if one of the disks goes belly up, the other one effectively takes its place. You can then replace the dead drive after normal work hours without any employee downtime. The likelihood of both disks failing simultaneously is just about zero, although disk mirroring doesn't protect you from failure of the disk controller (see Figure 8-3). Novell IntranetWare supports disk mirroring without any additional software.

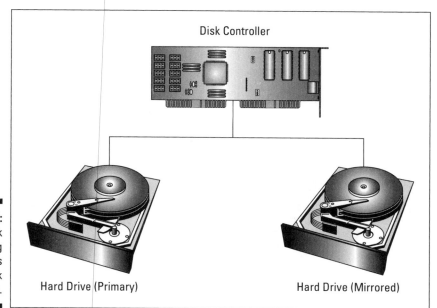

Figure 8-3:
Disk mirroring protects against disk drive failure.

Disk Controller

Hard Drive (Primary)   Hard Drive (Mirrored)

Disk duplexing

Disk *duplexing* is a refinement of mirroring and takes things a step further by not only providing twin disks, but also twin controllers and (usually) power supplies, so that if a controller or power supply fails, the server still works. (Duplexing is still considered RAID Level 1, however.) Novell IntranetWare and Windows NT Server both support disk duplexing with no additional software. Novell support is more sophisticated, allowing *split seeks* that send read requests to both disks — whichever disk can fetch the data first is the one the server uses.

Duplexing is better than mirroring, and with today's low-cost disks and controllers, it isn't too much more expensive than the SLED approach. Figure 8-4 shows the concept.

RAID Level 5

RAID Level 5 is the most popular form of RAID for larger servers. (RAID Levels 2, 3, and 4 don't see much use, so I don't discuss them.) You may want to consider RAID 5 as an alternative to duplexing, primarily because it doesn't require as many disk drives. With RAID 5, you need just one more disk than you use in a nonredundant situation, instead of twice as many. RAID 5 requires a minimum of three hard drives to work, and it normally uses a single disk controller, so it doesn't protect you from controller failure as duplexing does.

You can run RAID 5 in software (which demands a lot of the server's CPU resources) or in hardware (in the form of a RAID 5 disk controller that handles the processing chores). Windows NT Server supports software-based

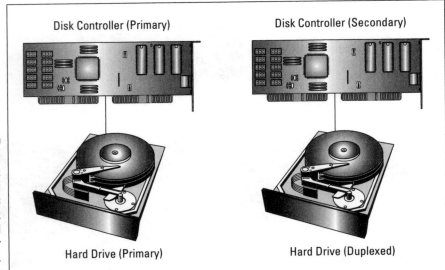

Figure 8-4: Disk duplexing protects against disk drive and controller failure.

Disk Controller (Primary)   Disk Controller (Secondary)

Hard Drive (Primary)   Hard Drive (Duplexed)

RAID 5 out of the box, although NT doesn't raise an alert if a drive fails, and you have to bring the server down to swap out a bad drive. You can add software to other Network Operating Systems in order to provide RAID 5 protection. RAID 5 disk controllers cost a lot more than regular controllers, but they're likely to outperform the software-based RAID feature that comes with Windows NT Server. However, RAID 5 disk controllers are less likely to outperform Novell-style duplexing.

My advice? If you run Windows NT Server, try the built-in software-based RAID and see if the performance is adequate; if not, go for a RAID disk controller. If you run Novell IntranetWare, use the built-in disk duplexing.

Adding a Network Interface Card

The physical procedure for adding a *Network Interface Card* (NIC) is the same as for adding a disk controller (see the first bullet in the "Adding disk drives" section earlier in this chapter). For a server, use a PCI slot. If you take my advice and buy NICs that you configure completely in software, either with a utility supplied by the NIC manufacturer or with a control panel in the Network Operating System, you don't have to muck about with jumpers or switches on the card. Otherwise, check the computer's manual or run its diagnostic test and find out which interrupts are available. Choose a free one and set the card to that interrupt number. If the card also requires memory addresses, follow the card manufacturer's suggestions stated in the manual. On a PC, D000 is usually free for the upper memory address, and 300 is usually fine for the base address. If these don't work, you'll have to yank out the NIC and try other possibilities. (You can begin to see why I favor cards that let you make all these settings in software!)

Installing a tape drive

If you buy a server with a built-in tape drive, it should work right out of the box. Otherwise, you have a decision to make: Do you want a tape unit that installs into the server, into a workstation, or directly onto the network?

- ✔ **If you put it into the server,** you get the fastest performance when backing up files from that server; however, if the tape drive fails, the server must come down in order for you to replace the drive.

- ✔ **If you put it into a workstation,** tape drive performance suffers when you do a server backup because the data has to cross the LAN cable; however, device failure isn't as big a deal because you only have to bring down one user workstation.

- ✔ **If you put it directly on the network,** you spend a little more, but the drive runs faster than a workstation-based device, and when it needs repair or replacement, no computers have to come down. You need a tape drive designed specifically to work directly on the network, known as a *net-direct device*. Such devices get their own *node* (location) on the network, instead of having to be installed in a workstation or server.

For a single-server network where users keep most of their data on the server, installing the tape drive in your server is probably best. When your network grows to two or more servers (or if it starts life that way), the net-direct drive may make the most sense.

Installing a tape drive into a server computer is very similar to installing a hard drive (see the "Adding disk drives" section earlier in this chapter). The tape drive slides into an empty bay inside the system unit, and you secure it with screws. Set the SCSI ID number, connect the drive to your SCSI controller daisy chain, and plug a terminating resistor into it if the tape drive is the last device in the chain (don't forget to remove the terminating resistor from the device that used to be last in the SCSI chain). You may also need to ground the device with a separate wire if the computer has plastic mounting rails instead of metal ones. Connect a power cable, and you're done.

Installing a net-direct tape drive is very simple. Just connect one end of a twisted-pair cable to the modular plug on the drive, the other to a network hub, and follow the vendor's instructions for installing the software.

Power backup connection

A power failure that cuts power to the file server can cause your files and directories to turn into complete mush, as well as cause users to lose precious data. Power failure can also throw duplexed disks out of sync, and make for a time-consuming recovery operation. Fortunately, protecting your server is fairly easy. The simplest (and cheapest) protection comes in the form of a battery, specifically, an *Uninterruptible Power Supply* (UPS), which connects between the AC wall outlet and the server (see Figure 8-5). You can buy these devices from manufacturers such as American Power Conversion, Best Power Technology, and Panamax (see Appendix B for contact information).

A good power backup unit does three things: It provides battery power to run your server for a while during a power cut; during normal operation, it conditions the AC power by filtering out electrical noise; and it provides surge protection so that voltage spikes don't damage your equipment.

You have to get the right size UPS for your server: If the UPS isn't beefy enough, its circuit breaker trips and you're left with no protection. American Power Conversion provides a handy sizing utility at `http://www.apcc.com/english/itool/size/index.htm`. Also, every time you add disk drives or other power-hungry devices to your server, take another look at the UPS rating to see if your power backup unit can handle the new load.

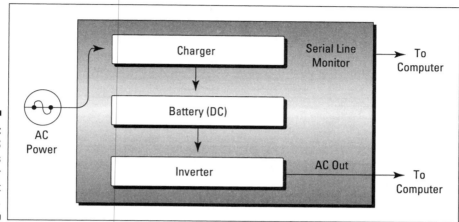

Figure 8-5:
A UPS
protects
your server
against
power cuts.

I know we're talking servers here, but don't forget to put a UPS on every critical network component. Hubs and network modems may also need power backup, as may selected workstations (the boss's computer comes to mind). You usually don't worry about printers, because a power cut doesn't hurt them, and a user can always print again later if the printer cuts off.

Installing a UPS is a simple matter of plugging it in and then plugging the server into the UPS. If you want to get fancy, you can install a cable between the UPS and a server serial port so that the UPS can tell the server about a power cut and the server can shut itself down in an orderly fashion. You have to install special software (usually provided by the UPS vendor) onto the server for this to work, but it's a good idea, especially if you leave your servers running at night (which you should definitely do, by the way, so that you can schedule unattended backups when nobody's working).

Server mirroring and clustering

Power backup doesn't protect a server from other sorts of faults, such as a memory module that suddenly develops amnesia. The next level of reliability, therefore, is to provide another server (or more) that can step into the breach when a primary server fails.

If your business is such that you can't afford for your LAN to be down even for the time it would take to bring a spare server online, you can consider *server mirroring* (see Figure 8-6) or *server clustering*. In either case, your network stays up and running if a server crashes or if you need to add memory or perform preventive maintenance on one of the servers. Whether the cost is worth it depends on how critical the server is to your business operations, but mirroring or clustering can kick LAN availability from the usual 95 percent up to 99 percent or better.

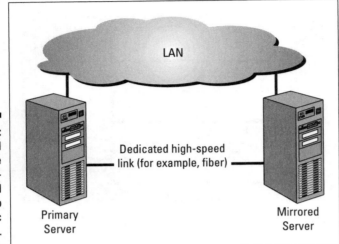

Figure 8-6:
Mirrored
servers use
a high-
speed
interface to
stay in sync
at all times.

A *mirrored server* (or *hot standby* server, as some call it) is a twin of its primary server, and does exactly what the primary server does. The two machines communicate via a high-speed link, such as a fiberoptic cable. If the primary server crashes, the mirrored server takes over without users noticing anything, but the mirrored server adds little to the network's processing power when both machines are running. The Novell server mirroring implementation is called *System Fault Tolerance Level III,* or *SFT III* for short.

A *server cluster* consists of two or more machines that appear as a single computer and share disk drives between them (you definitely want an external disk enclosure in this setup). If one server in the cluster fails, another picks up the slack. When all the servers are running, a cluster runs faster than a mirrored server setup. Microsoft plans to offer limited clustering capability for Windows NT Server via its Cluster Server (Wolfpack) product; NCR offers Lifekeeper as an NT clustering solution; and Vinca Corp. offers clustering solutions as well.

If you install an extra server to mirror or cluster with your primary server, buy one that's the same make and model. If the two machines connect via fiberoptic cable, you may be able to put the two servers at different ends of the office, so if a file cabinet falls over on one machine, the other's okay. In any case, you can get the two machines up and running yourself, but get some expert help installing and configuring the server-to-server link.

Installing Workstations

The procedure for installing workstations is just about identical to that for installing a server (see the section "Installing the Server" earlier in this chapter), with the following exceptions:

✓ **When you get everything installed and power up the workstation, it should run whatever operating system comes preinstalled (Windows 95, Windows NT Workstation, Macintosh, and so on).**

✓ **Workstations often come with a ton of software preinstalled, most of which you want to remove. (I cover this in Chapter 9.)**

✓ **You generally don't have to add a disk drive, memory, a tape drive, or power backup to a workstation computer.** If you do add a disk, it's probably not a SCSI variety but rather an *Enhanced Integrated Drive Electronics* (EIDE) disk. EIDE disks are a lot simpler to add, and your computer user's manual should contain detailed instructions.

✓ **You can mirror disk drives on important client workstations just as you do with servers, but the software may not come with the workstation operating system.** You may need to buy disk-mirroring software from a vendor such as Octopus Technologies.

✓ **You can use an ISA slot for the Network Interface Card, unless you expect the user to spend a lot of time using files on the server, in which case a PCI slot is faster (and therefore better).**

✓ **Users spend much more time at workstations than the network administrator spends at the server console.** Therefore, spend some time properly positioning the screens and keyboards to minimize physical fatigue. The top of the screen needs to be at about eye level, and the keyboard should create about a 90-degree angle at the user's elbows. I also highly recommend that you buy ergonomic keyboards that split the keys into two angled groups — they're a fully compatible replacement for original keyboards.

Connecting a Printer

Compared to installing a server or workstation, installing a printer is a breeze. If you buy a laser printer with a built-in Network Interface Card (which I recommend), you simply unbox the printer, install the toner cartridge per the manual's instructions, and connect an available network cable to the plug in the back of the printer. If your printer doesn't have a built-in network connection, you can either buy one for it, or use a device (such as the Castelle OfficeConnect print server) that hooks into a network cable on one end, and to a printer's parallel port on the other. Power up the printer and punch a button or two (which ones depends on your printer model — check the manual that comes with it) on the device's front panel to print a test page. The first one usually looks crummy, so print up a dozen or so until the toner cartridge gets happy and the quality looks good.

Most printers offer several zillion options you can set on the front panel, but if you use a Windows or Macintosh network, don't worry too much about these. You can set nearly all of these options in software when you configure the workstation printer drivers, as I discuss in Chapter 9.

Testing the Hardware

Everything's plugged in and seems to be working great. Now the time has come to make *sure* it's working great by doing a little hardware testing. You don't want to go to Chapter 9 until all your hardware checks out thoroughly.

Watch the messages that appear when you first turn the power on. Do you see any words like *invalid, incompatible, error,* or *failure?* If you see Invalid Incompatible Error Failure all in one digital breath, then you're *really* in trouble. (Gotcha.) A startup error indicates that the computer may not be passing its *POST,* or *Power On Self Test.* Make a note of the message (be sure to include any numbers that may identify the exact type of error) and call the manufacturer or reseller.

If you have one, install and run a good diagnostics program, such as the Norton Diagnostics that comes with Symantec Norton Utilities, to test workstation memory and processor functions as well as disk drives. Even easier, if your workstation comes with a test diskette, use that; it should even work with server machines if it's a boot diskette that you pop in before powering up.

Check the diagnostic lights on your hub. Refer to the hub user's manual to interpret their meaning. Do the same thing with the Network Interface Cards in your workstations; the light or lights are near the cable connection at the back of the computer. If any of these lights indicate a problem, you may have a bad Network Interface Card, cable, or hub. Do a little component swapping to troubleshoot (you may want to read Chapter 15 first).

Check diagnostic lights on other devices that you've installed: hard drives, tape drives, and so on. Get to know these lights. For example, the lights on the excellent Exabyte Eliant tape drive even tell you when it's time to pop in a cleaning cartridge.

For your servers and power-protected workstations, test your Uninterruptible Power Supplies (UPSs) by yanking the power cord out of the wall while the protected computer is running. (By the way, this test may be just about the most fun a network administrator can have in an evening.)

Chapter 9

Brew the Coffee and Set Up Network Services

In This Chapter

▶ Installing basic networking software on workstations and servers

▶ Sharing files and printers on a peer-to-peer network

▶ Organizing the server on a client/server network

▶ Creating user and group accounts to make life simple

▶ Setting up client/server network printers for easy user access

▶ Configuring workstations for easy and intuitive network access

*N*etwork services are all the things that you want your network to do for your users. Primary among them (and the focus of this chapter) are file and print services, which enable users to share programs, data files, and printers. (Communications services may also be important to your company, and just so you know, I deal with them in Chapter 10.)

"I do not like work even if someone else does it."
(Mark Twain, quoted in *The Portable Curmudgeon*, NAL Books)

One guiding principle towers over all others when designing network services: Minimize the amount of work required to keep them running. In a peer-to-peer network, this principle implies that you give all the network users the know-how they need to share, protect, and *unshare* directories and printers. In a client/server network, this means that you create a server file and directory structure that's easy to maintain over time, and that you build user and group accounts that make personnel changes easy to handle. In any sort of network, you can minimize ongoing administration requirements by setting up file and print sharing services so that they're easy and intuitive for network users. The best networks feel like an extension of the user's own local computer, just as a well made and properly sized tennis racquet feels like a natural extension of the player's arm.

Installing Basic Workstation Software

Before you can set up file and printer sharing on your LAN *(Local Area Network)*, you have to install the basic networking nuts and bolts on each user workstation so that the workstations can communicate across the net. If you remember the *Weadock Integrated Network Knowledge* (WINK) model from Chapter 6, the three layers of software you need are the *network driver,* the *transport protocol,* and the *network client.* You need these layers whether you're running a peer-to-peer or a client/server network.

Each type of workstation operating system (for example, Windows 95 or Windows NT Workstation) has its own procedures for installing these software layers. Depending on the manufacturer and reseller from whom you bought your computers, some or all of these pieces may already be in place. Just in case they're not, I go through a brief overview of installing these layers on a Windows 95 workstation. All the action takes place in the Net-work control panel Configuration tab (see Figure 9-1). Other computer systems use different commands, but the overall approach is the same. (Windows NT Workstation uses an almost identical sequence as Windows 95, with the exception that version 4.0 doesn't support Plug-and-Play.)

Figure 9-1:
The
Windows 95
Network
control
panel
is your
command
center for
installing
basic
workstation
networking
software.

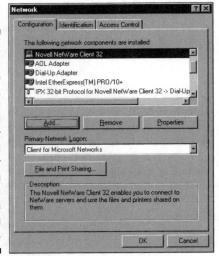

The network driver

The network driver is the software that speaks to the particular *Network Interface Card* (NIC) that you installed into the computer (or that the computer came with). Chapter 8 covers NIC installation.

If your NIC adheres to the Plug-and-Play standard, the first time you start Windows 95 after installing the NIC, Windows 95 states that it has found new hardware and is installing the software for it — when that happens, here's what you need to do:

1. **In the New Hardware Found dialog box, click** `Driver from disk provided by hardware manufacturer` **and then click OK.**

   An Install From Disk dialog box pops up.

2. **Pop the diskette that came with the NIC into the diskette drive, specify** `A:\` **as the path in the Install From Disk dialog box, and click OK.**

   The Select Network Device (or something similar) dialog box appears.

3. **Choose the correct NIC model and click OK.**

4. **Windows 95 now copies files from the diskette; if you are asked to insert the original Windows 95 CD-ROM, do so and click OK.**

5. **At the System Settings Change dialog box, click OK to restart the computer.**

If your NIC isn't a Plug-and-Play device, then the NIC installation process involves different steps:

1. **Open the Control Panel by clicking Start⇨Settings⇨Control Panel.**

2. **Double-click the Network icon.**

   The Network control panel appears.

3. **Click the Configuration tab if it isn't already in the foreground.**

4. **Click the Add button.**

5. **Click Adapter, and then click Add.**

   The Select network adapters dialog box pops up.

6. **Choose the NIC manufacturer and model in the Select Network adapters dialog box (see Figure 9-2).**

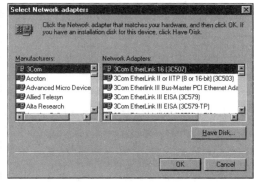

Figure 9-2:
Choose the NIC manu-facturer in the left window, and the model in the right window.

If the NIC appears in the list, then as soon as you select it and click OK, the computer asks you to pop in the Windows 95 CD-ROM so that it can get the necessary software. Otherwise, click the Have Disk button and put the diskette that came with the NIC into the diskette drive. Pick the correct model off the list that appears, and restart the computer when prompted to do so.

The NIC drivers on the Windows 95 CD-ROM may be old, so if you have a diskette from the NIC manufacturer, choose the Have Disk option even if the NIC appears in the Select Network adapters dialog box, and use the manufacturer's diskette.

After you restart Windows 95, go back to the Network control panel Configuration tab (Step 3 in the previous steps), click the NIC driver item (the green icon that looks like a letter "P") in the list of installed components, and then click the Properties button. The Resources tab shows the current hardware settings, and there should be no asterisks by any of them; if there are, you may have to change one or more settings to avoid a conflict with another device. You may have to select the cable type (click the Advanced tab in the Network control panel, and select the correct option under Transciever type) if you have a NIC with both coax and twisted-pair connectors.

As a final check, go to the System control panel Device Manager tab (Start⇨Settings⇨Control Panel, and then double-click the System icon) and find your new NIC by clicking the plus sign next to the Network adapters line (see Figure 9-3). Double-click your NIC and look for the message This device is working properly in the Device status box. If you see it, you're done! If not, you may have a conflict, in which case you can click the Resources tab and try a different interrupt or memory address setting (your NIC owner's manual should offer several suggestions). Or, you may not have seated the NIC fully in its slot. Finally, you may have a dead board — try another one to see if it works.

The transport protocol

If you're running IntranetWare for Small Business, Novell has created a handy program that automates the entire transport protocol *and* network client setup process. To run it:

1. **Pop the main IntranetWare CD-ROM into the workstation's CD-ROM drive.**

2. **Double-click the My Computer icon.**

3. **Double-click the CD-ROM drive icon (it shows a shiny disc).**

4. **Double-click the file CLNTINST.EXE.**

The famous and amazing CLNTINST.EXE program works its voodoo.

Figure 9-3:
Double-check your NIC installation in the System control panel.

Even if you're *not* using IntranetWare, the transport protocol layer is still easy to install:

1. **Open the Control Panel by clicking Start⇨Settings⇨Control Panel.**

   The main Control Panel window appears.

2. **Double-click the Network icon.**

   The Network control panel appears.

3. **Click the Configuration tab (if it isn't already in the foreground).**

4. **Click Add.**

   The Select Network Component Type dialog box pops up.

5. **Select Protocol.**

6. **Click Add.**

7. **Choose your Network Operating System (NOS) vendor in the left window, and the protocol you want in the right window.**

   Again, Windows 95 asks you to insert the Windows 95 CD-ROM so it can fetch the necessary files.

8. **Restart Windows 95 when prompted to do so by clicking OK in the System settings change dialog box.**

9. **Go back to the Network control panel Configuration tab (see the first three steps in this list).**

10. **Select the protocol in the list of installed components.**

11. **Click the Properties button.**

12. **Click the Advanced tab.**

13. **Set the *frame type*.**

    If you're running an Ethernet network and the IPX/SPX protocol, you need to set the *frame type* to whatever your server is using (most Ethernet networks use 802.2, but some use 802.3 or ETHERNET_II). If this setting doesn't match the other computers on the network, you can't communicate with them; it's a little like a language dialect (imagine someone from the Bronx trying to communicate with someone from London). The Auto setting in Windows 95 often doesn't work.

The network client

The third step is the easiest! Again, if you run the Novell CLNTINST program, it installs the Novell network client for you. Otherwise, go through the same drill as for the network protocol in the previous set of steps, but choose Client instead of Protocol at Step 5. At that point, each network client has its own particular options; for example, a Windows NT Server client installation requires that you specify whether to log on to a *domain controller* (a server that administers security), and if so, which one. After a restart, you can see your network server by double-clicking the Network Neighborhood desktop icon. If you haven't installed your server software yet, read on!

Installing the Network Operating System

If you buy a server computer for a client/server style network, it probably has the *Network Operating System* (NOS) preinstalled, with all three WINK software layers (see Chapter 6) snugly in place. I *highly* recommend going this route; this option wasn't available a few years ago, and speaking as someone who's done dozens of NOS installations (and consumed dozens of bottles of aspirin to relieve the pain), it's wonderfully convenient. If you don't, and you need to install a NOS onto a computer so that it can act as a server on your LAN, consider getting a consultant to do it *with* you. (I prefer "with" rather than "for" because watching an expert install your NOS is a useful educational experience.)

If you *really* want to do the installation yourself, you can do a fine job as long as you have some computer experience — just be patient and organized about it! Here's the typical sequence of events for installing a NOS:

1. **Read the installation instructions before you do anything.**

    When you're done, and you feel you understand the procedure fairly well, read 'em again.

2. Check the hardware requirements as specified by the NOS vendor.

Nothing, other than maybe being stood up at the altar, is as frustrating as getting 90 percent of the way through a NOS installation only to discover that you've run out of disk space, or that your NOS doesn't work with your Network Interface Card. For example, if you're installing Windows NT Server, you must make sure that *every* device in your system appears on the Microsoft Hardware Compatibility List, a little book that comes with the NOS. If you install Novell software, it works with a wide variety of hardware, but you may still want to double-check with a Novell reseller or consultant just to make sure, or check for the logo "Yes — It Works with NetWare" on product packaging or spec sheets.

3. Make key decisions about your disk setup ahead of time.

For example, if you have a single large hard drive, do you want to set it up so that it appears as two, or even three, hard drives to your users? Doing so may help you organize files according to who needs them. Conversely, if you have two or more hard drives, do you want them to appear as a single drive? Doing so is great if everyone needs the same files, and you simply need some major storage space for all your data.

Most small networks can simply set up each hard drive as an individual unit, but read the "Organizing the Server File Structure" section later in this chapter anyway. If you have a choice of file systems, such as with Windows NT Server, make that choice now. (By the way, for Windows NT, I strongly recommend NTFS (NT File System) rather than FAT (File Allocation Table) — see Chapter 5 for details.)

4. Find out the hardware settings your NICs and disks use.

On a PC, for example, you may need to know the *base address* and *interrupt* (IRQ) for the network card. Run the card's setup utility and write these settings down. If you use SCSI hard drives, note the base address and IRQ information for the SCSI controller, as well as the ID numbers of the controller and its connected disk or disks. If you use a SCSI controller from Adaptec, for example, the Adaptec EZ-SCSI program can tell you all of this information.

5. Have some diskettes on hand for creating emergency server boot files.

Some NOS installations let you create special diskettes you can use to start the server if the main hard drive becomes damaged. *Don't skip this step.*

6. Run the NOS installation program.

Unplug your phone, turn off your beeper, lock the office door, and allow plenty of time — at least three hours — for this operation. Running the installation program may not take that long, but you don't want to rush it. Read the online help for each step if you're unsure about how to answer a question. Do the installation during work hours so you can call your reseller, NOS manufacturer, friendly neighborhood consultant, or spiritual adviser if you run into trouble.

Above all, don't worry. If you make a mistake, you can always run the installation program over again.

Peer-to-Peer File and Printer Sharing

In a peer-to-peer network such as Windows 95, LANtastic, or a simple Macintosh network, file and printer sharing is simplicity itself. For starters, you don't have to worry about sharing programs, because for all practical purposes, you can't! These networks only share data files. So, you typically install application programs on every workstation that needs them — one at a time.

For the peer-to-peer procedures in this section to work on a Windows 95 machine, you have to set it up for share-level security:

1. **Click Start➪Settings➪Control Panel**

2. **Double-click the Network icon.**

3. **Click the Access Control tab.**

4. **Make sure that the** Share-level access control **radio button is selected.**

5. **Click OK.**

You also have to install the peer sharing service in the Network control panel Configuration dialog box, if it isn't already there. Here's how:

1. **Click Start➪Settings➪Control Panel.**

2. **Double-click the Network icon.**

3. **Click the Configuration tab.**

4. **Click Add to bring up the Select Network Component Type dialog box.**

5. **Choose the Service icon and click Add.**

   The Select Network Service dialog box appears.

6. **In the Manufacturers column on the left, select Microsoft.**

7. **In the Network Services column on the right, highlight File and Printer Sharing for Microsoft Networks.**

8. **Click OK.**

   You end up back at the Network dialog box Configuration tab (same place you were after Step 3).

9. **Click the button labeled File and Print Sharing.**

   The File and Print Sharing dialog box appears.

10. **Click both boxes in the File and Print Sharing dialog box, as shown in Figure 9-4.**

Figure 9-4:
The File and
Print
Sharing
dialog box.

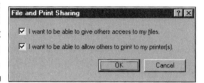

If you have to go through this procedure on several computers, here's a shortcut: skip Steps 4 through 8. The File and Print Sharing dialog box automatically installs the File and Printer Sharing for Microsoft Networks service. I show you the longer procedure in the preceding list so you know how to install other network services if the need ever arises, and so you understand where that new service entry in the Network control panel comes from.

Sharing data files

Sharing data files is up to the individual users, so you need to get everyone keyed in to the process. In a Windows 95 network, for example, here's how you do it:

1. **Double-click the My Computer desktop icon.**

2. **Double-click the drive icon that contains the folder to be shared.**

3. **Right-click on the folder to be shared.**

   A pop-up menu appears on-screen near your mouse pointer.

4. **Click Sharing.**

   A Properties dialog box appears, as shown in Figure 9-5.

5. **Click the Shared As radio button and give the folder a *share name*.**

   The share name is how the folder appears when other users browse the network via the Network Neighborhood desktop icon — it can be a different name than the actual directory name.

6. **Select an Access Type for the folder.**

   The default is Read-Only, meaning that other users can access, but not modify, the directory you share; or you can choose Full access, which lets other users add, modify, or delete the folder's contents. You can

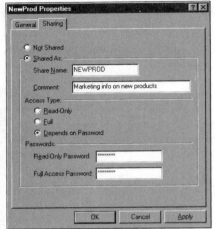

Figure 9-5:
Sharing a
directory in
Windows 95
involves a
single,
simple
dialog box.

add a password to either of these options, or even choose the Depends
on Password option in order to allow some people full access, and
others read-only access, depending on the password the individual user
has. The procedure is nearly identical if your workstations are running
Windows NT Workstation instead of Windows 95.

7. **Notify other users about the new shared resource, let the appropriate
   people know the password, and that's it!**

Sharing a printer

Sharing a printer connected to the workstation is just as easy as sharing
data files. In Windows 95:

1. **Double-click My Computer.**

2. **Double-click Printers.**

3. **Right-click the printer that you want to share (usually there's
   only one).**

   A small pop-up menu appears.

4. **Choose Properties from the pop-up menu.**

   The Properties dialog box for that particular printer graces your
   screen.

5. **Click the Sharing tab.**

6. **Give the printer a share name, and assign an optional password.**

   There's no such thing as read-only access to a printer, so you don't
   have the choice of whether to assign read-only or full access.

Organizing the Server File Structure

Setting up your server's file structure for sharing programs and data files is more complex on a client/server network than on a peer-to-peer network, but it also gives you far greater control over which users and groups can do what with those shared files.

Volumes, partitions, and directories

First, a word about terminology. In Novell networks, the main unit of storage on a server file system is called a *volume*. You can set up multiple volumes on a single physical hard drive, or you can set up a single volume that spans multiple physical hard drives. I don't generally recommend *either* for a small business network — you're best off setting up a one-drive, one-volume setup. In Microsoft networks, the main unit of storage is called a *partition,* but my advice is the same: Create one partition per physical drive. Most likely, this is how your network is set up if you buy a preconfigured server machine.

Directories, also known as *folders* (depending on who you talk to, what system they use, and how many ice cream sandwiches they ate for lunch), divide up the volume or partition in much the same way that manila folders divide up a filing cabinet drawer. After you install your Network Operating System, several directories already exist; their names and functions vary from one network to another. As you organize your server file structure, you create new directories for programs and data files. You can even create directories below other directories; for example, you may create a directory called APPS that contains subdirectories called WP, SPREADSHEET, DATABASE, and so on. Figure 9-6 illustrates this hierarchical structure.

Many modern networks, such as Windows NT Server, allow you to specify a particular file or directory using a *Universal Naming Convention* (UNC) path. Put two back slashes in front of the server name, and single back slashes in front of the volume, directory, subdirectory, and file name, like this:

```
\\SERVER1\VOLUME\DIRECTORY\SUBDIR\README.TXT
```

Today's networks and workstation operating systems make browsing network resources easy through the use of graphical windows like Network Neighborhood in Windows 95. Still, UNC paths are good to know about, because you're sure to run into UNC path notation at some point when administering your LAN. Incidentally, if you use Novell workstation software to access a Novell server, you see a similar, but somewhat different, notation for describing a file location:

```
SERVER1\VOLUME:DIRECTORY\SUBDIR\README.TXT
```

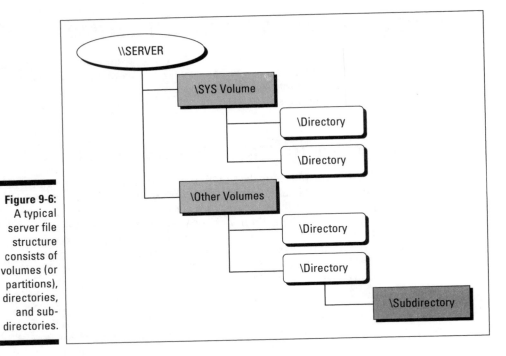

Figure 9-6:
A typical
server file
structure
consists of
volumes (or
partitions),
directories,
and sub-
directories.

You may be used to identifying programs and files with PC DOS notation, which uses a leading drive letter and colon before the directory and subdirectory (F:\DIRECTORY\SUBDIR\README.TXT). In this example, the drive letter F: substitutes for the server and volume names. You can still use this style notation with Novell and Microsoft servers, but you may not have to (see the section "What are drive mappings and do you need them?" later in this chapter).

Novell networks also use a special notation to describe the location of resources in the *NetWare Directory Services* (NDS) tree, which provides a hierarchical view of every doggoned thing in the network, including printers, users, and groups. If you use IntranetWare for Small Business, you may never need to master NDS notation, but the online documentation explains it in depth just in case.

System software

Remember that system software consists of not only the Network Operating System, but also all the various housekeeping and management programs you use to keep your network in great shape. Antivirus software, backup software, and administration programs for managing users, groups, and printers all fall into this category.

I suggest you keep all such system software programs in their own subdirectories, and all underneath a master directory (UTILITIES or something similar) that's different from the directories containing user programs and data files. The network administrator, and his or her understudy, are really the only people who need access to system software. Restrict that access to make it as *difficult as possible* for any nonadministrator to run system software and accidentally (or intentionally) trash a server.

Application software

You can easily add a new application program to your network in either of two ways: You can install it onto the server, and have users run (or *execute*) it from there, or you can install it separately onto each local workstation hard drive. The advantages of a server installation are that you can more easily maintain and upgrade the software because it all resides in a single location, and you can preset various options so that the program works the same way for everyone. The advantages of workstation installation are that the program runs faster, and that the installation procedure is generally simpler. I tend to favor server-based execution for networks of over a dozen users, and workstation-based execution for smaller LANs, but the choice is yours. Server-based execution is sometimes a better deal financially, depending on licensing policies of the product you want to install.

If you opt for server-based execution, the actual installation is usually pretty straightforward:

1. **Make sure you have a recent (for example, ten minutes old) full server backup, so that you can restore the server in case the installation goes awry.**

2. **Check to be sure that you have adequate disk space on the server (you can use Windows 95 Explorer to check).**

3. **Follow the application vendor's installation instructions for server-based execution.**

The most common *gotcha* is that you may need to log on as a network administrator or supervisor in order to have sufficient LAN permissions for the installation. A less common, but still frequent problem, is that you may need to temporarily disable your server's antivirus utility (remember to re-enable it immediately afterward!). The software vendor should guide you on these points in the installation instructions.

I like to install all application software in a subdirectory that I create under the server directory for which users already have read and execute permissions (such as SYS:\PUBLIC on an IntranetWare server, or C:\PROGRAM FILES on an NT server). This way, you don't have to manually add the new program's directory to the permission list for existing users and groups.

If you opt for workstation-based execution, installation is simpler, though more time-consuming. You just go from machine to machine, like a pollinating bee, performing a fresh install from CD-ROM each time. If you want to customize how the program works, for example by setting it to automatically check the network server when the user tries to open a data file, you have to do that separately for each computer.

Data files

Where users store their data is the last file system decision that you need to make. The basic choice is between private user areas on the server and shared public directories that you create for different workgroups or projects. Users may need their own private areas (called *home directories*) on the server for e-mail and for personal files they create. On the public side, it may be convenient to give everyone who's working on a particular project common access to a server directory containing all project-related files.

Typically, you set up a user's home directory when you create a new user account (see the next section, "Group Therapy: Creating User Accounts"). Home directories typically reside as subdirectories under a parent server directory named USERS. Each user has full rights to his or her home directory, which may appear as a separate drive letter on that particular user's computer (that is, Bill's H: drive is \\server\users\Bill, and Mary's H: drive is \\server\users\Mary).

You create project or departmental data directories using your network's file management utility, for example, Novell Easy Administration Tool (NEAT) for IntranetWare for Small Business, or Explorer for Windows NT Server. I suggest you create a master directory and call it something like PROJECTS. Then, you can create subdirectories beneath PROJECTS that pertain to individual projects. After you create the directories, you then need to make them available to the groups who need them (again, with NEAT or Explorer or whatever utility your network uses to grant directory permissions).

You can assign different permissions to different groups. For example, you may grant your financial people access to \\SERVER\PROJECTS\MERGER, your marketing people may need access to \\SERVER\PROJECTS\PR, and so on. Using a directory and subdirectory structure to divide out data files by workgroup makes sharing those files with only the people who need them much easier.

Of course, if your company has four people and everyone needs access to everything, you can share the master PROJECTS directory with the EVERY-ONE group, and all network users can then automatically access all subdirectories under PROJECTS. Even so, organizing your project data files into subdirectories allows users to find specific files more easily.

Group Therapy: Creating User Accounts

One of the most important tasks in setting up client/server network services is creating user and group accounts. If you do this right, future administrative chores, such as adding new users, become much easier.

Create user and group accounts using the NEAT or QuickStart programs in an IntranetWare for Small Business network; the NWADMIN program in a regular IntranetWare network; and either the User Manager for Domains program or the Administrative Wizards in a Windows NT Server network (see Figures 9-7 and 9-8 for a look at these utilities).

Figure 9-7:
The Windows NT Server Administrative Wizards includes tools to add user accounts and perform group management.

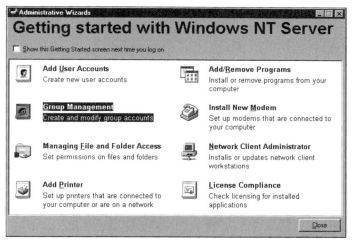

Figure 9-8:
IntranetWare for Small Business has the NEAT utility for creating, changing, and deleting users and groups.

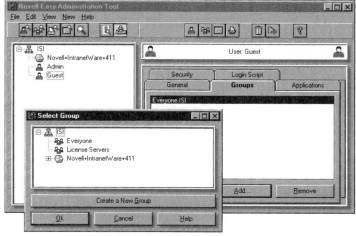

Start by creating a separate account for every user on the network. Each account has its own user name and password, a combination that unlocks all the network resources that you've determined that particular user should have permission to access. Giving each user a separate account is better for security, network usage tracking, and troubleshooting.

After you create user accounts for each employee, create user groups. My advice is to assign security restrictions at the group level rather than at the individual user level wherever you can. Even in a very small company, you are best off setting up a group for network administrators (one primary and one backup individual), another for general users who need to run application programs but not system software, and one more for consultants or contractors who may work with or on your network but who shouldn't have access to sensitive company data. Larger companies can set up additional groups by project or department. If you allow customers to run programs on your network when they visit your office, you need to set up a separate group for them as well.

The reason for using groups for assigning shared resources and security permissions is that most networks have fewer groups than users, so it's easier on the administrator. If you think and plan carefully about who needs what from the network, you can do all your directory sharing at the group level, and never have to modify the sharing setup for individual user accounts. See Chapter 11 for more on assigning security restrictions to directories and files.

Setting Up Network Printers

Network printers operate on a first-come, first-served basis — like the Department of Motor Vehicles, except faster. That means that if Carina tries to print (that is, she sends the printer a *print job*) while Cecily is already printing, the network must somehow put Carina's print job into a holding area where it waits until Cecily's job is done. That holding area goes by the name *print queue* (Microsoft just calls a print queue a printer), and the network service that manages the print queue is called the *print server*.

Running a print server on the same machine that also shares files is no big deal for a small network because queuing up print jobs and delivering them to the printer is a simple-minded task that the server CPU barely notices.

How you set up a network printer depends a little bit on how the particular printer model you have connects to your network. In the simplest case, you connect the printer to the server with a parallel cable, and use the Network Operating System's built-in setup utilities (shown back in Figures 9-7 and 9-8) to prepare the printer for sharing. (You have to specify the *port* that the printer is using, which is normally the first parallel port or LPT1: on a PC, and the printer make and model. Don't use a serial port such as COM1: — it's too slow.) The drawback to this approach is that parallel cables start to choke on data if they run longer than 12 feet, so you have to place your printer near your server. Such a setup isn't ideal, because you want the server to be in a low-traffic location so people don't spill coffee on it, sit on it, or knock it over.

You have two alternatives to connecting a printer directly to a server:

- ✓ **Hang the printer directly on the network.** If the printer model you have offers the *net-direct* option, you can connect it directly to the network, for example with a twisted-pair cable running to the hub. In this case, you can probably still use the network's built-in printer sharing utility. For example, on a Windows NT Server, you run the Administrative Wizards (Start➪Programs➪Administrative Tools➪ Administrative Wizards), choose Add Printer➪My Computer➪Add Port, and then select the option specified by your printer vendor from the Printer Ports dialog box (see Figure 9-9). You then finish the steps as prompted by the wizard.

- ✓ **Use a *standalone print server*.** A standalone print server is a sharing device that you can connect to the printer using a parallel cable on one end (to connect to the printer) and a network cable on the other. Standalone print servers sometimes require special software setup (as explained in their manuals), but may be worth the extra tweaking because they take over some print job processing brainwork from your network server for better network and printer performance. However, remember that every document must still flow through the parallel port, which can be the speed bottleneck. Also, you may have to install an additional network protocol, such as DLC (*Data Link Control*), on your LAN server to communicate with the standalone print server.

Figure 9-9:
Choosing the net-direct communications type.

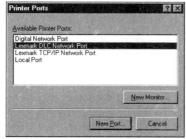

When giving your printer a share name, stick to eight characters and avoid spaces and nonalphanumeric characters (Fred is okay, $*| ( )^& is not). This strategy ensures maximum compatibility with whatever kind of user workstation computers you have. You can assign security to your shared printers, but you needn't bother unless you have a fancy color network printer that uses really expensive supplies.

Finally, no matter how you set up your network printer, you probably have to go around to each workstation and install the necessary software (for example, by double-clicking the Add Printer wizard in the Windows 95 Printers folder) so that the workstation can communicate properly with the particular make and model printer you've installed. You can set up Windows NT Server to skip this step, but not IntranetWare. Access these options in Windows 95 by right-clicking the printer in the Printers folder (after you've run the Add Printer wizard to install its software) and choosing Properties.

Configuring Network Clients

Two big topics on configuring network clients for ease of use are *drive mappings* and *desktop customization*. I don't much like the first and I love the second, but you need to know about both.

What are drive mappings and do you need them?

Drive mappings are simply associations that match up a network volume and directory with a PC DOS-style drive letter (F:, G:, and so on). You may need them if you run DOS programs on user workstations, because DOS programs generally don't know how to find network directories. Or, you may find drive mappings convenient if your network users are already familiar and comfortable with DOS-style path names.

However, you may not need drive mappings at all if your network users only run Windows 95 or NT programs. These programs can find shared directories via the Network Neighborhood icon in the regular File⇨Open dialog box that pops up every time a user wants to open a document.

If you install programs onto an IntranetWare server, you can use the Novell Application Manager and Novell Application Launcher (NAL) so that all server-based programs appear in a window when the user logs on (see Figure 9-10). In this scenario, you don't need drive mappings to run the programs; the user just double-clicks the program icons in the NAL window.

Figure 9-10: The Novell Application Launcher.

You can assign drive letters to specific directories in both Novell and Microsoft networks by writing a *logon script,* which is just a sequence of commands that runs automatically when the user logs on to the network. The details are beyond the scope of this book, but the tools you use are a text editor (such as Windows Notepad) and either User Manager (for Windows NT Server) or NEAT (for IntranetWare for Small Business). You can also assign drive letters on a computer-by-computer basis by running the Windows 95 Explorer and choosing Tools⇨Map Network Drive.

I suggest that you avoid using drive mappings unless you have some good reason for doing so. They're just one more thing to manage on your network.

Customizing the workstation

Setting up user workstations so that network resources are as easy to use as files and printers on the local computer makes the LAN administrator's job much easier. Here are just four examples of how to do this:

- ✔ **Create a workstation shortcut to the server application.** After you install an application program that runs from the server, create an icon or program menu selection for it on every user's workstation. For example, in Windows 95, you can add programs to the taskbar's Start menu. (Click Start⇨Settings⇨Taskbar, click the Start Menu Programs tab, and then click Add.)

   If you use IntranetWare, you can run the NetWare Application Manager to set up the new program as a separate network object, which appears automatically when users log on to their workstations and run the NetWare Application Launcher.

- ✔ **Standardize the Start menu.** If you want to get fancy, you can even store the Start menu on the network server, using the Windows 95 *custom folders* feature, so that it's the same for everybody. The Microsoft *Windows 95 Resource Kit* book provides the details.

- ✔ **Create user desktop icons that point to commonly accessed data directories on the server.** For example, do this in Windows 95 or NT Workstation by simply double-clicking Network Neighborhood, double-clicking the server icon, finding the folder you want, and dragging it to the user's desktop. (You can use the same technique for printers.)

- ✔ **Set up the workstation logon name and password, if you use them, to be the same as the user's network logon name and password.** (You can do this using the Windows 95 Passwords control panel.) This way, the user automatically logs onto the network when the operating system starts, and network resources are always available.

As you become more familiar with your particular workstation and network software, you're sure to find other ways to make using network resources simple and intuitive for your appreciative users. If you get really good at it, maybe your users won't give you fruitcake next December.

Chapter 10

Making Your Network Communicate

. . . .

In This Chapter

▶ Deciding between *remote control* and *remote node* dial-in access

▶ Setting up your network so that anyone can dial out through a shared communications link

▶ Getting ready to use e-mail and other network communications stuff

▶ Combining the best features of computer-based fax and dedicated fax machines

. . . .

*C*ommunication services enable your network to talk to the outside world, and they enable you to talk to your network when you're away from the office and a part of that outside world. In this chapter I lay out the basics of small business network telecommunications.

> **Mo•dem •com•mu•ni•ca•tions** (mo'dum' kuh'myoo'ni'kay'shuns) *n.*
> What you need if dem communications just ain't enough.
> (*Weadock's Practical Computer Dictionary*, not yet written)

Early office networks concentrated on providing file and printer sharing services without giving much thought to communications services. One reason is that a few years ago, dial-up modems were too slow to carry traffic much more complex than "Watson, come here, I want you." Another reason is that portable computers were portable in the same sense that a mobile home is portable. You could move them around, but you couldn't put one into an airplane's overhead bin without compressing your fellow passengers' luggage to the density of lead.

Today, companies can use a *Local Area Network* (LAN) to communicate electronically with contractors, suppliers, customers, and information services. Similarly, a business can make its network available to employees who are on the road, or who telecommute. Perhaps the best news is that neither feature costs very much at all. Large companies often install expensive dedicated high-speed lines, but modem technology has advanced to the point that a small company can achieve reasonably snappy communications over plain old phone lines for a fraction of what a dedicated data line costs. Achieving quick, reliable, secure, and convenient LAN telecommunications is more affordable than ever.

Communications software hasn't traditionally been an integral part of the typical *Network Operating System* (NOS), but it's getting to be that way. For example, Novell IntranetWare for Small Business ships with a bundled copy of NetWare Connect, and Microsoft Windows NT Server comes with a communication service called *Remote Access Service* (RAS — say "razz"). Expect to see even more integration of communications services in future versions of these and other client/server NOSs.

If you run a peer-to-peer network, you still have to install some add-on software to make shared dial-in and dial-out a reality. And no matter what sort of network you have, when it comes to faxing, sending is easy but receiving can be tricky.

Dialing In from Home or the Road

The first communication service you're likely to want is the ability to dial up your LAN from outside your office: from home, a customer site, a hotel room, or an airport. After you set up dial-in access, your employees can easily obtain any information your network contains — product data, inventory, "financials," customer history, contracts, sales forecasts, and so on — wherever they go. (Sure beats paper.) Also, dial-in access makes telecommuting both possible and feasible. So how do you set it up?

First, you need a modem in your office. I discuss the hardware in Chapter 7, but how you connect it depends on how you want remote users to dial into your LAN. You have two choices: *remote control* and *remote node*. Figure 10-1 illustrates the two different methods, which the following sections explain.

Remote control

Until the last two or three years, *remote control* was the most common way to dial into a LAN. You connect an office modem to a workstation computer in the office, not to a server. A user or administrator in the office runs a remote control software utility, such as Symantec pcANYWHERE32 (see Figure 10-2) or Traveling Software LapLink, on this workstation. The remote control software turns the computer into a *slave* or *host* machine (host *does* seem friendlier), sets the modem to auto-answer, and waits for an incoming call. The remote user runs the remote control software on his or her note-book, and sets it up to dial into the office computer.

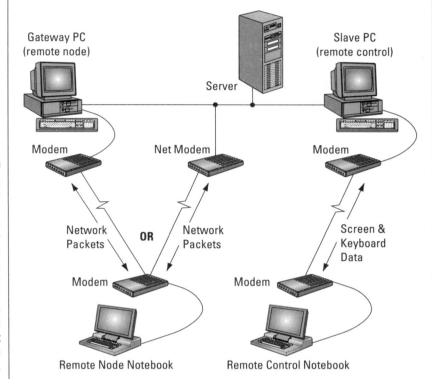

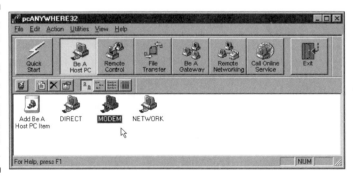

After the remote control software on both sides of the connection establishes the link, which may involve a separate password that the remote user
must enter, the remote machine becomes the *master,* basically taking over
the keyboard, mouse, and display of the slave machine. The remote user's
keystrokes and mouse actions travel across the phone link to the slave

computer, and the slave computer sends screen data back across the phone link, where it appears on the remote user's screen. The remote user can now do just about anything that he or she could do in the office, seated in front of the slave machine. However, the remote user doesn't have to have network software (transport protocol and network client) loaded on the remote computer, because the slave computer handles the network connection.

Remote control software, like Ted Koppel, has become very sophisticated over the years:

- ✔ **File transfer.** Remote control software typically supports file transfer in the background, so the remote user can copy files between machines while doing something else.

- ✔ **Modem callback.** The better programs also offer *callback* operation, in which the slave computer hangs up and calls the master computer back at a predefined number to protect against unwanted intruders. (This feature is not too useful for remote users who dial in from multiple locations, unless you want to be really slick and use a cellular modem.)

- ✔ **Security.** You can set up security levels that the remote control software uses to authenticate remote users, which is both an advantage (more secure) and a drawback (in that it's one more layer of security the LAN administrator must manage).

Perhaps the biggest drawback to remote control access is that you have to have a workstation computer at the office set up to answer the phone, something that the other method, *remote node,* doesn't require.

Remote node

Remote node setups actually extend the LAN out to the remote user. The remote computer user must have all the networking software that a local workstation would have, namely, transport protocol and network client. The phone link works almost exactly like a very slow network cable, and the remote user's software treats the modem like a very slow Network Interface Card (NIC). As with remote control, you must install remote node communications software on at least one office computer (which may or may not be a file server, as the next paragraph explains) and on every notebook that requires dial-in access.

Remote node access offers a lot of flexibility as to where you install an office modem:

✔ **You can connect a modem to a server in a client/server network.** Doing so doesn't require buying a separate computer, but this practice may make a busy machine even busier, depending on how hard you work your server.

✔ **You can connect a modem to a workstation computer that you designate for communications services.** The workstation can run a service such as NetWare Connect, Windows 95 Dial-Up Server, or Windows NT Remote Access Services to manage the remote user calls. The workstation becomes a portal or *gateway* into your network: The remote user doesn't necessarily see any of the workstation's files, but can see the rest of the network. You can even continue using the workstation as a regular office computer while it's handling incoming calls (the lingo here is *nondedicated communications server*). However, when the dial-up traffic exceeds one or two connections, you should probably dedicate the computer to handling calls and hide the keyboard.

✔ **Finally, if you buy a so-called *network modem* such as those sold by Shiva Corp., you can connect it directly to a LAN cable, and thus have the advantage of not tying up a computer.** Network modems cost a lot more than regular modems, but usually less than the dedicated workstation setup discussed in the previous bullet.

Windows 95 comes with remote node software, called *Dial-Up Networking* or DUN. The Microsoft Plus! add-on product (shipped together with Windows 95 on many PCs) provides the server component, as shown in Figure 10-3.

Figure 10-3:
The
Windows 95
Dial-Up
Networking
server can
make a
single
modem
available
for remote
node
dial-in.

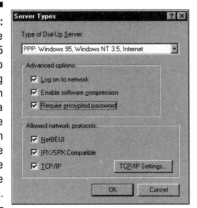

These days, companies use remote node access instead of remote control access for several reasons. First, screen and mouse performance is faster and smoother. Also, you can set up the notebook computer software almost exactly the same way you set up desktop software to make remote computing just as smooth as computing in the office. You don't have to allocate a slave computer and remember to activate its remote control software. Finally, neither users nor the LAN administrator has to worry about an extra layer of security because the remote node user logs on to the network with the same user ID and password as if he or she were sitting at a desk in front of a workstation.

In Chapter 9, I discuss installing application software onto the server as opposed to installing it onto user workstations. Although this setup works great for the reasons I cover in that chapter, it creates a hitch for remote computing: When connecting via remote node, executing programs that reside on the server is excruciatingly slow. The solution is to set up remote node clients with large hard drives so that they can install and run programs from the local drive rather than across the modem link.

Neither Windows 95 nor Windows NT Workstation allows you to run a remote node session and a local network session simultaneously if you're using the IPX/SPX network protocol. This may be a problem for telecommuters who have their own small network setup in a home office. The solution is to set up two different Windows hardware profiles in the System control panel (to get there, click Start⇨Settings⇨Control Panel, double-click the System icon, and then click the Hardware Profile tab). You can create one hardware profile to access a network via the modem, and the other via the Network Interface Card (NIC).

Modems for remote computing

Whether you choose a remote control or remote node connection, you have to set up your remote computer with a modem. The modem translates the digital signals that computers use into analog signals that the phone system uses, and back again (the term "modem" is short for **mo**dulator-**dem**odulator). Get a unit that can communicate at a speed of at least 33.6 kilobits per second, and that supports the Plug-and-Play standard if you use Windows 95 (or plan to use NT Workstation 5.0). Modem vendors include Hayes, Motorola, and U.S. Robotics (now part of 3Com), among many others. Nearly all modems today also come with fax capabilities (it costs about a dollar extra to burn fax features into the modem circuitry, so *modem* has really become synonymous with *fax/modem*).

Desktop computers

Most desktop computers come with a built-in modem, but if you need to add one, I usually recommend an *external* modem rather than an *internal* type.

For one thing, you don't have to dig into the system unit, and for another, you can watch the LED lights on an external modem to give you clues about your connection — such as whether it's establishing a high-speed link or a low-speed link (the *HS* light). I also like the fact that you can turn off an external modem to break the connection if your communications software crashes.

An external modem is easy to connect: Just attach a modem cable between the computer's serial port (usually a 9-pin "D" shell connector) and the modem's serial port (usually a 25-pin "D" connector). Then, connect a phone wire cable between the phone jack and the modem's LINE IN plug, and optionally connect a phone handset to the modem's PHONE plug so you can easily use the phone when you're not using the modem.

Portable computers

Many portable computers (formerly called *laptop* but now called *notebook* as sizes continue to shrink) have a built-in modem; it's easy to add one if yours doesn't. In the world of portables, space is at a premium, and an internal modem is more convenient than an external modem. Buy a *PC Card* modem that slides into a little credit card size slot in the side of the notebook, unless your notebook already comes with a built-in modem, or doesn't offer a PC Card slot. (*PC Card* is the new name for the PCMCIA standard, an acronym thought up by some nameless industry executive who, I think we can all agree, is one sandwich short of a picnic. PCMCIA stands for *People Can't Memorize Computer Industry Acronyms*. Okay, it really stands for *Personal Computer Memory Card Industry Association,* because these gizmos originally added memory to laptop computers.) Some notebooks, mostly older ones, can only accept an internal modem designed specially for that model notebook.

The PC Card modem connects to a modular phone jack into which you plug a regular phone cable. You can even buy PC Card modems that work with cellular phones, although the connection quality can be a problem for high-speed data communications.

Mobile Computing For Dummies by Cliff Roth (IDG Books Worldwide, Inc.) dives into the details of remote computing more deeply than I can here.

Dialing Out to the World

As soon as you get your network set up for inbound access, the next logical step is to set it up for outbound access. In some companies, outbound may be even more important. Dialing out to the world enables your business to

✔ Send e-mail messages to customers, suppliers, and contractors for faster communications at a lower cost than phone, mail, or fax

✔ Post updates to your company's World Wide Web site for promotion and customer service purposes

✔ Quickly obtain the latest software updates for your network to improve reliability and speed

✔ Search the wealth of information available through online information services and the Internet to keep informed about markets, customers, and competitors

Whether you connect to a private information service, such as America Online, CompuServe, or Prodigy, or to the public Internet, your small business network allows you to set up a modem or an *ISDN* (*Integrated Services Digital Network*) connection and share that hardware with every user on the LAN.

Just in case you haven't read Chapter 7 yet, ISDN connections are digital from end to end, run at up to 128 kilobits/second, and use special hardware at your office called a *terminal adapter* in place of a modem. You pay a monthly fee for the ISDN line, which your local phone company installs (pricing and availability vary by region).

For some specific ideas on setting up and taking advantage of an Internet connection, whip on over to Chapter 17.

Even though you can share the communications hardware for outbound dial-up access, you typically still have to install communications software on each workstation. If you dial a proprietary service such as CompuServe, you need to use the software provided by the proprietary service, as shown in Figure 10-4 (although CompuServe is currently changing to become an Internet-based service). If you access the Internet, you use a web browser such as Internet Explorer or Netscape Navigator. If you dial up bulletin-board systems (or *BBSs*), which are becoming less common but still have their uses (such as for updating software), you use a general-purpose dialer such as the little HyperTerminal program that comes with Windows 95.

How you set up sharing services for your dial-out link depends on whether you have a peer-to-peer or client/server network, as the following sections explain.

Peer-to-peer modem sharing

Some peer-to-peer networks, such as Artisoft LANtastic, include provisions for modem sharing right out of the box. Others, most notably Microsoft Windows 95, can share the fax part of a fax/modem, but not the data part. (Seems weird to me, too.)

Figure 10-4:
Proprietary
online
services,
such as
CompuServe,
usually
have their
own
software
that you
need to
install on
each
workstation.

Fortunately, Artisoft sells its modem sharing software, appropriately named ModemShare, as a separate product. You can buy licenses for 1, 2, 4, 8, or 32 shared modems. I've used ModemShare since its debut (two company buyouts ago!) as Modem Assist from Fresh Technologies, and it works reliably as long as your network runs the NetBEUI or IPX/SPX network transport protocol.

After you install the software, you simply set up your communications programs to connect to the shared modem using a non-standard serial port (such as COM4: on a PC), instead of a local physical port (such as COM1:). The computer that's directly connected to the shared modem is the *host,* and all the other computers are *clients*.

You probably won't run the TCP/IP transport protocol on a small peer-to-peer network, but if you do, take a look at the Internet LanBridge modem-sharing software from Virtual Motion. It works over NetBEUI, IPX/SPX, or TCP/IP networks. And if your interest lies primarily in sharing an Internet link, with a single Internet account and IP address, among multiple peer-to-peer LAN users that don't run TCP/IP, look at i.Share from Artisoft, which is a little less expensive than Internet LanBridge.

For more on transport protocols like IPX/SPX and TCP/IP, Chapter 6 is your ticket to ride.

With whatever software you use for peer-to-peer modem sharing, look for features such as compatibility with your communications programs, the ability to automatically retry connection requests if all the shared modems are busy, modem activity monitoring and logging, and the ability to use *multiple-port* or *multiport* modem cards (devices that include several modems on a single plug-in board).

Client/server modem sharing

Although you can buy standalone modem-sharing communications servers, today's client/server Network Operating Systems (NOSs) often come with the software you need to enable modem sharing, and using that software is often easier and cheaper than buying proprietary standalone communications servers.

One of the advantages that Novell IntranetWare for Small Business has over its bigger brother IntranetWare is that it includes a copy of the Novell modem sharing software — NetWare Connect — as part of the package. Windows NT Server comes with a modem sharing service called Remote Access Service (RAS). Both products let you install specialized multi-modem circuit boards into your server to create a *modem pool* (group of modems). Vendors of such boards include Digi International, Eicon, and NetAccess (see Appendix B).

Don't be confused by the fact that I mention NetWare Connect and RAS in the earlier section, "Dialing In from Home or the Road." These products support both inbound and outbound access.

NetWare Connect (NWC) comes with IntranetWare for Small Business, although you have to install it separately. Other Novell NOSs require that you buy it as a separate product. NWC is a solid piece of software that supports both outbound and inbound access (the inbound part can provide either remote control or remote node software). NWC can handle up to 128 modems, provides advanced activity monitoring, logging, and usage analysis, and lets you install modems into a server machine.

The Remote Access Service (RAS) that comes with Windows NT Server also supports outbound and inbound access, and it can handle up to 255 modems. RAS can do activity logging, but it requires editing the Windows NT Registry to activate (loosely defined, the NT Registry means a medium-sized headache), and doesn't provide as many activity logging features as NetWare Connect. However, it's an easy decision to use RAS if you've standardized on Windows NT Server as your NOS.

Whatever solution you choose for client/server modem sharing, the installation procedure involves first installing the software on the server, and then configuring the workstations so that they can find the shared modems when initiating a communications session. The vendors supply all the gory details with the products, but you can read books on the subject too. For example,

Windows NT Networking For Dummies by Ed Tittel and company (IDG Books Worldwide, Inc.) devotes two chapters to RAS. Installing the modems and software and testing everything takes about a day, but you don't really need a consultant to help you with this project.

Don't confuse me with the fax

Like the protagonist in one of my all-time favorite movies, *Local Hero,* many men and women in small business live and die by the fax machine. E-mail is slowly replacing the fax as the communication technology of choice when phone conversation is unnecessary, prohibitively expensive, or just too time-consuming with certain individuals. However, e-mail still suffers from too many competing standards, and the fax is a highly standardized method of communication.

- **The advantages of LAN faxing include:** better quality for documents that you fax directly from a computer program; less time wasted standing around at the fax machine; the ease of sending a fax to multiple recipients; and a lower phone bill if you schedule nonurgent faxes for sending during off-peak hours.

- **The disadvantages include:** a myriad of maddening compatibility problems between computer fax/modems and the several decades' worth of dedicated fax machine models in common daily use; no convenient way to automatically route incoming faxes to the correct LAN users; and no way to receive or send faxes if the network is down.

Once you install a fax program, faxing a document from a computer is as easy as selecting the fax device instead of a printer, as shown in Figure 10-5.

Figure 10-5: Faxing a computer document is easy in Windows 95. Just choose File⇨Print and specify the fax device instead of a printer.

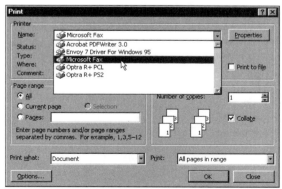

Using your LAN to handle fax chores has a certain appeal, but the technology is still somewhat immature even after years of development and use. I usually suggest to small companies that they set up the network for outbound faxing because it's so convenient, but also set up a dedicated fax machine for incoming documents. The dedicated machines are much less likely to give you a `Receive Failed` error and trash your entire fax just because the last millimeter of the last page didn't transmit properly. They also let you transmit an existing paper document that isn't formatted and stored on disk — an operation that, with a computer-only fax setup, requires an image scanner that your company may otherwise not need.

If you can squeeze it into the budget, invest in a high-quality fax software package. Symantec WinFax Pro, for example, offers a wide variety of features and settings. If you do a lot of network faxing, or if you don't already have any other fax/modem sharing software (such as Artisoft ModemShare or Microsoft RAS), you may want to look at WinFax Pro for Networks, which sets up a fax server with up to four modems.

One cool fax application your company may want to consider is *fax-on-demand* or *fax-back*. Your fax software may include fax-on-demand capability as part of the package (for example, WinFax Pro comes with TalkWorks). The idea is to create a round-the-clock automated document delivery service. Customers can call a special phone number; a fax server on your network answers, and then prompts the caller to key in a document code and a return fax number. The fax server then hangs up, calls the customer's fax machine, and faxes over the requested document. (A new caller can request an index of document codes and descriptions.) The document files can reside on the fax server computer or on a network server.

Part IV

Running the System: Networking versus Not Working

"WE OFFER A CREATIVE MIS ENVIRONMENT WORKING WITH STATE-OF-THE-ART PROCESSING AND COMMUNICATIONS EQUIPMENT; A COMPREHENSIVE BENEFITS PACKAGE, GENEROUS PROFIT SHARING, STOCK OPTIONS, AND, IF YOU'RE FEELING FUNKY AND NEED TO CHILL OUT AND RAP, WE CAN DO THAT TOO."

In this part . . .

In networking, as in cooking, construction, and sex, the difference between a highly successful project and a merely satisfactory one often comes down to the last 25 percent of the job. Your network is up and running, and there is a great temptation to call it a day (or a week or a month) and move on to other things. *Don't!*

Summon up another burst of energy and do what it takes to add an appropriate level of security to your network so that your company is protected against both accidental and intentional harm; then go the extra little bit to make your network perform at its peak. Chapter 11 lays the security groundwork. Then (and you have more time for this last task), give your network a tune-up, as described in Chapter 12, so that it runs at maximum speed. In Chapter 13, I offer some tips for the part-time network administrator on how to manage and maintain your network over time, so that it runs just as effectively a year from now as it does today.

Chapter 11

Healthy Paranoia: Keeping Your Network Secure

● ●

In This Chapter

▶ Determining how much security your network needs

▶ Setting up physical security (they can't hurt what they can't touch)

▶ Protecting your network against computer viruses

▶ Using the many security tools available in today's client/server networks

▶ Protecting workstations and dial-up network links

● ●

"Thieves respect property. They merely wish the property to become their property that they may more perfectly respect it." (G. K. Chesterton, *The Man Who Was Thursday*)

Andrew Grove, the successful president and CEO of Intel, wrote a book titled *Only the Paranoid Survive*. Keeping that phrase in the back of your mind pays off when rigging your network for daily business. Your network faces many threats to its (and your) well-being: threats of accident or intent, which may come from within or from without your company.

Some small business managers I've known have expressed their belief that "We're a small company, so we don't really need LAN security." The reality is that as a small company, you may need *more* LAN *(Local Area Network)* security than a big company, especially if you rely heavily on your network for daily operations or to provide data for executive decision-making. One big accident, upset employee, mischievous data burglar, or pesky computer virus is all it takes to put the future of your entire business at risk. A more realistic attitude to take is: "We're a small company, so we need to be extra careful about LAN security."

Fortunately, network security isn't terribly difficult to set up. The trick is to provide the level of security that your organization requires, while making that security as *invisible* (that is, unobtrusive) as possible to the user, and spending no more time and money than is really necessary.

Figuring Out How Much Security You Need

Your business may not be involved in an industry fraught with industrial espionage. You may trust your company's employees as though they were family members. Nevertheless, you still probably need security if any of the following situations describes your network:

- ✔ You don't want every network user to have access to every bit of information stored on your network.

- ✔ Your network incorporates modems and remote access.

- ✔ You work with outside contractors who occasionally use your network.

- ✔ Your company may one day fire someone.

- ✔ You install software on your network.

- ✔ You exchange data files with other companies.

- ✔ Your company employs human beings, a species known to make occasional errors such as polluting the earth, taxing capital gains, and hitting the wrong key on a computer keyboard.

The degree of security that you need depends on the degree to which any of the previous statements holds true. For example, you need to pay more attention to user and group account security if you have a lot of confidential data on your server than you do if you have very little confidential data stored there. The following sections describe the steps a typical small company needs to take in order to put reasonable computer security in place. I don't cover the extraordinary measures you may need if you have exceptionally stringent security needs beyond guiding you to some of the books in Appendix B and suggesting you consult with a computer security expert. Retinal scanners are way cool, but most companies don't need one.

Before I dive in to specific types of network security, I need to make one key point. Although, as Figure 11-1 shows, security consists of several distinct parts — physical security, antivirus measures, server security, and remote access security — your security plan needs to be a balanced whole, and you must evaluate the plan's effectiveness by the strength of its weakest element. For example, putting a lot of effort into mastering and using your Network Operating System's security features, and then not educating users about how to choose good passwords, is a little like building a thick steel box and then putting a toy plastic padlock on it.

Physical Security

Physical security means limiting physical access to network computers and devices in order to prevent both accidental and intentional damage. Physical security is a good place for you to start, because it's inexpensive and effective against many types of threats. Physical security measures include the following:

- ✔ Installing door locks to the office or room where the server resides
- ✔ Putting the server in a low-traffic area
- ✔ Removing and locking up the server keyboard
- ✔ Removing diskette drives from user workstations
- ✔ Destroying media containing electronic files before tossing them in the trash (hammers still have a place in the world of computers)

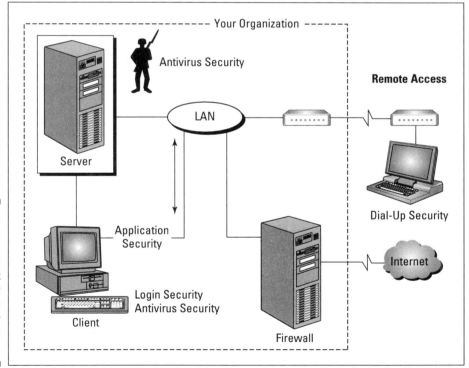

Figure 11-1: Places where you need to think about security issues. This chapter discusses each item.

✔ Placing user workstations where others can easily see them

✔ Bolting computers to desktops so burglars can't steal them without taking the whole desk also (a sure tip-off to passersby)

✔ Keeping your office locked after hours

✔ Installing alarm systems

You may need to consider physical security measures for servers, workstations, network hubs, and even printers, if the data they print may be confidential. Typically, however, physical security concentrates on the file server; the need for printers to be easily accessible usually overrides the fact that they may print the occasional sensitive document (see Figure 11-2). Consider physical security for the parts of your network that permit remote access, too, such as modem servers.

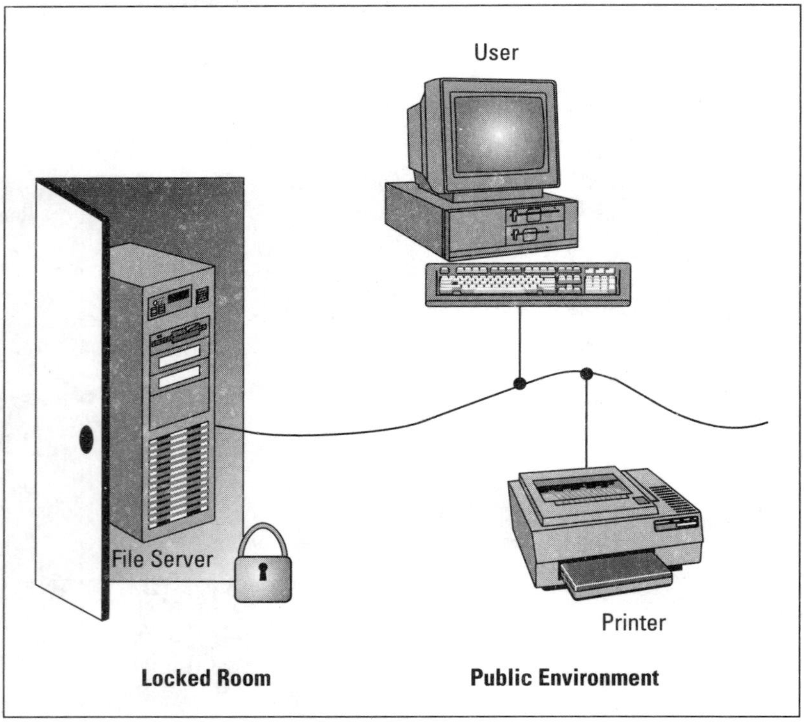

Figure 11-2:
Physical security usually begins with file servers. Companies place printers near users for convenience, but users rarely need physical access to a server.

User

File Server

Printer

Locked Room   **Public Environment**

Virus Prevention

A computer *virus* is a program that spreads copies of itself throughout a computer and/or network by attaching those copies to *host* files (usually program files, also known as *executable* files). Viruses may perform a number of more or less disruptive actions in addition to irresponsibly reproducing themselves, much like certain lesser mammals. Thousands of viruses exist and new ones (Symantec, maker of the popular Norton AntiVirus software, estimates the figure at three) crop up every day. Their creators are generally intelligent but misguided sorts who gain a false sense of power from writing programs that cause harm. I say "false" because, at least to my way of thinking, true power is the power to create rather than destroy.

That last sentence sounds way too serious for this book, so to counterbalance it, here are two fictitious computer viruses reported on the Internet:

- ✔ **The Dan Quayle virus** addse ane ee toe everye worde youe typee.

- ✔ **The Ross Perot virus** makes loud noises on all your computers before it suddenly quits. If you don't remove it, the virus does the same thing four years later.

The main virus categories are as follows (I'm being serious again now):

- ✔ **Boot sector viruses,** such as *Michelangelo,* infect the boot sector of a hard drive or diskette and may also infect the *partition table* or "Master Boot Record." These are usually workstation based rather than server based. Merely *booting* (starting up) the computer is all that's necessary to activate a boot sector virus.

- ✔ **File infector viruses,** such as *Jerusalem,* typically infect application programs. These viruses often add themselves to the code of the host file, increasing its size enough for an antivirus utility to detect the change, but may be otherwise unnoticeable. These can spread over a network and are activated when the host program is executed.

- ✔ **Macro viruses,** such as *Concept,* are the most recent form. These are miniature programs designed to run inside a particular application program. They typically replace the normal, benign action of a particular program command with an abnormal and destructive action.

Within each primary category, several other classifications exist. *Time bomb* viruses wait for a prespecified date or time delay before taking action. *Stealth* viruses take steps to conceal their presence. *Polymorphic* viruses change their code to an encrypted pattern when they're not executing.

Multipartite viruses have characteristics of both file infectors and boot sector viruses. *Logic bombs* wait for a specific event to activate a virus, such as the disappearance of an employee from the payroll database (remember the evil programmer in *Jurassic Park*). And so on, *ad nauseam*.

In the good old days, all you had to worry about was infection of programs. Today, because the line is blurring between data and program, you have to worry about data files as well. For example, a user downloads a word processing document from an outside source. When the user opens this data file in a word processing program, the data file may run a little program called a *macro,* which (if it's actually a *macro virus*) can cause damage to other data files the user works with later. The problem becomes worse if users spend a lot of time accessing the Internet, because the *viewers* or *plug-in* programs that let a web browser automatically run certain kinds of files can potentially activate data files that may be infected with a virus.

Some Internet sites with useful virus information are `http://www.cheyenne.com`; `http://www.drsolomon.com`; `http://www.mcafee.com`; `http://www.ncsa.com`; and `http://www.symantec.com`. Also, if you have access to CompuServe or an Internet search service, search for VSUM.EXE, a fine shareware virus database by Patricia Hoffman.

I'm telling you all this in order to convince you that viruses are real, bad, and real bad. In an interconnected world, when you compute with someone, you compute with every computer that person has ever computed with (to borrow a phrase). You need to protect your network against viruses, with both technology and policy, as I discuss in the following sections.

Antivirus software

Antivirus software does three things for you:

- ✔ **It helps prevent a virus from infecting your system in the first place.** The software recognizes hundreds of viruses by maintaining a database of virus fingerprints, or *signatures*. It can scan new files that a user downloads from an external source, or places into a diskette drive, and raise an alert before the user even copies or executes the program.

- ✔ **It provides an early warning system**. Antivirus software can detect a virus that slips through your early warning system and quickly alert your administrator, who can then repair and disinfect the affected file before the virus spreads and forces a costly network shutdown.

- ✔ **It helps you recover from a virus attack**. Good antivirus software can clean, repair, and disinfect the computer, or at least tell you when to throw in the towel and restore from a clean backup.

Effective antivirus technology runs software on both servers and clients. Some companies believe that they achieve complete protection by running antivirus software on the file server. However, you really need to protect every node on the network that — either through a diskette drive or modem — allows data input.

Some of the questions to ask when shopping for antivirus software include

✔ **How many different viruses can the software detect?**

✔ **How frequently does the vendor issue updates so that the software can catch new viruses?** You need to update your antivirus software monthly, at least.

✔ **How much of a pain is it to apply such updates?** The really slick software provides a one-click update procedure, as does Symantec Norton AntiVirus (see Figure 11-3).

Figure 11-3:
Norton
AntiVirus
LiveUpdate
automatically
connects to
Symantec's
Internet
site and
downloads
new virus
information.

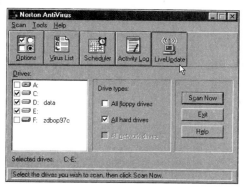

✔ **Can the software detect viruses it doesn't already know about?** Good utilities watch for suspicious activity, such as software attempting to write to a hard disk's boot sector. Nevertheless, antivirus software is always more effective when it uses an updated list of *virus signatures* — the telltale fingerprints that identify known offenders.

✔ **Can the software detect viruses in compressed files?** Novell IntranetWare and Microsoft Windows NT Server both use automatic file compression in order to conserve server disk space.

✔ **How prone is the software to false alarms?** These are a real pain.

✔ **What ways can the software tell me about an alarm?** A network message, a pager alert, a Strip-o-Gram sent to the office, and so on, are ways the software can alert you. (The Strip-o-Gram feature costs extra.)

✔ Can the software be set to scan particular files or directories (or particular types of files, such as EXE and DLL) more often than others?

✔ What information does the software's log file provide? And can you understand it?

✔ Does the software kill my network in terms of speed? Some antivirus software does. Benchmark it (see Chapter 12) to find out.

Antivirus software vendors include Cheyenne Software (a division of Computer Associates), Seagate Software, and Symantec Corporation, among many others. See Appendix B for contact information.

Antivirus procedures

Technology alone isn't enough to combat viruses effectively. You also have to have reasonable and widely followed antivirus *policies and procedures* in place. For example:

✔ **Scan all new workstations for viruses.**

✔ **Only install software from shrink-wrapped boxes.**

✔ **Decide whether computer games are allowed in the office.** Games transmit more viruses than most other kinds of software, because some of the game authors think viruses are "cool" and because people tend to copy games more often from their home machines to office machines.

✔ **Restrict users from booting workstations from diskette.** The rare exception is when a LAN administrator must boot a computer from diskette in order to safely disinfect a machine, such as with the *rescue diskettes* that many antivirus utilities create.

✔ **Assure that your company won't discipline or hold accountable those who report a virus, unless they're responsible for introducing it and are in violation of your policies and procedures.**

✔ **Help users protect their portable and home computers.** Companies don't just do this out of the goodness of their hearts; many employees work at home on their own computers and then unwittingly bring in to the office the virus that little Timmy picked up when he downloaded the latest beta of the game *Parents In Bondage*.

You need to have a procedure in place for recovering from a virus if you get hit. The usual steps are as follows:

1. **Rule out all other possibilities.**

2. **Quarantine the affected computer, and thus the virus.**

How to tell when you've been hit

So how do you know when a virus has inconsiderately attacked your network? Aside from receiving an alert message from your antivirus utility, some of the warning signs include the following:

- ✔ Keyboards act weird (some keys don't work, or don't do what they should).

- ✔ Displays behave oddly (they change to unusual colors, letters slowly slide to the bottom of the screen, and so on).

- ✔ Hard drives fill up much faster than normal.

- ✔ Programs slow down dramatically.

- ✔ Data files disappear into thin air, or won't open (the common Windows *Concept* virus causes users to unwittingly save documents as templates, which users can't open anymore thereafter).

- ✔ Messages appear on user workstations, advocating political positions on use of the Cannabis plant, wishing you a happy Friday the 13th, or saying things like, "This is what you get for firing me, you ingrates!". (Actually, virus authors rarely use words like *ingrate*, but you get the idea.)

Users tend to assume that odd computer behavior is somehow *their* fault, but often it indicates virus infection (troubleshooters, take note!). Educate your users about virus signs and to report suspicious behavior to the LAN administrator immediately.

---

3. **Identify the virus.**

4. **Remove the virus.**

5. **Repeat the process for all computers from which the virus may have come, and to which it may have spread.**

6. **Take measures to ensure against a repeat of the infection.**

Your antivirus software vendor can provide more details on how to perform these steps using its product.

Server Security

Security consultants tend to focus on servers for good reason: Servers are where you keep most of your critical programs and data files.

User-level versus share-level security

Share-level security, the kind most peer-to-peer networks use, associates passwords with particular network resources (files, directories, printers, and so on) rather than with individuals. In this setup, any user on the network has the authority to share any file on his or her computer with anyone else on the network — no one person or policy controls how security is implemented.

This sort of decentralized security is poor security in the minds of many network managers, which is why peer-to-peer networks are usually used in organizations where security isn't a big deal. In Chapter 4, I mention that the number of passwords users have to remember in a share-level security setup is larger than in a *user-level setup* (see next paragraph), and that fact alone increases the risk that users write their passwords down somewhere. Another risk is that users simply assign blank passwords to all shared resources.

User-level security works on the model of assigning an account and a password to each network user, and then controlling what network resources those users can access by using a central administrative utility. Client/ server networks, such as IntranetWare and Windows NT Server, use user-level security. Although they also provide options to add resource-centric security (such as making a file or directory read-only) where appropriate, they typically don't assign passwords on a resource-by-resource basis.

Because share-level security in peer-to-peer networks is so simple (I explain how it works in Chapter 4), I focus here on user-level security in client/ server networks — which is simultaneously more complex and more complete.

Client/server security

In this section, I give you eight tips for implementing user-level security no matter what kind of network you use, and incredibly brief summaries of the security mechanisms available in IntranetWare and Windows NT Server. The specific steps to put client/server security into practice in your network are available in the online or printed documentation that you get with your Network Operating System. However, by reading this section first, you arm yourself with the basics — and you get some suggestions from a guy who's been there and done that, many times.

An octet of tips

Try to assign all of your file server permissions at the group level, and then add and delete users from those groups as appropriate. This way is much easier than trying to track the permissions of every individual user in your business.

Along the same lines, when assigning restrictions to directories and files, try not to go down to the file level. Assign restrictions by directory, and organize your directories so that different users don't need different access privileges to files within the same directory.

Keep your Network Operating System updated with vendor patches and maintenance releases — many of these updates are designed to boost security, or even fix security holes.

Use the *auditing* and *logging* features built into your network software to help you identify break-in attempts. Auditing and logging programs create files that record a history of network activity, viewable with a supplied utility or simple text editor. Look for two or three incorrect logon attempts in a row; legitimate users may mistype a password once, but rarely three times, unless they're on something. You can even set your server to lock out an account if a user enters an incorrect password *X* times in a row, forcing the user to go to the administrator to reactivate the account.

Remove the relevant LAN account(s) immediately after an employee leaves your company, or at least change the user ID and password if you want the employee's replacement to have the same privileges and don't want to re-create the account.

If the network administrator changes a user account's privileges during troubleshooting, the administrator must remember to change the account back when finished.

Special LAN-based security measures include *watchdog programs* that automatically log users off the network after a specified number of minutes of inactivity. These programs can help avoid the he-went-to-lunch-and-forgot-to-log-out syndrome. An unattended but logged-in workstation is a major security hole.

Programs to test your LAN-based security are a good idea. The Unix world offers the Security Administrator Tool for Analyzing Networks (SATAN — I'm not kidding). Windows NT Server and NetWare shops can look at the Kane Security Analyst (see Appendix B), which knows about and looks for common security holes in these operating systems. Also, the Windows NT Resource Kit contains a program called C2 Manager that graphically shows your security holes and fixes them on request.

IntranetWare security in two pages or less

Novell IntranetWare offers a wide range of tools for the network administrator wanting to lay down some server security. Your biggest challenge in implementing IntranetWare security is mastering all the options available to you. In a nutshell, the IntranetWare security mechanisms include the following:

- ✔ **Logon security.** This first line of defense deals with user names, passwords, and logon restrictions; the operating system stores this information in the NDS (NetWare Directory Services) database. You manage logon security with NEAT (NetWare Easy Administration Tool) in IntranetWare for Small Business, and with the NWADMIN program in a regular IntranetWare installation (that is, not the Small Business product).

- ✔ **Trustee rights.** This is where you allow specific users or groups rights to specific files and directories. Novell calls this security measure *trustee rights* because the user becomes a trustee of the directory to which he or she has access. The trustee rights include *read, write, create, erase, modify, file scan, access control,* and *supervisory.* You can assign a new user the same trustee rights as an existing user through what Novell calls *security equivalences* (Mary can do whatever Bob can do). Again, NEAT and NWADMIN are the tools you use to assign or change trustee rights.

- ✔ **Effective rights.** These are the trustee rights that take effect because they're not blocked by what Novell calls an *Inherited Rights Filter,* or IRF. The IRFs are specific to each server directory, and they basically limit what a user can do when he or she doesn't have a specific trustee right to access a particular file or directory.

- ✔ **Attribute security.** This lowest level of IntranetWare security assigns special properties or attributes to individual directories and files, regardless of whatever trustee rights a user may have to those directories and files. For example, you can assign a group of files the *read-only attribute* to ensure that users can't modify or delete them. (However, users with the *modify* trustee right can change those file attributes, so trustee rights and attribute security can overlap. Got that?)

- ✔ **NDS security.** NetWare Directory Services introduces two new types of rights to go along with its tree-structured view of the entire network: object rights and property rights. *Object rights* specify what one object in the NDS tree can do with another object; object rights consist of the *browse, create, delete, rename,* and *supervisor* rights. *Property rights* specify what users can do with a particular object's properties.

With these five tools at your disposal, you can make an IntranetWare server as secure as you need it to be — even up to the standards of the U.S. Department of Defense. An administrator of a small network should start with logon security, trustee rights, and attribute security before worrying about the other two. The NEAT program is much easier to use than NWADMIN and is one of the nicest things about IntranetWare for Small Business (see Figure 11-4).

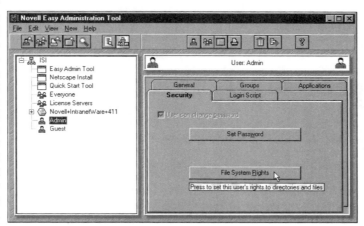

Figure 11-4: The Novell Easy Administration Tool presents a hierarchical view of the network on the left, and lets you set security options on the right.

Windows NT Server security in two pages or less

Windows NT Server offers strong, multifaceted security as does IntranetWare, and it has many similar elements, with a few wrinkles:

- ✔ **Logon security.** User names, passwords, and access restrictions constitute logon security, just as in IntranetWare. The tool to use is the NT User Manager or User Manager for Domains (see Figure 11-5).

- ✔ **User and group rights.** NT Server comes with a number of convenient, predefined users and groups, which you can view and modify in User Manager for Domains. User Manager for Domains is where you begin when designing an NT security system, crafting groups and users and assigning rights on the system to those groups and users via the Policies menu. (*Rights* in this context means "things you're allowed to do with the server," and there are too many to list here.)

Figure 11-5:
The
Windows
NT Server
User
Manager
for Domains
Account
Policy
dialog box
enables
your
administrator
to specify
several
kinds of
logon
security.

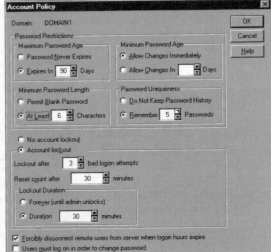

✔ **Share permissions.** You then move to the Server Manager (or, alternatively, Explorer) to specify shared resources (*shares*) on the network and which users and groups you want to have access to those resources. You can specify *no access, read, change,* and *full control* when creating a share. Some consultants recommend leaving the share permission at full control, and managing group and user access with directory and file permissions (see next item).

✔ **Directory and file permissions.** NT Server allows an administrator to set permissions at the directory and file level. The tool to use is the Windows NT Explorer, which is very similar to the Windows 95 Explorer. You simply log on as an administrator, run Explorer, right-click the particular directories or files, and then choose Properties. You then click the Security tab and choose Permissions. The file and directory permissions you can set are *read, write, delete, execute, change permission,* and *take ownership.* Microsoft also provides a number of permission groupings that combine these individual permissions in different, commonly used ways for convenience at the directory level.

✔ **System policies.** NT Server allows you to create system policies (using the appropriately named System Policy Editor) that restrict a number of functions that users can perform from their desktops. See "Workstation Security" later in this chapter for more on the concept of policies.

Format server hard drives with the *NT File System* (NTFS) rather than the *File Allocation Table* (FAT) file system in order to take maximum advantage of the Windows NT security features (specifically, file-level attribute security).

Most small companies set up NT Server to use a single domain. If you want to set up multiple domains (which incidentally require multiple servers as *primary domain controllers*), you have to create a *trust relationship* between them in order for users on one domain to access resources on another domain. For very large companies, the Novell NDS database is undeniably more convenient than Windows NT domain security, but small businesses shouldn't really feel the difference. Anyway, if you're big enough to need directory services on an NT Server network, you can buy NDS for NT from Novell. NT 5.0 will feature *Active Directory,* essentially a big wizard that makes trusts in the domain model work like the tree structure in NDS.

Please pass the word

Whether you use peer-to-peer networking and share-level security, or client/server networking and user-level security, passwords can help secure your network. They're more important with user-level security because a single password unlocks more resources, but passwords can help buttress share-level security, too. The big problem with passwords is the same as with lottery tickets: Most of them are no good.

Users share passwords with each other like dirty secrets. They pick passwords that are easy to remember and therefore easy to guess, and they write their passwords down. Contractors and consultants get passwords that administrators fail to cancel when the jobs are finished. Users who leave the organization may enjoy password access for months — or even years — later.

LAN administrators can program their networks to enhance password security by taking the following steps:

- ✔ **Make users change their passwords periodically by forcing expiration after a specified number of days (30 to 90 is typical), which requires the user to enter a new, unique password.**
- ✔ **Don't allow employees to log on with the same account.** For best security, every user needs to have a unique account name and password.
- ✔ **Restrict password accounts to specific times of the day.** This is especially important for visitors and contractors.
- ✔ **Force a minimum password length.** For example, Windows NT Server defaults to 6 characters but can go up to 14.

✓ **Specify a maximum number of incorrect logon attempts.** If the incorrect logon attempts exceed the set number, lock out the account for at least 30 minutes afterward (to foil *crackers*, people trying to break into your network).

✓ **Require unique passwords that no one else on the network is already using.** Also, set the minimum time for how soon the user is allowed to change the password again after having been forced to change it by server security. Doing so keeps users from flipping back to the old password right away.

✓ **Remove the default passwords that come with preconfigured LAN user accounts.** These include Guest, Supervisor, or Administrator (even better, rename those accounts to other, less well-known names).

User education on password selection can help, too. For example, users should choose passwords that

✓ **Aren't in the dictionary**

✓ **Have numbers and punctuation marks, as well as both uppercase and lowercase letters**

✓ **Don't have anything to do with the user.** For example, don't use the user name spelled backward, the user name spelled *forward* — I've seen this more often than you'd think — part of a user name, the name of a user's relative, and so on.

✓ **Are reasonably easy to remember through the use of mnemonic devices**

The password *Uf2bdis!* ("You have two beady eyes!") is okay; *myhusbandbob* is not. The network administrator's account should have an especially long and hard-to-guess password.

Application security

The application programs you run may come with their own product-specific security features, and a wide variety of them exists. Just remember the following:

✓ **Application security is an *added layer* only.** Product-specific application security is in addition to whatever LAN-based or web server-based security you may have set up, not in place of it. By the same token, if you feel your LAN-based security is sufficient, don't use application security. You don't have to use it just because it's there.

> ✔ **Too many passwords actually encourages a *less* secure network.** If every application you use has its own set of user IDs and passwords, in addition to whatever network passwords you've set up, users are likely to write all those passwords down on sticky notes and paste them onto their computer monitors. Or, users may figure out ways to combine all those passwords into a *password cache* (such as that provided automatically by Windows 95) that a single logon password unlocks. Too much security becomes no security.

Some of your applications may deal with information that you must keep private by law, such as some types of human resources data (who has a drug problem, for example), or information that may facilitate employer discrimination. Check with your legal counsel to identify information that requires strict access control by law, and then either slap tight security on that information and related applications, or don't put the sensitive data on your network at all.

Workstation Security

After you secure your server or servers, take a look at user workstations. Today's network-ready microcomputers often ship with powerful software that can modify other computers on the network. For example, a Windows 95 PC can potentially link to another Windows 95 PC and change all the hardware and software settings on that machine — a nice capability for your network administrator, but not something you want anyone else using.

Whereas network-level security controls what users can do with shared files, programs, and printers, workstation-level security controls what users can and can't do with the files and programs on their own computers and (as in the preceding paragraph's example) on other workstations. If you run Windows 95, Windows NT 4.0, or newer versions of those products on user computers, you can use a feature called *system policies* to lock users out of certain tasks. You can use system policies regardless of whether your server runs IntranetWare, Windows NT Server, OS/2 Warp Server, or just about anything else.

You can set systemwide policies that apply for all network users, or group policies that apply different restrictions based on the user's membership in different network groups. Microsoft also makes available, via its Internet site (www.microsoft.com), a *Zero Administration Kit* that makes setting system policies a little easier. Some of the Windows books in Appendix B provide details on setting system policies. Figure 11-6 shows you what the Policy Editor looks like — you can get to it at ADMIN\APPTOOLS\POLEDIT on the Windows 95 CD-ROM.

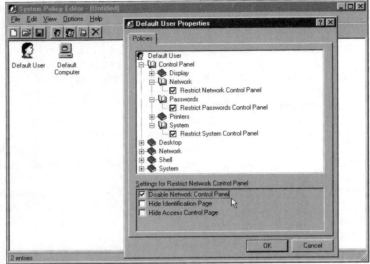

Figure 11-6:
The
Windows 95
System
Policy
Editor.

Whatever tool you use to limit user capabilities on local computers, you need to consider restricting the following types of activities:

- ✔ **Installing new software**
- ✔ **Changing the network setup**
- ✔ **Setting up the workstation to permit dial-up access**
- ✔ **Running administrative tools** (for example, the Registry Editor in Windows 95 and Windows NT Workstation)

Several consulting clients of mine remove diskette drives from user workstations. This practice isn't feasible in all situations, but it increases security by preventing users (or visitors or intruders) from booting the computer from diskette, installing programs or data files from diskette, and copying network files to diskette. If you take this step and need employees to work from home periodically, provide dial-up access, as discussed in Chapter 10.

Remote Access Security

This section takes a look at ways to prevent unauthorized users from linking into your network from remote locations, whether via the public Internet or via modems that connect directly to your network.

Dial-up security

If your business has a lot of portable computing going on (telecommuting, dial-up access, and so on), you need to pay attention to dial-up security. The three aspects of dial-up security worth considering are *power-on passwords, callback modems,* and *encrypted logon.*

A *power-on password* is one that a user creates using the notebook computer's setup program — having one in place means that the computer won't let an unauthorized user even get to square one. When the computer is turned on, the computer asks the user for a user name and password. Without authentication, the computer doesn't do a thing. There are ways around power-on passwords, such as removing the tiny, internal battery that stores the password information, but most notebook thieves don't have the time to bother with them.

Callback modems work like this: A user dials up your server, provides an identifying code, and then hangs up. The server looks up the user's phone number, which is cross-referenced to the identifying code, and calls the user back. Then the user's modem answers the phone, the user logs onto the network, and then starts working. "But wait," you say. "What if the user is on the road, and has a different number than usual?" One solution is for the traveling user to have a cellular modem with a fixed number.

Notebooks often use connection software that transmits unencrypted logon information (user ID and password). In theory, an electronic eavesdropper monitoring the dial-up line can sniff out that account information, and then gain access to the network by going to the office and posing as a copier repairperson. If the connection software has an option to *encrypt logon* passwords (as, for example, Windows 95 Dial Up Networking does), then enable this feature. You may also want to ask the phone company to assign an exchange prefix to your dial-up lines that differs from the office's regular prefix. A cracker has a tougher time guessing seven numbers than four.

One additional level of dial-up security encrypts *all* the communications between the remote user and the network, not just the logon process. The technology that enables this security measure is called *Point-to-Point Tunneling Protocol,* or PPTP. Microsoft Windows NT Server 4.0 supports PPTP. For PPTP to work, the remote user needs to have a communication program, such as Windows 95 Dial-Up Networking, that also supports PPTP.

Securing an Internet link

If your network links to the public Internet, you may need to put several security measures in place:

> ✔ **Limit user ability to connect to the Internet.** Maybe not everyone in your company should have Internet access. Your LAN administrator needs it, certainly, and so may market researchers, but other employees may not need a license to surf.
>
> ✔ **Limit user ability to connect to certain sites.** You may want to limit access to certain sites that appeal to our baser human instincts, or are likely to waste a ton of time.
>
> ✔ **Restrict all (or most) Internet users outside your organization from linking to your network.**

A *firewall* is a mechanism for protecting a trusted network (usually, your LAN) from an untrusted network (usually, the Internet) to which it connects. The firewall can help prevent access by unauthorized outsiders, and it can also lay restrictions on what parts of the Internet internal users can go visit. Firewalls can usually restrict outbound communications by user ID or by IP (Internet Protocol) address. Think of a firewall as a single, defensible connection from one network into another.

A simple firewall may simply limit Internet communications to e-mail and deny all Web traffic in either direction. Another simple sort of firewall is a *packet-filtering router* that only permits communication between the Internet and a certain chunk of your LAN. The most complex, and effective, firewalls use something called a *proxy server*.

Proxy servers don't permit direct communication between the Internet and your internal network. Instead, they act as a store-and-forward repository. The proxy server examines incoming traffic from either direction, sees if that traffic meets its predefined criteria, and if so, passes it to the requesting computer — it acts as a *proxy* between two communicating computers that think they're connecting directly, but really aren't.

Proxy servers hide your workstation IP addresses from the outside world — the proxy server has its own IP address, which is all that the external users see, and it can forward traffic to the appropriate internal IP addresses, which only the proxy server knows about.

Firewalls may be separate, standalone servers running firewall software, or add-on software that installs onto an existing web server. For example, Microsoft Internet Access Server is a software-only firewall that plugs into Internet Information Server (IIS) running on a Windows NT Server machine. Some popular firewall vendors include Check Point Systems, Raptor Systems, Secure Computing Corp., and Trusted Information Systems (see Appendix B for contact information).

Chapter 12

Your Business Moves Fast and So Should Your Network

"**S**peed, it seems to me, provides the one genuinely modern pleasure." (Aldous Huxley, *Music at Night and Other Essays*)

One of a small company's biggest advantages is speed, and you don't want your computer network to diminish that advantage by slowing you down. Today's computer hardware may be a zillion times faster than that of 20 years ago, but today's software is a zillion times more demanding, too. I find that network delays on a modern *Local Area Network* (LAN) aren't dramatically different from the delays on the old time-sharing system I cut my programming teeth on back in college two decades ago. (What you can *do* on a modern LAN is amazingly more advanced, however. I could never have played Duke Nukem or Tomb Raider on that old Digital Equipment Corp. time-sharing computer.)

Here's why I devote an entire chapter to improving LAN speed: The human brain, when it hasn't atrophied from overexposure to television and radio talk shows, works faster than most of us realize. If a computer network takes much more than a second or two to respond to a user action, the user is already thinking about something else by the time the network reacts. Or, sometimes, the user's brain shifts into a slower gear during the wait (technical term: to *zone*), and has to upshift when the information arrives. In either case, the user can't work at full tilt. Working on a slow computer network is a bit like crossing the Rockies on a moped; you get where you want eventually, but it takes more work and time than it should.

Nobody functions at top speed all the time, but in every business, situations arise when time is critical, such as when Galactic Ventures, Inc., offers to place a huge order if you can generate a detailed quotation by the end of the day. You want your people to rise to the occasion, and you want your computers to be right in there with them.

One other quick point: You may be installing a network where, previously, you've had a number of individual (*standalone*) computers. Be aware that information moves more slowly across a network cable (*between* computers) than it does *within* a standalone computer. Your employees are sure to notice that any data on a server takes longer to retrieve than data on local hard drives. You want to wring as much speed out of your network as you can, to minimize the degree to which your employees hate the network because it's slow compared to what they're used to.

Hot-Rodding Your Network 101

Specific speed tips depend on the particular software and hardware you run on your network. However, the principles stay the same, and they're worth understanding before you dive into the particulars of your situation.

Four pillars of wisdom

One: Computers, and particularly computer networks, rarely run at maximum speed right out of the box. Hardware and software vendors can't know the exact size of your network, what programs you intend to run on it, and what aspects of network performance (printing, opening data files, performing backups, and so on) are most important to you.

Two: Performance tuning only takes you so far. You can wax a canoe till it's as slick as a Washington politician, but it won't outrun a motorboat. Rarely is the difference between a tuned network and a nontuned network as great as 50 percent, so condition your expectations accordingly. Chapters 2 and 7 offer guidelines to help you start with appropriately fast hardware; this chapter helps you wring the most out of it, and keep it fast over time.

Three: When you can't tune something and you can't replace it, see if you can work around it. Print those big reports at night, after making sure that the paper tray's full. If data backups take a long time, do them at night, too. Ditto for month-end and year-end accounting close procedures. Performing these types of network-intensive tasks at night (that is, after 5:01 p.m. for a big company, after midnight for a small business!) means that fewer employees are around to get burned by the network slowdown.

Four (and arguably most important): A computer network is only as fast as its slowest part. When you talk about performance tuning, *balance* (sometimes called network *load distribution*) is everything. Your first order of business, then, is to find the *bottlenecks* — places where network traffic hits a speed bump, or, for my British readers, a "sleeping policeman."

Find the bottlenecks

The three places where bottlenecks can lurk are at the server, in the *plumbing* (cabling and hubs), and at the user workstations. Usually, performance tuners (like piano tuners, but with pocket protectors) tackle these three areas in the stated order. Professional consultants start a speed overhaul at the server almost by reflex. However, the location of your network's bottlenecks may vary. Save time and money and fix the big problems first, wherever they are; find them by talking to users and running tests.

Interview the users

Network users can tell you a lot about where to direct your hot-rodding efforts. For example:

> ✔ **Ask users whether their computers seem noticeably faster or slower at different times of the day.** Do things run a lot faster when most employees are at lunch? If the answer is yes, you're almost certainly looking at server or network plumbing performance.

> ✔ **Ask users about the speed differences between different programs.** If graphics-oriented applications like desktop publishing programs generate most of the complaints, you may have a bottleneck at the workstation video circuit. A new $100 video board may do the trick. Another possibility is that the computer doesn't have enough memory to store an entire graphic, and a RAM infusion could be the solution.

> ✔ **Ask users about different types of operations.** Is printing horribly slow? What about opening files on the network server? Starting programs in the morning? Saving documents to disk? The answers can point you in the right direction.

After the users give you a good feel for where performance problems seem to be, you can roll up your sleeves, get scientific, and start running benchmarks and experiments.

Benchmark and experiment

Benchmarks are standardized tests that you can run on a computer system to see how it performs compared to other systems, or compared to itself with different settings or equipment. You can get free benchmark test software from computer magazines like *PC Magazine* and *Byte*. (See Figure 12-1.)

You can download the current version of Ziff-Davis Labs' benchmarking utilities on the World Wide Web at `http://www1.zdnet.com/zdbop`. The Byte benchmarks are at `http://www.byte.com`.

When you run a benchmark on a computer or a network, you can compare the results you get with published results for similar systems to see if you're in the same ballpark. (The magazines that supply benchmark software also supply results for a variety of hardware and software combinations.) If your network rates relatively close to the published results, you may decide that your computers and network are healthy, and decide not to worry much about performance tuning. If not, you may have a performance bottleneck that you need to find and fix.

You can also use benchmark software to tell you the effect of your tuning changes. You typically do this by running the benchmark software to check how your computer or network runs today and obtain what is called a *baseline*. Then you make a software or hardware change to your network and run the benchmark again to see the effect. When you find a change that seems to make a positive difference, you can make it permanent.

Some tips on running benchmarks:

- ✔ **Change only one thing at a time between benchmark runs, so you can determine the effect of that change by itself.**

- ✔ **Make sure you keep all variables (number of programs running on the computer, number of users logged in to the network, and so on) identical between runs, so you're comparing apples to apples.**

- ✔ **To be a little more scientific, run your benchmarks more than once for each scenario and average the results.** Be on the alert for wide variances between runs under supposedly identical conditions: Variables that you haven't controlled may affect the results (for example, users may log on to the network from home while you're testing).

- ✔ **Use the most up-to-date benchmark software you can get.** Product manufacturers figure out how to optimize their products for popular benchmark software, but not necessarily for *performance*. After the manufacturers tune their products to the benchmarks, the benchmarks are useless.

You can also perform various experiments, with or without a benchmark utility. For example, to find out whether performance problems pertain to the workstation itself, or to the network (server plus plumbing), try copying a data file (preferably a large one) to the user's hard drive, and have the user work with the "local" data file for a few minutes. If the user still reports slow speed, you may need to tune the workstation, for example by defragmenting the hard drive or by adding RAM. On the other hand, if the speed is much better, you're dealing with either server or traffic issues.

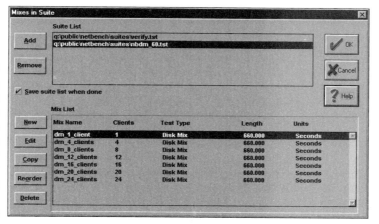

Figure 12-1:
Ziff-Davis
Labs
offers the
NetBench
program for
checking
network
performance.

Fight no small battles

Remember the Hydra monster of Greek mythology? Whenever Hercules chopped off one of its heads, two would instantly grow in its place, ultimately forcing Hercules to kill the Hydra with a small thermonuclear device. LAN tuning is similar. Once you find (and fix!) the most important network performance bottleneck, two smaller bottlenecks appear.

Tuning a network for performance by making configuration changes, and then measuring the effect of those changes, is an ever-smaller spiral that never seems to end. Users rarely say, "Gee, you don't need to spend any more time on performance tuning, the network's fast enough to suit me," and you always have some way of making your computer network run slightly faster. Your network administrator may even take a certain pleasure in tuning the LAN, which can be a fun and gratifying intellectual exercise. Here, then, are two guidelines I often use to help ensure a favorable return on your time and money investment when hot-rodding your network:

✔ **Don't buy new hardware that boosts performance less than 20 percent in a particular area (file transfer, graphics, and so on).** If a new *Network Interface Card* (NIC) is advertised to be 50 percent faster than what you have, by all means consider it, but don't buy a new workstation hard drive because it claims to run 10 percent faster than the existing one. Small steps in performance usually aren't worth the money in an industry that makes big leaps every couple of years.

✔ **Don't spend more than a day working on software settings that boost performance less than 10 percent.** You can easily get bogged down mastering the many detailed software settings that ultimately don't do much for you in terms of speed. Get some guidance from manuals, magazines, or vendors as to which settings make a significant difference and which don't (the remaining sections of this chapter offer several suggestions, as well).

Monitor performance

Your network's usage profile — number of users, peak activity times, and so on — may change over time, changing performance along with it. The only way to keep your LAN in shape is to monitor performance on a regular basis, track the changes, identify the problems, and then deal with them. More scientific system managers use performance monitoring as a way to predict future capacity requirements.

Most *Network Operating Systems* (NOSs) have built-in or *bundled* (included) performance monitoring utilities. These utilities can give you an overall view of how the server's doing and track resource use over time so that you can see what happens during a typical minute, hour, or day. Windows NT Server comes with a Performance Monitor that enables you to track just about every performance-related quantity imaginable, as does the Novell Monitor utility. You may also want to check out third-party performance monitoring software; for example, NConsole from Avanti Technology, Inc. (see Appendix B) for Novell NetWare server monitoring.

Network monitoring isn't just for client/server networks, either. For example, if you use Windows 95 servers on a peer-to-peer network, you can use the handy little System Monitor program to collect network information (choose Start⇨Programs⇨Accessories⇨System Tools⇨System Monitor). The System Monitor program isn't as fancy as the Windows NT Server Performance Monitor, but it doesn't really need to be, and in some ways, it's easier to use. The bytes/second and memory values for the Microsoft Network Server category provide information on traffic and memory use attributable to server functions, as shown in Figure 12-2.

A good network administrator gets to know the network's characteristics by running performance monitoring software regularly. Doing so helps the administrator identify abnormal situations (such as a defective, or *chatty*, NIC) and correct them.

Server Tuning

You probably ask quite a bit of your network server. In a typical client/ server LAN, servers share files, printers, modems, and CD-ROMs. Servers also impose and enforce user security, handle data and program backups, stand guard against viruses, enable you to play multiuser computer *Battle-ship,* and keep detailed logs of what happens on the network. If you have a peer-to-peer network, the machines sharing frequently accessed files and printers must also provide workstation functions for their designated users. Servers work hard, and may need the occasional tweak here and there to stay quick and alert enough to do what you ask of them.

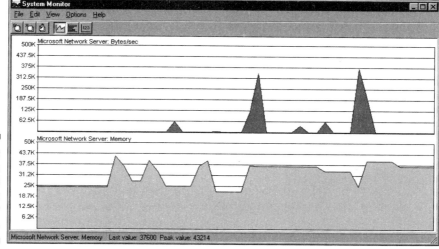

Figure 12-2:
The
Windows 95
System
Monitor
program.

Assuming that you've already bought and installed a machine to act as your primary server, whether in a peer-to-peer setup or a hybrid client/server and peer-to-peer setup (see Chapter 4), what can you tune to make it go faster? The usual candidates are the CPU, memory (RAM), disk, and communications.

CPU

Certain programs tend to tax a LAN server's CPU (*Central Processing Unit*) — e-mail and database programs are good examples. Fortunately, if you find that you underbought the server CPU, you're not necessarily stuck. You may have one or more of the following three options:

✔ ***Symmetric MultiProcessing* (SMP).** For example, Microsoft Windows NT Server enables you to throw up to four microprocessors into one box to ramp up server brainpower. Novell IntranetWare also supports SMP through an add-on software module called SMP.NLM that can handle 32 CPUs(!). Servers that support SMP don't run twice as fast when you throw a second CPU into the server — often, 50 percent faster is all the performance boost you see. On most systems, you get the biggest jolt going from one CPU to two; more CPUs cost the same but don't deliver as much additional oomph. Also, you have to run programs on the server that know about SMP; programs that don't take advantage of SMP run solely on the first CPU. (32-bit Windows programs, for example, *do* take advantage of SMP when running on a Windows NT Server.)

✔ **CPU upgrade.** Sometimes you can do chip surgery and replace an older, slower microprocessor with a newer, faster one. Chip replacement can be a valid option, but an upgrade may not exist for your CPU — in part because some new CPUs require *motherboard* (the computer's main circuit board) changes also. You may want to consult with an experienced technician who can peek at the motherboard and decide if the CPU is upgradable. Again, the performance boost you get is not directly relative to the CPU speeds, because simply upgrading a CPU doesn't upgrade all the circuitry surrounding it.

✔ **Level 2 cache.** Most CPUs spend a good portion of their day sitting around waiting on memory transfers. *Level 2 CPU cache memory* is very fast (and, on a per megabyte basis, very expensive) memory that sits between the CPU and the main chunk of slower memory (the 32, 64, or 128MB you hear about when I talk about "server RAM"). Many computers come with 256KB of L2 cache, but they can often accommodate 512KB, which enables the computer to feed the CPU with information more rapidly. For $100 or so, you can give your server CPU a speed boost on the order of 10 to 15 percent. As with a CPU upgrade, some motherboards support additional L2 cache and some don't; check with the manufacturer or an experienced technician. (For more on how cache memory works, see the next section.)

RAM

Servers need RAM for two things: to hold the Network Operating System (NOS) software itself, and to provide *memory buffers* for NICs and disks. You can check the first item by looking at the specification sheet for the NOS — the minimum amount of memory stated there is enough to run the network. However, the minimum amount of RAM to run the network may not be enough to provide adequate space for the second item, *buffers,* which require a bit of explanation. . . .

Servers temporarily store files and directories in chunks of RAM called *buffers* to increase speed, because getting information from RAM is *many* times faster than getting it from a disk drive. Disk buffering, or *caching* (pronounced "cashing"), is the act of saving recently retrieved information in a special chunk of memory called the *cache* (French for "hiding place") where the computer can get to it much faster if it needs that same information again in the next few seconds.

The whole idea behind caching is that computers tend to go back to the same place for information over and over again. You can think of caching as somewhat like bookstores putting the bestsellers in a special display at the front of the store where customers can find them faster. (The Level 2 CPU cache I discuss in the previous section is another example, but in that case, the computer caches RAM instead of the hard drive.) In addition to read caching, a server can also buffer data that it ultimately plans to *write* to the hard drive, in order to buy a little time so that the server can write to the disk when things aren't too busy and even out the workload a bit.

Communications buffers are, again, chunks of memory, but they act as a way station, or combination in-box and out-box, for incoming or outgoing network traffic while the server is busy doing other tasks. Communications buffers cache the NIC, while disk buffers cache the disk drives. Figure 12-3 illustrates disk and communications buffering.

Usually, tuning RAM on a server means simply adding more, until your performance monitoring utility reports that the *hit rate* — the percentage of time that the server can find the data it needs in a memory buffer instead of having to perform an actual disk read or write — is above 90 percent.

If you use Novell IntranetWare (or IntranetWare for Small Business) as your server, run the performance monitor to see if the *LRU sitting time* statistic is at least 15 minutes (LRU stands for *Least Recently Used*). If not, you probably need RAM.

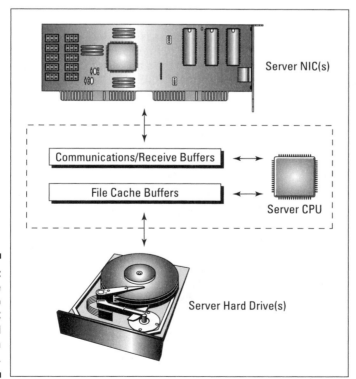

Server NIC(s)

Communications/Receive Buffers

File Cache Buffers

Server CPU

Server Hard Drive(s)

Figure 12-3:
Servers use RAM to buffer NIC traffic and disk data transfers.

The total amount of RAM you need depends on the server operating system that you run. For example, Microsoft Windows NT Server needs more RAM than IntranetWare to provide the same level of performance. If you run NT and you have less than 64MB, you can probably run the server faster by adding RAM. If you run Novell IntranetWare and you have less than 32MB of RAM, ditto. The right amount of memory also depends on the programs you run, how many users you have, how many disk drives, how many printers, and so on.

Although modern NOSs like Novell IntranetWare and Microsoft Windows NT Server do a good job of managing file and communications buffers automatically, you can tune these settings manually and sometimes enjoy better performance. The details are beyond the scope of this book, and setting these server performance variables is a great candidate for outsourcing. A specialist can spend a couple of hours analyzing your network and making performance enhancements that may take your part-time network administrator a week just to read about.

Disk

Tuning server disks generally involves fixing file system problems using the operating system's repair utility, such as Novell VREPAIR and Microsoft ScanDisk. You also want to regularly *defragment* disks, that is, consolidate files so that all their pieces are physically adjacent and the server doesn't have to hunt all over the disk platter for files that are stored in bits and pieces (see Figure 12-4). (Nearly all computer operating systems written in the last four decades automatically chop up, or *fragment,* files so that those files can fit on disks having only scattered pockets of free space. When disk space used to cost big bucks, fragmenting was an important virtue, because it allowed computers to use nearly all the available disk space.)

Sometimes the operating system comes with a defragmenter, and sometimes, as with Windows NT Server, you have to buy a separate utility (Diskeeper from Executive Software International is the market leader). Despite Microsoft claims to the contrary, NT Server *does* suffer from fragmentation. In either case, setting up a regular schedule for tuning the disks is a great idea. Some programs defragment continuously in the background whenever the server isn't too busy.

Here are some other disk performance tips:

✔ **Update your disk driver.** The *disk driver* is the bit of software that the NOS uses to talk to the hard disks. Network vendors are always tweaking these drivers for better performance and reliability. Keep them up to date with a quarterly check of the vendor's Web site. (I've seen performance jump as much as 30 percent with an updated driver.)

✔ **Tweak the block size.** You may want to change the *disk block size* for better speed. For example, increasing the block size to 64K on Novell IntranetWare servers usually improves speed. However, be aware that this operation may require a full backup and restore of the disk. The idea is that the computer has to read each block separately, so if the blocks are larger, the computer has less work to do — it's quicker to move 100 apples in 2 boxes of 50 rather than in 10 boxes of 10.

✔ **Do some *load balancing*.** Server audit logs can tell you which programs and data files users access most frequently; spread these files around on different disks to minimize wait times. On a Windows NT Server, for example, put the page file (an often-accessed system file) on a disk that doesn't get much other activity.

✔ **Turn off read-after-write (RAW) checking in software.** Turning off RAW is fine if your disk drives and controllers already perform such checking in hardware (many do). The command to turn off RAW in IntranetWare, for example, is `SET ENABLE DISK READ AFTER WRITE VERIFY = OFF`. See Chapter 7 for more on the RAW deal.

✔ **Clean house every now and then.** Most small business servers are like overcrowded attics or garages; so much stuff accumulates there that finding what you're looking for often takes much more time than it should. By migrating unneeded files to tape or optical disk or whatever backup medium you use, you let the server more quickly find the programs and data files that your employees need. Chapters 7 and 13 discuss data backup procedures.

Communications

The NIC in your server is the computer's link to the network. If you have a fairly new and fast one sitting in a high-speed motherboard slot (such as a *PCI* slot, which is short and white), you're in good shape. NICs older than a couple of years, or sitting in a slow motherboard slot (such as an *ISA* slot, which is long and black) are good candidates for upgrading.

✔ If you replace an older NIC with a newer one, try buying one that uses a technique called *bus mastering* (see Glossary) to pump data in and out of the server faster and with less CPU overhead.

✔ Sometimes, simply updating the software that the server uses to talk to the NIC — the NIC *driver* — can boost performance dramatically.

In faster servers, even a quick NIC can be a bottleneck. In such cases, you can reconfigure your network so that you have two or even three NICs in a single server, or you can deploy multiple servers (see next section).

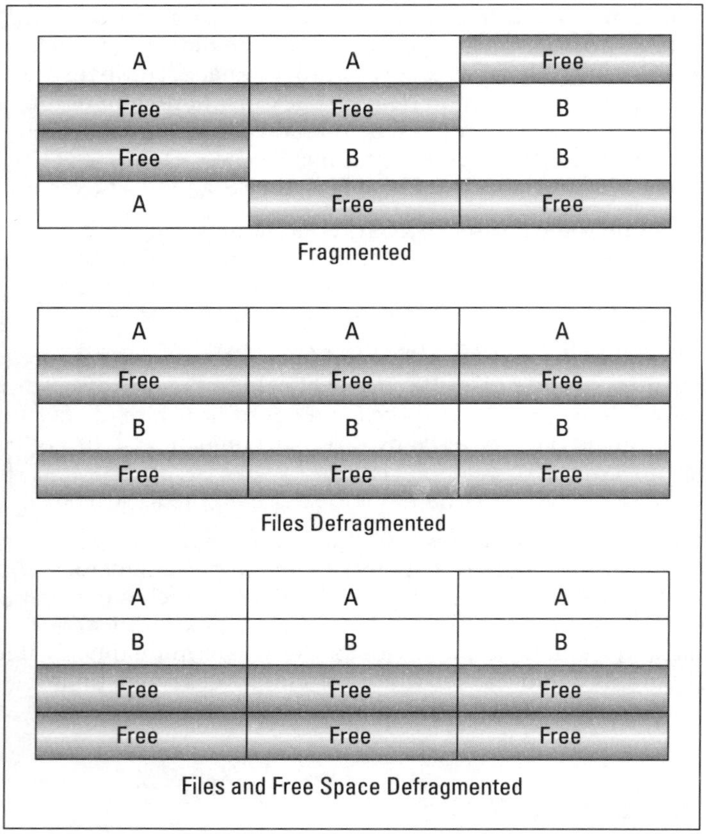

A	A	Free
Free	Free	B
Free	B	B
A	Free	Free

Fragmented

A	A	A
Free	Free	Free
B	B	B
Free	Free	Free

Files Defragmented

A	A	A
B	B	B
Free	Free	Free
Free	Free	Free

Files and Free Space Defragmented

Figure 12-4: Defragmenting reassembles files so that they reside in physically adjacent places on the disk. Complete defragmenting also consolidates the disk's free space.

Infrastructure Tuning

The relative importance of tuning your network *plumbing* — that is, the type and layout of your NICs, hubs, and cables that join your computers together — depends on the answers to several questions:

- ✔ Do your users do a lot of graphics and desktop publishing work?
- ✔ Do you run programs from a server instead of from each user's computer?
- ✔ Do you store most data files on a server instead of on user workstations?
- ✔ Do you need to connect to remote computers such as those on the Internet, or other company offices?
- ✔ Do you have fairly old NICs and hubs?

If you find yourself answering "yes" to several of these questions, and if your user interviews and network benchmarks indicate that your workstations run quickly but network activities run slowly, some infrastructure tuning may be in order. This section presents the more common techniques for tuning small business networks.

Segmenting the network

You can divide your network into multiple segments, and configure it so that each computer doesn't see every single network message, and traffic congestion becomes less severe. For example, the art department may have to send images back and forth all day, but they may not need to exchange data with accounting more than once a month.

You typically *segment* (that is, chop up) a network with a device called a *bridge*. The bridge allows data traffic to flow between the two network halves it creates, even though the bridge introduces a slight delay for packets that must cross it. And on either side of the bridge, data traffic congestion is reduced. You can also use a somewhat more expensive device called a *router,* which is more sophisticated than a bridge and has the ability to send or redirect data traffic to the least crowded routes. Some hubs come with a built-in bridge; they're called *multisegment hubs*. If you have one of these, you don't need a separate bridge or router.

Another way to segment a network is to put two NICs into your server computer and connect each to a different hub. In this arrangement, the server itself becomes the bridge or router. Check your server and Network Operating System documentation to see if this is an option.

When you segment an existing network, try to balance the load on the different segments. Use your network monitoring utilities (see the "Find the bottlenecks" section in this chapter) to rank users by how much network traffic they generate, and then go down the list and assign every other user to a different segment.

For a bit more information on bridges and routers, see Chapter 7.

Adding a server

Often, the best way to improve a server's performance is to give it a sibling: Add another machine and divide the chores between the two. You can split server chores across multiple machines in two primary ways:

- ✔ **Divide files and applications by type:** For example, put file and print services onto one server, e-mail and database services onto a second one. Personally, I like this approach, because it's easier to design and tune each server for performance. A database server, for example, should have more CPU firepower than a file server.

- ✔ **Divide files and applications by department or function:** For example, put finance and accounting on server A, manufacturing and sales on server B. You may want to do things this way if you want different groups to take responsibility for their own servers.

If you don't have a dedicated server (for example, you're running a peer-to-peer network), and network performance has slowed down dramatically, you may need to set up a computer to do nothing other than share frequently used files. You can do this without changing your network software; just put the busiest files on a computer that no one uses for other tasks.

You can even dedicate a separate machine to handle the bulk of your company's printing chores. If you do this, make sure the machine you connect to your shared printer has a high-performance parallel port (the techie names, which all mean pretty much the same thing, are *ECP, EPP,* and *IEEE 1284* — I'll spare you the definitions this time). The computer doesn't have to be the sharpest pencil in the box — printer sharing doesn't require much computer brain power — but the parallel port does need to be fast.

Replacing a bad NIC

If the network suddenly runs more slowly than it did the day before, and you notice that turning off one specific workstation seems to fix the problem, you may have a bad NIC that's spewing unnecessary traffic and bogging things down for everyone. (Technicians quaintly call such a card *chatty.*) Replace the card and the network should instantly return to normal speed.

Shifting into a higher gear

If you use regular old Ethernet (speed limit: 10 Mbps) for desktop communications and your user interviews and benchmarks suggest that traffic is a bottleneck, one option is to move up to *Fast Ethernet.* Fast Ethernet is up to ten times faster, depending on how many users are on the network.

You don't have to perform the transition to Fast Ethernet all at once. You can start by replacing server and workstation NICs with *combo cards* that can work at either speed, and when you're ready, upgrade your network hubs.

Installing an Ethernet switch

An Ethernet switch is a hub that specifically sets up dedicated (nonshared) communications circuits between two computers — a neat trick, given that Ethernet is a shared-medium signaling method where theoretically every computer can get to the cable whenever it wants. Ethernet switches are more expensive than regular hubs. As a cost and performance compromise, you may want to look at a switch that offers a Fast Ethernet connection to your server, but regular Ethernet connections to workstations.

Replumbing the printer

If users complain of slow printing speed, you may need a quicker connection to the printer. Putting a NIC inside a laser printer, rather than connecting the printer's parallel port to a device that translates between the parallel port and the network, may provide a noticeable speed boost. Even today's faster parallel ports are much slower than network cable speeds, and the parallel port can be a bottleneck — especially when your employees print documents with graphics.

Printers often work faster when they have more memory, too. When I threw an extra 8MB of memory into the laser printer I use on my network, it started spitting out graphics documents almost twice as fast as it did with the original 2MB.

If for some reason you're running a network printer across a serial cable, I can guarantee that you can improve printing speed by switching to a parallel cable or a direct network connection.

Connecting to the outside world

If your network connects to the outside world — such as the Internet or an online service like CompuServe or America Online — that connection is often a bottleneck. Small businesses that don't expect to move locations anytime soon may want to install an ISDN (*Integrated Services Digital Network*) line to enjoy a faster connection speed than is possible with dial-up modems and regular phone lines. The phone company runs and installs the ISDN line to your office (for a fee, of course), and then bills you monthly for usage. You then connect your network to the ISDN line with an additional piece of hardware called an *ISDN terminal adapter*.

If you stick with a regular phone line, you may be able to improve connection speeds by getting the latest high-speed modem. 33.6 kilobits per second (Kbps) modems meeting the popular *V.34* standard are commonplace and inexpensive as I write this, so if your modems run at slower speeds, an inexpensive upgrade may be smart. Even faster modems that transmit at

33.6 Kbps but receive at a zippier 56 Kbps may give you an added speed boost, but check with your Internet Service Provider or online service to make sure that they support the higher speed. Also check to see which of the two competing 56 Kbps methods the service supports: *K56flex* or *x2*.

Some 28.8 Kbps modems can be beefed up to 33.6 Kbps speed with a free software upgrade that you can download from the modem manufacturer's Web site and then run on your computer to update the modem's *firmware* (software-on-a-chip). Some vendors send you a physical chip upgrade, which involves modem surgery and isn't as convenient.

Workstation Tuning

Workstation performance tuning involves some of the same steps as server tuning, along with a few different ones.

Network software

See whether you're running the most efficient *transport protocol* and *network client software* on user workstations — the transport protocol and network client software link the user computer to the network (see Chapter 6). For example, Power Macintosh systems perform noticeably better with the newer Open Transport TCP/IP software than the older, slower MacTCP. For another example, if you use Microsoft Windows 95 with Novell IntranetWare, you may find that Novell Client32 software works faster than Microsoft NetWare client software.

Next, check whether you've set up that client software optimally. For example, Windows 95 PCs perform better when they only load the network software components that they absolutely need, that is, when installers remove components in the Network control panel that aren't necessary. (You reach the Network control panel by clicking Start⇨Settings⇨Control Panel and double-clicking the Network icon.)

How do you discover tricks like these? Spend time with magazines and books, read tech tips on your network vendor's Internet site, make a bunch of phone calls during your free support period, and if you don't have time for all that, hire experts to help.

Memory

The amount of RAM a network user needs varies with the type of computer and operating system (Sun SPARCstation, PC with Windows 95, PC with Windows NT, and so on). However, a good guideline is to have no less than

16MB of main memory and go with 32MB if you can do so without straining the budget. The point of diminishing returns for performance on a Windows 95 PC running typical office applications is usually 32MB, so adding beyond that amount probably won't have much speed impact.

Workstations perform disk *buffering,* or *caching,* much like servers do (see "Server Tuning" earlier in this chapter). Depending on the operating system you run on your workstations, you may be able to tune the cache for better performance. For example, Windows 95 lets you change cache settings by setting your computer up as a mobile, desktop, or server computer:

1. **Choose Start⇨Settings⇨Control Panel.**

2. **Double-click the System icon.**

3. **Click the Performance tab.**

4. **Click the File System button.**

5. **In the Typical role of this machine list box, choose** Network server **to optimize caching for machines with more than 16MB of memory,** Desktop computer **for machines with exactly 16MB, and** Mobile or docking system **for machines with less than 16MB.**

The preceding procedure doesn't work properly if you have an earlier version of Windows 95 (the "0" or "a" releases — check the version number in the System control panel that pops up at Step 2). You can fix Windows 95 so that the procedure does work as it should, but the steps are too involved to describe here, so I modestly point you to my own *Bulletproofing Windows 95* (McGraw-Hill, 1997), which helps network administrators set up Windows 95 for maximum speed and reliability.

Communications

The workstation's physical network link can be a speed bump, especially for users who do a lot of work with server files. If the workstation has a high-speed expansion slot where a NIC can plug in, such as a PCI slot, use a NIC that can take advantage of that type of slot.

The good news here is that high performance workstation NICs are inexpensive. A hundred dollars a seat is usually all you have to spend to ensure the user-to-network link isn't a bottleneck.

Video

One of the best ways to soup up a workstation's performance is to improve its ability to handle display information, especially nowadays when even the most mundane, text-oriented programs have to look colorful and detailed to be competitive (and, therefore, have to tax the computer's display circuitry). You can do this several ways:

✔ **Set the resolution and color depth options for speed, using a bench-mark program such as WinBench.** *Resolution* is how many dots or *pixels* the computer paints on the display; *color depth* is how many colors the computer can display at one time. Usually you can make a workstation faster by going to a lower resolution (for example, to 800 x 600 pixels from 1024 x 768) and by reducing the color depth (for example, to 256 colors instead of 16.7 million). WinBench is shown at work in Figure 12-5; see the *Navigate* icon in the "Benchmark and experiment" section earlier in this chapter for how to get it.

✔ **Update the video *driver* (the software that the operating system uses to "speak" to the display).** Newer drivers often run faster than the older ones that your computer may automatically install. You can get new drivers from the computer vendor's Web site if the video capability is integrated on the motherboard, or from the video card manufacturer's Web site if the computer uses a plug-in circuit card for video.

✔ **Buy a new, faster video circuit card.** Just make sure you get one designed for the kind of work you do. Video cards that perform well for multimedia (digital video, computer animation, and so on) may not be the best performers for general business use (word processing, spread-sheet, database). Check computer magazines for reviews and bench-mark test results. If you have an available PCI slot in the computer, a PCI video card can run faster than an ISA card.

The type of computer monitor you use has almost no effect on video speed, except inasmuch as the monitor dictates the display color depth and resolution.

Figure 12-5:
The
WinBench
program for
Windows
PCs
features a
benchmark
test that
puts your
workstation's
graphics
circuitry
through its
paces.

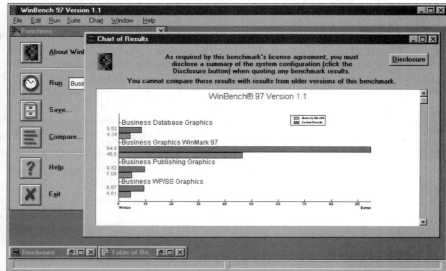

Chapter 13

Managing Your Network without a Network Staff

APPLIANCE SALESMAN:
"You'll like this range, Mrs. Burns. For instance, you put in a roast, you set the oven control, and then you go out all day. When you come home at night, the roast is done."

GRACIE:
"Haven't you got one where I don't have to go out?"

(George Burns and Gracie Allen, quoted in *Laughing Matters*, Gene Shalit, ed., Doubleday)

Whether you're talking about ovens or networks, the more automatic, the better. In this chapter, I describe ways to make your network run itself (at least to an economically reasonable extent), so that your network administrator can set the controls and "go out all day" — keeping the pager handy, of course, just in case the roast tries to escape. As with cooking, though, some aspects of network management just can't be automated, and probably shouldn't be. Therefore, I also clue you in to the jobs your administrator must perform, both initially and on a regular basis, in order to ensure a smooth-running system.

In my experience at least, many small companies have terrible network management procedures, if they have any at all. (Network management is one thing big companies tend to do well.) If you automate the management chores that you *can* automate, and get very organized with the rest so that they become a matter of routine (that is, automate your brain), your small business network is sure to enjoy high uptime, good problem recoverability, low ongoing costs, and excellent user (and manager) satisfaction.

Some things you can't control: your boss, big-picture business cycles, commuter traffic, or your love life. But, by gum, you *can* control your network. Table 13-1 summarizes network management, and the sections that follow elaborate on each item.

Table 13-1	Network Management Made Simple
Task Description	*When to Do It*
Create a network standards document that reflects both industry and company standards	During the network design phase
Set up a support network for yourself (people, books, CD-ROMs, Internet resources; see "Building a Support System")	At installation, and whenever adding new products
Educate users on spotting common problems and reporting procedures for when they come across a potential problem	At installation, and whenever adding new products
Create a disaster recovery plan document (see "Hoping for the Best, Planning for the Worst") and review it with every employee	One month after installation if not sooner, and update it annually thereafter
Create a schedule for backing up servers and workstations (the next four rows give an example)	Immediately after installation
Perform a full server backup	Weekly, for most companies
Perform a differential server backup (see "Backing Up the Server")	Daily, for most companies
Perform full workstation backups	Monthly, for most companies
Perform differential workstation backups (see "Backing Up Workstations")	Weekly, for most companies
Add a new user (see "Adding and Removing Users")	As soon as a new employee or contractor starts work
Remove an existing user (see "Adding and Removing Users")	As soon as an employee or contractor leaves, voluntarily or otherwise
Install or remove software (see "Managing Your Software")	As business needs require, weighing the risks and costs of new programs against the practical benefits the programs offer

Task Description	When to Do It
Check for updates (see "Updating software") to Network Operating System (NOS), workstation operating system, device drivers, and applications (with the exception of antivirus software — see next item)	Quarterly
Check for updates to antivirus software	Monthly
Evaluate network usage by viewing server log files and interviewing users; add capacity if necessary (see "Adding Capacity")	Quarterly; earlier if problems arise
Set up alerts so that the NOS can automatically send the administrator bulletins if common server problems occur (see "Setting Up Automatic Alerts")	Immediately after installation
Perform server and workstation diagnostics and preventive maintenance (such as scanning disks for errors; see "Conducting Regular Checkups")	Monthly

Being a Standard-Bearer

The closer you keep your *Local Area Network* (LAN) in line with industry standards, the easier it is to manage. You get better support from vendors and consultants. You have a better chance of finding solutions to network problems on the Internet. You can take better advantage of technical innovations, which vendors tailor first for standardized, mainstream systems because it's more profitable for them to do so. You can obtain replacement parts more easily. You have a wider variety of software from which to choose as your company grows and changes. And you also have more choices in products that can automate network management chores.

The problem is that the computer industry has more standards than Rodney Dangerfield has jokes (incidentally, he's at http://www.rodney.com on the Internet). So, adhering to *industry* standards isn't enough. You need to write some of your own company standards, too, as Figure 13-1 illustrates. Some examples may include

✔ Using the same hardware and software platforms for all workstations (for example, the Intel/Windows combination)

✔ Buying *Network Interface Cards* (NICs) from the same vendor (3Com, Madge, whomever), and preferably the same model as well

✔ Configuring all the computers on your LAN to use the same network language *(protocol)*, be it IPX, TCP/IP, or what have you

✔ Standardizing on a single word processor, spreadsheet program, database program, Internet browser, and so on for all users (even if some of them whine and stomp the floor)

Big companies can sometimes justify a hodgepodge of products because they have so many different kinds of users, and those users may have very specific needs that justify a particular product. More often, the podge of hodge arises from many years of decentralized and even *random* purchasing policies. You're not in that boat, so take advantage of the fact, and build a highly standardized and consistent LAN.

Write down your company standards — the document can be as short as a page. Make sure that

✔ The boss gets behind it, and

✔ Anyone who may ever go out and buy something for the network gets a copy.

Ideally, all network-related purchasing decisions go through the network administrator, whether that's you or someone else, so that someone can consistently help to enforce the standards you write.

Building a Support System

A network administrator, especially one who has other responsibilities in the business, needs a support system: resources — both human and otherwise — to turn to when a situation arises that's outside the administrator's expertise. (In the early days of a novice administrator's first network management experience, situations that require outside help may be more the rule than the exception.) Remember the famous words of poet John Donne: "No mayonnaise in Ireland." (No woman is, either, for that matter.)

Human resources

The wealthiest person I ever met outside the oil bidness once shared the secret of his financial success with me: "I'm not particularly smart, I just listen very carefully to people who are smarter than me in their areas of expertise." So who are the people a LAN manager can listen to?

Day-to-day users

Some of the folks the LAN manager can turn to are the people who use your computer system day in and day out. They know how the system looks,

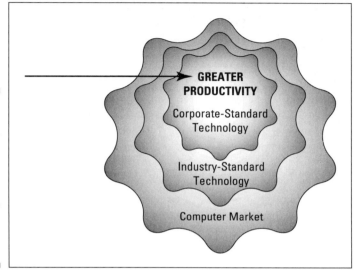

Figure 13-1:
Adhering to industry standards is smart; setting up your own company standards is even smarter.

feels, tastes, and smells in the normal course of running the application programs. Educate your users as to when they should call you for help and how to report problems in a detailed and useful way. (For more on this concept, take a look at Chapter 15.)

Vendor tech support analysts

Although free vendor tech support may only apply for the first 30 to 90 days after you make your first call, you can sometimes establish a relationship with a technician, whom you can later contact by e-mail at no charge. In some cases, if your business relies heavily on a particular product, an annual technical support subscription may be worth the money to you. In any case, make good use of that free support period!

Internet newsgroup subscribers

You can reach expert users, other network administrators, and even vendor technicians via Internet *newsgroups*. Internet newsgroups essentially serve as open discussion forums, usually on a very specific topic, such as a particular hobby, television show, or, as concerns your network, software products.

Sometimes you can get answers by simply reading the message *threads* (queries and replies) already there when you first get to the newsgroup site; if not, you can post your own query and see if you get useful responses. You can connect to newsgroups as long as you have newsreader software. With Microsoft Internet Explorer or Exchange, you may need to install *Internet Mail and News* separately, but newsreader software comes with Netscape Navigator and Netscape Communicator. Here are a few newsgroups to get you started:

- ✔ **General networking topics:** `comp.dcom.lans.ethernet,` `comp.dcom.net-management, comp.dcom.servers, comp.protocols`
- ✔ **LANtastic:** `comp.os.lantastic`
- ✔ **NetWare and IntranetWare:** `bit.listserv.novell,` `comp.os.netware, comp.sys.novell`
- ✔ **Windows 95:** `comp.os.ms-windows.networking.win95,` `microsoft.public.win95.networking`
- ✔ **Windows NT Server:** `microsoft.public.windowsnt,` `comp.os.ms-windows.nt`
- ✔ **Apple Macintosh:** `comp.sys.mac`

To find newsgroups that pertain to your particular interests, visit `http://www.dejanews.com` on the Web and use the Deja News Interest Finder. You can also read newsgroup messages from Deja News, but it isn't as convenient as dedicated newsreader software. In addition, if you need more help with newsgroups and other Internet features, check out *Small Business Internet For Dummies* by Greg Holden (IDG Books Worldwide, Inc.).

Inhuman resources

People are wonderful resources, but you can't always find the right ones or gain immediate access to them. In such situations, make sure that you have good product documentation, CD-ROM support libraries, access to World Wide Web sites, and a few books and magazines in your bag of tricks.

Product documentation

The software industry is shipping products without paper manuals these days. Everyone seems to be doing it — Computer Associates, Microsoft, Novell, and the list goes on. (Symantec is usually a happy exception.) CD-ROM-based documentation is important as an adjunct to paper documentation, but not as a replacement for it.

You can't read a CD-ROM in an easy chair or on a train, bus, or plane, and you can't highlight the important parts or make notes in the margins. Online documentation is harder on the eyes than printed material, and you can't use CD-ROM manuals at all if your only CD-ROM drive is on the network and the network's down. Maybe electronic manuals save paper, but if ever there were a productive use of paper, it's to provide detailed software product information to customers.

By all means, install the online documentation. The keyword search capability is handy as long as you're somewhere that you can use it (see Figure 13-2), and if you have room to copy the files from CD-ROM to your server, access becomes even more convenient. But also buy the printed manuals if they don't come with your software. You don't have to buy one manual for each user; small groups (up to three or four people) can share the printed manuals — you just need to set aside a convenient community space for the purpose. And of course, users don't need manuals for software that only the network administrator uses.

Order printed documentation from Microsoft at `http://www.microsoft. com/mspress/`, and from Novell at 512-834-6905. For other vendors, check the two dozen little scraps of paper that ship with the software for a phone number. Incidentally, you can get to the Novell manuals through the Web at `http://www.novell.com/manuals`.

CD-ROM references

Above and beyond the online documentation that vendors provide with their software are separately sold CD-ROM reference libraries. Here are two that you may find useful:

- ✔ **Computer Select,** from Information Access Company (800-419-0313, 212-503-4400), costs $1,250/year, which ain't small potatoes. However, this reference library contains a year's worth of about 100 periodicals, either in full text or abstract, is updated monthly, and comes with its own easy-to-use search engine. The product also includes the Data Sources directory of computer companies, software, and hardware products, plus a glossary of technical terms — it's a great research tool.

- ✔ **TechNet,** from Microsoft Corporation (800-344-2121), costs $295/year and has grown into a remarkably useful resource for businesses that run primarily Microsoft products. TechNet includes the Microsoft knowledge base of tech support notes, system software updates, resource kits, service packs, and white papers on specific topics. But wait, there's more: You also get 25 percent off all Microsoft Press books.

Vendor Web sites

The World Wide Web is an excellent source of technical support databases that you can consult. Here are a few vendor Web sites to check out:

- ✔ **LANtastic, i.Share, and ModemShare:** `http://www.artisoft.com`

- ✔ **Macintosh support:** `http://www.info.apple.com/supportline`

- ✔ **Microsoft site search facility:** `http://search.microsoft.com` (choose the `Support` button)

- ✔ **Microsoft Knowledge Base, a collection of keyword-searchable tech support Q & As:** `http://www.microsoft.com/kb`

- ✔ **Novell Support Connection:** http://www.support.novell.com

Commercial books and magazines

Product manuals are great, but they aren't likely to warn you about problems or deficiencies with the product. Go to the bookstore for this sort of

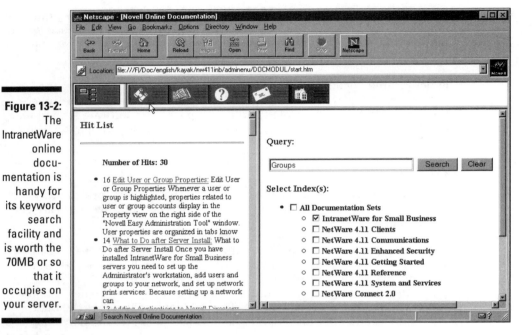

Figure 13-2:
The
IntranetWare
online
docu-
mentation is
handy for
its keyword
search
facility and
is worth the
70MB or so
that it
occupies on
your server.

information (I recommend some titles in Appendix B). Just watch out for
commercial books that do little more than rehash the vendor manuals. If you
know the titles you want, you can usually save 10 to 30 percent off list prices
by shopping online bookstores (such as http://www.barnesandnoble.com
and http://www.amazon.com).

Magazines have a quicker publishing turnaround time than books, so they
can be great for up-to-the-week information. I list a few good ones in Appendix B, but select no more than two or three to scan on a regular basis. Head
to a good newsstand or bookstore to get an idea of the ones you need.

Hoping for the Best, Planning for the Worst

Disaster recovery planning certainly includes a solid backup strategy,
as I cover in the next section, but it goes beyond that. Planning for the
worst deals with all the procedures and policies that pertain to any sort of
disaster — computer viruses, fire, flood, earthquake, plague, or somebody
losing the only office key. (I deal with preventing computer viruses in
Chapter 11, but as for *preventing* the rest, you may want to consult the
religious tome of your choice.)

Though you may not be able to prevent the next natural disaster, you *can* prepare for one. If your organization already has a disaster recovery plan, great — look it over to see if you need to do anything different or extra for your computer network (you probably do). If not, grab a good book on the subject — I like Patrick Corrigan's *LAN Disaster Prevention and Recovery* (Addison-Wesley) — and write something down. Repeat this process annually.

You may want to consider issues like an alternate location where you can set up shop if your main office becomes inaccessible; getting a quick hardware loan or rental from a local company; which programs and data files to load first on the alternate equipment; and so on.

Backing Up the Server

Backing up a computer simply means making a copy of the data the computer contains so that if the primary storage device (usually a hard drive) fails, you can replace it and reload the data from your backup medium (usually tape, but see Chapter 7 for other choices). The only bad thing about backing up your computers is that you can't do the same with your brains. I'm convinced that for every new thing I learn, I forget something else to make room. I know a lot more about computers than I did in 1980, but much less about the Highland Peoples of New Guinea, which is probably okay as the Highland Peoples of New Guinea probably don't know a damned thing about the Colorado Writers of Computer Books, either.

A smart backup routine is like fire insurance for your home: You probably won't ever need the insurance, but if you do, you'll need it *badly*. In a client/ server network, users typically store most, if not all of their data on the central server, so that's the most important machine to protect. Here are some elements of a good data backup procedure:

- ✔ **Store at least one set of backups off-site.** A different building is a good idea. Safe deposit boxes are fine, but unavailable on weekends.

- ✔ **Back up frequently, preferably daily, and maybe even more often if the data changes frequently.**

- ✔ **Don't back up everything each time if you don't need to.** *Differential* backups copy everything that has changed since the last *full backup* — see Figure 13-3. You can perform a complete server restore using the most recent full backup and the most recent differential backup in combination.

You may also hear about something called an *incremental backup* in which you back up only those files that have changed since the last incremental backup. I advise against this method, because the head- ache is cumulative: If your last full backup was 30 days ago, and all you

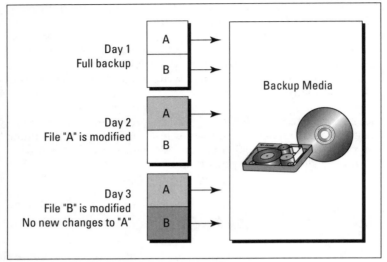

Figure 13-3:
Many companies perform a full backup weekly, and a differential backup daily.

Day 1
Full backup

A

B

Day 2
File "A" is modified

A

B

Day 3
File "B" is modified
No new changes to "A"

A

B

Backup Media

have is incremental backups since then, you may need 30 different tapes to get a crashed server ready for business again.

✔ **Use a tape drive that handles *write verification* (also called RAW, or Read-After-Write) in *hardware*.** This means you can turn the feature off in the software, saving lots of time. Drives from Exabyte and Seagate, among others, have this feature.

✔ **Consider the time it takes to restore the data.** Tape drives can be slow if you only need to recover a single file and that file happens to be at the end of the tape. Some organizations back up their most critical data to another hard drive for speedy recovery, in addition to backing it up to tape or other removable media for off-site storage.

✔ **Be wary of data compression.** Compressed backups can be more sensitive to *media flaws* (physical glitches in the disk or tape). On a related note, be wary of data compression on hard drives, too; server file compression is normally reliable, but workstation file compression (such as Microsoft DriveSpace) is less so.

✔ **Use *redundancy options* provided by your backup software to help protect against media flaws.** With redundancy, which writes error recovery data to the target media, you can often work around such flaws and reconstruct the data if something went awry.

✔ **Don't perform backups when users are working.** The backup operation stresses the network and makes it unbearably slow for employees.

✔ **Consider media life.** Tapes, disk cartridges, and even optical disks all have finite lifetimes, although *CD-Recordable* (CD-R) discs last longer than most other media (see Chapter 7). Throw out old media well before the manufacturer's estimated lifetime, and pay attention to manufacturer recommendations on how many times you can write over the media as well as to the media's longevity in years.

The best advice I can give you on server backups is to get a good third-party software program rather than rely on the backup utility that comes with your NOS. The Novell SBACKUP utility and the Microsoft NT Backup program are okay in a pinch, but they have *serious* limitations. NT Backup, for example, can be configured (with the help of the Scheduler service) to do an unattended nighttime backup, which is the only way to go, in my opinion, but it doesn't offer automatic recovery options if the backup operation hits a glitch at 3:00 a.m. (the more sophisticated backup programs do). Cheyenne ARCserve from Computer Associates and Backup Exec from Seagate get high marks; the single-server editions are cheaper than the "enterprise" (multiple-server) editions.

Backing Up Workstations

You have several choices for backing up user workstations:

- **Suggest that users back up their computers to diskette.** (For example, it would take 605 diskettes to back up the computer I'm using to write this book.) Ask them to work for free, while you're at it.

- **Don't do a workstation backup at all, and tell users that any data files they want to protect, they should store on the server.** If a workstation hard drive crashes, user data is safe on the server. However, restoring application software onto a new drive can take a long time.

- **Equip every workstation with a tape drive and backup software, and run a scheduling program to perform backups automatically.** Options include the Scheduler that comes with Symantec Norton Antivirus, and the free InstantOn utility from Intel at `http://developer.intel.com/ial/inston/sched.htm`. However, users still have to change tapes, and you have to buy a tape drive for every computer.

- **Get a portable tape drive that hooks to a computer's parallel port, and periodically run around from machine to machine, backing up workstations.** The advantage is that you don't buy every computer a tape drive; the disadvantage is that backups are manual and you have to run around like a network administrator without a head.

- **Perform workstation backups across the network, using the high-capacity tape drive you use for server backups.** You can alternate between full and differential workstation backups.

All but the first are legitimate approaches; the last may be the most automatic and least expensive. After all, you already have a tape drive for the server, and it's probably a good, fast one. You already have the server backup software, too, and most good server backup utilities come with workstation backup features. You can even schedule workstation backups for after hours, when the relatively slow speed of moving all that data across the wire doesn't matter. To make the workstation backup procedure simpler, designate a particular master directory on workstation computers (for example, `C:\USERDATA`) to be backed up across the network, and advise all users that they need to put data files somewhere under that directory to guarantee that they'll be backed up. (And advise them to leave their machines on at night!)

Adding and Removing Users

You may need to create a new user account whenever your company hires a new employee or contractor. You need to remember to always remove or modify (change the password) an existing user account immediately when an employee or contractor leaves, even when the departure is amicable. Business is business, and security is security. Setting an account expiration date when you create the account is smart insurance.

Adding and removing users is more complicated in a peer-to-peer network situation because every shared resource (file, directory, printer) may have a separate password. When someone new comes on board, you have to give that person a list of share names and associated passwords. When someone leaves, you need to change all the passwords to shared resources that the person who's leaving used or knew about.

If you're clever when you set up users and groups, you don't have to go through a lot of explicit permissions stuff when you create a new user. Make the new user a member of the group or groups that pertain to that user's job function, and all the security permissions naturally fall into place because the user automatically has permissions to the resources that the group or groups have permissions to. See Chapter 9 for more on users and groups.

Managing Your Software

Software management consists of adding new programs, keeping the current ones up to date, and removing old ones. It can be a big job, but it's less so if you stay organized and disciplined.

Adding new software

Chapter 9 covers typical procedures for installing software onto your LAN. Here, I just recap the following tips:

✔ **Decide whether you want the program to run from the server or from user workstation hard drives.** (In a peer-to-peer network, the latter is your only practical choice for most business applications.)

✔ **If you plan to run the program from a server, back up the server before installing a new program.** Log on as the network administrator, and install the software into a public area on the server so you don't have to assign permissions to it manually afterward. Finally, set up user workstations so that they can access the new program, either with drive mappings, menu options, desktop icons, or an application delivery utility such as NetWare Application Launcher.

✔ **If you plan to run your new program from workstation hard drives, do a test installation first and document every step.** Check whether the installation creates problems for any other applications on a typical user workstation. Try loading a sample data file, printing it, and saving it. Once you're satisfied, repeat the installation on each user machine, following the exact same steps to ensure consistency. If you set up all your workstations with the same or very similar hardware and operating system, installing applications consistently is infinitely easier.

If you have over a dozen or so users on your network, you may want to look into specialized utilities that can help automate the software installation process. Microsoft Systems Management Server, Hewlett-Packard OpenView Desktop Administrator (formerly Symantec Norton Administrator for Networks), and Seagate Desktop Management Suite are popular products in this category. Some of these products require you to perform a test install over the network onto a user workstation, which the installation manager monitors in exact detail and can then repeat for other workstations. "Cloning" installations in this way is a slick capability, but these products can be a bit difficult to use as well as somewhat expensive. Incidentally, Windows NT Server 5.0 will include some application distribution features.

Updating software

Software isn't perfect when you get it, and it never will be. Software is just too complicated for vendors to test all possible situations ahead of time. Fortunately, vendors generally try to fix the worst problems as they go along. Unfortunately, software vendors don't do a very good job of telling customers about the fixes. They expect customers to periodically check the vendor Web sites to see what new fixes the vendor has posted for public use.

BIOS

The *BIOS (Basic Input/Output System)* is software-on-a-chip that loads into memory even before the operating system. The BIOS handles low-level data transfer between disk drives, printers, keyboards, monitors and memory.

The BIOS also provides an important piece of the Plug-and-Play puzzle for workstations (such as Windows 95/98) that support Plug-and-Play standards.

You can imagine that a problem with the BIOS software can have widespread effects, because it loads on every computer. Such problems can also be tough to diagnose. Fortunately, most vendors offer periodic fixes to the BIOS software, usually via the computer manufacturer's Web site. The fixes usually take the form of a program you run one time on each computer. However, bargain-basement computers may require you to replace the BIOS in the form of a chip on the motherboard (a good reason to avoid them).

Operating systems

No matter what kind of network you build, users have an *operating system* (OS) running on their computers, be it Windows 95, Windows NT Workstation, the Macintosh OS, OS/2 Warp, Unix, or something else. In every case, the operating system vendor issues periodic fixes, or *patches,* to correct problems that the vendor or other customers have discovered. Some vendors are more organized about this than others. For example, Novell has traditionally done a good job numbering their NetWare patches and documenting what each patch fixes. Microsoft has not been quite so organized: *Windows* magazine editor Fred Langa coined the delightful term *dribbleware* to describe the somewhat chaotic manner in which Microsoft releases small patches to Windows 95.

Sometimes, the cure is worse than the disease, and the trade press is full of stories about operating system patches that create more problems than they fix. Just as with new software versions, wait until a patch is out for a month or two, and if you don't see any horror stories in the press, install it.

Device drivers

Device drivers are the little programs that let computers communicate with devices — mainly, the display, printers, disks, and Network Interface Cards (NICs). Device manufacturers update these guys all the time. Stay current in order to avoid possible problems. Do a quarterly check on all the device drivers in your network, both server and workstation.

Applications

Many computer users, and even some network administrators, don't know that most application software vendors issue minor fixes and patches to their software in between so-called "major" releases. (For example, did you Microsoft Office 97 users know that Microsoft has issued a *Service Pack* — Microspeak for a maintenance release — to fix program bugs?) Check software vendor Web sites at least quarterly.

Some applications leave junk behind when you upgrade them, so the vendor recommends you remove the old version first and then install the upgrade. Netscape Navigator is an example. The "read me" text file that accompanies the upgrade software is your best guide on this point.

Remove

Only in recent years have application software vendors begun to provide removal (deinstallation) programs for their small business products. (You can easily check to see which applications have automatic removal programs on a Windows 95 or NT PC by running the Add/Remove Programs wizard in the Control Panel — see Figure 13-4.) The practice still isn't universal, and the deinstallation programs sometimes don't do a thorough job. The administrator may need to do some manual cleanup after removing a program: remove files, directories, and (in the Windows 95/98/NT world) Registry entries. (The Registry is a central database that contains information about installed programs.)

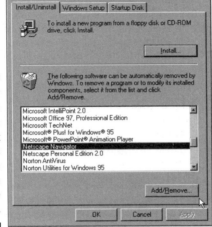

Figure 13-4: Windows 95 and NT PCs list programs that you can remove with a single mouse click.

Failing to thoroughly remove a program wastes disk space and can slow down workstations. However, deinstallation can be a tricky job: Some program files work with two or more programs, and if you remove them, you can unintentionally render other applications unrunnable.

Commercial utilities exist to help you remove application programs thoroughly, whether they include their own deinstall utility or not. For example, Uninstaller from CyberMedia (formerly MicroHelp) is a good choice for Windows systems (see Appendix B), as is CleanSweep from Quarterdeck.

If you don't use a commercial deinstall utility, check with the vendor to see if you can get a fax or e-mail detailing the steps necessary to exorcise the vendor's product ("Software, I cast thee *out!*"). Vendors get asked this question so often that nearly all of them provide such a checklist on request. Check the free fax-back number or Web site for this info so the vendor doesn't hit you up for a technical support "incident."

Adding Capacity

Capacity can mean many things on a computer network: server or workstation memory, server or workstation disk space, dial-in or dial-out communications links (modems plus phone lines), tape or optical backup units, printers, and even network transmission capacity.

Listening to network users can help you identify capacity problems ("I can never dial in to the network from the road because the line's always busy"), but by the time someone complains, chances are that a problem has already existed for awhile. I suggest a quarterly review of all network capacity aspects, so you can add capacity before users really need it. Here are a few tips to guide you:

✔ **Hard disk capacity.** When you add disk capacity (don't ever let a disk get over 90 percent full), put in a new hard drive that's at least twice the size of whatever hard drive is in the computer already. The labor cost outweighs the device cost. Further, though many computers limit the *number* of new hard drives you can add, they often don't limit the *size* of each drive.

✔ **Server RAM.** Check your network server's *cache hit rate*. For example, in IntranetWare, you choose Cache Utilization in the MONITOR utility and look at the Long Term Cache Hits statistic. If it's less than 90 percent, add memory to the server. You want the cache hit rate to be high, meaning that your server is reading from faster RAM instead of the slower hard drive, and you have to have plenty of RAM (and therefore a larger cache) to reach a high hit rate.

✔ **Server disk space allotments for each user.** If certain users consistently hog server disk space, consider implementing disk quotas that restrict users to a certain number of megabytes, until you can add enough capacity to please everyone. The capability is built into IntranetWare, but unfortunately not Windows NT Server, for which you have to get extra software such as Quota Manager from New Technology Software.

✔ **Tape backups.** When you add tape backup capacity, try to get a unit that can back up your entire server onto a single tape, so that the backup can proceed unattended at night.

✔ **Network transmission capacity.** When you need more transmission capacity, consider installing an Ethernet switching hub (also called a *switch*) to replace your regular hub. An Ethernet switching hub may be cheaper than upgrading your hub and everyone's Network Interface Card to Fast Ethernet (see Chapter 7 for more info).

Setting Up Automatic Alerts

One of the smartest things a network administrator can do is program the network to raise a red flag (or whatever other color flag that strikes fear and trepidation in the hearts of network administrators) when a problem arises. For example, with Windows NT Server, you can set up administrative alerts by running the Server Manager utility, double-clicking the server computer, clicking the Alerts button, and keying in the name of the administrator's account. (You can also define administrative alerts in the Performance Monitor, where you can specify the precise resource to be monitored as well as the alert trigger level.) The server then automatically notifies the administrator of problems with access, security, power, and printing. (The Server Manager online help file provides the details.) Third-party tools offer more capabilities, customizability, and cost. Intel LANDesk Server Manager is an example.

Conducting Regular Checkups

A big part of responsible network management is performing regular, periodic diagnostics and preventive maintenance on your network computers. Sophisticated Network Operating Systems can tolerate certain kinds of problems without shutting down, but the administrator needs to check the server periodically and correct these noncritical errors before they stack up and become critical, like straws on the proverbial camel's back.

Some diagnostic utilities come with the computer operating system, but you may want to supplement these tools with more sophisticated ones, such as Intel LANDesk Management Suite or Novell ManageWise, that perform more thorough tests and offer better online help. For example, the Windows NT Diagnostics program doesn't do much in the way of reporting disk or network errors (it doesn't tell you if a drive in a multiple-drive set fails); it offers no online help to speak of, and neither does the NT Network Monitor. The NT Event Viewer is handy in that it can alert you to problems that may affect network reliability and speed. The disk scanning facility (right-click a drive icon in Explorer and choose Properties⇨Tools⇨Check Now) fixes some noncritical file system problems — although you may have to restart the server to run it.

The diagnostic utilities and tools that come with IntranetWare are generally more mature than those that come with Windows NT, and they include VREPAIR, which fixes file system problems, and DSREPAIR, which fixes problems in the NetWare Directory Services security database. You also want to run the Novell MONITOR program (type **LOAD MONITOR** at the server console), choose Disk Information, and check the number of redirected blocks for each disk. This number shouldn't change from month to month — if it does, you may have a bad disk drive or controller. The NETADMIN utility lets you view the server error log, which can also alert you to disk or communication problems.

Part V
The Part of Tens

The 5th Wave® By Rich Tennant

"THE ENTIRE SYSTEM IS DOWN. THE COMPUTER PEOPLE BLAME THE MODEM PEOPLE WHO BLAME THE PHONE PEOPLE WHO BLAME IT ON OUR MOON BEING IN THE FIFTH HOUSE WITH VENUS ASCENDING."

In this part . . .

The Part of Tens is a standard feature of ...*For Dummies* books, and this one includes four chapters. The first one, Chapter 14, is required reading for small companies who can't afford to waste money; in it, I offer ten great tips to help you hold down computing costs. Read Chapter 15 when problems arise, or (even better) beforehand, so that you have a troubleshooting plan of action in place. Chapter 16 presents ten reasons to build a special type of network called an *intranet,* currently the hottest trend in network computing, and of interest to you if you have multiple office locations. Finally, Chapter 17 lists ten ways you can use your network to connect to the public Internet and develop new markets for your products and services.

In the spirit of the Part of Tens, here's the one and only quiz question in the book: What's a ten-letter word for small business computer power? (Hint: It starts with *n* and ends with *ing.*) It's not the only word you need to know to succeed in business, but now that you know what it means and how to do it, your odds just went up considerably. Good luck!

Chapter 14

Ten Techniques to Lower Your Networking Costs

· ·

In This Chapter

▶ Cutting future network expansion costs

▶ Trying and buying software on the cheap

▶ Saving with warranties

▶ Leveraging your training dollars

· ·

*T*hroughout this book, I try to provide some tips for minimizing the size of
the checks your company must sign in order to create a first-class
network. On the theory that you can't be too thrifty, here are ten more for
good measure.

"The capitalist is a rational miser." (Karl Marx, *Das Kapital*)

I don't always agree with Karl, but in this quotation, he's on the Marx. When
I finished writing the sections of this book that deal with a lot of cost issues,
primarily Chapters 2, 5, and 7, I realized that I had an embezzler's dozen of
other money-saving ideas that don't seem to fit neatly anywhere else. I've
shoehorned these ideas into this little chapter, which is not as important as
those other chapters, but which still may save your company enough
pfennigs for you to justifiably request a raise at your next performance
review.

Expect to Expand

One of the thriftiest things you can do when laying out for a new network is
to follow Glenn's Rule of Computer Economics #12:

*When you can buy a product that allows for expected future growth at a
marginal cost (less than half of what you'd otherwise pay later), buy it.*

In other words, if buying a 16-port hub would cost you $100 more than buying an 8-port hub, but a second 8-port hub would cost over $200 later, you're ahead of the game buying the extra capacity up front. This rule is often applicable to hard drives as well as hubs. I'm looking at a catalog right now that sells a 1.2GB drive for $180 and the same model in a 2.5GB size for $220. The $40 cost difference is much less than half the cost of another $180 drive, so if I think I might need more than 1.2GB in the next couple of years, I'm best off getting the 2.5GB size now.

Some alert readers may be thinking, "Hey, Glenn, I understand what you're saying, and by the way I'm really enjoying your lucid and highly entertaining book, but computer hardware's always decreasing in price. The $180 drive may be much less expensive two years from now when I need it." While that's true, don't forget the labor cost, time cost, and downtime cost of installing the new hardware later — these costs are likely to cancel out any price decrease.

My rule isn't as scientific as it could be, but it's usually good advice and it's also easy to remember. (Incidentally, Rules #1 through #11 don't exist, but this is a book about computer products, so I can start numbering things wherever I want.)

Read Reviews

You could buy one new computer product a day and still not own them all after 250 years. That's a lot of products (around 100,000). How on earth can you choose the best values?

Books like this can help a little. Other books can help, too (I mention some in Appendix B). But to get the greatest deals on software and hardware, spend $20 a year and subscribe to a good computer magazine that covers the sort of computers you use. When the magazine reviews products that you're thinking of buying, see what the review recommends for value-conscious buyers. Appendix B of this book also lists some magazines to consider.

Magazine reviews aren't flawless or absolutely comprehensive, and you may disagree with them occasionally, but they can certainly help you get good value for your dollar.

Try Trialware

Say you need a new software program. After you create a short list based on input from friends, colleagues, consultants, magazines, or all of the above, take the program candidates out for a spin. You're much less likely to be dissatisfied with your purchases later (at which point they may not be returnable). Here are three approaches to trying before buying:

✔ **Download a free trial version from the vendor's Web site.** Trial software normally has some significant limitation: You can't save files, for example, or the software expires after 30 days, but it's fine for evaluation purposes. Some companies, such as Symantec, post trial versions of just about every product they sell. Having a quick Internet link helps with the downloads, but some products are just too darned big to download even then, in which case you can e-mail the vendor and request a trial version on CD-ROM. You may have to pay a little for shipping and handling, and some vendors won't be able to accommodate you, but many will.

✔ **Buy a *Not-For-Resale* (NFR) version.** Some software vendors sell NFR copies (also called *evaluation* copies) direct to anyone who asks, and the price is usually around 10 to 20 percent of the street price. Other vendors may require you to be a software reseller in order to buy NFR software. In any case, be honest and buy the commercial product (with whatever site license agreement is appropriate for the number of users you have) if you test and like the NFR product. NFR software is meant only to help you decide whether you want to buy the full product or not, which (incidentally) explains why you can neither get tech support for NFR software nor upgrade it when a new version appears. If free trialware isn't available, NFR software is the next best thing to acquaint you with a program.

✔ **Verify that the vendor has a no-questions-asked 30-day return policy and then buy the product outright, preferably using a credit card.** Install the software program, work with it, and if you love it, keep it. If you don't, return it by registered mail and have the vendor credit your account.

When trying new software, you're best off installing it on a test workstation, just in case the installation creates a problem that interferes with other software on the same machine. You can use a comparatively slow computer for a test workstation, and you can even buy a used machine to be your test computer, as it won't receive heavy use.

Buy Bundles

One great way to save money on software is to watch for the best *bundle* deals. A bundle is a collection of software that ships with a hardware product, such as a computer, modem, or network hub. Manufacturers offer bundles to help differentiate their product from the very similar products their competitors sell.

The software bundled with computers nowadays can be almost overwhelming in quantity. You can easily buy a computer with a 1.5GB hard drive, one-third of which is already filled with bundled programs. Some of these programs are for home use, but some — web browsers, diagnostic utilities, personal information managers — may have valuable business applications. Certain vendors even sell office application suites, like Microsoft Office, with new computers. You can save $200 or $300 right there.

Before you buy hardware, ask what else comes in the box. The bundle deals may just help you decide between two otherwise similar products, and trim your software bill in the process.

Cash in on Competition

The computer biz is getting more competitive all the time, and every software manufacturer wants you to switch to their product if you're using a competing one. What software firms often do these days is offer special *competitive upgrade* prices. For example, if you own a copy of Apex Software's e-mail program, you may be able to buy Nadir Software's competitive product for a whole lot less than the regular retail price. Mail-order catalogs often advertise these competitive upgrades, but retail stores and superstores rarely do.

Competitive upgrades may not sound like such a hot deal, as you essentially buy two programs when you ultimately intend to use just one, but they're good to know about if you're unhappy with software you have now and intend to switch anyway. Also, you may be able to work the system a little, as the following tip explains.

Find out what programs qualify for the competitive upgrade. You may be able to buy a copy of the cheapest one, get the competitive upgrade to the product you really want, and still save money (even hundreds of dollars, depending on the software). You may like the cheap software so well that you don't care about the competitive upgrade anymore. If you do get the competitive upgrade, you may be able to sell the cheap program to someone else ("Nvr used, stl in bx"), and save even more.

Competitive upgrade software can be a pain if you ever need to reinstall it, because you may have to first reinstall the software from which you upgraded.

Watch Warranties

Computer hardware usually comes with a warranty of from one to five years. If you keep track of when you buy hardware and if you hang on to your receipts, you can save money — sometimes several hundred dollars — if a device fails under warranty.

What many customers don't know is that some of the devices *inside* the computer have a longer manufacturer's warranty than the computer itself. Many hard drive companies warrant their products for three to five years, even if the computer that the hard drive comes in has only a one-year warranty. Workstation hard drives aren't terribly expensive, but 300 bucks is 300 bucks, and the hard drives your server uses may cost much more.

If you have to return a device by mail for in-warranty replacement, as you typically must do with hard drives, call the manufacturer and get a *Return Materials Authorization* (RMA) number first. You need to put this number on the outside of the box, or the vendor may simply ship the package right back to you without even looking at it. Also, send the device with a carrier that can track the package and verify delivery.

Documentation is key. I once requested that a certain manufacturer (which shall remain nameless, but which has the same initials as Icelandic Business Machines) replace a $1,100 in-warranty hard drive by mail. The company instead sent a technician to my office and then billed me $3,300 for parts and labor. After several phone calls and letters and months, the company (famous for its Personal Computer) voided the charge, but only because I was able to scrounge up the proof of purchase. The fact that the drive had a five-year warranty, and the model was only a year old, was amusingly irrelevant. Most manufacturers are easier to deal with than this company (whose nickname is Big Blue), but keep the paperwork anyway.

Laser printers have warranties, too, but be careful. If you use reconditioned toner cartridges, or if you hook a laser printer up to a mechanical "A/B" switch (which you really don't need now that you have a network!), you may invalidate the warranty.

Cruise in the Current

Someone you know and respect may at some point tempt you to invest in outdated or nonmainstream technology for your business network. A consultant may tell you that you can pick up a complete ARCNet LAN for practically nothing (so you'll have more dollars in the budget for consulting services). A friend who works for another company may confide that that company is unloading an old minicomputer for pennies on the dollar (because no one else is willing to buy it). Or, heck, maybe someone you don't know and don't respect, such as a computer store salesperson, may try to push weird but "innovative" products (with fat resale margins).

Don't do it. Old computers don't run modern software well, and you probably can't fix them when they break. Unpopular technologies, which may not be around next week, make you vulnerable to owning orphaned products that no one supports. Outdated technologies lock you out of tomorrow's improvements.

Be a bold pioneer in the business your company has chosen as its focus, be an individual in the way you dress and eat and live, but be a conformist when it comes to computer networking. Your colleagues may yawn when you tell them you've just set up a network with Novell IntranetWare, Windows 95 or 98, IBM-compatible PCs, Microsoft Office, and twisted-pair Ethernet. I say let them yawn, and may they choke on the gnats that fly into their mouths. Everything from user training to future expansion becomes cheaper and easier when you swim in the technology mainstream. Dare to be boring — and profitable.

Hire Out Headaches

Time is money, and one of the best ways to save time when designing, installing, and managing a Local Area Network is to hire out the jobs that don't make sense for you to master in-house. Yes, you have to pay someone to do these jobs if you don't do them, but a day of someone else's time may be much less expensive than a week or two of yours. Here are some good outsourcing candidates:

- Testing existing network wiring (good cable test equipment costs thousands of dollars; why buy it?)
- Running twisted-pair and/or fiber cable through walls and plenums, and installing a patch panel in a wiring closet
- Setting up automatic IP addressing systems, such as Dynamic Host Configuration Protocol (DHCP), in a TCP/IP network

✔ Designing custom database programs for your business operations

✔ Hosting an Internet Web server

✔ Designing an Internet Web site

You may run into a few other possibilities. My point is that you can always hire people to do anything that you find a little difficult or time-consuming. Use this book to help you do what you're comfortable doing and what seems fun and interesting, and contract out the rest of it (see Chapter 3 for more on choosing and using consultants).

Rethink Rebates

The computer industry is becoming almost as fond of rebate promotions as the car industry is. A reliable source informs me that the 50 largest computer companies have gotten together and hired a guy named Herbert to handle the 10,000 rebate requests that hardware and software customers send in each day, with the strict condition that Herbert will instantly lose this lucrative contract if he doesn't accurately process at least one request each month.

Here are some tips on rebates:

✔ **Don't make buying decisions based primarily on promised rebates.** By all means apply for them, because they can be significant ($200 per computer isn't unusual), but recognize that you may not see the dollars for many months.

✔ **Make copies of any receipts you send to claim your rebate.** You may need to resend them. And do send every last bit of documentation that the promotion requires. The fulfillment houses routinely put incomplete rebate requests into the round file.

✔ **If you don't get your rebate within the store's product return time window, don't go through the usual customer service channels because you don't have time for that.** Call a marketing vice president at the company sponsoring the rebate. Tell the VP that you want your money pronto, or you're returning the products. I've done this half a dozen times (and it works).

Cross-Train Colleagues

Training is a big expense, but you may not need to spend quite as much as you think. For example, you may be able to do some *cross-training* within your company. Here's what I mean:

- Have your network administrator hold periodic classes for employees on how to use the network effectively, troubleshoot common problems, perform backups, and so on.

- Identify people in your company who are experts with a particular program, and have them give talks for your employees that explain some of that program's more useful tips and tricks. Your financial people may be very familiar with the spreadsheet program your company uses, for example. Administrative assistants typically know the word processing program well. Sales staff get expert with e-mail.

- Send a small number of designated trainees to different classes and seminars and have them share what they learned with other employees when they return, instead of sending everyone who may benefit. (This technique also helps ensure that the person you send to a seminar actually pays attention.)

Chapter 15

Ten Network Troubleshooting Tips

In This Chapter

▶ Using the troubleshooting methods the pros use

▶ Asking the right questions of yourself and your users

▶ Stocking and swapping components to save time

▶ Taking troubleshooting one step further to eliminate recurrences

*I*f the automobile had evolved the same way the computer has, a Mercedes-Benz would now cost $100, get a thousand miles to the gallon, and spontaneously combust every six months. Computer networks, even small, simple ones, break from time to time: sometimes dramatically, sometimes in minor yet irritating ways. This chapter offers ten troubleshooting techniques for attacking network problems with minimum time and minimum cost.

"I never guess. It is a shocking habit." (Sir Arthur Conan Doyle's famous detective, Sherlock Holmes, in *The Sign of Four*)

Guesses, hunches, and suspicions can pay off for network troubleshooters who have enough years of experience to ground their speculations in reality. However, many small business Local Area Network (LAN) administrators don't have the benefit of such experience.

No problem. Your LAN troubleshooter can heed Sherlock Holmes's advice and reject guessing in favor of a stepwise, analytical approach. As long as the troubleshooter has a plan laid out ahead of time, it can substitute for experience to some degree — especially if someone with experience suggests the plan, as I do in the following ten tips. So polish up your magnifying glass and read on; you're about to become a professional LAN sleuth.

Get the Lay of the LAN

You may be able to troubleshoot a network of three or four users without any documentation (though I don't recommend it). However, as soon as your LAN grows larger than a few users, proper notes are sure to save you time when tracking down a problem. For example, if a problem occurs on one computer but not another, and your notes show that one machine has 16MB of RAM while the other has 32MB, you may have the clue you need. If your network map indicates which computers connect to which hubs, and you notice that the users reporting problems are all connected to the same hub, your map has probably helped you solve your case.

I suggest you keep all your network documentation in one place, such as a loose-leaf binder. Good documentation needs to include the following items:

- ✔ **Physical map:** a graphical map of the physical network (computers, printers, hubs, cables, what hooks to what, and so on)

- ✔ **Logical map:** a graphical map of the logical network (users, groups, shared resources, and so on)

- ✔ **Hardware inventory:** brand, model, CPU type, memory, disk space, Network Interface Card, printer make and model, hub make and model, and so on

- ✔ **Software inventory (including version numbers):** workstation operating system, Network Operating System, application software, and so on

- ✔ **Configuration details:** transport protocol, computer addressing, Control Panel settings, and so on

Chapter 9 discusses mapping your LAN and some software tools that partially automate the process.

Suspect Everyone

My favorite Inspector Clouseau line from the *Pink Panther* movies is "I suspect everyone . . . and I suspect no one." (I don't know what it means, but then, he didn't either — he just wanted to appear profound.) When troubleshooting your network, start by suspecting *everyone and everything*.

When you start working on a network problem, you automatically and subconsciously draw an imaginary dotted line around the part of the network where you think the problem resides. Often, the user reporting the problem helps determine where you draw that dotted line ("I'm having a PC problem" or "This program isn't working"), which may be a good or a bad thing depending on the user's expertise level. If you start with too restrictive a problem boundary — that is, you draw your dotted line around too narrow a piece of the network — you risk wasting the time you spend trying to zero in on a problem that actually lies elsewhere in the network.

Always troubleshoot network problems from the outside in, and start big: Draw your mental problem boundary line around the entire system (and maybe even part of Kansas) and then eliminate large parts of that system by asking questions and running tests. Ideally, each question or test eliminates roughly half the possibilities, allowing you to zero in on the root cause as quickly as possible. The following sequence illustrates the concept:

- ✔ **Could the problem be related to utility-supplied power or problems in the phone network?** If you have Uninterruptible Power Supplies (UPSs), you may be able to rule out AC power problems, but only if you install a UPS on every network device (server, hub, workstations, modems, and so on).

- ✔ **If the problem doesn't relate to the power or phone grids, does it affect every user on the network?** If so, the problem may be with a hub, cable, or server, but it probably isn't with a particular workstation.

- ✔ **If the problem affects only one user, does the problem relate to that user's network account, or to his or her particular workstation?** Test this by logging on to a different workstation with the same user ID and password. If the problem persists, it's a network account problem; otherwise, it's a problem with the user's computer.

- ✔ **If the problem only occurs when the user logs on to his or her usual computer, does it occur when the user runs any application program, or just one?** If the problem affects more than one program, it may relate to the user's hardware, or the workstation operating system. If the problem affects only one program, then it has to do with the configuration of that program on the user's machine, assuming other network users run the same program successfully.

- ✔ **If the problem's with system software, what's unique about the system software setup for that user?** For example, what device drivers does that user have that no one else has? What Control Panel settings are different?

You get the idea by now. By starting general and working your way down to specific, you never have to retrace your steps. (Well, almost never.)

Interview the Victims

The more detail a crime victim can remember, the quicker the authorities can nail the crook. A few minutes spent interviewing (not grilling!) the LAN user who reports the problem can provide key clues. Some important questions to ask the user include the following:

> *Has the action you were trying to perform when you noticed the problem ever worked in the past, or is this something new you're trying to do with the network?*

If the user's action is a new activity, the problem may be that the proper software options aren't installed. For example, a spell check fails if the online dictionary isn't available, and a spreadsheet calculation can fail if the correct formula libraries aren't installed.

> *Has anything changed on your computer recently — have you installed software, removed software, modified any settings, spilled coffee into the system unit, and so on? If so, what changed? Can you provide the details of what you did?*

The answer to this question can direct your attention to the effect of the change, which you can then reverse to see if the problem disappears. Sometimes users hesitate to admit that they changed anything on their systems ("I would *never* change anything, no way, nosiree"), whether out of fear of reprisal ("We *told* you never to do that!") or fear of looking silly ("Why on earth did you do it *that* way?"). A good troubleshooter tries to gain users' confidence by assuring them that it doesn't matter what they did, the concern right now is to get their systems functioning again. You can also exercise some good diplomacy and phrase this question carefully; "What have you done to your computer *now?*" is not the way to enlist a user's help.

> *Can you remember what you were doing the moment before you noticed the problem? Did it occur when you logged on, when you tried to print, when you tried to save a file to a network directory, or when you switched from one program to another?*

This question is key. The answer tells you where to spend your time: looking at the network logon script, checking the print server, checking disk space, or what have you.

> *Did the computer report an error message, and if so, do you remember what it said, or did you write it down somewhere?*

Error messages can provide clues to the problem's cause, even if they don't necessarily point to it precisely. You can search a vendor's technical documentation for elaboration on specific error messages. You may even provide your users with a *problem log* form that "helps" (that is, *requires*) them to record more details than they may otherwise.

> *If the problem is intermittent, does it seem to occur at certain times rather than others? For example, does it occur toward the end of the day, when your computer's been on for a few hours?*

Some hardware problems occur more often when components, such as memory modules, are hot. Also, on some computers, software can gradually run low on memory if the computer has been on for a few hours or days, due to software design inefficiencies called *memory leaks*. A problem that occurs first thing in the morning may relate to heavier network traffic as employees hit the office and log on, in which case you may suspect Network Interface Cards or cabling.

When did you start drinking in the morning?

If you actually ask this (which I recommend only in the most informal circumstances), a quick-witted user may reply, "When my computer started acting up," in which case your comeback is, "Pour me a shot, then. Looks like I'm gonna need it." If you're going to be a network gumshoe, you may as well act like one.

Sometimes you may want to interview the neighbors, too. If you suspect a networkwide problem, ask other users if they've noticed whether the network has been performing unusually slowly. A bad Network Interface Card on one computer can send out lots of unnecessary traffic (known as a *packet storm*) that degrades network speed for everyone.

Reconstruct the Crime

Reconstructing the crime is analogous to duplicating the network problem. Re-create the circumstances that caused the event, and see where it leads you. If you can get the problem to reoccur, you're more than halfway to a solution.

When you duplicate the reported problem, you can be much more careful about observing the results — after all, you expect the problem to occur, and the reporting user didn't. Even if the user didn't jot down the detailed error message, you can. You can also change some of the variables: See if the problem happens no matter which network ID you use, for example, or which network printer you use. Vary the application, vary the physical network port, vary the workstation software settings (but one at a time!). Most important, take concise notes so you can refer to them later; remembering exactly what you did is not always easy.

Even if reconstructing the crime doesn't point you to an exact solution, it's useful information if you have to call in some help later on.

If you *can't* duplicate the user's problem, you may be tempted to assume that the problem's "fixed itself," and to attribute the problem to a unique and unusual combination of events and circumstances, including sunspots and El Niño. Document the problem anyway; if it does rear its ugly head again, you may be able to detect a pattern.

Pull the Ol' Switcheroo

Two out of every three Erle Stanley Gardner mysteries I've read involves a weapons switch at some point. And similarly, the ol' switcheroo is one of your most potent LAN troubleshooting techniques. After you zero in on a problem to the extent that you suspect a particular computer, printer, monitor, keyboard, NIC, or whatever, abandon the intellectual for the practical and swap the suspicious component with a "known good" spare. No faster way exists to determine whether a particular component is bad.

Once the bad component is off your LAN, you can return it to the vendor if it's under warranty, and the replacement becomes your new spare — and you don't experience downtime waiting for the replacement to arrive. If the bad component isn't under warranty, it probably doesn't make sense to repair it; repair costs usually meet or exceed replacement costs for computer devices, and you typically don't get as good a warranty (if you get one at all) when you get a part repaired, either.

So, have some spares on hand for components you consider likely to fail. Make sure the spare parts work by testing them before you put them in the "spares" box; nothing leads you down the wrong path faster than a spare part you assume is good, but in reality doesn't work. Here's my list of spare parts no network administrator should be without — make sure you have at least one of each (or even a spare PC that includes everything I list here):

- ✔ Patch cables that link computers to wallplates, or, if you don't use wallplates, cables long enough to connect the furthest computer to a hub

- ✔ BNC "T" connectors, unions, and terminating resistors (if you use coaxial cable)

- ✔ Network Interface Cards, one spare for each type you have in your LAN (ideally, you only use one type, so you only need one spare)

- ✔ Server disk drive controllers, that is, SCSI host adapters, one spare for each type you use in your servers (which, again ideally, means one spare)

- ✔ Workstation hard drives, typically the EIDE type, with capacity equal to or greater than the largest workstation hard drive in your LAN

- ✔ Server hard drives, typically the SCSI type, with capacity equal to or greater than the largest server hard drive you use

- ✔ Workstation power supplies (usually integrated with a fan unit)

- ✔ Server power supplies (ditto)

You may not be able to afford a spare hub, but if you have more than two or three hubs in your network, a spare is a good idea if you have the money. Some companies purposely leave one or two ports vacant on each hub, both to make bad-port identification easier and to provide short-term growth capacity. You may also consider a spare server if network downtime could cost your business dearly; it doesn't have to be terribly expensive if you put the server disk drives in a separate enclosure.

Keep any spare circuit boards, such as NICs, in the antistatic bags in which they originally shipped (or buy new ones at Radio Shack). These bags protect the circuit boards from dust and static electricity, both of which can render your spare parts useless.

Keep a small toolkit with your spare parts to help you install them. You should have an assortment of screwdrivers, including a "Torx" screwdriver for notebook computers and Compaq desktops — make sure the screwdrivers are *not* magnetic. Tweezers come in handy too, as does a pair of needle-nose pliers, a Swiss army knife, a socket set designed for computers (sometimes the screwdriver doesn't give you enough grip), and a small flat file. I don't use cable tools myself, because I think it's cheaper and better in the long run just to throw away a bad cable and replace it, but that's a judgment call.

Consult with the Crime Lab

Police often rely on sophisticated crime labs to analyze physical evidence. As a network troubleshooter, you need a crime lab, too, even if it contains no actual chemicals and only occupies a single bookshelf near your cubicle or office. What should it contain?

- ✔ **Technical manuals for the products you use in your network.** Note that technical manuals may not come with the product, but you can often order them separately.

- ✔ **Commercial books covering the products you use.** Sometimes, these are even better than the technical manuals the vendors provide. Appendix B lists some books you may find useful.

- ✔ **Technical magazines, but only if you have a way to search them electronically.** Getting information from magazines quickly is too difficult unless you can get a CD-ROM with the text contents in digital form. You may still want the physical magazines, for the graphics and charts that CD-ROM products usually omit.

- ✔ **Aspirin.** This makes for a bit of humor that users are sure to chuckle over good-naturedly when you leave two pills on their desks with a note saying, "Here's your solution! Call me in the morning!"

- **CD-ROM troubleshooting databases, for example, from Microsoft or Novell.** The beauty of these is that you can search by keywords, phrases, and cryptic error messages. See Appendix B for details.

- **A computer linked to the Internet.** The network administrator needs Internet access even if no one else in the company has it. Many software and hardware vendors make technical support services available through the World Wide Web, and through newsgroups where customers post details about their problems and help each other when possible.

Your LAN troubleshooting crime lab can be an excellent investment, reducing user down time and helping you avoid incurring phone support "incident" charges.

Get a Confession

Sometimes the best troubleshooting approach is to let the network tell you what's wrong. Many network devices actually do try to submit a confession — "Yes, I'm broken, fix me!" — but you have to understand their language. Most often, this means understanding the meaning of the little status lights on the physical device.

LEDs *(Light-Emitting Diodes)* are a network troubleshooter's best friend. You find them on hubs, Network Interface Cards, modems, keyboards, hard drives, diskette drives, tape drives, and optical drives. They can tell you a lot about a hardware problem, if you know how to interpret them. Here are a few guidelines:

- **On hubs.** Network hubs vary somewhat, but usually they have at least one LED indicating that a particular port is on-line and active. Sometimes hubs have error LEDs that light up when the hub detects a problem on a particular port; other hubs use normally green LEDs that go yellow to indicate trouble.

- **On NICs.** Network Interface Cards usually have an LED that burns steadily if everything's okay, and flashes or goes dark if a problem exists with the NIC or the cable to which it connects.

- **On computers.** When you start a computer, the diskette drive LED should flash for a moment (if a diskette drive exists on the system) and so should the keyboard LEDs. If these lights don't flash, the computer may have a problem with its main circuit board.

- **On hard drives.** Shortly after starting a computer, the hard drive LED should flicker vigorously while the operating system software loads into RAM. No activity here may indicate a dead hard drive or controller, or invalid information in the computer setup program.

> If a computer's hard drive light or diskette drive light comes on and stays on, the chances are good that a NIC or other new device is using the same interrupt that another device in the computer is using. You may have to change interrupt assignments (see Chapter 8). Another possibility is a reversed hard drive cable.

Many laser printers and some servers go beyond mere LEDs and provide a front-panel LCD (Liquid Crystal Display). The LCD panel can provide valuable error information if you're having problems, and (unlike the error messages that workstation computers display) the LCD panel messages are almost always correct. Usually, the error is a numeric or alphanumeric code, so hang on to that manual; it could save you a lot of troubleshooting time.

Call in the Feds

Network administrators (or their backups — every administrator should train a backup in case of absence) often fix problems without outside help. However, any good troubleshooter puts a time limit on solo work. The actual limit depends on how busy the troubleshooter is, how important the problem is, and how expensive outside help is. Generally, if you haven't figured something out in an hour or two, the probability that you'll ever figure it out starts sliding steeply. Remember the time-honored Glenn's Rule Of Troubleshooting (GROT), which I just made up: If it's happening to you, it's probably happened to someone else, and the vendor has probably heard it — and solved it — before.

Calling vendor technical support can be expensive, especially if you pay by the hour, so you want to get your ducks in a row before you call. Be prepared to provide the full litany of details on the problem: product version numbers, hardware and software configuration details, when the problem does and doesn't occur, what you've done to try to fix it, and so on. Also, try not to vent your frustration on the support analysts. They get a lot of that, and if you remain polite, cooperative, and open to suggestions, they tend to work harder on your behalf.

Exceptions to the GROT do occur, and tech support analysts may not have any earthly idea as to what's causing your problem. In this case, they invariably suggest the same thing: *Reinstall the software.* Doing so may fix the problem, but it's a last resort because you'll never know why it fixed the problem, it can take a long time (you may have to reconfigure all the settings), and it's an easy out for the support technician. Politely but firmly ask to "be escalated to second-level support" (the real tech support industry term!) before accepting this solution. A less time-consuming fix may exist, and the person you're working with just may not know about it. In most companies, the first person you speak to is a Junior Troubleshooter; you may need the Grizzled Veteran.

Sometimes, even the vendor's top tech support gurus can't crack a case. In that situation, you may be able to make a software or hardware change. For example, if you find that an upgrade to your accounting software no longer handles sales tax correctly, and no one can figure out how to correct the problem quickly, you may be able to undo the upgrade and reinstall the most recent version of the software that does work correctly. Similarly, if you buy a new-and-improved Network Interface Card that for some weird reason just doesn't work in your LAN, send it back and buy a simpler NIC model that does. You're not actually fixing the problem so much as sidestepping it, but the users don't care as long as they don't have to remember to do anything different or special. A problem avoided is a problem solved.

No vendor tests new products in every possible combination, and therefore every change to a working computer system (like every change to an ecosystem) invites problems. Perform only those upgrades that promise significant benefits.

Rehabilitate the Offender

After the cop nabs the crook and the court hands down a conviction, the story generally ends — at least in novels and television shows. In real life, that's when the story should begin, because — without slighting the work of the sleuths and prosecutors — the toughest challenge is rehabilitating the offender. LAN troubleshooting is similar: Get the user's computer working again, and you may think you're done, but you're not. To really beat the problem you just solved, you have to take steps to ensure that it doesn't occur again. For example:

- ✔ **Provide additional training.** Did a user procedure error cause the problem? If so, maybe a little user education is in order. When one user makes a mistake, you have to ask yourself if other users are likely to do the same at some later date. The usual answer is yes.

- ✔ **Take a close look at the products you're using on your network.** Did premature hardware failure cause the problem? If you see a lot of failures, maybe you need to rethink your purchasing policies. Going with the lowest priced components may not be the cheapest strategy in the long run. (If you contract for the government, you may have no choice. If you don't, be thankful that you have the option of spending more money and getting more reliable parts.)

- ✔ **Consider preventive maintenance.** Did an incorrect software setting on a user workstation cause the problem? If changing the setting on one machine fixed the problem, you may want to consider changing it (or at least checking it) on everybody's machine.

✔ **Make sure the problem isn't a symptom for a larger systemwide problem.** Did a faulty cable cause the problem? If you see more than one such incident, you may want to get the cable installer out to test the whole system, and make any repairs if needed (especially if the job's still under warranty).

Set Up a Neighborhood Watch

The most important function of a police officer may be to help citizens prevent crime in the first place. Similarly, the most important function of a chapter on troubleshooting may be to give you a list of things that can help you avoid trouble. Get everyone in your network neighborhood to follow these routine network procedures, and you'll have fewer troubles to shoot:

✔ **Watch for viruses.** Everyone should know the common signs of computer viruses and promptly report suspicious computer activity, such as a workstation that flashes the message YOUR COMPUTER IS NOW A USELESS HUNK OF JUNK — ELVIS LIVES on the screen (see Chapter 11 for more on viruses).

✔ **Watch for error messages.** Users should report all error messages to the LAN administrator right away, even if those messages don't seem to impair users' ability to go about their business, and even if they offer an "ignore" option.

✔ **Be alert — the world needs more lerts.** Before reporting a problem, users should check all power cords and power switches and cable connections, to avoid wasting time and, more important, looking like a dolt.

✔ **Don't touch the self-destruct button.** Users shouldn't delete (or try to delete) any file unless they own it, they know no one else is sharing it, and they know *exactly* what that file is and does.

✔ **Tarzan say: Change loincloth good, change settings bad.** Users shouldn't change their computer hardware or software setup without first checking with the network administrator (except for minor cosmetic changes such as screen wallpaper or icon font size).

✔ **My biggest turn off . . .** No one should turn off a workstation without closing all programs, logging off the network, and following the proper shutdown procedure (for example, Start⇨Shut down in Windows 95). Similarly, no one should turn off a server computer without making sure that no one is logged on. If the server is idle and it needs to be shut down, be sure to follow the server's shutdown procedure.

✓ **No touchy the connections.** No one should connect or disconnect a computer to or from a network cable when the network is running and the computers are powered on. (More generally, no one should connect any computer device to any other computer device unless both are turned off.) Strategically placed yellow high-voltage warning stickers can make your point.

Chapter 16

Ten Appealing Features of Intranets

. . . .

. . . .

*A*n intranet can be a fine addition to your basic file-, printer-, and program-sharing network as a way to give your employees convenient access to text and graphics documents from multiple locations. In this chapter, I discuss ten of intranetting's key benefits.

> **in•tra•net** (in'tru'net') *n.* What the Internet would look like if it grew up and got a job. (*Weadock's Practical Computer Dictionary,* not yet written)

An *intranet* is a miniature, private Internet living within the borders of your own company — kind of like a company wide web instead of a World Wide Web — that uses the same languages and protocols that the public Internet uses. On an intranet, employees run web browser software, like the popular Netscape Navigator or Microsoft Internet Explorer, and connect to a web server that you maintain for your company's exclusive use. Intranets can also run other software you find on the public Internet, such as newsgroups and e-mail. Intranets can connect to the public Internet, but they don't have to, and many don't.

Intranets are very hot right now in medium and large companies, partly because the technology is good at tying together a bunch of different, largely incompatible computer systems and giving them a common face, or *front end.* As a small company that is most likely building a new computer network from the ground up, you probably don't have the problem of tying together many different computer systems. However, you may wish to consider an intranet for its other advantages. This chapter sets forth ten of the more important ones.

To be fair, intranets have disadvantages, too. The primary one is that, unlike the public Internet, you cannot search a typical intranet for computer jokes such as "This amn keyboar oesn't have any 's."

If all the work your company does takes place in a single location, or if your company has a dozen or fewer employees, you may want to skip this chapter. Most likely, in these cases, you won't benefit from having an intranet. Also, if you don't use the TCP/IP *(Transmission Control Protocol/ Internet Protocol)* language for your network (see Chapter 6), setting up an intranet is a bit of a hurdle, although not impossible.

If you read over this chapter and decide that intranetting may be appropriate for your business, check out *Building an Intranet For Dummies* by John Fronckowiak, and *Intranet Publishing For Dummies* by Yours Truly (both from IDG Books Worldwide, Inc.).

Fast

You can build a small intranet quickly — with a little expert help, getting a new intranet up and running in a week or two is not out of the question.

The reason for the quick setup time for an intranet is that you probably already have most of the pieces in place: a network running the TCP/IP language, a dedicated server computer, and a bunch of client computers. Intranets don't need separate network cable. Heck, you may not even have to install a new computer.

If your intranet gets more than occasional use, giving the web server program its own computer (a *dedicated server*) though not necessary, can really improve intranet performance. The appropriate computer depends on the number of users, how often they access information, the amount of graphics on the web pages, and the presence or absence of fancy programming. Companies with simple intranets can happily run a web server on a $3,000 computer.

Building your intranet may require that you do nothing more than

- ✓ Install a web server program onto an existing network server computer
- ✓ Install a web browser program onto each workstation
- ✓ Design the web pages that convey the *content* you wish to distribute electronically
- ✓ Show employees how to use the browser software

In order to create your intranet content, you may be able to convert existing computer files into intranet-ready format using programs you already have (see the "Easy" section later in this chapter).

If you want to spend even less time building your intranet, you can buy a complete intranet server in a *box* — a computer equipped with a web server, page design tools, and even prebuilt business applications! A new intranet doesn't get much easier than this. Vendors of intranets-in-a-box include, among others

 ✔ IntraNetics (no final product name at this writing, $5,000 to $7,000)

 ✔ Lotus (Domino Intranet Starter Pack, $1,700)

 ✔ Whistle Communications Corp. (Interjet 100, $2,000)

Cheap

Novell IntranetWare, Microsoft Windows NT Server, and many other network products already come with a "free" web server. The Novell and Microsoft servers are not flimsy freebies — they're competent, full-featured products. Unix shops can download the popular Apache web server for free (point your web browser to `http://www.apache.org`), and various other free, shareware server products are available for the download. Netscape offers a range of web servers, from the simpler FastTrack Server ($295) to the industrial-strength Enterprise Server ($1,295), that aren't free but do provide a lot of features for the dollar.

On the workstation side, you can get the Microsoft Internet Explorer web browser free (it comes with Windows 95) or you can pay a small sum (around $50) for Netscape Navigator or Communicator. You may already have a version of Internet Explorer preinstalled on your workstation computers.

Page design tools are inexpensive, too — many good ones cost less than $200. Bottom line: If you already have a TCP/IP network in place and you run a network that comes with a bundled web server, you can add basic intranet publishing capabilities to your network for under $500, plus whatever you pay someone to help you set it up — an incredible bargain, even in an industry known for incredible bargains.

Universal

Small companies often enjoy the luxury of having the same computer (some people may say *single platform*) for every user on their *Local Area Network* (LAN). One problem with companies that practice *telecommuting,* however, is that employees don't necessarily have the same kinds of computers at home as in the office. If you've ever tried to tap into a PC network using a home Macintosh that you bought to help Johnny learn to read (and to let you play a little Myst or 7th Guest while Johnny plays in the street), you know what I mean.

If you don't know about Myst or 7th Guest, please forget I said anything. They're fascinating games that rank right up there with chess and home redecorating in the world-class time sinkhole category.

The good news for prospective intranetters is that almost any computer built in the last ten years can connect to your company intranet. Employees can run web browser software on home PCs, Macintoshes, Unix workstations, you name it. Netscape even recently announced plans to make its web browser run on toaster ovens and dishwashers.

Easy

Intranets are easy to develop. You can create a demo intranet without even installing a web server: Just create some web pages, link 'em together, throw 'em into a public directory on an existing file server, and point a workstation browser at the main page.

A fully functioning intranet isn't much more complex than a demo if all you need to do is distribute information. You can develop an intranet with a variety of page design tools and publishing applications, such as

- Adobe PageMill
- Macromedia Backstage Internet Studio
- Microsoft FrontPage
- SoftQuad HoTMetaL Intranet Publisher

Many office automation programs (word processors, spreadsheets, and so on) include a command to export a data file to the HTML *(HyperText Markup Language)* format that web browsers understand. Alternatively, a variety of conversion tools like InfoAccess HTML Transit and Net-It Software Net-It Now! can translate existing computer files into formats viewable by intranet users.

Intranets are not only easy to develop, they're also easy to use. The command buttons on web browsers are almost as simple as the controls on your home VCR: go backward, go forward, stop. The most complicated thing about a web browser is typing in that first address (called a *Uniform Resource Locator* or URL): `http://pub.acme.com/intranet/home.html` or something similar. However, users only need to type such an address once, and then add it to their browser's list of "favorite places." And once a user connects to an intranet page, all further navigation is of the point-and-click variety. In addition, today's browsers let you drop the `http://` part altogether, letting you keep the keyboard acrobatics to a minimum.

Structured

An intranet is a good way to add structure to a LAN because you can easily create web pages that contain links (called *hyperlinks*) to other web pages, data files, and even programs. Hyperlinks are little places on a web page where a user can click the mouse to go somewhere else. A hyperlink can be an underlined word or phrase, a graphical button, or a particular area inside a larger graphical image. The web designer (or *webmaster*) determines where hyperlinks appear, what they look like, and where they lead to. You can place hyperlinks wherever you want, and include descriptive text on the web page that tells the user where the links go. All the user has to do is click on the link and the intranet does the rest.

The great thing about hyperlinks is that they can bring together data files or programs that may reside in various different locations on your LAN, without the user having to hunt down those precise locations. Here are a few tips on designing a well-structured intranet:

- ✔ **Provide a way home.** Include a link to the main intranet page, or *home page,* on every subsidiary page so the user can easily return to an anchor location. Some designers advocate placing a home page link at the top and at the bottom of every page.

- ✔ **Let users know where links lead.** When you add a hyperlink, make sure that you describe it thoroughly enough so that users don't accidentally go places they don't want to go.

- ✔ **A map can lead the way.** An *image map* is a graphical image that contains hyperlinks. Page design tools generally enable you to create image map *regions* that link to different locations. You can build a graphical map of your intranet site with an image map, and include a link to this site map on every page.

✔ **Index long pages with *bookmarks*.** *Bookmarks,* also called *anchors,* enable easier navigation of a long page. Typically, bookmarks are nothing more than text hyperlinks at the top of a page that point to specific locations further down the page. For example, in a directory of employee names, you can include bookmarks for each letter of the alphabet at the top of the page so that users can easily find the person they are looking for.

Instantaneous

When you distribute information on paper, a delay exists between the actual printing of the document and when people receive it. That delay isn't significant in a small office, but if some employees work from home, or if you have sales reps who basically work on the road, the time discrepancy can mean that important information doesn't get to everyone who needs it as quickly as you like.

Intranet publishing, on the other hand, is instantaneous: After you publish a document by placing it on a web server, all employees with access to your business network can see that document immediately, regardless of physical location.

Thrifty

One of the best features of intranets is their ability to save the costs associated with paper documents: the paper itself, printing, binding, handling, and mailing. Small companies don't generate as much paper as big companies, but your employees may still spend more time (and money) at Kinko's than you like. Ask yourself whether you may be able to put some of that paper-based information onto an intranet and save some bucks.

Human resources material can account for a big part of even a small company's paper bill. You probably distribute some sort of employee handbook to new hires that details policies on employment, employee records, payroll, working conditions and hours, drug and alcohol use, business travel, leaves of absence, employee conduct, disciplinary actions, and so on. Specialized software, like Policies Now! from KnowledgePoint, can help you build an online manual containing all this information, and put that manual on your intranet. When the policies change, you don't have to reprint anything — just modify the online manual and send an e-mail to everybody alerting them to the change.

You can also use your intranet to publish information about employee benefits like vacation time, sick days, employee discounts on company products or services, insurance policies, retirement plans, the allotted four square inches of lunch sack space in the communal refrigerator, and so on. Then there's the company schedule, with key financial and operational dates. Just about anything you currently put on paper, you can put on an intranet — and for less dough.

 With software like Adobe Acrobat, a slick $300 tool for creating so-called *portable electronic documents,* you can even create searchable document files with slick text-and-graphics formatting that rival anything you can do on paper.

Profitable

An intranet can be a handy sales and marketing tool, especially if your sales staff visits customers at their locations. A salesperson can dial into your intranet from a customer site, using either a customer's phone jack or a cellular link, and have immediate access to useful product, customer, and sales support information. For example

- ✔ **Spec sheets and configuration details** to help salespeople understand the product and assist customers in making an appropriate choice

- ✔ **Product photographs or illustrations** that salespeople can show customers online

- ✔ **Current price lists and ordering terms** that enable your sales reps to make accurate quotations on the spot

- ✔ **Sales presentations** in a computer slide show format, such as Microsoft PowerPoint, that reps can download from your intranet with a single mouse click, and then "play" for customers on a laptop equipped with an LCD *(Liquid Crystal Display)* panel or LCD projector

- ✔ **Competitive analyses** that showcase the strong points of your company's products or services in comparison to those of Brand X

- ✔ **Sales and marketing bulletins** that can replace the paper documents you normally send to inside and outside sales reps

Intranets permit quick, global changes to sales-related documents; relieve sales staff from having to keep track of quite as many pieces of paper; and let you easily reach geographically dispersed sales reps.

Figure 16-1 shows the primary screen for a sample sales and marketing intranet system. This screen demonstrates how an intranet organizes different informational pages or programs, so that the user clicks on whatever information he or she wants at a given moment.

Figure 16-1:
Sales staff
who go on
the road
frequently
can dial into
your
intranet
from hotel
rooms or
customer
offices to
obtain a
variety of
helpful
information.

Helpful

One of an intranet's best uses is to provide helpful information for using programs on the network. Because intranets are so easy to use, they're well suited to providing more complex information about programs that aren't terribly easy or intuitive.

A technical support intranet (see Figure 16-2) can present online software and hardware documentation, frequently-asked questions and answers (called *FAQ* documents), and even electronic forms for users to submit questions and problems to the network administrator. An intranet is also a great way to distribute software on an as-needed basis. You can create a *download page* with links that users can click to receive software updates, utilities, and even complete programs.

Many new software products come with help files in HTML (HyperText Markup Language) format. Licenses permitting, you can put such HTML files onto your intranet with no conversion or reformatting.

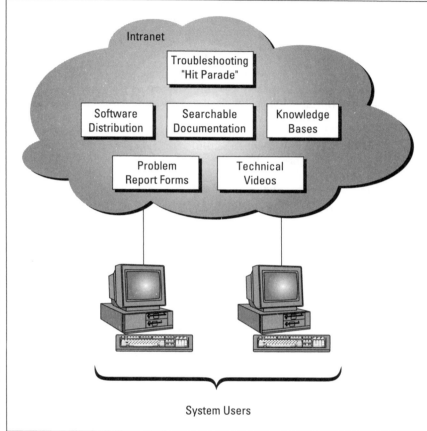

Figure 16-2:
Possible
components
of a
technical
support
intranet,
which
has the
advantage
of being
available
around the
clock —
unlike your
LAN admin-
istrator.

Connectable

Last but not least in this brief recital of intranet advantages is the ability to connect to other *systems,* such as databases you may have already set up, and to other *users,* such as customers and suppliers.

To databases

Most small businesses use intranets primarily for one-way document publishing, but you can also use your intranet to retrieve, present, and even modify data stored in network databases — your intranet becomes a form of *middleware,* interacting on the one hand with users through web pages, and on the other hand with databases through custom programs. You may want to build such an intranet, for example, if you already have a Microsoft Access database containing product price information, and you want to put that price information onto an intranet web page to make it available to sales reps in the field.

Integrating an intranet with a database may be beyond the technical ability of your part-time network administrator, as it usually involves at least a little bit of programming. Database integration is a good candidate for outsourcing (see Chapter 3).

Products you may wish to explore for database integration (see Appendix B for more details) include

- Allaire Cold Fusion
- Borland IntraBuilder
- Expertelligence WebBase
- Macromedia Backstage Internet Studio
- Microsoft FrontPage 98 and Internet Information Server
- NetObjects Fusion
- Netscape Enterprise Server and FastTrack Server

To customers and suppliers

You can make your intranet available to those outside your own organization, such as customers, suppliers, or even the general public, at which point your intranet gets a new name: *extranet*. Extranets (think of them as intranets that can answer incoming phone calls) are more complex and demanding to build than intranets because of the increased importance of security, reliability, performance, and professional design. Extranets may also have database-publishing features and may incorporate software to handle transactions like order processing.

Using an intranet for transaction processing is a little different than using the public Internet for the same purpose (see Chapter 17). You may be able to ensure tighter security with an intranet, and you can also control system availability and performance more directly because you manage the extranet server in your own office.

Start with an internal project like a simple one-way document publishing intranet before embarking on an extranet that the outside world will see. Make your mistakes where they won't be quite as embarrassing, and where you are free to experiment.

Chapter 17

Ten Ways to Do Business Using the Internet

● ●

In This Chapter

▶ Realizing the potential of your business on the Internet

▶ Setting up your own Internet site (it's easier than you think)

▶ Using the Internet to connect with customers in new ways

▶ Finding new markets with the World Wide Web

● ●

*Y*ou can't read a magazine or watch television anymore without bumping into references to the Internet. (I've even seen Internet references in bathroom graffiti, a sure sign that it's become a permanent part of modern culture.) In this chapter, I offer ten ways you can turn the Internet craze to your company's business advantage, using your new computer network.

> "The Internet is the most important single development in the history of human communications since the invention of 'call waiting.'" (Dave Barry, *Dave Barry in Cyberspace*, Crown)

Also known as the "information superhighway," or more accurately, the *information ball of yarn,* the Internet (see Figure 17-1) is a sprawling collection of over 40 million computers linked in a global network. The Internet (or for short, the *Net*) was originally just for military and academic use, but has now grown to include all manner of private, public, and commercial uses.

Each computer on the Internet has its own unique network address (called an *IP address*) to identify it to other computers, and speaks the same basic communications language: TCP/IP, or *Transmission Control Protocol/Internet Protocol* (see Chapter 6). The millions of Internet computers connect to each other via a complex network of communication links (some fast and some slow), managed by computerized traffic *routers* (which function like information traffic cops).

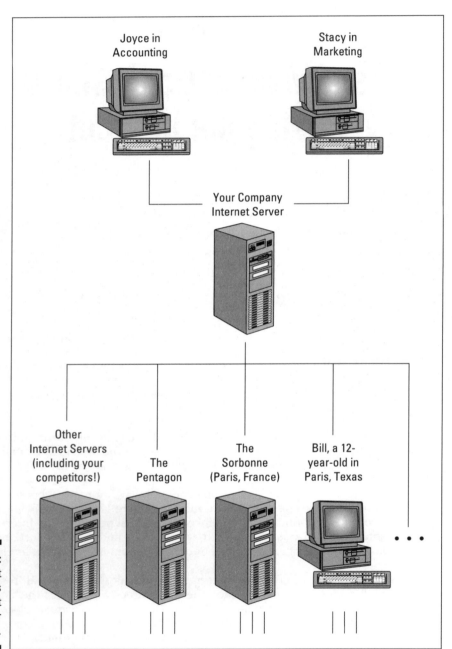

Figure 17-1:
The Internet
is Earth's
largest
computer
network.

An Internet-connected computer that makes information available for others to access is called a *server,* and a computer that reads that information is called a *client.* Because of the way the Internet is set up, any computer connected to the Internet can be a server, a client, or both. If you've already read Chapter 4, this is another way of saying that the Internet is essentially a huge *peer-to-peer* network.

The part of the Internet that generates the most interest among businesses is the *World Wide Web,* or simply the *Web* for short. (*World Wide Wait* and *Weird Wild Web* are frivolous variations that I won't mention.) You can think of the Web as the graphical face of the Internet, because it can present pictures as well as text. It can also present sounds, digital videos, and even programs, to the user.

The Web may get the most press, but it isn't the only part of the Internet you should know about. The Internet's most common use is for plain old e-mail. Another popular Internet service is the *newsgroup,* a sort of electronic discussion group. You can use both to the benefit of your business.

If your interest is piqued by this chapter, take a look at *Small Business Web Strategies For Dummies,* by Janine Warner, and *Small Business Internet For Dummies,* by Greg Holden. In addition, *Small Business Internet Directory For Dummies,* by Esau Barchin and Edward Craig, can point you to some Internet resources that may help your business. All three books are from IDG Books Worldwide, Inc.

Since the Internet mutated from its role as strictly an academic and military network, businesses have been grappling with the problem of how to take advantage of its exploding popularity. Here are ten ideas to get you started.

Research Your Market

The Internet can be a very useful market research tool. First, of course, you have to connect your network to it.

Connecting to the Internet, in three pages or less

Assuming all you want to do is use the Internet for information access, rather than set up a Web presence of your own (which I discuss in a minute), you have to make two decisions: who provides your Internet access, and how you connect with that provider.

You have two options for gaining access to the Internet:

- ✔ **You can use an online service (such as America Online or CompuServe).** Unlimited access for a flat monthly fee (say $20) may be more cost-effective than paying by the hour (some services offer both plans).

- ✔ **You can use an Internet Service Provider (ISP).** ISPs are companies like PSINet, MindSpring, and AT&T WorldNet that offer Internet connections as their main business. Most ISPs charge you something to set up your account, and then provide unlimited access for a flat fee (again, usually in the $20/month ballpark).

You have four options for how you connect to either an ISP or online service:

- ✔ **Leased line.** A small business can install a direct *leased line* connection to the Internet. A leased line is great for speed, but the cost may not be justified by the amount of time your employees actually spend using Internet services. You also have to buy specialized equipment to link your *Local Area Network* (LAN) to the leased line. A variety of leased lines exist; ISDN *(Integrated Services Digital Network)* lines run at 128 Kbps, while a more expensive T1 connection runs about ten times faster.

- ✔ **Satellite link.** You can set up a *satellite link*. I know, this sounds really expensive, but you may find that it actually costs a lot less than a leased line. It's also fun, when your big-company friends are crowing smugly at happy hour about all their slick computer gear, to say "Yeah, leased lines are okay, but we prefer our satellite dish. More buffalo wings?" Check with the companies that provide satellite TV services; some of them now sell Internet access at surprisingly competitive rates.

- ✔ **POTS.** You can use a POTS dial-up link. (*POTS* is a fun acronym for Plain Old Telephone System.) A telephone connection is the least expensive way to go, and the slowest too, but modem manufacturers keep finding ingenious ways to wring more speed out of POTS lines. One gotcha here is that the phone lines your business uses may not accommodate your maximum modem speeds in practice. A chat with the local phone company can help you understand why, and whether you can do anything about it.

- ✔ **Cable modem.** In some (still limited) communities, you can connect to the Internet over the same coaxial cable that the cable TV companies use. The upload speed maxes out at 768 kilobits per second and download speed peaks at a blazing 5 to 6 megabits per second, depending on traffic — all for about $40 a month more than basic cable TV service. A great deal if you can get it.

In any of these scenarios, you don't need to have a modem at every user's workstation in order to provide each of them with Internet access. One link connected to the network — be it leased line, satellite, or POTS — is all you need. Yet another benefit of having a small business network!

Depending on the access provider you choose, you may have to deal with the fact that the Internet runs on the TCP/IP networking language. If your network runs TCP/IP already, you're set. Otherwise, you can go one of two ways. You can install TCP/IP software on your workstations, which isn't all that hard but can be a bit of a chore if you're only doing it to gain Internet access. Or, you can set up a *gateway* computer (see Figure 17-2) that lets you link to the Internet without changing your workstation setups — a slicker approach if you don't mind a slight decrease in speed. Gateway vendors include FTP Software, Bay Networks, and Novell (in the full IntranetWare product, though, not the Small Business version).

Figure 17-2:
An IPX-
to-IP
gateway
allows
every
computer
on a Novell
network to
connect to
the Internet.

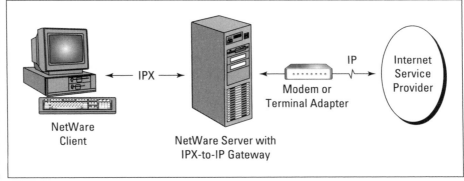

NetWare
Client

IPX

Modem or
Terminal Adapter

NetWare Server with
IPX-to-IP Gateway

IP

Internet
Service
Provider

The last piece of the puzzle is to install a *web browser* on every user's workstation. The browser is the application a user runs to view Internet Web pages (and intranet web pages, as I discuss in Chapter 16). Depending on the kind of computers you have, you may very well already have the software. You can also find browser software on the CD-ROM included with this book.

Doing research on the Net

After you have Internet access, you can perform a variety of market research activities. All you have to do is type the correct URL (that is, the web address — it stands for *Uniform Resource Locator*) in your web browser's location window, and then follow the on-screen instructions.

You can connect to your main competitors' Web sites, if they have them, and see what those rascals are up to. You can also study public information sources on competitors, customers, and contractors, such as the so-called *10-K* forms that provide financial information required by the government. The Securities and Exchange Commission (http://www.sec.gov) maintains these records in its EDGAR database *(Electronic Data Gathering And Retrieval)*.

You can search Internet newsgroups with the free Deja News search utility, at `http://www.dejanews.com`.

You can also read and search online business periodicals, such as the following:

- **The interactive *Wall Street Journal*** (`http://interactive.wsj.com`) is $49 per year at this writing, or $29 if your company already subscribes to the print version. The service includes the useful *Markets Data Center*, a customizable *Personal Journal* where you can specify the keywords, companies, and columns you want to see, and a search facility that goes back 14 days. The site also offers a subscription to the interactive *Wall Street Journal's Publications Library* to search past history for hundreds of business periodicals, although the cost ($1 per citation, $3 per article retrieved) adds up fast.
- ***Business Week*** has an online edition (`http://www.businessweek.com`) that you can browse the current version for free.

And you can search the entire Web from any of the popular free Internet search sites, including the following:

- AltaVista (`http://altavista.digital.com`)
- Excite (`http://www.excite.com`)
- HotBot (`http://www.hotbot.com`)
- Lycos (`http://www.lycos.com`)
- Yahoo! (`http://www.yahoo.com`)

For a good guide to Web-searching techniques, see *World Wide Web Searching For Dummies* by Brad Hill (IDG Books Worldwide, Inc.).

As long as you have one connection between your LAN and the Internet, all of your network users can connect to Internet research facilities.

Find New Partners

One side benefit of outfitting your network for Internet access is the possibility of finding other companies in related or complementary businesses with whom you can partner and extend your marketing reach. If your company sells specialty coffee beans on the West Coast, you may join forces with a distributor that handles the Midwest. If you sell rare books all over the U.S. from your Atlanta headquarters, you may want to work together with a Canadian company and even combine your catalogs. If you market home-brew beer-making kits, you may set up a cooperative marketing agreement with a company that sells home wine-making kits.

You still have to go through the usual due diligence in checking out potential business partners; after all, anyone with $20 a month to spend can establish a Web presence. But you may just find a valuable business partner through the Internet that you would never discover any other way.

Set Up a Web Site

Web servers are computers that host Web pages, and they generally run some flavor of Unix, or Microsoft Windows NT Server operating system. These days, many network operating systems come packaged with a Web server. For example, Windows NT Server 4.0 and higher comes with Microsoft Internet Information Server (IIS). The Apache Web server is the most popular on the Internet; it runs on Unix and is free for downloading at http://www.apache.org.

As a practical matter, however, most small businesses don't set up their own in-house Internet Web server. Doing so requires a costly high-speed data connection, a router, and some fairly sophisticated technical know-how. Small companies are usually better off contracting with an outside company to provide *Web hosting services,* meaning that you contract with an ISP to store your Web site on their server. Fortunately, most Internet Service Providers also offer Web hosting services — and at a much lower cost than you could do it in-house.

Online services such as CompuServe and America Online offer Web hosting services for personal pages as well, and these can be very inexpensive, or even free if you already subscribe to the information service. However, think twice before using a personal Web hosting service for your business. The site address can end up being quite long; you may not be able to expand your site; you may not be able to host secure transactions for electronic commerce; and you may not receive the level of technical support you need.

You can contract out Web site design, as well. You may already have someone on staff who can design a sharp and effective Web site, but Web design requires a special blend of technical and aesthetic skills. Professionals who do such work every day may be able to do it faster and better. They also don't have to be at your office to do the work.

If you do decide to design your own Web site, here are a few tools that can be a great help (see Appendix B for contact information):

- Adobe PageMill
- Macromedia Backstage Internet Studio
- Microsoft FrontPage

You don't have to have a computer network in order to establish a Web site, but it can help a great deal — especially if you design your site in-house. If you provide Internet access via your network, every user in your company can view your Web site and contribute ideas for enhancing it. You can even delegate responsibility for different pages to different employees, who can perform their own modifications and updates, and then submit the new files to your ISP via your LAN and its Internet link.

The site design tools mentioned in the previous list all have built-in forms for submitting (or *uploading,* as it's called) Web site files to the ISP host computer, and your ISP can give you specific instructions for how to fill in the blanks in your site design program's submission form.

You need a domain name that uniquely identifies your Web site to other Internet computers. A small company concerned with projecting a solid, stable image should get its own unique domain name (such as www.xyz.com). A company that's watching the budget closely can save $100 and piggyback onto an existing ISP domain name to create a name such as www.w3.xyz.com, which is a bit longer, a bit less convenient, and a notch lower on the prestige scale.

Here are the steps to follow, in a nutshell, if you want your own unique name:

1. **Pick one or more domain names you like for your servers.**

   You may want to consider choosing more than one name to reserve, as the fee isn't large ($100 per name for two years, as I write this) and the good, short names are disappearing fast.

2. **See if the names are already taken.**

   An easy way to do this is to connect to http://rs.internic.net/cgi-bin/whois and specify the name you want. If someone else has it, that company's name and contact information appears on the screen.

3. **Follow the instructions at the InterNIC registration authority's Web site (**http://rs.internic.net/rs-internic.html**) to register domain names and network numbers.**

   The details are all there in the form of *Frequently Asked Questions* (FAQ) documents and procedural flowcharts. You can fill out the templates online, and send your check by mail.

After your company is up on the Web, you can put just about any kind of information onto your site for all to see (and hear):

  ✔ **Text** (for example, a list of frequently asked questions about your company and its wares)

  ✔ **Graphics,** including color (such as product photographs)

✔ **Binary data files** (such as catalogs)

✔ **Programs** (such as self-running product demos)

✔ **Links to other Internet locations** (for example, companies you partner with, or who market products or services that complement your company's offerings)

✔ **Digital audio** (such as the CEO's recent speech on strategic direction)

✔ **Digital video** (for example, how to assemble a subassembly from parts)

Promote Your Wares

The Internet can be a great way to promote your company's products or services on a worldwide scale. Anybody in the world with Internet access can visit your Web site and learn more about your business.

Many kinds of promotion exist, and probably the least effective (especially on the Internet) is the out-and-out "Buy our product *right now* — it's the best!" school of advertising. Hundreds of companies have discovered that Internet users prefer being persuaded to being hyped. Some techniques for friendly persuasion include the following:

✔ **Inform your site visitors.** Describe your products or services so that customers can understand them and choose from among them. If possible, provide enough information so that customers can make a purchase decision. For example, demonstrate how your products or services offer advantages over your competitors'.

✔ **Post testimonials from satisfied customers.** Get permission to use their real names and company names; the public is suspicious of anonymous testimonials such as "ABC Company's investment advice made me rich!" – G. W., Old Dime Box, Texas. (This town really exists, although G.W. may not.)

✔ **Demonstrate your product.** Offer case studies of your products or services in action — especially when they're complex or abstract.

✔ **Post a company newsletter.** Newsletters can increase customer confidence by publicizing your business's success and growth. They can also help personalize your company by including employee articles.

✔ **Offer a way to get more information.** Provide a form where customers can sign up to receive the company newsletter, in either physical or electronic form.

The temptation to splash big, full-color photographs on a promotional Web site is a big one, but many customers may not have a fast Internet connection. Those big graphics can take a long time to appear over a slow link, and may actually turn prospective customers off instead of on. Make any clickable site maps also available as text-only links as a courtesy to those who turn off Web graphics for speed and to the visually impaired, who use screen-reading audio software that can't process graphics.

Get Noticed: Register with a Search Service

Once your Web site is up and running, you want Internet users to be able to find it — for example, when they perform a search using keywords that describe what your business does. With hundreds of new Web sites appearing each *day* (that's not a misprint), most Web users rely heavily on search services to help them find sites of interest.

You can wait around a few months for the primary Internet search services to send out a program called a *spider* to *crawl* your site — that is, inspect it and automatically add to the services' index what seem to be the keywords that describe it. Or, you can be a little more proactive and register your site with those services. I recommend the latter. You get registered much sooner, and you can specify the keywords you want, rather than hope that the spider guesses the best ones.

If you're counting pennies, you can register with each search service individually, which is usually free. Just access their Web sites (see the "Doing research on the Net" section in this chapter for addresses of the more popular services) and click on the links that take you to the registration form. (Sometimes these links say Add URL or something similar.)

A much faster way is to pay a *registration service* to handle the individual registrations for you. The cost typically ranges from $50 to $200, but you don't have to spend your own time filling out online forms. Also, a good service registers you with dozens or even hundreds of search services — more than you would register with if you do the work yourself.

Some of the registration services you may want to check out include

✔ Postmaster at http://www.netcreations.com/postmaster
✔ Register It! at http://www.register-it.com
✔ Submit It! at http://www.submit-it.com

Choose a registration service that allows you to easily re-register your site when it changes in some significant way — for example, when your company offers a new category of products or services.

Get Noticed the Sequel: Use That URL

Registering your site with the popular Internet search engines is just the beginning. Use your URL whenever and wherever you can to lure potential customers:

- ✔ Reprint your letterhead and business cards to include your Web site address.
- ✔ Display that URL prominently on product packaging and customer newsletters.
- ✔ Print it on those promotional highlighter pens, calendars, and golf caps that you give out at trade shows.
- ✔ Stitch it into your underwear, if you're social by nature.
- ✔ Include it in the signature block of any e-mail that you send over the Internet or other service (such as America Online or CompuServe).

 Many e-mail programs, for example Microsoft Outlook, as shown in Figure 17-3, allow you to create a signature block, or *sig file* (so-named because the file usually ends in the .SIG suffix) that automatically appends to every message you send. This is a convenient way to ensure that your Web site address always appears in e-mail messages that you send.

Another great technique is to *cross-link* your site with other relevant and noncompetitive sites: contractors, suppliers, companies you have cooperative marketing agreements with, and so on. Cross-linking simply means that you include a link to someone else's site on your Web pages in exchange for a link to your site on theirs. Trading links doesn't cost anything, it enhances the value of your Web site, and it provides more avenues for potential customers to see your cyberspace storefront.

 Check out the Link Exchange (http://www.linkexchange.com) for possible cross-link partners in addition to the ones you can think of yourself. You may also consider buying ad space at the top of pages that people often visit. Yahoo! and other big sites sell ads that link to the advertiser's home page.

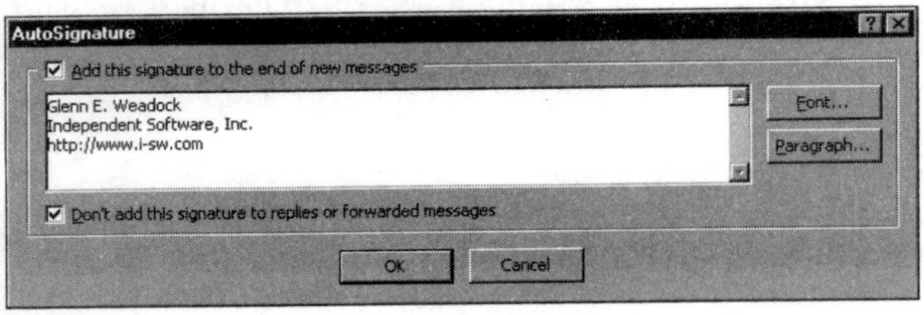

Figure 17-3:
The
Microsoft
Outlook
Auto-
Signature
feature.

Take Orders

You don't have to be able to take orders for products or services via your Web site in order for it to be a great marketing tool. Customers can visit your Web site, compare your products with the competition, learn about the particular product they need, and then send e-mail or phone your office to actually place an order.

However, if you have a product for sale, Internet-based ordering can supplement your more traditional methods for accepting customer orders. It can be convenient for customers who don't need more information than your Web site provides in order to make a purchase decision. Internet order processing also reduces the likelihood of clerical errors, because the customer keys in the information directly on a Web page form (such as the one in Figure 17-4).

Probably the biggest issue for electronic commerce is data security. Many customers are leery about giving out a credit card number over the Internet. Some businesses deal with the problem by letting the customer submit order details over the Net, and including a phone or fax number on the Web page that customers can call to provide the credit card number. Other companies go to some lengths on their Web sites to explain the measures they've taken to ensure electronic security. The second approach probably isn't as effective unless most of your customers would understand what *Secure Sockets Layer* means (it's a way to conduct communications securely over the Internet).

In any case, get some technical help from your Internet Service Provider if you decide to set up online ordering. Many ISPs offer special services for this exact purpose, and they can explain the various options for setting up your site to handle electronic commerce (quite a few exist at this writing).

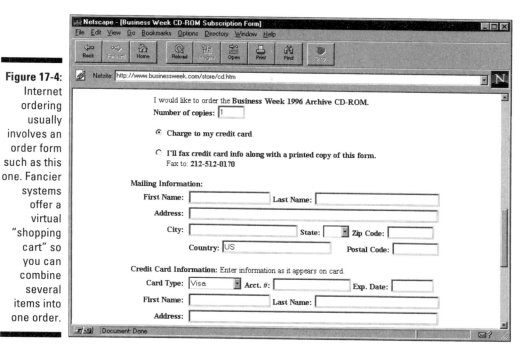

Figure 17-4:
Internet
ordering
usually
involves an
order form
such as this
one. Fancier
systems
offer a
virtual
"shopping
cart" so
you can
combine
several
items into
one order.

If you use your Web site for order processing, make the process as seamless and simple as possible. Hire someone to do a little server-side programming to calculate shipping and handling costs as well as taxes, rather than ask your customers to figure these amounts themselves.

Your salespeople may work on commission or commission-plus-salary, and you may not want them to resent your Internet site because it siphons away their livelihood. One possible solution is to allocate commissions from Internet sales to each salesperson equally. You may also want to review any distribution agreements you have to ensure that an Internet direct-order site doesn't violate those agreements.

Answer Common Questions

If your customers tend to ask a lot of the same questions of your sales or customer service representatives, you may be able to create a FAQ (Frequently Asked Questions, pronounced *fack*) page on your Web site (see Figure 17-5).

A Web FAQ can help keep your employees from having to answer repetitive and common questions, such as:

- ✔ What are the details of your customer satisfaction guarantee?
- ✔ How do you normally ship products?
- ✔ What's your policy and procedure on product returns?
- ✔ What trade associations does your company belong to?
- ✔ How do I determine who my sales rep is?
- ✔ How can I establish a credit account?

Depending on the type of business you're in, you may want to develop specialized FAQ pages. For example, if you sell doughnut-making equipment, you can create a tech-support FAQ that explains how to set the equipment controls to avoid doughnuts that are too squishy or too firm. You can create multiple FAQ pages and link them to a central FAQ page for easy user navigation.

Solicit ideas from your salespeople as to what material makes sense to place on a FAQ page; they're the ones in direct contact with the people asking the questions.

Figure 17-5:
A
Frequently
Asked
Questions
page
usually
uses simple
text format
and a
different
type style
for the
questions
and the
answers.

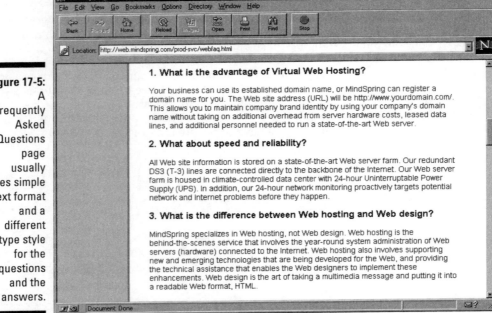

Provide Added Value

Companies large and small are discovering that one great way to get customers to come back to your Web site on a regular basis is to offer some sort of bonus for doing so. The possibilities include

- A straight percentage discount for electronic customers who order online, or who mention your Web site when calling your company
- Special deals on bundled products or services, such as time-limited promotions
- A free "Chia pet" shipped with the customer's order
- Advance information on new products or services your company offers

You can also add value to your company Web site by including links to related helpful Internet sites. For example, you can link to books carried by Internet bookstores such as Amazon (http://www.amazon.com).

Another idea is to offer downloadable software that can help customers in some way, and even prequalify them for a new product. For example, one of the satellite television vendors offers a downloadable calculator via its Web site. The calculator lets you key in a zip code and then tells you where you must point your satellite dish. The prospective customer who hasn't bought a dish yet may not have a direct line of sight to the satellite, in which case he or she can discover the problem with the calculator and won't waste sales reps' time asking about pricing plans and programming options.

Develop a Community of Users with a Newsgroup

You may find it helpful to host your own company *newsgroup* on the Internet, even if you don't host a Web site. (Newsgroups sometimes go by the name *Usenet newsgroups*.) A newsgroup is a sort of distributed, electronic bulletin board. You can install a newsgroup server on your Web site, and make the newsgroup available to your customers for them to exchange messages with each other and with you.

A visitor to your Web site can post a message to the newsgroup, for instance, "Anyone having problems glazing donuts with the new DonutMaster 3000?" Then, other visitors can respond. Maybe one of your DonutMaster 3000 customers already figured out a solution and posts it as a response, or maybe your own design expert can post a response for all your customers to read.

Setting up a newsgroup server on the public Internet can be a bit of a complex undertaking, requiring connections (or *feeds*) to and from other newsgroup servers on the Usenet. You don't have to go through that drill, however. You can build a *private news server* that doesn't link to other Usenet servers, but just provides discussion group capabilities for those who connect to your Internet site. For an example, see Figure 17-6.

Your Internet Service Provider may be able to help you get a private news server off the ground. If you're hosting your Internet site in-house, vendors of news server software include Microsoft, NetManage, and Netscape (see Appendix B for contact information).

Figure 17-6: A user with Netscape Navigator connecting to a private news server at Asymetrix Corp. Note the hierarchy of messages and responses in the upper-right window.

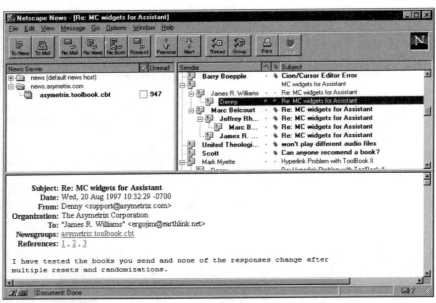

Part VI
Appendixes

The 5th Wave® By Rich Tennant

©RICHTENNANT

NETWORK MGR

"AND JUST WHAT THE HECK PART OF THE NETWORK DID YOU SAY YOU'RE FROM?"

Appendix A
Glossary

This glossary defines most, if not all, of the technical terms in this book. Definitions are listed under the acronyms rather than the expanded term. Cross-referenced terms are in **bold italics** — note that occasionally, multiple cross-referenced terms appear in a row, for instance, ***NetWare Directory Services*** where ***NetWare*** and ***Directory Services*** both have their own entry.

4mm tape (also known as Digital Audio Tape, or DAT). These popular Sony-licensed tape drives offer high capacity and good price/performance using small cartridges (2.9" x 2.1" x 0.4"). Cartridge capacity ranges from 4 to 24 ***gigabytes,*** and the speed of data transfer goes up to 2.4 ***megabytes***/second.

8mm tape. Exabyte, Seagate, and Sony make 8mm tape drives that offer higher tape capacity than ***4mm tape*** drives on slightly larger cartridges (3.75" x 2.5" x 0.5"). Cartridge capacity ranges from 7 to 25 ***gigabytes,*** and the speed of data transfer ranges from 0.5 to 6 ***megabytes***/second.

10Base-2. The standard for thin shielded ***coaxial Ethernet cable;*** usually ***RG-58*** cable with ***BNC***-type connectors. The "10" means 10 ***megabits***/second speed, and the "Base" means ***baseband*** network. Maximum ***segment*** length is 185 meters.

10Base-5. The standard for thick shielded ***coaxial Ethernet cable*** (also called yellow garden hose, ***ThickNet,*** or thick ***Ethernet***). The "10" means 10 ***megabits***/second speed, and the "Base" means ***baseband*** network. Maximum segment length is 500 meters.

10Base-T. The standard for ***twisted-pair Ethernet cable,*** either shielded or unshielded. The "10" means 10 ***megabits***/second speed, and the "Base" means ***baseband*** network. Maximum segment length is 100 meters. See also ***STP*** and ***UTP***.

10Base-F. The standard for ***fiberoptic Ethernet cable***. The "10" means 10 ***megabits***/second speed, and the "Base" means ***baseband*** network.

100Base-T. See ***Fast Ethernet***.

100Base-VG. A network ***protocol*** developed by Hewlett-Packard and AT&T; runs ***Fast Ethernet*** over all four ***twisted pairs*** in ***Category 3 cable***. The "100" means 100 ***megabits***/second speed, and the "Base" means ***baseband*** network.

AAUI (Apple Attachment Unit Interface). A special connector Macintoshes use to connect to an ***Ethernet*** network. See also ***AUI***.

Account. Just like a bank account lets you access your money, a network account typically allows a user to gain access to certain programs and data areas on the network, and verifies the identity of that user via an ***authentication*** process.

Adapter. A circuit board, such as a ***Network Interface Card,*** that plugs into a computer's ***motherboard***.

Administrator. See ***supervisor***.

Airwall. A physical separation between two computer networks, such as a company's internal network and the company's ***Internet server***. An airwall makes it just about impossible for an Internet ***cracker*** to penetrate your network. Two unconnected networks are said to have an airwall between them.

AMP (Asynchronous or Asymmetric Multi-Processing). An option, built into certain ***operating systems,*** that splits ***CPU*** duties between two ***mirrored servers*** — one handling input/output traffic and the other handling network services, such as file sharing. See also ***SMP***.

Anonymous login. A ***login*** to a ***server*** in which the user does not specify a network user name, or specifies the user name anonymous. Often used for public ***FTP*** file ***download*** sites on the ***Internet*** or on an ***intranet***.

ANSI (American National Standards Institute). One of the primary U.S. computer standards organizations.

Antivirus program. ***System software*** that monitors your ***network*** for computer ***viruses,*** alerts a ***supervisor*** if it finds one, and may or may not be able to remove the virus from the network.

API (Application Program Interface). A defined set of commands or "calls" that *application programs* use to communicate with underlying services, software, or devices. A programmer uses API calls when creating a program. Because each *operating system* has its own distinct API, programs written for the Mac won't run on a Windows PC unless the programmer rewrites them to use the Windows API.

Applet. 1) A small, single-purpose program, often designed to run "inside" another program; usually refers to small Windows accessory programs or to *Java* programs that run inside a web *browser.* 2) A runt apple.

AppleTalk. The Apple networking standard, also used to connect single Macintoshes to printers. AppleTalk runs at 230 *kilobits*/second maximum, which is pretty slow, but the *Ethernet* variant (*EtherTalk*) runs at 10 *megabits*/second.

Application program. Software that enables users to perform useful tasks with the computer. Word processors and spreadsheets are examples of application programs. See also *data file.*

Application server. A *network server* that provides specialized functions such as communications, *database* management, or file *backup.* Lotus Notes is typical of *application programs* that run on application servers so they don't have to be installed on each computer. Application servers typically have their own *dedicated* computer.

Archives. Permanent copies of data files, such as tax records, for long-term storage, for example for one or several years.

ARCNet (Attached Resource Computing Network). A *network* system developed by Datapoint, known for low cost and easy installation, but no longer popular. ARCNet can handle 255 *nodes* and runs at 2.5 or 20 (ARCNet-Plus) *megabits*/second with a token-passing *protocol.* See also *token.*

ATM (Asynchronous Transfer Mode). A way to transfer data on a *network* that offers high speed and the ability to prioritize traffic. ATM is considered too expensive to bring to desktop *workstations,* but many organizations are using it for a *backbone* in larger networks.

Attachment. A data file or program sent along with an *e-mail* message.

Attenuation. The weakening of a signal (for example, in a cable) over distance or time.

Attribute. See *file attribute.*

AUI (Attachment Unit Interface). Usually, a connection between a *workstation Network Interface Card* with a 15-pin plug and a *ThickNet coaxial cable.* Macintoshes use a special connector called an *AAUI* to connect with Ethernet networks.

Authentication. The process of checking that a user who supplies a given name and password is in fact a legitimate *network* user.

Autochanger. A tape or optical disc drive with the ability to switch tapes or discs by itself (just like a CD changer in a car stereo system).

Autorun. In *Windows 95,* a feature that permits a properly configured *CD-ROM* to automatically run programs and install *drivers* when the CD-ROM is inserted into the drive.

Average access time. 1) How long the *hard drive* read/write head takes to find a specific location on the disk, in *milliseconds.* The smaller this number, the better. 2) How long a computer takes to transfer a *byte* to or from *memory.*

Backbone. The part of a large *network,* typically a communications channel connecting *servers,* that manages most of the traffic and links multiple *Local Area Networks* together. Small networks may not have a backbone.

Back-end. The part of a computer system that *supervisors,* rather than users, work with directly. Just as a business may have a front office that customers see and a back office where work gets done, computer systems can have a *front-end* (such as a user running *Windows*) and a *back-end* (such as a *server* running a *database*).

Backup. 1) To create a copy of files on a computer, either for long-term storage or to provide a way to recover from hardware failure. 2) The tapes or disks created by a backup operation, also called a "backup set."

Backup agent. A program that runs on a computer (usually a workstation) with files to be backed up and that communicates over the *network* with the computer running the main *backup* program (usually a server). Backup agents allow a server to back up a workstation on the same network. The agent determines which files need to be backed up and feeds them to the main backup program when requested.

Bandwidth. The data-carrying capacity of a data communications *channel.*

Base I/O address. A *Network Interface Card* setting that defines a part of *memory* used by the card to move data between the *network* and the computer in which it's installed. See also *NIC, RAM start address.*

Baseband. Single-signal, unmodulated transmission of digital information. Baseband *Local Area Networks* are typically *Ethernet* or *Token Ring* and are limited to fairly short cable runs.

Bastion host. A *server* computer that connects to the public *Internet,* with security mechanisms in place to protect any internal *networks* from Internet *crackers.* See also *firewall.*

Baud rate. A measure of *modem* speed. Not the same as the *bit*-per-second rate, the baud rate represents how often the data-carrying analog wave changes. Modems can send more than one bit for each change in the wave shape, so the bits/second rate usually exceeds the baud rate.

Beaconing. In *Token Ring networks,* an alert signal that is broadcast by a *NIC* that has detected a problem, such as a computer that is not passing the token. See also *token.*

Binary file. A data file that a user can't read or modify without a particular software *application,* in contrast to a *text file.*

Bindery. In *NetWare* 3.*x*, the files that contain user, *group,* and *print server* information, including security information. *NetWare Directory Services (NDS)* takes over bindery responsibilities in NetWare 4.*x*.

Bindery emulation. A feature of *NetWare* 4.*x* that permits *application programs* to interact with users and *groups* in the same manner they did under NetWare 3.*x*.

Binding. The process of logically connecting a *network transport protocol* to a *Network Interface Card* driver, or a network *client* to a transport protocol; usually done at computer startup. You may have the network software installed, but it doesn't run until you bind it to the NIC, usually through an *operating system* control panel. Usually, when you install network software, the bindings are set automatically, but not always.

BIOS (Basic Input/Output System). *ROM*-based software that loads before the *operating system* and handles low-level data transfer between disk drives, printers, keyboards, *monitors,* and *memory.* The BIOS also includes the *POST* (Power-On Self Test) program. Devices such as video adapters and disk controllers typically have their own BIOS in addition to the computer BIOS.

Bit. Short for **b**inary dig**it**, the smallest unit of computer data, consisting of a one or a zero. Eight bits are usually needed to make a *byte,* which represents one alphanumeric character, though sometimes a byte may contain seven or nine bits (*bps* stands for bits per second).

BNC (British Naval Connector). 1) A bayonet-type dual-pin cylindrical connector used most often in *ThinNet coaxial cable* environments. Typically a cable connects to a *NIC* via a BNC-type "T" connector; unions and right-angle connectors are also available. 2) In London, an umbilical cord.

Boot. 1) The process a computer goes through when it starts and loads the *operating system* into *memory.* 2) What you use to kick a *crashed* computer.

BootP (Bootstrap protocol). Technology from the *Unix* world that allows the system to make on-the-fly *IP address* assignments from a predefined pool of addresses as users connect to a *TCP/IP* network. See also *DHCP.*

BRI (Basic Rate Interface). 1) The most common type of *ISDN* connection, consisting of two digital voice-and-data channels and one digital-only signaling channel for control. The BRI is designed for an individual line connection over standard copper telephone lines. 2) A misspelled cheese.

Bridge. A device that connects one *network* to another, usually the same type (for example, *Ethernet* to Ethernet), and passes data between the two. Usually, a bridge is simply a computer with two *Network Interface Cards* in it, but they don't necessarily use the same cable type.

Broadband. Multiple-signal transmission of digital and analog (for example, voice and video) data on different frequency channels. Broadband transmission can span longer distances than *baseband.*

Broadcast. To send information to all networked *clients.* For example, *servers* broadcast their availability periodically to let *workstations* know they're online. You can also broadcast an *e-mail* message by sending it to everyone on a list.

Brouter. A device that can perform both *bridge* and *router* functions.

Browser. The software tool users run to "browse" *intranet* and *Internet* web *servers*. Browsers speak *HTTP* and present web documents in a *GUI*. Browsers provide some navigation controls and may offer security and performance features. Netscape Navigator and Microsoft Internet Explorer dominate the browser market.

Buffer. A temporary storage location for data in transit; usually used to smooth out data transfer between devices capable of operating at different speeds.

Bus. A data highway inside a computer. Traffic flows on buses that connect all the computer's component parts: *CPU, memory,* storage devices, keyboard, *monitor,* and *NIC.* (If the speed of the bus drops below 55 *megahertz,* the network explodes — but only if Sandra Bullock plays your IS manager.) See also *EISA, ISA,* and *PCI.*

Bus mastering. A feature of high-performance computer circuit boards that allows them to temporarily take control of the computer and shuttle data around without *CPU* intervention. Bus mastering is generally used by disk controllers, network adapters, and video cards — it's most important on *servers.*

Bus topology. A *network* layout in which a single cable, terminated at each end by an electrical component called a resistor, connects all *workstations.* Inexpensive for very small networks, but cable failure renders the whole segment inoperable.

Byte. A chunk of computerized data corresponding to one alphanumeric character; comprised usually of eight *bits.*

Cable tester. A device for testing a *network* cable to make sure it's okay to carry traffic — not too long, not too noisy, and so on. Much like pay-per-view television, you don't necessarily need to have one of your own, but it's good to know someone who does.

Cache (pronounced "cash"). 1) An area on a disk that stores recently read data or data that is considered likely to be read again soon. *Network servers* and *workstations* typically perform caching automatically, but if enough *RAM* isn't installed, the cache doesn't work as well. 2) An area of relatively expensive, high-speed *memory* that stores data recently read from slower main memory (*RAM*). Network servers typically have up to 512 *kilobytes* of cache memory, while workstations typically have from 128 to 512 kilobytes.

CAD (Computer-Aided Design or Computer-Aided Drafting). Software (such as AutoCAD) and hardware (such as powerful graphics *workstations*) that handle traditional product design and drafting functions on the computer.

Callback modem. A security *modem* that returns a call. You first call the callback modem, and then it calls you back at a predetermined number, based on a password you enter on the first call.

CAN (Campus Area Network). Two or more *Local Area Networks* that connect across multiple nearby buildings. A CAN with a broken cable is referred to as a CAN'T (joke).

Category 1 cable. *Twisted-pair cabling* suitable for voice transmission, but not for digital data, according to the Electronic Industry of America's performance standards.

Category 2 cable. Inexpensive *twisted-pair cabling* that can move data at up to 4 *megabits*/second.

Category 3 cable. *Twisted-pair cabling* that can move data at up to 10 *megabits*/second, or higher with four-pair cable configurations.

Category 4 cable. *Twisted-pair cabling* that can move data at up to 20 *megabits*/second; often used for *Token Ring networks.*

Category 5 cable. Presently the most expensive and flexible grade of *twisted-pair cabling,* Category 5 can move data at 100 *megabits*/second and higher, making it suitable for *Fast Ethernet, ISDN,* and *ATM* connections.

CBT (Computer-Based Training). *Application programs* that offer interactive, self-paced user training by providing information in either text or graphical form and then providing a way for the user to validate the training, for example, by passing a self-paced test.

CD-R (Compact Disc-Recordable). Recordable *CD-ROM* technology has replaced *WORM* (Write-Once, Read-Many) optical formats and is rapidly dropping in price. CD-R provides about 650 *megabytes* of data storage per optical disc and is a good candidate as a medium for data *backup.*

CD-ROM (Compact Disc-Read Only Memory). An optical disc, similar in appearance to an audio CD, that stores about 650 *megabytes* of digital computer data. Users can read, but not modify or erase, data on CD-ROMs.

Centronics port. The longtime *parallel port* standard, specifying both hardware (a 36-pin socket) and signalling method. Centronics parallel ports can handle 200 *kilobits*/second throughput, though the cables are limited to 12 feet (longer cables can sometimes work okay).

Certificate. A digital, *encrypted* document that verifies that a computer is what it says it is and provides the public key for that computer. Obtaining a digital certificate (from a central authority, such as Verisign) is a part of implementing *SSL* security on an *intranet* or over the *Internet.* See also *public key encryption, SSL.*

CGI (Common Gateway Interface). A standardized method for a web *server* to pass instructions and data along to an external program (such as a mail *router, database* connector, or *search engine*) and for that external program to return information to the user via *HTML.*

CGI script. A program called by an *Internet* or *intranet* web *server* at the request of a *browser* program — for example, to process the data in a user-submitted form. See also *CGI.*

Channel. 1) Any communications link between two devices. 2) In the *SCSI* specification, a *host adapter* and its connected *peripherals. Duplexed* drives use two parallel SCSI channels. Some definitions of "channel" also include the power supply.

CHAP (Challenge-Handshake Authentication Protocol). A password *encryption* technique that makes eavesdropping on a network to pick out passwords and user names virtually impossible.

Chat. To communicate "live" over the network with another user.

CheaperNet. See *ThinNet.*

Circular definition. See *definition, circular.*

Class 1. A *Group III* fax standard extension allowing the control of *fax modem* functions using commands similar to the commands used by computers to control data *modems.*

Class 2. A *Group III* fax standard extension similar to *Class 1,* that allows the *fax modem* to take over some of the connection chores from the *CPU.*

Client. 1) A *workstation* that connects to a shared resource on a *server.* A **network** client, for example, can be a user workstation running *Windows 95, OS/2 Warp, Unix,* or Macintosh software. 2) An *application* running on a client workstation, such as a *database user interface.* 3) The layer of network software that enables a computer to connect to a particular kind of *NOS.* 4) The combination of client hardware and software.

Client/server computing. A type of processing based on a simple, stable control relationship between two cooperating programs, which usually run on two separate computers.

Client/server network. A *network* (such as *NetWare* or *Windows NT Server*) in which a *dedicated* computer handles resource-sharing responsibilities, such as file and printer sharing, for *client* computers (user *workstations*).

CMIP (Common Management Information Protocol). The *ISO*'s (International Standards Organization) *network* management standards.

Coaxial cable. *Network* cabling with a central insulated copper conductor, a braided, jacketed shield, and a plastic or plastic-and-Teflon cover; typically used for its superior resistance to *electromagnetic interference* and its ability to

handle 100 *megabits*/second data rates. Coaxial cable is more costly than *twisted-pair cable. Hubs* often connect to each other with coaxial cable. See also *10Base-2, 10Base-5.*

Collision. What happens when two *network clients* try to send information *packets* across the network cable simultaneously. Collisions cause a loss of data and slow the network by requiring a retransmission.

Communication buffers. *Server memory* devoted to *caching NIC* read-and- write activity. Servers with too little memory and too few communication buffers don't work well.

Communications server. A network *server* that shares *modems* or *fax modems* for inbound access, outbound access, or both. Communications servers manage *queues* and assign devices much like *print servers* do and they may be *dedicated* or nondedicated.

Concentrator. Typically, a *network* device linking *workstations* in a physical *star topology;* often used synonymously with *hub.*

Conditioning. 1) Improving AC line power quality by correcting variations in voltage waveform and frequency. 2) Improving telephone line quality by reducing *noise.*

Console. The *monitor* and keyboard at a *network server.*

Contention. When two programs vie for the same *resource,* for example, an *Ethernet* cable.

Continuity. The quality of an unbroken electrical pathway, for example, in a network cable. One of the simplest functions of a *cable tester* is to test continuity.

Controller. 1) A circuit board that controls a computer device. For example, a *SCSI host adapter* can act as a *hard drive* controller. 2) The person in your company who tells you that the network you want is too expensive.

CPU (Central Processing Unit). The microprocessor inside a computer's *system unit* that manages most of the computing and data traffic. The Intel Pentium, Motorola PowerPC, and DEC Alpha are examples of CPUs. CPU is often improperly used to refer to a computer's *system unit*.

Cracker. Someone who attempts to gain unauthorized access to a computer or *network* with ill intent.

Crash. The event that causes a computer system or *application* to stop working suddenly, immediately, and irreversibly.

Crosstalk. Interference from an adjacent wire or cable.

CSMA/CD (Carrier-Sense Multiple Access/Collision Detection). The *Ethernet* standard for arbitrating cable access by multiple devices and for dealing with *collisions.* CSMA allows computers to transmit any time they sense that the network is available; two *nodes* trying to transmit simultaneously each detect the collision, wait a random amount of time, and then retry, sort of the same way people use an inexpensive speakerphone.

Daisy chain. A string of two or more computer devices connected together in a row (A to B, B to C, and so on). *SCSI hard drives* can connect in a *daisy chain,* and so can many *hubs.*

DAT (Digital Audio Tape). See *4mm Tape.*

Data file. A computer file that contains information you create. A word processing document and a spreadsheet sales forecast are data files. See also *application program.*

Database. A collection of related information stored in a computer, such as a sales history or customer list, that a user can search, edit, add to, delete from, and print. See also *DBMS.*

Database server. A specialized *server* that accepts requests from *clients* and then selects data from a *database* to send across the *network* to satisfy those requests.

DBMS (DataBase Management System). An *application* that handles data entry, validation, updating, querying, reporting, and archiving.

DC2000. A quarter-inch tape "minicartridge" standard measuring 3.25" x 2.5" x 0.6" that is used with QIC-40 and QIC-80 tape drives. See also *QIC* and *QIC-Wide.*

DC6000. A quarter-inch tape "full-cartridge" standard measuring 4" x 6" x 0.675" and used with higher capacity QIC tape drives. See also *QIC* and *QIC-Wide.*

Decryption. The process of decoding an encrypted file or message. See also *encryption.*

Dedicated. 1) Said of a computer devoted to one specific task exclusively. For example, a *network server* that cannot or does not double as a user *workstation* is a dedicated server. 2) What you have to be to read this book cover to cover.

Dedicated line. See *leased line.*

Definition, circular. See *circular definition.*

Defragment. To reassemble a file on a disk so that all of its bits and pieces are physically adjacent. Defragmenting improves performance of disks and disk *caches,* and special *system software* exists to handle the job automatically.

Device driver. Software that enables a computer to communicate with a particular input or output device; for example, a mouse or a *NIC.* Device drivers interpret computer data and provide the commands or signals needed by the device — they become an extended part of the *operating system.*

DHCP (Dynamic Host Configuration Protocol). A *Windows*-compatible software utility that allows a *server* to make on-the-fly *IP address* assignments from a predefined pool of addresses as users connect to the *network.* See also *BootP.*

Differential Backup. A *backup* scheduling method calling for periodic backups of all files that have changed since the last *full backup.* A file *restore* requires two backup sets: the last full backup and the last differential backup.

Digital Audio Tape. See *4mm tape.*

DIMM (Dual Inline Memory Module). A circuit board holding memory chips. DIMMs use a 168-pin connector to plug into the *motherboard.*

DIN (Deutsche Industrie Norm, or Deutsche Institute für Normung). Standards for circular plugs and sockets like the *PC* keyboard connector. More widely used in the Macintosh world.

Directory. An organizing structure that a computer *operating system* uses to group files and, optionally, other directories together; synonymous with *folder.*

Directory services. *Network* software that makes *resource* information (such as user names and addresses) available to everyone on the network. *NDS* (NetWare Directory Services) is an example.

Diskless workstation. A computer without diskette drives or *hard drives.* Reduces security risks both outbound (confidential data) and inbound (*virus*-infected files). See also *network computer.*

DLT (Digital Linear Tape). DLT is a half-inch format using cartridges about twice the size of *4mm tape* and *8mm tape* with supporting capacities from 10 to 35 *gigabytes*/second and transfer rates of 1.25 to 5 *megabytes*/second. DLT is gaining rapid market acceptance, but still lags behind 4mm and 8mm drives in popularity.

DMA (Direct Memory Access). A process wherein data transfers between devices don't require the direct involvement of the computer's *CPU,* and instead are managed by a separate processor (for example, on a disk *controller*). Hard disk *backup* programs often use DMA for better performance.

DMI (Desktop Management Interface). A *network management system* offered by the DMTF (Desktop Management Task Force). Similar in concept to *SNMP; memory*-resident "agents" can report on *workstation* configurations and problems. See also *NMS*.

DNS (Domain Name Service). A software program for matching up computer *IP addresses* such as 207.68.137.40 with easier-to-remember names, such as acme.pub.com.

Domain. A group of *servers* and *workstations,* or "subnetwork," governed by a single security *database;* intended to ease *network* management. *Windows NT Server* uses the domain concept.

DOS (Disk Operating System). The most popular *operating system* for IBM-compatible *PCs* until *Windows 95* became popular (earlier versions of Windows still used DOS).

DOS partition. On a *NetWare server,* the disk *partition* from which the *server boots.* See also *DOS* and *partition.*

Dot-matrix printer. A printer that creates characters by striking an inked ribbon with a matrix of fine metal pins; rarely used today, except to print multipart forms.

Download. To copy a file from one computer to another, in the direction toward the user initiating the copy. See also *upload.*

DPI (Dots Per Inch). A measure of a computer *peripheral*'s resolution. Computer *monitors* typically have a dpi rating of 72 to 96; laser printers typically have a dpi rating of 300, 600, or 1,200. The higher the dpi, the crisper the image.

Driver. See *device driver.*

DUN (Dial-Up Networking). Microsoft's remote access software for *Windows 95, Windows NT Workstation,* and *Windows NT Server,* allowing remote *PCs* to connect to a *LAN* over phone lines. Synonymous with *RAS.* See also *remote node.*

Duplexing. A *network server* reliability technique using redundant disk *controllers* and drives to protect against the failure of either component. Each drive has the same data as all the others so that if one crashes, another drive still has your data.

EC-1000. A software upgrade for *QIC*-80 tape drives permitting an uncompressed capacity of 400 *megabytes* on 1,000-foot tapes.

ECC (Error Correction Coding). A technique often used by *backup* software that adds redundant information to a backup set to permit rebuilding of records damaged due to media (tape) failure.

ECP (Extended Capabilities Port). See *IEEE 1284.*

ECU (EISA Configuration Utility). A program used to define operating characteristics for circuit boards installed in *EISA* bus slots. See also *EISA.*

EDI (Electronic Data Interchange). Intercompany standards for exchanging information such as orders and inventory.

EIDE (Enhanced IDE). An extension to the IDE (Integrated Drive Electronics) standard permitting larger disk drive sizes, more devices per connector, and faster data transfer rates. EIDE is the most common kind of *hard drive* in *workstations.*

EIS (Executive Information System). A read-only computer system or *application program* that provides access to corporate data, usually in a summarized and graphical form.

EISA (Extended Industry Standard Architecture). A *bus* usually found in high-powered desktop computers and network *servers.* EISA machines have programs to configure adapters in software; they also support *bus mastering.* See also *ISA* and *PCI.*

EISA Configuration Utility. See *ECU.*

E-mail. Electronic mail, one of the best uses of a *network;* permits network users to send, receive, forward, print, and organize messages.

E-mail attachment. See *attachment.*

E-mail server. Generally, a *network server* running an *e-mail post office* program; the server may or may not be *dedicated* to e-mail services.

EMI (Electro-Magnetic Interference). Typically, *noise* from fluorescent lights and dimmer switches, which can mess with data communications.

Encryption. The mathematical massaging of data characters to make them unintelligible to unauthorized viewers. Most encryption schemes rely on keys to decode encrypted data at the receiving end. See also *public key encryption, private key encryption.*

Enhanced Parallel Port. See *IEEE 1284.*

Enterprise. 1) A whole business: branch offices, subsidiaries, offshore tax shelters in the Caymans, and all that other good stuff. 2) Often used to denote the most expensive and powerful versions of software *application programs.*

EPP (Enhanced Parallel Port). See *IEEE 1284.*

Ethernet. A very popular 10 *megabits*/second networking standard using either thick *coaxial cable,* thin coaxial cable, or *twisted-pair cable.* Ethernet handles *network* traffic using a data *collision*-detection scheme. See also *CSMA/CD* and *Fast Ethernet.*

Ethernet II. An *Ethernet* variant specifying a *frame* type compatible with *TCP/IP,* early versions of *AppleTalk,* and Digital Equipment Corporation *networks.*

Ethernet SNAP. An *Ethernet* variant specifying a *frame* type with an extension for compatibility with later versions of *AppleTalk.*

EtherTalk. AppleTalk over *Ethernet;* see *AppleTalk.*

Extended Capabilities Port. See *IEEE 1284.*

FAQ (Frequently Asked Questions). A document featuring a list of common questions and their answers.

Fast Ethernet. 100 *megabits*/second *Ethernet* that can run on standard *twisted-pair cables,* but requires updated *network* hardware. Multimedia *application programs* run better over Fast Ethernet. Maximum *segment* length is 100 meters.

Fault tolerance. Said of computer systems that can operate without interruption during a software or hardware component failure.

Fax modem. A *modem* that can send and receive faxes.

FDDI (Fiber Distributed Data Interface, pronounced "fiddy"). A *token*-passing *network protocol* that can manage 100 *megabits*/second data rates and long distances (2 kilometers on fiberoptic cable). FDDI has better immunity to cable failure than *Token Ring,* but costs more.

FEP (Frequently Encountered Problems). A document featuring a list of common problems and their solutions.

Fiberoptic cable. Glass or plastic light conductors having high transmission rates (over 150 *megabits*/second) and the best *noise* immunity of all cable types. Fiber is not subject to *crosstalk* or *attenuation.* Because it uses light rather than electrical signals, it's also very secure from electronic eavesdropping.

File attribute. Information stored with a computer file that describes the file in some way; for example, most *NOSs* allow a *supervisor* to mark a file with the attribute of "read-only," meaning that a user cannot modify or delete the file.

File server. A *network server* that shares files among users.

File system buffers. *Server memory* devoted to *caching* disk read-and-write requests. Servers with too little memory and too few *file system buffers* don't work very fast.

Firewall. Any system or group of systems that implements and enforces an access control policy between two *networks.* Firewalls can run on their own special computer, or on the same computer as a web *server.* See also *proxy server.*

Flag. To mark a file with a *file attribute.*

Folder. See *directory.*

Form. A part of a *database* program, Internet web page, or other *application program* with various places for the user to enter information onscreen.

Frame. The envelope of control, addressing, and error-correcting information around a *packet.* *Ethernet* frame types include ETHERNET_II, ETHERNET_SNAP, ETHERNET_802.2, and ETHERNET_802.3. An incorrect frame type results in "Server Not Found" errors.

Front-end. The part of a computer system that users work with directly; sometimes synonymous with *UI* (User Interface). See also *back-end.*

FTP (File Transfer Protocol). A *TCP/IP* program designed for copying files of various types between computers. Most *browsers* support FTP for *downloading.*

Full backup. A *backup* of all the files on a computer's *hard drive* or drives, bar none. See also *differential backup* and *incremental backup.*

Gateway. 1) A *router* that interconnects completely different *networks,* or networks and mainframes, by translating *protocols.* 2) A software tool that provides access between two *e-mail* systems.

GFS (Grandfather — Father — Son). A *backup* media rotation strategy employing three generations of media.

GIF (Graphics Interchange Format, pronounced "jif"). A compressed graphics file format developed by CompuServe and characterized by small file sizes and a maximum palette of 256 colors. One of two graphics file formats typically used on *intranets* and the *Internet.* See also *JPEG.*

Gigabit Ethernet. Gigabit Ethernet runs 10 times faster than *Fast Ethernet,* and 100 times faster than plain vanilla *Ethernet.* Gigabit Ethernet is worth considering for *network backbone* connections and server-to-server *links.*

Gigabyte (abbreviated GB). A measure of data storage capacity equaling 1,024 *megabytes,* or roughly a billion *bytes.*

Group. A collection of *network* users who have the same permissions for shared *resources.*

Group III. The most common fax communications standard, specifying 203 x 98 dots (standard) or 203 x 196 dots (fine) resolution with data compression and 9600 bits/second. (Group III bis provides for 14.4 *kilobits*/second transmission.)

Groupware. Software designed to facilitate the cooperative, collaborative efforts of multiple people working together. Typically includes *e-mail* and scheduling features.

GUI (Graphical User Interface, pronounced "gooey"). Software, such as Microsoft Windows, that presents a graphical "face" to the user, as opposed to a text-mode interface like the *DOS* command line or a simple text mainframe terminal. See also *UI.*

Handshaking. A communications *protocol* that prevents data overrun between two devices operating at different speeds, such as a computer and a printer or a computer and a *modem.* *Hardware* handshaking uses a *dedicated* wire for this purpose and is more reliable at high speeds; *software* handshaking uses control codes over standard data lines. In the context of *modems,* handshaking determines the best speed, error-correction, and compression options to use.

Hard drive (also called "hard disk"). A computer storage device in which a stack of magnetic disks spins at high speed in a sealed enclosure. Hard drives retain information even when no power is supplied to them, unlike *RAM.* Hard drives can be written to, erased, and rewritten a large number of times. Capacity is measured in *megabytes* or *gigabytes.* See also *average access time, EIDE,* and *SCSI.*

Help Desk. An organizational unit responsible for answering users' technical questions and helping with computer problems in order to maximize employees' productivity and minimize downtime. Small businesses are more likely to call software vendors' Help Desks than to have their own.

Helper program (also called *plug-in*). A program that a web *browser* can use to process a particular type of data for example, to decode and play a sound file or video clip that the browser by itself doesn't know how to read.

Hit. A file access on a web page. A single visitor may generate several hits, because each displayed graphic file counts as another hit. See also *visit.*

Home page. An *HTML* web page that serves as a jumping-off point for a user's *intranet* or *Internet* excursion, usually presenting a table of contents with *links* to other pages or systems.

Hop count. How many *NIC*s a *network* data *packet* crosses during its route from source to destination. After a certain number of hops, typically 16, the transmission may not complete and the sending machine must resend.

Host adapter. The *controller* card on a *SCSI* device chain. Host adapters are available for *ISA, EISA, MCA, VESA,* and *PCI buses.*

Hot fix. The ability for an error to be corrected, or a problem repaired, without interrupting operations. *NetWare* disks support this for bad disk sectors, as do many *SCSI* hard drives. Also called a *"hot swap"* when you are talking about removing/exchanging entire components such as *RAID* hard drives.

Hot swapping. 1) The ability to replace a component without powering it or its host computer down; a feature of some *RAID* disk subsystems and *PCMCIA* cards. 2) What some couples did in the '60s.

HTML (HyperText Markup Language). The most popular coding method for defining documents on *intranets* and on the *World Wide Web.* HTML permits the web page author to specify approximately where text, graphics, and *links* appear, and what they do (if anything).

HTTP (HyperText Transfer Protocol). The *client/server protocol* that manages *links* between pages on a web server. Servers and *browsers* "speak" HTTP, which underpins the *World Wide Web* and company *intranets.*

Hub. A network device to which two or more cables connect in a *star topology.* Hubs may be separate devices or plug-in circuit boards; they also may or may not include *network*-management software ("intelligent hubs" or "managed hubs"). So-called *switching hubs* can provide better network performance. Most hubs also boost signals and act as a *repeater.* The upper component of a hub enclosure is called a "hub cap" (groan). See also *stackable hub.*

Hyperlink. A highlighted text area or graphic in a document that takes the user to a different, related place in the same document, or to another document, when clicked with a mouse.

Hypermedia. The extension of the *hypertext* concept to multimedia data types. Hypermedia *links* can be graphical, like little button icons or *image maps.* Hypermedia targets can be text, sound, graphics, or video.

Hypertext. A document, such as an online help file or a web page, that contains *hyperlinks*. As the term is traditionally used, hypertext links and targets (documents to which the links point) are both text.

IEEE (Institute of Electrical and Electronic Engineers). A computer and telecommunications standards-setting body with over a quarter of a million members.

IEEE 802.2. The *Ethernet* standard that *NetWare* 4.*x* uses by default. A modification of 802.2 called *Ethernet SNAP* adds *AppleTalk* compatibility. See also *Ethernet.*

IEEE 802.3. The formal name for the "raw *frame*" Ethernet standard (also known as StarLAN). See also *Ethernet.*

IEEE 802.5. The formal name for the Token Ring standard. See *Token Ring.*

IEEE 1284. A high-performance *parallel port* standard, providing for higher data transfer rates and better bidirectional communication compared to the traditional *Centronics port* standard. See also *ECP, EPP.*

Image map. A web page graphic that may have multiple "clickable" regions on it, each of which acts as a *hyperlink.*

Incremental backup. A *backup* scheduling method calling for periodic backups of all files that have changed since the previous backup. Incremental backups require less space on backup media than *differential backups,* but are less convenient in the event that you need to restore the files.

Intelligent hub. See *hub.*

Internet. The world's largest computer *network,* the Internet was originally just for military and academic use but has now grown to include all manner of private, public, and commercial uses. Physically, the Internet is a collection of millions of computers that each has its own unique network address to identify itself to other computers. Each computer on the Internet speaks the same basic communications language — *TCP/IP.* These computers connect to each other via a complex network of communication links managed by computerized traffic *routers.*

Internet Network Information Center. See *InterNIC.*

Internetwork. A *network* with more than one *segment,* possibly with different cabling, speeds, *NOSs,* and so on, typically connected by one or more *routers.*

InterNIC (Internet Network Information Center). A federally funded organization that registers and keeps track of the *domain* names for computers that connect to the *Internet,* and provides Internet-related information to the public.

Interrupt. A signal to the *CPU* from a device that needs attention, usually to service an input or output demand (such as a keystroke or a file save request).

Intranet. A "company wide web," that is, a *TCP/IP* computer *network* that shares information to company employees, using tools such as *e-mail* and web pages. Intranets use *Internet* technologies such as *HTTP, HTML,* and *FTP,* but usually forbid or restrict access to the public Internet. Normally used by businesses with at least a couple dozen employees, or one whose employees are geographically spread out.

IntranetWare. A recent version of Novell *NetWare,* with *intranet* software included.

I/O (Input/Output). Said of devices or operations that involve the flow of information into, or out of, a computer.

IP (Internet Protocol). The part of the *TCP/IP networking protocol* set that handles addressing and routing.

IP address. The numerical address of a particular computer on the *Internet* or an *intranet,* consisting of four numbers separated by periods. Each computer on a *TCP/IP network* needs a unique IP address. See also *IP, BootP, DHCP, DNS,* and *WINS.*

IPX (Internet Packet eXchange). A message routing *protocol* used by *NetWare networks.* See also *SPX, TCP/IP,* and *NetBEUI.*

IRQ (Interrupt ReQuest line). Basically a hardware "hot line" that devices, such as *NICs,* use to snag the attention of the *CPU.* No two devices in an *ISA-bus PC* may share the same IRQ simultaneously, though *MCA, PCI,* and *EISA* machines permit interrupt sharing under specific circumstances.

ISA (Industry Standard Architecture). The *bus* introduced by the IBM PC-AT computer. Used in most IBM-compatible *PCs,* for devices (such as sound cards) that don't need the speed of *local bus* connections. See also *EISA, MCA,* and *PCI.*

ISDN (Integrated Services Digital Network). Allows voice, fax, data, and video on the same *network,* and has much higher speeds than regular voice lines. Telephone companies in major North American cities offer ISDN connectivity, although it's still more popular in Europe.

ISO (International Standards Organization). The ISO is headquartered in Geneva and produces the *OSI* (Open Systems Interconnect) *network* model, among other standards.

ISP (Internet Service Provider). An organization that offers *Internet* connectivity, usually for a monthly fee. ISPs offer web hosting services for both *Internet* and *intranet* use.

Java. A programming language developed by Sun Microsystems to be *platform*-independent, secure, portable, and familiar (it's based loosely on the C++ programming language). Java is becoming popular on the *Internet* and on company *intranets* because it shifts processing chores from *servers* to *clients,* and because it works on many different kinds of computers.

JPEG (Joint Photographic Experts Group). A graphic file type featuring adjustable compression and the ability to display millions of colors. JPEG is one of two graphic file formats used on *intranets* and the *Internet.* See also *GIF.*

Jumper. A small metal and plastic block that, when placed over two protruding metal pins on a circuit board, makes a connection and switches a setting on or off. The trend is for circuit board manufacturers to permit all settings to be made by running a software program, but you may still find circuit boards that use jumpers, in which case tweezers come in handy.

Kilobit (abbreviated Kb). 1,024 bits, where a *bit* is a zero or one.

Kilobyte (abbreviated KB). 1,024 bytes, where a *byte* is a character equivalent to one letter or number.

LAN (Local Area Network). A *network* containing *servers, workstations,* cable, and software all connected together within a relatively small geographical area.

Landmark Backup. A *backup* performed before a major *LAN* event, such as an *application program* upgrade or end-of-year accounting close procedure. Also called "milestone" backup.

LANfill. Where you dump old *networking* equipment.

LANtastic. A popular network from Artisoft, most often used in *peer-to-peer networks* but also usable with a *dedicated server.*

Laptop. A portable computer, larger than a *notebook* computer but smaller than a lunchbox.

Laser printer. A printer that creates high-quality pages by transferring electrically charged toner particles from a photosensitive drum onto a page, and then fusing those particles to the page at high temperature. A laser beam strikes the drum before it picks up the toner particles, determining where toner sticks to the page.

Leased line. A telephone line leased from a common carrier and dedicated for exclusive, round-the-clock service between two locations; also called "dedicated line" or "dedicated circuit." May be *conditioned* for better data capability.

Legacy system. An old system.

License. Typically, the right to use a software product in a particular way. Software isn't sold — it's licensed, a subtlety that is sometimes confusing and often legally ambiguous. *Network Operating Systems* generally come with licenses that specify how many users can simultaneously connect to a *server.*

Link. See *hyperlink.*

Local bus. A *bus* running at higher speeds — often at the *CPU*'s clock rate — and possibly wider data pathways than the computer's standard bus; useful for video, disk, and network adapters. See also *PCI.*

Locking. In a *DBMS,* the act of preventing other users from updating a field or record while one user is already doing so. Locking maintains the data's validity. A few non-DBMS programs also use locking.

Log in (on). To identify oneself to the *network,* usually by keying in a user name and password, in order to use shared network *resources* such as files, printers, and programs. The noun or adjective is usually spelled "login" or "logon."

Log out (off). To remove oneself from participation in the *network.* A *workstation* user may log out and still be able to work on the workstation; the user just doesn't have access to shared network *resources.* The noun or adjective is usually spelled "logout" or "logoff."

Logical map. A *network map* showing *servers, groups,* and users, sometimes including server public and private *directories.* See also *physical map.*

Login script. A *text file* containing a sequence of commands that run when a user *logs in* to the *network.* Some networks permit different login scripts for different *groups* of users or even individual users.

LPT port. See *parallel port.*

MAN (Metropolitan Area Network). A *network* that covers a city or a portion of a city.

Managed hub. See *hub.*

Map. To associate a **network resource** (such as a printer or **directory**) with a logical name (such as a local **port** or drive letter). For example, the LPT2: device on a **PC** may map to a shared network printer instead of corresponding to a printer that's physically connected to the **workstation's** second **parallel port.** Mapping has become less necessary now that many **operating systems** understand **UNC paths.**

MAU (Multistation Access Unit). 1) The **hub** to which computers in a **Token Ring** network connect. Also called **MSAU.** 2) **Media Access Unit,** an **Ethernet hub.**

MCA (Micro Channel Architecture). The **bus** used in certain IBM PS/2 computers (and few others). MCA boards are software-configurable.

Megabit (abbreviated Mb). About 1 million **bits,** a bit being a one or a zero. Usually used for specifying how fast data moves across a **network;** for example, **Ethernet** has a maximum speed of 10 **megabits**/second (Mbps).

Megabyte (abbreviated MB). A measure of data storage capacity equaling 1,024 **kilobytes,** or roughly a million **bytes,** a byte being equivalent to one letter or number.

Megahertz (abbreviated MHz). One million cycles per second, or, more meaningfully, a comparative way to rate **CPU** speeds. A 200 MHz CPU isn't necessarily twice as fast as a 100MHz CPU, though, so the comparison is only approximate.

Memory. See **RAM.**

MIB (Management Information Base). Configuration data files used by the **SNMP (NMS** Network Management System**)** to manage **network** devices.

Microcomputer. Originally, a small, self-contained, general-purpose computer with a single, primary **CPU.** The definition is now stretching to include computers with more than one CPU; for example, **Windows NT Workstation** can support two CPUs on a microcomputer, and **Windows NT Server** supports up to four CPUs. The IBM **PC,** Apple Macintosh, and Sun SPARCstation are examples of microcomputers.

Middleware. In a **client/server network,** software that mediates and standardizes the connections between different parts of the system's communications pathways. If you have two different **database** systems and you want all users to be able to work with both, you may need middleware.

MIF (Management Information File). Configuration data files used by the **DMI (NMS** Network Management System**)** to manage **network** devices.

Millisecond. A thousandth of a second; typically used to rate **hard drive average access times.**

MIME (Multipurpose Internet Mail Extensions). A set of extensions to the original **Internet e-mail** standards that allows users to send and receive data types other than text.

Mirroring. A **network** reliability technology that uses redundant disk drives (each disk drive has the same data on it) sharing the same **controller.** Mirroring protects against drive failure but not controller failure. See also **duplexing.**

Mission-critical application. An **application program** that is essential to the functioning of the business.

Modem. Short for **mo**dulator-**dem**odulator, a modem converts digital computer signals to analog signals that phone lines can handle and vice versa.

Monitor. A computer screen. On **notebook** computers, the screen is integral to the computer and is simply called a **display** or **display panel.**

Motherboard. A computer's main circuit board; also called the system board. If you try to be Politically Correct and call this a parentboard, nobody will know what you're talking about.

MPR (MultiProtocol Router). A software-based external **routing** solution from Novell.

MSD (MicroSoft Diagnostics). An old utility that comes with **Windows** and can help identify **IRQ**s, **RAM** addresses, and other details of a particular **PC.**

MTBF (Mean Time Between [Before] Failures). A statistical measure of how long one can expect a hardware component to operate reliably before a problem arises; usually given in **POH** (Power-On Hours).

MTTR (Mean Time To Repair). How long it takes, on average, to fix something.

Multitasking. When a computer manages two or more simultaneous tasks or programs. For example, a user can **download** a file in the background and write a memo in the foreground.

Name space. A **NOS** option that permits the storage of files on a **server** using different file systems.

NCP (NetWare Core Protocol). A set of procedures **NetWare** uses to deal with all network-related **client** requests. See also **SMB.**

NDIS (Network Driver Interface Specification, pronounced "EN-diss"). A standard developed by Microsoft and 3Com for network **device drivers. Windows 95** uses NDIS 3.1 drivers, which support **Plug-and-Play.**

NDS (NetWare Directory Services). A naming system for *NetWare* 4.*x networks* that includes all network resources in a tree-structured hierarchy.

Nerd. A usually derogatory term for someone who already knows all the definitions in this glossary. Considered passé today because computer experts, particularly those who write books, are often well-rounded, attractive, and socially sophisticated.

NetBEUI (NetBIOS Extended User Interface, pronounced "NET-booie"). A high-speed, non-routable *network* transport *protocol* that controls access to file and print sharing. Often used for small, informal networks not expected to grow large. See also *TCP/IP, IPX.*

NetBIOS (Network Basic Input/Output System). *Network* software that handles redirection of input/output requests to network *resources.* Made popular by IBM and Microsoft, and required for certain *application programs.*

NetBIOS Extended User Interface. See *NetBEUI.*

NetBIOS name. The name of a computer in the Microsoft *networking* scheme.

NetWare. A popular *NOS* from Novell. Recent versions have the trade name *IntranetWare.*

Network. Two or more computer systems connected to enable communication or *resource* sharing; the sum total of *clients, servers,* and interconnecting infrastructure. Often informally used as a synonym for *LAN.*

Network adapter. See *NIC.*

Network computer. A computer with no local disk space; a network computer loads all programs and data from the *network.* Also called "Network PC" and "NetPC."

Network drive. A disk drive shared with other *network* users.

Network Interface Card. See *NIC.*

Network modem. A *modem* (such as those made by Shiva) that connects directly to a *network,* rather than indirectly to the network via a *server* or *workstation* computer.

NIC (Network Interface Card, pronounced "nick"). A plug-in circuit board that connects a computer to a *network* and manages data transfers between the two. The speed (such as 10 or 100 *megabits* per second) and width (such as 16 or 32 *bits*) of the connection help determine a network's perceived performance.

NLM (Netware Loadable Module). An extension to the *server operating system* that provides

added capabilities, such as the ability to interact with disk and network *controllers,* detect *viruses,* provide foreign *name space* support, or perform *backups.*

NMS (Network Management System). Software, such as *SNMP,* that enables a *network supervisor* to control, configure, and troubleshoot network devices without having to be physically present at the device.

Node. A device that connects to a *network,* be it a *workstation,* printer, *network modem,* or what have you.

Noise. Any electrical or magnetic interference that may disrupt data transmission. See also *EMI, RFI.*

NOS (Network Operating System, pronounced "noss"). The core *system software* running on a *network server.* Examples include Novell *NetWare,* Microsoft *Windows NT Server,* and Banyan *VINES.*

Notebook. A portable computer, the size of a large and unusually heavy notebook. Notebooks are smaller than *laptops.*

Notwork. A network that's down.

NT (*Windows NT,* for New Technology). The high end of the Windows product line, targeted for network *servers* (NT Server) and high-end Windows *workstations* (NT Workstation).

OCR (Optical Character Recognition). The process of converting a scanned document from a collection of tiny dots into a text document that a computer word processor or editor can understand.

ODBC (Open DataBase Connectivity). The most widely supported standard for open *database middleware,* initially developed by Microsoft. All major relational *DBMS*s support ODBC — DBMS vendors supply their own ODBC software.

OLE (Object Linking and Embedding, pronounced "oh-LAY"). A Windows technology that allows not only the creation of compound documents with data originating from more than one program, but also the editing of cut-and-pasted data using the data's originating *application program* without leaving the host program.

Operating system. The basic software that allows a computer to interact with users, manage files and devices, and communicate over a *network. Windows 95, Unix,* MacOS, and *OS/2 Warp* are all operating systems. Those designed for network *servers,* such as *NetWare* and *Windows NT Server,* are called *NOS*s (Network Operating Systems).

OR (Organizational Role). In *NetWare Directory Services,* an object specifying a position within an organization that may be occupied by different individuals at different times. The Netware NWADMIN program can assign users to ORs on an as-needed basis, which is a good way of handling part-time workers.

OS/2 Warp. IBM's *PC workstation operating system,* which never caught on in the market-place against the Microsoft Windows juggernaut, although devotees maintain that it offers better reliability than *Windows 95.* IBM continues to enhance OS/2 Warp, which contains *peer-to-peer networking* capabilities.

OS/2 Warp Server. A *client/server NOS* from IBM that competes with Novell *NetWare* and Microsoft *Windows NT Server.* OS/2 Warp Server runs with *NetBIOS* and *TCP/IP.*

OSI (Open Systems Interconnect). A seven-layer **network** model established in 1984 by the *ISO* (International Standards Organization) to help enable network software developers to create programs at each level independently. Small business network managers don't need to memorize the OSI model unless they want to pass a Microsoft or Novell certification test.

Packet. The unit of data transfer on a *LAN;* a chunk of data packaged for transmission in a way specific to the **network protocol** being used.

Parallel port. A *microcomputer* connection, used typically for printers, in which each *bit* of a *byte* has its own wire. Eight bits travel simultaneously, like traffic on an eight-lane freeway. See also *Centronics port, IEEE 1284.*

Partition. A portion of a disk set aside as a separate and distinct logical device, for example having a separate drive letter, or set aside for a separate *operating system.*

Patch. A modification to software that corrects a problem.

Patch cable. Typically, a short *network* cable connecting a *workstation* to a *wallplate* or a *hub* to a *patch panel.*

Patch panel. A panel consisting of neat rows of sockets, usually wall-mounted in a *wiring closet,* where several *network* cables from various offices or cubicles meet en route to a *hub.*

PC (Personal Computer). A *microcomputer* for individual use; a *workstation.* The abbreviation PC has come to indicate an IBM-compatible *microcomputer.*

PC Card. See *PCMCIA.*

PCI (Peripheral Component Interconnect). An Intel-developed high-performance *local bus* used for video, disk and *NIC.*

PCL (Printer Control Language). A standard developed by Hewlett-Packard for controlling its line of *laser printers.* Originally more oriented to text processing than *PostScript,* PCL levels 5 and 6 offer many of PostScript's capabilities.

PCMCIA. 1) **Personal Computer Memory Card Industry Association,** a group that standardized PCMCIA devices, now called "PC Cards." *Note-book* computers can use a PCMCIA *NIC* to connect to a *network.* 2) Acronym for "People Can't Memorize Computer Industry Acronyms."

PDL (Page Description Language). A set of device-independent commands for printers. See also *PostScript* and *PCL.*

Peer-to-peer network. A type of *network* in which no computer acts as a *dedicated server,* but in which every computer may share attached printers and local files, with network processing occurring in the background. *LANTastic, Windows 95,* Personal *NetWare, OS/2 Warp,* and Mac OS offer peer-to-peer networking. Generally suitable for small groups (2 to 20) with few security requirements.

Pentium. A *CPU* made by Intel Corporation and widely used on IBM-compatible *PCs.* Variants include the Pentium Pro, which works faster with 32-bit software such as *Windows NT Server,* and the Pentium II.

Peripheral. A computer device outside a computer's *system unit.* Peripherals include keyboards, mice, printers, *modems,* and so on.

PhoneNet. An inexpensive *network* wiring method developed by Farallon for Macintosh computers.

Physical map. A *network map* showing device locations (computers, printers, *servers, routers,* and so on) and interconnections. See also *logical map.*

Platform. A computer *operating system,* or the combination of the operating system and underlying hardware.

Plenum cable. *Network* cable with fire-resistant coating required by most fire codes for installation through walls and across ceiling plenum spaces.

Plug-and-Play (often abbreviated PnP). A set of standards that ease the configuration of hardware devices by automatically detecting device characteristics and setting *resources* and *interrupts.* A full implementation requires PnP compatibility at all levels, from the *BIOS* through the *operating system* to the *device driver.*

Plug-in. See *helper program.*

POP (Point of Presence). A telephone number that provides access to a public data *network* (such as the *Internet*).

Port. A socket on the back of a computer or *peripheral* used to connect it to some other computer or peripheral.

POST (Power-On Self Test). A program, residing in a computer's *BIOS,* that runs at the time the computer is turned on and checks the computer's vital signs.

Post Office. The drop-box facility for an *e-mail* system. The Post Office may be a physical subdirectory residing on the *supervisor's* computer, or on a *server directory.*

PostScript. A device-independent *PDL* (Page Distribution Language) rom Adobe Systems, used to control printers and,on some *workstations,* displays; known for sophisticated graphics handling.

Power conditioning. Usually, line voltage surge suppression, waveform regulation, and battery backup capability all rolled into a single box. Power conditioning "cleans" the electricity that comes from the power plant so that your computers run more reliably. *Network servers* should have power conditioning. See also *surge protector, UPS.*

PPP (Point-to-Point Protocol). 1) A standard for communications across relatively slow links (such as dial-up phone lines), and the usual *protocol* for *Windows 95 DUN* (Dial-Up Networking). 2 What you must do after too many cups of coffee.

PPTP (Point-to-Point Tunneling Protocol). Supported by *Windows NT Server* 4.0 and available as a free download for *Windows 95,* PPTP *encrypts* and packages remote access traffic — for example, by users connecting to your *network* from home via a dial-up connection.

PRI (Primary Rate Interface). A commercial *ISDN* installation consisting of 24 digital channels in the U.S., and 31 in Europe. In the U.S. version, 23 of the channels carry data and the 24th is used for commands.

Print server. 1) The part of a *NOS* that manages the *queuing* and printing of documents over the *network.* 2) A computer handling print services.

Protocol. A set of rules, specifications, or standards that controls and manages the creation, maintenance, and termination of data transfer between computers.

Protocol analyzer. A program, or an entire computer system, that listens to a network cable and collects data about *network* traffic; used for troubleshooting and tuning a network.

Proxy server. A *server* that permits no direct traffic between one *network* and another, but, for security reasons, acts as a store-and-forward device for data or messages meeting predefined criteria. If, for instance, you're on a network with a proxy server and you *browse* to an Internet Web page, the proxy server actually picks up the Web page, checks it to see if it meets security needs, and then sends it down the network to you. Proxy servers may forward permitted data or messages automatically, or only on request from another computer. See also *firewall.*

Private key encryption (also known as *symmetric encryption*). An encryption scheme in which each individual has a private secret key that is used for both encryption and decryption. See also *encryption, public key encryption.*

PSTN (Public Switched Telephone Network). The expanded acronym says it all.

Public key encryption (also known as *asymmetric encryption*). An encryption scheme in which each individual has a private secret key and a published, public key. A sender looks up the recipient's public key and uses it to encrypt a message, and the recipient uses the private key to decrypt it. See also *encryption, private key encryption.*

QFA (Quick File Access). A standard that requires support from both the tape drive and the *backup* utility in order to work, QFA is a method for repositioning a tape to the start of a file or *directory* up to 50 times faster than systems without QFA. Most top-line backup utilities and high-capacity tape drives support QFA.

QIC (Quarter-Inch Committee). An organization that creates standards for magnetic tape drives using 0.25" wide tape. QIC-40 offers 40 to 60 *megabytes* of uncompressed storage depending on tape length, and QIC-80 offers 80 to 120 megabytes. Defined standards go all the way up to 13 *gigabytes,* however, and many QIC variants exist. See also *EC-1000, QIC-Wide,* and *Travan.*

QIC-Wide. A Sony-developed extension to the *QIC* standard that uses 0.315" wide tape and boosts capacity from 20 to 75 percent over regular 0.25" wide tape.

Queue. Any kind of waiting or holding location; typically, the list of documents waiting to be printed on a *print server*.

Quiet. Said of a network with no users logged in and a minimal number of running programs. *Backup* operations don't skip as many files when performed on a quiet LAN, because fewer files are open (and many backup programs don't back up open files).

RAID (Redundant Array of Inexpensive Disks). A way to improve *network* reliability, usually involving vendor-specific hardware and software, that spreads *server* data across multiple disks (which may not be all that "inexpensive"). RAID 1 is the same as disk *mirroring* and also covers *duplexing.* RAID 5 is the most popular type; it's more expensive than *duplexing,* but has more potential for performance and reliability enhancement. See also *SLED.*

RAM (Random Access Memory). Chip-based *memory* in a computer, which is both faster and more expensive than disk-based memory (*hard drive*). A computer's RAM contains the currently active programs and data files, and its contents start empty every time the computer restarts. *Network servers* need more RAM than user *workstations* do.

RAM Start Address. Required to be assigned at installation by some, but not all, *NICs*, this is the starting address in the computer's *memory* space that the NIC uses to handle computer-to-computer data transfers. The chunk of *RAM* used is normally 16 or 32 *kilobytes,* and must not conflict (overlap) with memory ranges used by other devices.

RAS (Remote Access Services). See *DUN.*

RAW (Read-After-Write). Verifying that the data on a storage device (such as a *server hard drive*) is accurate by reading the data immediately after it is written. RAW is faster when implemented by the hardware, as in a high-performance disk *controller.* Better *backup* utilities and tape drives also perform RAW.

Relational database. A *DBMS* (DataBase Managment System) that stores data in tables with columns and rows. Relational databases support an almost infinite number of relationships among data records. For instance, in a relational database of customers, you may be able to look up entries by name, state, area code, or any other bit of included information.

Remote control. A remote computer that links indirectly into a network by taking over a local, *networked* computer via *modem.* This technique depends on the availability of a "slave computer" at the main office that can accept an incoming call from the remote computer. Keyboard, screen, and mouse data cross the dial-up link, but the actual computing takes place on the slave computer. See also *remote node.*

Remote node. A remote computer linked directly into a network via *modem.* Remote node computers function just as if they were logged in on-site, in that *network packets* cross the dial-up link. The Windows 95 *DUN* is a remote node connection.

Repeater. A simple *network* device that boosts incoming signals so that they can be sent a longer distance. Repeaters do not look at *packets* or *protocols;* they just amplify and recondition every *bit* they receive and then retransmit.

Resource. Any computer drive, *directory,* printer, or other *peripheral* that can be shared among *network* users.

Restore. To copy a file from a secondary location back to its original location; the reverse of *backup.*

RFI (Radio Frequency Interference). For example, noise from radios and televisions.

RG-58A/U. *ThinNet Ethernet coaxial cable.*

RG-62. *ARCNet* cable.

Ring topology. A *network* layout in which computers connect via a closed loop of *NICs*. In *Token Ring* networks, the ring topology may reside entirely inside the *hub,* with the actual cabling in a *star topology* radiating from the hub.

RJ-45. The 8-pin connector type usually used in *twisted-pair cable 10Base-T networks;* similar to a phone plug, but wider.

ROM (Read-Only Memory). A computer *memory* chip or storage device that permits reading information, but not changing or deleting it. See also *BIOS, CD-ROM.*

Root directory. The top-level *directory* on a disk or *volume.*

Router. A *network* device, more sophisticated than a *bridge,* that can send or redirect data traffic to the least crowded routes by examining data *packet* destination addresses. Multiple networks connected by routers form *internetworks.*

SCSI (Small Computer Systems Interface, pronounced "scuzzy," not "sexy"). A high-performance device connection system (such as for *hard drives*) commonly used in *network servers.* See also *EIDE.*

Search engine. A computer utility that allows users to search for content on a *workstation,* a *network server,* an *intranet,* or the *Internet* by specifying key words or phrases.

Segment. A discrete portion of a *network.*

Segmentation. Dividing a *LAN* into multiple *segments,* also called *subnets,* usually to increase performance. Segmentation or "subnetting" may increase the *network supervisor*'s burden for the overall network.

Serial port. A *microcomputer* connection, used typically for *modems* but also occasionally for printers and mice, in which each *bit* of a *byte* travels sequentially down a single wire. Serial ports are slower than *parallel ports.*

Server. 1) A computer that provides *network* services, such as *web, file, print, communication, name space, directory,* security, or *application services.* In *peer-to-peer networks,* a server is any computer that is sharing a local *resource* over the network, and any given computer may be both a server and a *client* for different resources. 2) A program providing services to a client application, for example, a *database server.* 3) The combination of server hardware and programs.

Share-Level Security. A *network* security model in which a *supervisor* assigns names, passwords, and access privileges on a per-*resource* basis. See also *user-level security.*

SIMM (Single Inline Memory Module). Today's most popular *RAM* packaging type. A 16 x 9 SIMM uses nine 16-*megabit* chips to provide 16 *megabytes;* most current SIMM packages use a 72-pin connector.

SLED (Single Large Expensive Disk). A single high-capacity, high-performance *hard drive,* usually in a *network server.* If it *crashes,* you're in trouble. See also *RAID.*

SLIP (Serial Line Interface Protocol). A communications standard similar to *PPP* but less efficient.

Slot. 1) In *network* parlance, a network connection such as a user *license.* Certain *print servers* also use a slot (that is, they count as a user in terms of the maximum licensed number of connections) if they connect directly to a hub. 2) A *motherboard* connector into which you can plug a circuit board, such as a *NIC.*

SMB (Server Message Block). A *network protocol* for handling *workstation* requests on Microsoft networks such as *Windows NT Server.* See also *NCP.*

SMP (Symmetric MultiProcessing). An option, built into certain *operating systems,* that splits processing duties between two or more *CPUs. Windows NT Workstation,* for example, supports two CPUs in the same computer. See also *AMP.*

SMTP (Simple Mail Transport Protocol). The basic *TCP/IP protocol* for *e-mail* exchange.

SneakerNet. Walking disks between two computers in order to transfer files; considered gauche in the age of *networking.*

SNMP (Simple Network Management Protocol). A popular standard that developed in the *Unix* world; used for managing *LANs.* SNMP specifies a *protocol* for communication between a management *console* and *network* devices.

Solaris. A popular *Unix operating system.*

SPARCstation. A popular *Unix* computer line made by Sun Microsystems.

Spool. Actually an acronym for *Simultaneous Peripheral Operations On Line,* a spooler is a program that reroutes print output to a disk file before sending it to a printer. Spooling at a server lets multiple users print multiple documents that go to a common directory to wait their turn at the printer. Spooling at a workstation lets the user regain control of the computer more quickly after submitting a print job, and aids in reprinting a document if the printer is busy or hangs.

SPX (Sequenced Packet Exchange). Runs over *IPX* and provides error checking and flow control to make sure *packets* reach their intended destination and reach it intact. Used instead of *NetBIOS,* and commonly required by data *backup* and communications *application programs.*

SQL (Structured Query Language). A set of commands for requesting information from *databases;* very popular among *DBMS* vendors in *client/server networks.*

SSL (Secure Sockets Layer). A standard method of providing *encrypted* data transmission between an *Internet* or *intranet browser* and web *server.*

Stackable hub. A *hub* that you can easily connect with other hubs, usually but not necessarily with a *coaxial cable,* to form a *daisy chain* that the network thinks is a single hub. Some stackable hubs can connect with each other using *Fast Ethernet* for better performance.

Star topology. A network layout in which *network* connections extend in a star from a central point, like spokes on a wheel. See also *bus topology* and *ring topology.*

STP (Shielded Twisted Pair). 1) A type of *network* cable, with braided metal shielding similar to that used in *coaxial cable;* used where *EMI* (Electro-Magnetic Interference) may present problems. STP is more common with *Token Ring* than *Ethernet* networks. See also *UTP.* 2) Michael Jackson and Lisa Marie Presley.

Stream. To begin playing as soon as a *download* operation begins, instead of only after the download is completed. For example, streaming audio starts playing as soon as the user opens a web page containing a sound file.

Striping. The process of spreading data across multiple physical disk drives, called a *stripe set,* in order to make them appear as a single unit of storage. *Windows NT Server* supports disk striping.

Supervisor. Also called *administrator,* a *network* supervisor is someone with no security restrictions — that is, one who can create user accounts, assign security restrictions to other users and *groups,* install and remove software, and so on.

Surge protector. A device that is supposed to protect computer equipment from voltage spikes, although tests show that most inexpensive ones don't. See also *conditioning, UPS.*

Swapfile. An area of *hard drive* space used by the *operating system* (for example, *Windows*) as a low-speed supplement to *RAM.* The swapfile runs much more slowly than RAM but avoids an "out of memory" error.

Switch. See *switching hub.*

Switching hub. An intelligent device that establishes *dedicated* connections between individual computers on a *LAN,* instead of forcing all computers on the *network* to share a single connection.

System software. A computer's *operating system* plus any housekeeping utilities, such as *backup* utilities and *antivirus programs.*

System unit. The main box of a computer, housing the *motherboard,* other circuit boards, the *CPU, memory,* the power supply, cooling fan, a speaker, and internal disk drives. Desktop system units sit horizontally, while tower system units stand vertically.

TCO (Total Cost of Ownership). What computer systems really cost, as opposed to their price tags. TCO includes training, support, communications, and data acquisition. The *network computer* is an attempt to reduce TCO.

TCP/IP (Transmission Control Protocol/Internet Protocol). A set of *network protocols* for file transfer, network management, and messaging — the public *Internet* and company *intranets* use TCP/IP. TCP/IP is popular in the educational, engineering, and governmental areas; it was developed in the early '70s by the Defense Advanced Research Projects Agency. TCP breaks apart and reassembles *packets* in the correct order, and resends if errors occur; IP handles routing and transmission.

Terminator. 1) The resistor used at each end of a *network* cable *segment* to minimize electrical reflections. A 50-ohm terminator is used in *ThinNet* systems, while a 96-ohm terminator is used with *ARCNet* schemes (an ohm is a measure of electrical resistance). 2) In the *SCSI bus,* a resistor that serves pretty much the same function. SCSI buses require termination at each end of the *daisy chain* and don't permit terminators elsewhere. 3) A movie Bob Dole wouldn't have said he liked even if he'd actually seen it.

Text file. A data file consisting of nothing but standard alphanumeric characters that a user can read with a wide variety of *application programs.*

ThickNet. An *Ethernet* cabling scheme using 0.4" diameter *coaxial cable.*

Thin client. A type of *client/server network* system that puts only the *UI* (User Interface) component on the *client,* keeping all the process logic and data storage on the *server.*

ThinNet. An *Ethernet* cabling scheme using *RG-58*A/U type shielded *coaxial cable,* which is thinner than the older *ThickNet* cable, but still thicker than *UTP.* ThinNet cable typically uses *BNC*-type connectors.

Timeout. Said to occur when a device or program fails to perform an action within a predetermined maximum time limit.

Token. A unique sequence of (typically) 24 *bits* that confers the right to access a *token*-passing *network* and includes origin and destination data.

Token Ring. A 4- or 16-*megabits*/second *network* standard promoted by IBM and noted for predictable response and fault tolerance, as well as somewhat higher cost than *Ethernet.* A sending computer waits for an empty token to circulate to its location, where the computer fills the token with destination and message information. All computers monitor circulating tokens to determine if any are targeted to them; if so, the computer retrieves the token data and resets the token to an empty state. See also *token.*

Topology. The shape or layout of a network cabling and/or signalling scheme; common topologies include *bus topology, ring topology,* and *star topology.*

Tower of Hanoi. A *backup* media rotation strategy, more sophisticated than *GFS,* that permits *supervisors* to select which days to do backups, how many media sets (for example, tapes) to use, and how long the oldest backup can be.

Transceiver. A device used to connect a *NIC* with a *coaxial Ethernet bus cable.* The transceiver may be a separate device connecting to the NIC via a short cable, or it may be onboard the NIC.

Transport protocol. A protocol specifying the network language; computers in a network must speak the same transport protocol to communicate. Examples include *TCP/IP, IPX/SPX,* and *NetBEUI.*

Travan. A popular, inexpensive 3M-developed tape standard using 0.315" tapes with longer lengths and higher densities than regular *QIC* tapes. Travan capacities range from 800 *megabytes* to 10 *gigabytes,* competing with low-end *4mm tape* (*DAT*) drives, and can move data at rates from 10 to 20 megabytes/minute. Travan does not perform *RAW* verification and is slower than *4mm* or *8mm tape.*

TWAIN (Toolkit Without An Interesting Name). A serious standard (despite the acronym) put together by scanner manufacturers to allow all compliant scanning programs to work the same way (as far as the user is concerned).

Twisted-pair cable. Popular *network* cable using twisted pairs of phone wire; may be shielded or unshielded. The twists reduce unwanted signals. See also *Category 1, 2, 3, 4,* and *5 cable, STP,* and *UTP.*

UI (User Interface). The UI is concerned with getting information from the human user into the computer, or from the computer out to the human user. The UI includes data entry, automated data capture, character display, and graphical display.

UNC Path. The **Universal Naming Convention** for a network file or print *resource,* in the format \\server\queue or \\server\volume\directory.

Universal Naming Convention. See *UNC Path.*

Unix. A computer *operating system* originally developed at AT&T Bell Labs. Most *Internet* and *intranet* technologies were developed in the *Unix* world, and it's still a popular operating system for high-performance *servers.*

Unmanaged hub. See *hub.*

Upload. To copy a file from one computer to another, in the direction away from the user initiating the copy. See also *download.*

Upper memory. In IBM-compatible *PCs,* a *memory* range between 640K and 1024K for use by devices such as *NICs* and video cards.

UPS (Uninterruptible Power Supply). A *backup* device that provides power to a *server, workstation,* or other device continuously from its battery, which, in turn, is constantly being recharged from AC line power. If you experience a power cut, the UPS continues supplying power and lets you shut down your computer gracefully.

URL (Uniform Resource Locator). The address that points users to a specific *Internet* or *intranet* service, usually *HTTP* or *FTP,* and location (web page, file to *download*). Every *link* on a web page has an associated URL. Example: http://www.novell.com is the URL for the Novell Web site.

User-level security. A *network* security model whereby *supervisors* create user names, passwords, and *resource* access privileges, and security is established on a per-user basis. See also *share-level security.*

UTP (Unshielded Twisted Pair). The least expensive type of cabling for *Ethernet Local Area Networks*, using what is essentially phone cable and available in 2-pair, 4-pair, or 6-pair configurations. Used in *10Base-T networks* where electrical interference isn't a big problem.

VESA (Video Electronics Standards Association). Typically used to refer to the VESA *local bus* (formerly VL-bus), which provides higher performance than the standard *ISA* bus for video, disk, and *NICs. PCI* has overtaken *VESA* in popularity.

VINES (VIrtual NEtwork System). A *client/server network* from Banyan Systems that has enjoyed popularity in the *Unix* world, VINES is more common in large networks than in small ones.

Virtual memory. A technique for allowing programs to access *memory* addresses that correspond to disk space instead of *RAM.* The Windows *swapfile* is an example of virtual memory.

Virus. A computer program intended by its creator to cause mischief or outright damage. Usually, a virus is designed to spread from one computer to another, something a *network* usually makes very easy. Most viruses take various steps to conceal their existence until they can fulfill their creator's evil intent. Viruses usually attach to other program files. See also *antivirus program.*

Visit. A web page user session. A user who goes to an *Internet* or *intranet* site and displays a single *HTML* file and four graphics files in a web *browser* has generated one visit but five hits. See also *hit.*

Volume. A disk *partition,* or collection of partitions, that appears to *network* users as a single drive — even though an actual *hard drive* may contain multiple volumes, and a volume may span multiple actual hard drives.

VOM (Volt-Ohm-Milliammeter). An inexpensive test device often used to measure *continuity* and resistance, and to check that network cable is installed properly. Professional cable installers use tools that are more sophisticated than VOMs (one reason I recommend do-it-yourselfers contract out cable installation).

Wallplate. A wall-mounted *network* plug.

WAN (Wide Area Network). *LAN*s connected across large distances, usually via communications *protocols* running on satellite, microwave, or *Internet* links.

Web. See *WWW.*

Web browser. See *browser.*

Webmaster. An individual primarily responsible for the design and management of a web site.

Welcome page. See *home page.*

Windows. A family of *operating systems* from Microsoft that puts a graphical face onto the computer, enables users to run multiple programs at once, and eases the copying and pasting of data between programs. Versions in current use include Windows 3.1, Windows for Workgroups 3.11, *Windows 95, Windows NT Workstation,* and *Windows NT Server.*

Windows 95. A very popular *operating system* choice for new small business *networks,* Microsoft Windows 95 can be used as both a *workstation* operating system and as a *peer-to-peer* network.

Windows NT Server. A *NOS* (Network Operating System) from Microsoft featuring relatively easy installation and management and strong security. Windows NT Server 4.0 and higher use the same *UI* (User Interface) as Windows 95.

Windows NT Workstation. A *workstation operating system* from Microsoft for *PC*s requiring high performance, high security, or high reliability; more expensive than *Windows 95,* in both price and hardware requirements.

WINS (Windows Internet Naming Service). Software that matches up *IP addresses* with computer names, called *NetBIOS names,* in the Microsoft *network* system. The NetBIOS names are easier for users to remember than IP addresses.

Wiring closet. A utility closet where *network hubs* may reside, possibly along with telephone equipment.

Workgroup. A team of individuals that commonly works together and needs to share programs, files, and printers. See also *group.*

Workstation. Generally, a user computer. So-called scientific or engineering workstations are higher-powered computers capable of handling powerful, demanding software such as *CAD.*

WWW (World Wide Web). Born in 1993, the multimedia face of the *Internet.* Web pages can include color graphics and even sound and video. They can also include convenient and automatic *links* to other Web pages. The Web is based on the *TCP/IP, HTTP,* and *HTML* standards.

WYSIWYG (What You See Is What You Get). The goal of matching printed documents precisely with their on-screen appearance.

Zero-slot network. A *network* that doesn't use *NIC*s, but uses built-in computer *parallel ports* or *serial ports* instead. Much slower than networks that do use NICs, and somewhat less expensive.

ZIF (Zero Insertion Force). Said of *CPU* sockets that permit the easy removal and replacement of a microprocessor chip (like a *Pentium* or DEC Alpha) through the use of a clamping lever.

Zip drive. A popular cartridge disk device developed by Iomega, holding about 100 *megabytes* in a $15 removable cartridge about the size of a *CD-ROM.* A higher-capacity, similar unit called a Jaz drive, also made by Iomega, is becoming popular as a *backup* device. I recommend Zip and Jaz drives for workstation backups only.

Zip file. An *archive* created with the PKZIP or WinZip compression utility and that a user may decompress with PKUNZIP or WinZip. Commonly used with *e-mail attachments* and remote computer connections to save time and reduce *network* traffic.

Appendix B
References and Resources

● ●

In This Appendix

▶ Contact info on companies and products mentioned in this book
▶ Books
▶ Magazines

● ●

*Y*ou've made a great start toward setting up a small business network by buying (and, I hope, reading!) this book. In this appendix, I point you toward other resources that can take you further.

Companies Mentioned in This Book

This section provides Internet addresses, phone numbers (both the free-in-the-USA "800"/"888" variety and toll numbers for the convenience of my international readers), and physical addresses for the companies I mention in this book.

I tested over three dozen software and hardware products during the research for this book, and I've worked with many more products than that during the course of my consulting and teaching activities. However, I don't have firsthand experience with every single product or company listed here, so appearance in this list is not a purchase recommendation.

3Com Corp.
http://www.3com.com
800-NET-3COM, 408-764-5000
5400 Bayfront Plaza, P.O. Box 58145
Santa Clara, CA 95052-8145

Adaptec, Inc.
http://www.adaptec.com
800-934-2766, 408-945-8600
691 South Milpitas Boulevard, Milpitas, CA 95035

Adobe Systems, Inc.
http://www.adobe.com
800-833-6687 (main) 800-272-3623 (Acrobat)
415-961-4400, 408-536-6000
1585 Charleston Road
Mountain View, CA 94039-7900

Allaire Corp.
http://www.allaire.com
888-939-2545, 617-761-2000
One Alewife Center, Cambridge, MA 02140

American Power Conversion Corp.
http://www.apcc.com
800-800-4APC, 401-789-5735
132 Fairgrounds Road
West Kingston, RI 02892-9906

The Apache Project
http://www.apache.org

Apple Computer, Inc.
http://www.apple.com
800-776-2333, 408-996-1010
1 Infinite Loop, Cupertino, CA 95014-2084

Artisoft, Inc.
http://www.artisoft.com
800-846-9726, 520-670-7100
2202 N. Forbes Boulevard, Tucson, AZ 85745

Bay Networks, Inc.
http://www.baynetworks.com
800-8-BAYNET, 408-988-2400
P.O. Box 58185, 4401 Great America Parkway
Santa Clara, CA 95052-8185

Best Power Technology
http://www.bestpower.com
800-356-5794, 608-565-7200
P.O. Box 280, Necedah, WI 54646

Borland International, Inc.
http://www.borland.com
800-932-9994, 408-431-1000
100 Borland Way, Scotts Valley, CA 95066-3249

Checkpoint Software Technologies, Ltd.
http://www.checkpoint.com
800-429-4391, 617-859-9051
1 Militia Drive, Lexington, MA 02173

Cheyenne (Division of Computer Associates International, Inc.)
http://www.cheyenne.com
800-243-9462, 516-465-5000
3 Expressway Plaza, Roslyn Heights, NY 11577

Cisco Systems, Inc.
http://www.cisco.com
800-553-6387, 408-526-4000
170 W. Tasman Drive, San Jose, CA 95134-1706

Claris Corp.
http://www.claris.com
800-544-8554, 408-987-7000
P.O. Box 58168, 5201 Patrick Henry Drive
Santa Clara, CA 95052-8168

Compaq Computer Corp.
http://www.compaq.com
800-345-1518, 281-514-0484
20555 State Highway 249, Houston, TX 77070-2698

Computer Associates International, Inc.
http://www.cai.com
800-225-5224, 516-342-5224
One Computer Associates Plaza
Islandia, NY 11788-7000

Corel Corp.
http://www.corel.com
800-772-6735, 613-728-8200
1600 Carling Avenue, The Corel Building
Ottawa, ON, CANADA K1Z 8R7

CyberMedia, Inc.
http://www.cybermedia.com
800-721-7824, 310-581-4700
3000 Ocean Park Boulevard, Suite 2001
Santa Monica, CA 90405

Digi International, Inc.
http://www.dgii.com
800-344-4273, 612-912-3444
11001 Bren Road E, Minnetonka, MN 55343

Digital Equipment Corp.
http://www.dec.com,
http://www.digital.com
800-344-4825, 508-493-5111
146 Main Street, Maynard, MA 01754-2571

Eicon Technology Corp.
http://www.eicon.com
800-803-4266, 972-239-3270
14755 Preston Road, Suite 620, Dallas, TX 75240

Exabyte Corp.
http://www.exabyte.com
800-EXABYTE, 303-442-4333
1685 38th Street, Boulder, CO 80301

Executive Software, Inc.
http://www.execsoft.com
800-829-4357, 818-547-2050
701 N. Brand Boulevard, 6th Floor
Glendale, CA 91203-1242

Fluke Corp.
http://www.fluke.com
800-443-5853, 206-347-6100
P.O. Box 9090, Everett, WA 98206-9090

FTP Software, Inc.
http://www.ftp.com
800-282-4FTP, 508-685-4000
100 Brickstone Square, 5th Floor
Andover, MA 01810

Hewlett-Packard Company
http://www.hp.com
800-752-0900, 415-857-1501
3000 Hanover Street, Palo Alto, CA 94304

IBM Corporation
http://www.ibm.com
800-426-3333, 914-765-1900
Old Orchard Road, Armonk, NY 10001-3782

InfoAccess, Inc.
http://www.infoaccess.com
800-344-9737, 425-201-1915
15821 NE 8th Street, Suite 200, Bellevue, WA 98008

Informix Software Inc.
http://www.informix.com
800-331-1763, 415-926-6300
4100 Bohannon Drive, Menlo Park, CA 94025

**Intel Corp. (Personal Computer Enhancement
Division)**
http://www.intel.com
800-538-3373, 503-629-7354
5200 N.E. Elam Young Parkway
Hillsboro, OR 97124-6497

Intrusion Detection Inc.
http://www.intrusion.com
800-408-6104, 212-348-8900
217 East 86th Street, Suite 213
New York, NY 10028

Iomega Corp.
http://www.iomega.com
800-697-8833, 801-778-1000
1821 W. Iomega Way, Roy, UT 84067

KnowledgePoint
http://www.knowledgepoint.com
800-727-1133, 707-762-0333
1129 Industrial Avenue, Petaluma, CA 94952-1141

Lotus Development Corp. (a division of IBM)
http://www.lotus.com
800-346-1305, 617-577-8500
55 Cambridge Parkway
Cambridge, MA 02142-1295

Macromedia, Inc.
http://www.macromedia.com
800-457-1774, 415-252-2000
600 Townsend Street, Suite 310 W
San Francisco, CA 94103-4945

Microsoft Corp.
http://www.microsoft.com
800-426-9400, 206-882-8080
One Microsoft Way, Redmond, WA 98052

MicroTest, Inc.
http://www.microtest.com
800-526-9675, 602-952-6400
4747 North 22nd Street, Phoenix, AZ 85016-4708

Motorola, Inc. (Mobile Computing Products Division)
http://www.mot.com/MIMS/ISG
800-365-6394, 205-430-8000
5000 Bradford Drive, Huntsville, AL 35805-1993

Netaccess, Inc.
http://www.netacc.com
800-950-ISDN, 603-898-1800
18 Keewaydin Drive, Salem, NH 03079

NetManage, Inc.
http://www.netmanage.com
408-973-7171
10725 N. De Anza Boulevard, Cupertino, CA 95014

NetObjects, Inc.
http://www.netobjects.com
888-449-6400, 415-482-3200
2055 Woodside Road, Suite 250
Redwood City, CA 94060

Netscape Communications Corp.
http://home.netscape.com
800-638-7483, 415-254-1900
501 E. Middlefield Road, Mountain View, CA 94043

Novell, Inc.
http://www.novell.com
800-453-1267, 801-222-6000
1555 North Technology Way, Orem, UT 84757

Octopus Technologies, Inc.
http://www.octopustech.com
800-919-1009, 215-579-5600
1717 Langhorne Newtown Road, Suite 402
Langhorne, PA 19047

Oracle Corp.
http://www.oracle.com
800-633-0596, 415-506-7000
500 Oracle Parkway, Redwood Shores, CA 94065

Panamax
http://www.panamax.com
800-472-5555, 415-499-3900
150 Mitchell Boulevard, San Rafael, CA 94903-2057

Primavera Systems, Inc.
http://www.primavera.com
800-423-0245, 610-667-8600
Two Bala Plaza, Bala Cynwyd, PA 19004

Qualcomm, Inc.
http://www.qualcomm.com
800-544-4977, 619-587-1121
6455 Lusk Boulevard, San Diego, CA 92121-2779

Quarterdeck Corp.
http://www.quarterdeck.com
800-354-3222, 310-309-3700
13160 Mindanao Way
Marina del Rey, CA 90292-9705

Raptor Systems Inc.
http://www.raptor.com
800-9-EAGLE-6, 617-487-7700
69 Hickory Drive, Waltham, MA 02154

SCO (Santa Cruz Operation, Inc.)
http://www.sco.com
800-SCO-UNIX, 408-425-7222
P.O. Box 1900, 400 Encinal Street
Santa Cruz, CA 95061-1900

Seagate Software (Information Management Group)
http://www.seagatesoftware.com
800-877-2340, 800-663-1244 (Canada), 604-681-3435
1095 W. Pender Street, 4th Floor
Vancouver, BC, CANADA V6E 2M6

Seagate Technology, Inc.
http://www.seagate.com
800-SEAGATE, 408-438-6550
920 Disc Drive, Scotts Valley, CA 95066-4544

Secure Computing Corp.
http://www.borderware.com
800-692-LOCK, 612-628-2700
2675 Long Lake Road, Roseville, MN 55113

SoftQuad, Inc.
http://www.softquad.com
800-387-2777, 416-544-9000
20 Eglington Avenue, W., 12th Floor
Toronto, ON, CANADA M4R 1K8

Sun Microsystems, Inc.
http://www.sun.com
800-821-4643, 800-821-4642 (CA), 415-960-1300
2550 Garcia Avenue
Mountain View, CA 94043-1100

SunSoft, Inc.
http://www.sun.com/sunsoft
800-SUN-SOFT, 512-345-2412
2550 Garcia Avenue
Mountain View, CA 94043-1100

Sybase Inc.
http://www.sybase.com
800-879-2273, 510-922-3500
6475 Christie Avenue, Emeryville, CA 94608

Symantec Corp.
http://www.symantec.com
800-441-7234, 408-253-9600
10201 Torre Avenue, Cupertino, CA 95014-2132

SyQuest Technology, Inc.
http://www.syquest.com
800-245-CART, 510-226-4000
47071 Bayside Parkway, Fremont, CA 94538

Tally Systems Corp.
http://www.tallysys.com
800-262-3877, 603-643-1300
P.O. Box 70, Hanover, NH 03755-0070

Trusted Information Systems Inc.
http://www.tis.com
888-FIREWALL, 301-854-6889
3060 Washington Road, Route 97
Glenwood, MD 21738

Vinca Corp.
http://www.vinca.com
800-934-9530, 801-223-3100
1815 South State Street, Suite 2000
Orem, UT 84058

Virtual Motion, Inc.
http://www.virtualmotion.com
415-778-0100
185 Berry Street, Suite 4200
San Francisco, CA 94107

Visio Corp.
http://www.visio.com
800-446-3335, 206-521-4500
520 Pike Street, Suite 1800, Seattle, WA 98101-4001

Whistle Communications Corp.
http://www.whistle.com
415-577-7000
110 Marsh Drive, Foster City, CA 94404

Yamaha Corp. of America (Systems Technology Division)
http://www.yamahayst.com
800-543-7457, 408-467-2300
100 Century Center Court, Suite 800
San Jose, CA 95112

Books

These titles are worth a look next time you find yourself lost among the rows of computer books at your local bookstore-slash-coffeehouse — or wandering cyberspace bookstores like http://www.amazon.com.

Bulletproofing NetWare
Mark Wilkins and Glenn E. Weadock
McGraw-Hill
336 pages, $34.95

Bulletproofing Windows 95
Glenn E. Weadock
McGraw-Hill
350 pages, $34.95

Intranet Publishing For Dummies
Glenn E. Weadock
IDG Books Worldwide, Inc.
384 pages, $29.99 (includes CD-ROM)

LAN Disaster Prevention and Recovery
Patrick H. Corrigan
PTR Prentice-Hall
310 pages, $29.95

***Networking For Dummies,* 2nd Edition**
Doug Lowe
IDG Books Worldwide, Inc.
384 pages, $19.99

Networking with NetWare For Dummies
3rd Edition
Ed Tittel, Deni Connor, and Earl Follis
IDG Books Worldwide, Inc.
408 pages, $19.99

Novell's Guide to IntranetWare Networks
Jeffrey F. Hughes and Blair W. Thomas
Novell Press
1,079 pages, $59.99 (includes CD-ROM)

Running Microsoft Windows NT Server 4.0
Charlie Russell and Sharon Crawford
Microsoft Press
615 pages, $39.95

TCP/IP For Dummies, **2nd Edition**
Marshall Wilensky
IDG Books Worldwide, Inc.
432 pages, $24.99

Windows NT Networking For Dummies
Ed Tittel, Mary Madden, and Earl Follis
IDG Books Worldwide, Inc.
360 pages, $24.99

Magazines

Magazines should supplement your book diet. Here are a few that cover networking technology. Many of these periodicals can keep you up on current trends with a quick skim of each issue.

Byte: The Magazine of Technology Integration
http://www.byte.com
603-924-9281
One Phoenix Mill Lane, Peterborough, NH 03458

Computerworld
http://www.computerworld.com
508-879-0700
500 Old Connecticut Path, Framingham, MA 01701

Information Week
http://techweb.cmp.com/iw
516-562-5051
600 Community Drive, Manhasset, NY 11030

Infoworld
http://www.infoworld.com
800-457-7866
P.O. Box 1172, Skokie, IL 60076

Internet Magazine
http://www.zdimag.com
800-825-4237
One Park Avenue, New York, NY 10016-5802

LAN Times
http://www.lantimes.com
800-525-5003
1900 O'Farrell Street, Suite 200
San Mateo, CA 94403

Network Computing
http://techweb.cmp.com/nc
516-562-5882
600 Community Drive, Manhasset, NY 11030

Network World
http://www.networkworld.com
800-643-4668, 508-875-6400
151 Worcester Road, Framingham, MA 01701-9524

PC Magazine: The Independent Guide to Personal Computing
http://www.pcmag.com
212-503-5255
One Park Avenue, New York, NY 10016-5802

PC Week
http://www.pcweek.com
617-393-3700
10 Presidents' Landing, Medford, MA 02155

Software Magazine
http://www.sentrytech.com
508-366-8104
One Research Drive, Suite 400B
Westborough, MA 01581

Windows Magazine
http://www.winmag.com
516-733-8300
One Jericho Plaza, Jericho, NY 11753

Windows NT Magazine
http://www.winntmag.com
800-621-1544, 970-663-4700
P.O. Box 447, Loveland, CO 80539-0447

Appendix C
About the CD-ROM

● ●

*H*ere's some of what you can find on the *Small Business Networking For Dummies* CD-ROM:

✔ Novell IntranetWare For Small Business trial version

✔ Executive Software, Inc. Diskeeper Lite defragmentation utility

✔ A trio of useful networking tools from Artisoft, Inc.

The enclosed blockbuster CD-ROM contains over 600MB of software for you to experiment with as you develop your small business network. It includes freeware, shareware (which you should pay for and register if you decide to continue using it after and evaluation period), and trialware (tryout versions of commercial software).

System Requirements

Make sure your computer meets the minimum system requirements listed below. If your computer doesn't match up to most of these requirements, you may have problems in using the contents of the CD.

✔ **A PC with a 486 or faster processor.**

✔ **Microsoft Windows 95 or later or Microsoft Windows NT 4.0 or later.**

✔ **At least 16MB of total RAM installed on your computer.**

✔ **At least 300MB of hard drive space available to install all the software from this CD. (You'll need less space if you don't install every program.)**

✔ **A CD-ROM drive, double-speed (2X) or faster.**

✔ **A monitor capable of displaying at least 256 colors or grayscale.**

Using the CD

To install the items from the CD to your hard drive, follow these steps.

1. **Insert the CD into your computer's CD-ROM drive.**

2. **Click Start➪Run.**

3. **In the dialog box that appears, type** D:\SETUP.EXE.

   Most of you probably have your CD-ROM drive listed as drive D under My Computer. Type in the proper drive letter if your CD-ROM drive uses a different letter.

4. **Click OK.**

   A license agreement window appears.

5. **Since I'm sure you'll want to use the CD, read through the license agreement, nod your head, and then click the Accept button. After you click Accept, you'll never be bothered by the License Agreement window again.**

   From here, the CD interface appears. The CD interface is a little program that shows you what is on the CD and coordinates installing the programs and running the demos. The interface basically lets you click a button or two to make things happen.

6. **The first screen you see is the Welcome screen. Click anywhere on this screen to enter the interface.**

   Now you are getting to the action. This next screen lists categories for the software on the CD.

7. **To view the items within a category, just click the category's name.**

   A list of programs in the category appears.

8. **For more information about a program, click the program's name.**

   Be sure to read the information that is displayed. Sometimes a program requires you to first do a few tricks on your computer, and this screen will tell you where to go for that information, if necessary.

9. **To install the program, click the Install button. If you don't want to install the program, click the Go Back button to return to the previous screen.**

   You can always return to the previous screen by clicking the Go Back button. This allows you to browse the different categories and products and decide what you want to install.

   After you click an install button, the CD interface drops to the background while the CD begins installation of the program you chose.

10. **To install other items, repeat Steps 7, 8 and 9.**

11. **When you're done installing programs, click the Quit button to close the interface.**

You can eject the CD now. Carefully place it back in the plastic jacket of the book for safekeeping.

What You'll Find

This section lists the CD-ROM's contents by manufacturer. On a Windows 95 or Windows NT machine, all you have to do is pop the CD-ROM into the drive and detailed instructions for installing the software appear on your computer screen.

The publisher and I have taken all reasonable precautions to ensure that these files are neither damaged, nor infected by a computer virus. Even so, perform the usual safety chores before installing any software: Make sure you have a current backup of your hard disk, and scan any program files for viruses before running them.

Networking Tools

Artisoft, Inc.

I include three Artisoft products:

i.Share 2.5 is a 30-day trial version of this communications utility for sharing one Internet connection among all network users without requiring each to have TCP/IP software. (Windows 95, Windows 3.*x*)

LANtastic 7.0 is the popular peer-to-peer network software for Windows 95, Windows 3.*x,* and DOS. The trial version expires 45 days after you install it. (Windows 95, Windows 3.*x*, DOS)

ModemShare 7.0 is a 30-day trial version of this communications utility for sharing one or more modems among all network users for both inbound and outbound access. (Windows 95, Windows 3.*x*, DOS)

Cheyenne

ARCServe 6.5 for Windows NT Server is a trial version of Cheyenne's industry-leading server backup utility. (Windows NT Server)

Novell, Inc.

You get a fully-functional two-user trial version of *IntranetWare for Small Business!* To unlock it, you need to create a license disk, the files for which you can download from `www.novell.com/intranetware/products/ smallbiz/promos/2-user.html`. (This site also contains full documentation, which you should read before installing the software.)

When installing IntranetWare For Small Business onto a hard drive, either start with a fresh empty hard drive, or remove and store any programs and data that you want to keep. The usual first step is to boot from a boot diskette and install MS-DOS on a relatively small (about 32MB) partition on the hard drive. Make sure that when you install MS-DOS, you include the drivers for your CD-ROM. Now you are ready to install IntranetWare For Small Business:

1. **Start the computer in DOS mode.**

2. **Pop in the CD.**

3. **Change to the CD drive letter by simply typing the drive letter followed by a colon (usually** D:) **at the DOS prompt.**

4. **Type** INSTALL**, and follow the on-screen prompts.**

    Online help is available at nearly every step.

When you're done, you have a two-user version of Novell IntranetWare for Small Business! You can set up client machines individually using the CLNTINST.EXE program on the CD. Note that for space reasons, the NetWare Connect for Macintosh software is excluded.

Internet/Intranet Tools

Adobe Systems, Inc.

I include two Adobe programs:

A tryout version of *PageMill 2.0*, the popular Web page creation tool, may interest you if you decide to get involved in hosting a Web site or creating a company intranet. (Windows 95 and NT)

The *Acrobat Reader* is necessary for viewing the online documentation on Artisoft products. (Windows 95 and NT)

Microsoft Corp.

Internet Explorer for Windows 95 is one of the two most popular Web browsers. I include version 3.02, which is not subject to the Java controversy that has led Sun Microsystems to sue Microsoft over version 4.0. (Windows 95)

Nico Mak Computing, Inc.

WinZip 6.3 is a shareware file compression and decompression utility that's handy for moving files over modem links. (Windows 95 and NT)

Qualcomm, Inc.

Eudora Light is a freeware version of the popular *Eudora Pro* e-mail software from Qualcomm. (Windows 95 and NT)

Office Productivity Tools

Authentex Software Corp.

ThunderBYTE is an antivirus utility designed to protect against viruses transmitted by e-mail. (Windows 95 and NT)

Executive Software, Inc.

The *Diskeeper Lite* defragmentation utility keeps Windows NT Server disks running at top speed; this is a freeware version. (Windows NT Server)

Symantec Corp.

I include two Symantec programs:

Act! 3.0 is a 30-day trial version of the premiere PC information manager. (Windows 95)

Norton Antivirus 4.0 is a 30-day trial of the most popular workstation antivirus utility. (Windows 95)

That's it — all the goodies we could fit onto a single CD! Have fun and happy networking.

If You've Got Problems (Of the CD Kind)

I tried my best to compile programs that work on most computers with the minimum system requirements. Alas, your computer may differ, and some programs may not work properly for some reason.

The two likeliest problems are that you don't have enough memory (RAM) for the programs you want to use, or that you have other programs running which are affecting installation or running of a program. If you get error messages like Not enough memory or Setup cannot continue, try one or more of these methods and then try using the software again:

- **Turn off any anti-virus software that you have on your computer.** Installers sometimes mimic virus activity and may make your computer incorrectly believe that it is being infected by a virus.

- **Close all running programs.** The more programs you're running, the less memory is available to other programs. Installers also typically update files and programs. So if you keep other programs running, installation may not work properly.

- **Have your local computer store add more RAM to your computer.** This is, admittedly, a drastic and somewhat expensive step. However, if you have a Windows 95 PC or a Mac OS computer with a PowerPC chip, adding more memory can really help the speed of your computer and allow more programs to run at the same time.

If you still have trouble with installing the items from the CD, please call the IDG Books Worldwide Customer Service phone number: 800-762-2974 (outside the U.S.: 317-596-5430).

Index

Notes

Notes

Notes

Notes

Notes

IDG Books Worldwide, Inc., End-User License Agreement

READ THIS. You should carefully read these terms and conditions before opening the software packet(s) included with this book ("Book"). This is a license agreement ("Agreement") between you and IDG Books Worldwide, Inc. ("IDGB"). By opening the accompanying software packet(s), you acknowledge that you have read and accept the following terms and conditions. If you do not agree and do not want to be bound by such terms and conditions, promptly return the Book and the unopened software packet(s) to the place you obtained them for a full refund.

1. **License Grant.** IDGB grants to you (either an individual or entity) a nonexclusive license to use one copy of the enclosed software program(s) (collectively, the "Software") solely for your own personal or business purposes on a single computer (whether a standard computer or a workstation component of a multiuser network). The Software is in use on a computer when it is loaded into temporary memory (RAM) or installed into permanent memory (hard disk, CD-ROM, or other storage device). IDGB reserves all rights not expressly granted herein.

2. **Ownership.** IDGB is the owner of all right, title, and interest, including copyright, in and to the compilation of the Software recorded on the disk(s) or CD-ROM ("Software Media"). Copyright to the individual programs recorded on the Software Media is owned by the author or other authorized copyright owner of each program. Ownership of the Software and all proprietary rights relating thereto remain with IDGB and its licensers.

3. **Restrictions on Use and Transfer.**

   (a) You may only (i) make one copy of the Software for backup or archival purposes, or (ii) transfer the Software to a single hard disk, provided that you keep the original for backup or archival purposes. You may not (i) rent or lease the Software, (ii) copy or reproduce the Software through a LAN or other network system or through any computer subscriber system or bulletin-board system, or (iii) modify, adapt, or create derivative works based on the Software.

   (b) You may not reverse engineer, decompile, or disassemble the Software. You may transfer the Software and user documentation on a permanent basis, provided that the transferee agrees to accept the terms and conditions of this Agreement and you retain no copies. If the Software is an update or has been updated, any transfer must include the most recent update and all prior versions.

4. **Restrictions on Use of Individual Programs.** You must follow the individual requirements and restrictions detailed for each individual program in the "Appendix C: About the CD-ROM" section of this Book. These limitations are also contained in the individual license agreements recorded on the Software Media. These limitations may include a requirement that after using the program for a specified period of time, the user must pay a registration fee or discontinue use. By opening the Software packet(s), you will be agreeing to abide by the licenses and restrictions for these individual programs that are detailed in the "Appendix C: About the CD-ROM" section and on the Software Media. None of the material on this Software Media or listed in this Book may ever be redistributed, in original or modified form, for commercial purposes.

5. **Limited Warranty.**

    (a) IDGB warrants that the Software and Software Media are free from defects in materials and workmanship under normal use for a period of sixty (60) days from the date of purchase of this Book. If IDGB receives notification within the warranty period of defects in materials or workmanship, IDGB will replace the defective Software Media.

    (b) **IDGB AND THE AUTHOR OF THE BOOK DISCLAIM ALL OTHER WARRANTIES, EXPRESS OR IMPLIED, INCLUDING WITHOUT LIMITATION IMPLIED WARRANTIES OF MERCHANTABILITY AND FITNESS FOR A PARTICULAR PURPOSE, WITH RESPECT TO THE SOFTWARE, THE PROGRAMS, THE SOURCE CODE CONTAINED THEREIN, AND/OR THE TECHNIQUES DESCRIBED IN THIS BOOK. IDGB DOES NOT WARRANT THAT THE FUNCTIONS CONTAINED IN THE SOFTWARE WILL MEET YOUR REQUIREMENTS OR THAT THE OPERATION OF THE SOFTWARE WILL BE ERROR FREE.**

    (c) This limited warranty gives you specific legal rights, and you may have other rights that vary from jurisdiction to jurisdiction.

6. **Remedies.**

    (a) IDGB's entire liability and your exclusive remedy for defects in materials and workmanship shall be limited to replacement of the Software Media, which may be returned to IDGB with a copy of your receipt at the following address: Software Media Fulfillment Department, Attn.: *Small Business Networking For Dummies,* IDG Books Worldwide, Inc., 7260 Shadeland Station, Ste. 100, Indianapolis, IN 46256, or call 800-762-2974. Please allow three to four weeks for delivery. This Limited Warranty is void if failure of the Software Media has resulted from accident, abuse, or misapplication. Any replacement Software Media will be warranted for the remainder of the original warranty period or thirty (30) days, whichever is longer.

    (b) In no event shall IDGB or the author be liable for any damages whatsoever (including without limitation damages for loss of business profits, business interruption, loss of business information, or any other pecuniary loss) arising from the use of or inability to use the Book or the Software, even if IDGB has been advised of the possibility of such damages.

    (c) Because some jurisdictions do not allow the exclusion or limitation of liability for consequential or incidental damages, the above limitation or exclusion may not apply to you.

7. **U.S. Government Restricted Rights.** Use, duplication, or disclosure of the Software by the U.S. Government is subject to restrictions stated in paragraph (c)(1)(ii) of the Rights in Technical Data and Computer Software clause of DFARS 252.227-7013, and in subparagraphs (a) through (d) of the Commercial Computer–Restricted Rights clause at FAR 52.227-19, and in similar clauses in the NASA FAR supplement, when applicable.

8. **General.** This Agreement constitutes the entire understanding of the parties and revokes and supersedes all prior agreements, oral or written, between them and may not be modified or amended except in a writing signed by both parties hereto that specifically refers to this Agreement. This Agreement shall take precedence over any other documents that may be in conflict herewith. If any one or more provisions contained in this Agreement are held by any court or tribunal to be invalid, illegal, or otherwise unenforceable, each and every other provision shall remain in full force and effect.